THE POETICS OF AMERICAN SONG LYRICS

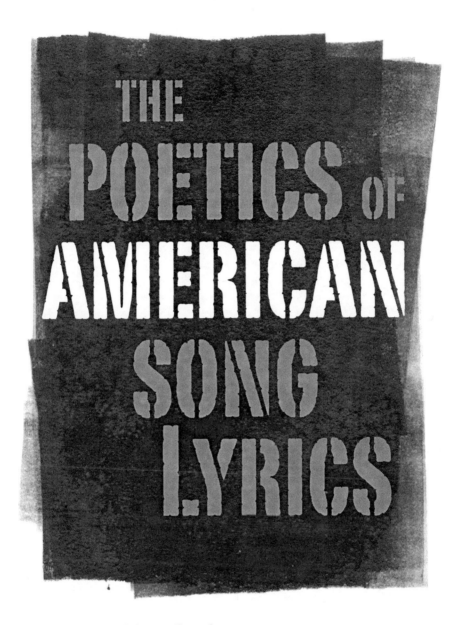

THE POETICS OF AMERICAN SONG LYRICS

Edited by Charlotte Pence

University Press of Mississippi   Jackson

www.upress.state.ms.us

The University Press of Mississippi is a member of the Association of American University Presses.

Permission Acknowledgments:

The editor gratefully acknowledges the publications where a few of these essays were previously published, sometimes in slightly different forms. They include Gordon Ball's "A Nobel for Dylan?" in *Oral Tradition*; Adam Bradley's "Rap Poetry 101" from his *Book of Rhymes: The Poetics of Hip Hop*, published by Basic Civitas 2009; David Caplan's "Reduced to Rhyme: On Contemporary Doggerel" in *Antioch Review*; and Peter Guralnick's "The Triumph of Icarus: Sam Cooke and the Creative Spirit" in the *Oxford American*.

The author would also like to thank:

ABKCO Music, Inc. for permission to quote Sam Cooke's lyrics from "Nearer to Thee" and "You Were Made for Me," both written by Sam Cooke and published by ABKCO Music, Inc.

Ram's Horn Music for permission to quote from "Tangled Up in Blue" written by Bob Dylan, Copyright © 1974 by Ram's Horn Music, renewed 2002 by Ram's Horn Music. All rights reserved. International copyright secured.

"It Don't Mean a Thing" © 2010 by Kevin Young. "Locomotive Songs" reprinted from *Jelly Roll: A Blues* published by Alfred A. Knopf. © 2003 by Kevin Young. Both reprinted by permission of the author. All rights reserved.

"What I'll Do?" by Irving Berlin. © Copyright 1924 by Irving Berlin. © Copyright Renewed International Copyright Secured. All Rights Reserved. Reprinted by Permission.

"To a Friend Whose Work Has Come to Triumph," from *All My Pretty Ones* by Anne Sexton. Copyright © 1962 by Anne Sexton, renewed 1990 by Linda G. Sexton. Reprinted by permission of Houghton Mifflin Publishing Company. All rights reserved.

Yusef Komunyakaa, five lines from "Woman, I Got the Blues," six lines from "Rhythm Method," from *Pleasure Dome: New and Collected Poems* © 2001 by Yusef Komunyakaa. Reprinted by permission of Wesleyan University Press.

First printing 2012   ∞

Library of Congress Cataloging-in-Publication Data

The poetics of American song lyrics / edited by Charlotte Pence.
 p. cm. — (American made music series)
 Includes bibliographical references and index.
 ISBN 978-1-61703-156-4 (cloth : alk. paper) — ISBN 978-1-61703-191-5 (pbk. : alk. paper) — ISBN 978-1-61703-157-1 (ebook) 1. Songs—Texts—History and criticism. 2. Poetics—History. 3. Poetry—Authorship. 4. Lyric poetry—History and criticism. I. Pence, Charlotte.
 PN1059.S7P64 2012
 782.42164'0268—dc22   2011016103

British Library Cataloging-in-Publication Data available

Come said the Muse,
Sing me a song no poet has yet chanted,
Sing me the universal.
—From "Song of the Universal" by Walt Whitman

CONTENTS

Introduction xi

INTRODUCTION

Not many editors can pinpoint the exact moment a specific project began, but I can say for certain that it was September 12, 2003, the day Johnny Cash died. I was living in Nashville, teaching composition and poetry writing at Belmont University where 27 percent of the entering freshmen[1] are part of the Mike Curb College of Entertainment and Music Business. The university sits on a hill that hovers at the end of Music Row, those legendary two streets that Nashville record labels and studios call home. When students miss class at Belmont, the reason often involves the words "touring schedule." Essentially, the music business is an extension of the campus, and there I was teaching poetry and having students ask if they could bring their guitars to class for backup as they read their "poems" for the class to critique.

I was a bit confused as to how to approach these songwriters in my poetry class who viewed poems and songs as one and the same. It was at this moment of my questioning that Johnny Cash died and one of Tennessee's senators, Lamar Alexander, gave a speech on the Senate floor about the loss.[2] Differing politics aside, I wanted to read anything I could about Cash. The speech began as expected by praising Cash, and then suddenly, I was directly implicated. Senator Alexander asked outright why Tennessee English professors, including those at Belmont specifically, were not writing criticism on songs nor teaching songs in literature courses. Immediately, I thought of many reasons why most professors did not do that. How could one discuss song lyrics without the music that was intended to accompany the lyrics? What would be the language of analysis? How was a literature professor qualified to talk about songs? And what criteria was behind this conflation between poetry and songs? I decided to investigate all of this and created a course at Belmont titled the Poetics of Country Music.

The class not only filled immediately, but the students' enthusiasm for the topic carried them through the entire semester. They spent more time researching their essays than any class I had taught before because their own passion for certain bands and artists drove them. They asked that I teach poetic meters and forms so they could learn more about what a poem does versus what a song does. Furthermore, I found they had a solid sense of how to articulate rhythm and prosody once they framed these concepts within lyric writing.

The main problem with the course occurred with assigning readings. There was an astonishing lack of articles that analyzed the content and techniques of song lyrics. Instead, writing focused on the cultural, sociological, and political impact of lyrics, such as *Music and Culture*, edited by Anna Tomasino (Longman Topics Reader, 2005), *A Boy Named Sue*, edited by Kristine M. McCusker and Diane Pecknold (University Press of Mississippi 2004), and *Da Capo Best Music Writing* published each year since 1999 (Da Capo Press). The focus of these writings revolved not around the construction or deconstruction of lyrics, but the effects of lyrics on our culture such as the sexual suggestiveness of some artists' work or other topical issues such as downloading.[3] While those issues are undeniably worthy of discussion, little focus was given to the poetics of the genre, its elements of craft, and its similarity and adaptation from literary poetry. The books I found that did analyze issues of lyrical composition were mainly designed for the budding songwriter such as *Tunesmith: Inside the Art of Songwriting* by Jimmy Webb (Hyperion, 1999), *Songwriting: Essential Guide to Lyric Form and Structure* by Pat Pattison (Berklee, 1991), and *The Rapper's Handbook: A Guide to Freestyling, Writing Rhymes, and Battling* by Emcee Escher and Alex Rappaport (Flocabulary, 2006). Two other common approaches were historical and biographical, with titles like *Can't Stop, Won't Stop: A History of the Hip-Hop Generation* (St Martin's, 2005), *Studio A: The Bob Dylan Reader* (W.W. Norton, 2004), and *The Rolling Stone Illustrated History of Rock and Roll: The Definitive History of the Most Important Artists and Their Music* (Random House, 1992).

Two genres of music in which the lyrics have received some close, critical explication is rap and hip hop. Something about rap and hip hop creates a dialogue quite similar to that found in contemporary poetry and its books on poetics.[4] Similarities within contemporary poetry and rap might be part of the reason for the similarity of poetic-oriented analysis. In his introduction (reprinted here) to *Book of Rhymes: The Poetics of Hip Hop*, Adam Bradley writes that "while rap may be new-school music, it is old-school poetry. Rather than resembling the dominant contemporary form of free-verse—or even the freeform structure of its hip hop cousin, spoken word, or slam poetry, rap bears a stronger affinity to some of poetry's oldest forms, such as the strong stress meter of *Beowulf* and the ballad stanzas of the bardic past" (xv).[5] *To the Break of Dawn: A Freestyle on the Hip Hop Aesthetic* by William Jelani Cobb (New York University Press, 2007), *Check the Techniques: Liner Notes for Hip-Hop Junkies* by Brian Coleman (Villard, 2007), and *Critical Essays on Rap Music and Hip-Hop Culture* by William Eric Perkins (Temple University Press, 1996) are just a few of the many books that analyze the techniques and aesthetics of rap and hip hop. But these findings seem the exception that proves the rule.

Although it is no secret that many poets and songwriters maintain a tightly braided relationship, too few scholars have examined the link between songs and poetry in any real depth. H. T. Kirby-Smith is one of the few to do so. In one chapter to his book *The Celestial Twins: Poetry and Music through the Ages* (University of Massachusetts Press, 1999), he connects how Walt Whitman, Emily Dickinson, and Langston Hughes—arguably the first three poets to give the United States a distinctive poetic voice—were heavily influenced by music. To shape her wonderfully gnomic poems, Dickinson used common measure adapted from hymns, and Hughes often utilized the twelve-bar blues form, as in "The Weary Blues." Some scholars such as Robert D. Faner claim opera was Whitman's major influence, but others claim it did not influence his work at all; Kirby-Smith takes more of a middle ground. Whitman was inspired by music, as the many references in his *Poetry and Prose* let us know: "But no human power can thoroughly suppress the spirit which lives in national lyrics, and sounds in the favorite melodies sung by high and low" (Whitman, quoted in Kirby-Smith).

What I continued to discover, then, was that the shared heritage and history of these two arts had been too often ignored. *The Poetics of American Song Lyrics* is the first collection of academic essays that treats songs as literature by bringing to song lyrics a level of artistic and critical appreciation that has been too often reserved for other art forms such as the novel, poetry, and drama.

As a whole, the essays identify intersections between poems' and songs' literary histories as a way to elucidate the connections between the two genres. This direct comparison is certainly not the only way to approach songs as literature. It is simply one way to begin the discussion, and also to locate points of synthesis and separation so as to better understand both genres and their crafts. The essays reflect a remarkable diversity of styles and perspectives, but, as a whole, the book is indebted to the school of New Criticism for its emphasis on close reading and to the field of Cultural Studies for its championing of pop culture texts as being worthy of critical attention.

The first section of the book provides a variety of perspectives on the poetic history and techniques within songs and poems, and the second section focuses on a few prominent American songwriters such as Bob Dylan, Bruce Springsteen, and Michael Stipe. While the collection offers a range of musical genres and songwriters, it is not meant to be comprehensive. (For example, Tin Pan Alley writers are not included here, although no one would deny their influence on contemporary songwriting.)

One common idea that many contributors feel compelled to address—and *should* address in a collection like this—is whether songs are poetry. In almost every essay, one will find either an implicit or an explicit answer to this question. Lamar Alexander asserts yes, echoing what many have said about Bob Dylan and Hank Williams. Wyn Cooper provides himself as an example that songs can be poems, since his poems have been turned into songs. Brian Howe identifies the tangled weave of poetry and song in Leonard Cohen's body of work. And Gordon Ball analyzes the Nobel Prize in literature's qualifying standards to argue that Bob Dylan must be considered as a recipient.

Much of what is at stake in these arguments seems to be cultural cachet.

When we argue that song lyrics are poetry, often what we mean is that song lyrics deserve the same respect, the same attention, the same care we might put into reading a poem. This may be why the comparison between poems and songs only moves in that one direction. While songwriters often claim that their work is poetry, poets themselves seldom insist that their poems are songs unless they are intentionally signaling that a poem is striving to offer a visionary quality, a sensation beyond the words themselves as in William Blake's *Songs of Innocence and Experience*, Walt Whitman's *Song of Myself*, or John Berryman's *The Dream-songs*.

Considering all of these concerns, Pat Pattison, who teaches both poetry and songwriting (and is world renowned for songwriting—having taught Gillian Welch, for example) at Berklee College of Music, lists how songs differ from poems in his essay that emerges largely from his own vast personal experience and education. Claudia Emerson's essay is comfortable with the intricacies of the question, yet at the same time, one suspects the question itself does not pique her interest since it does little to increase the rich experience of listening to a poem or a song. She points out what one of her mentors, H. T. Kirby-Smith, has said on the subject: "While we should consider poetry's 'indebtedness to music,' we must also recognize its decisive 'separation from it.'" Some essays (such as my own and Jill Jones's) reveal how songwriters (in both cases country songwriters) employ techniques that long have been associated with Renaissance poets such as Shakespeare. But the application or adoption of technique from one genre to another need not suggest that the two genres are exactly the same.

My own opinion is that—for all the reasons and more that Pat Pattison explains in his essay "The Similarities and Differences Between Song Lyrics and Poetry"—songs are a distinct genre with several considerations that contemporary literary poetry does not share. And the best definition of what is a song and what is a poem may be the one we intuit: a song needs music to complete it; a literary poem does not. Or, as Bob Dylan suggests: "If I can sing it, then I know it's a song. If I can't, then I call it a poem." But to say that the two have differences is not to say that either one is more or less deserving of cultural cachet or critical study in the classroom.

While all the essayists share the belief that songs deserve critical attention, how each writer chooses to approach this concern partly depends on his or her background. Twelve out of the twenty-four contributors in this collection are poets, most of whom also teach poetry: David Caplan, Wyn Cooper, David Daniel, Claudia Emerson, Beth Ann Fennelly, Keith Flynn, Jesse Graves, Brian Howe, David Kirby, Tony Tost, Kevin Young, and myself. The fact that half of the contributors are poets is not a coincidence. With the background in analyzing as well as implementing poetic techniques, these contributors readily see the inner workings of songs. The collection also benefits from showcasing the work of literature professors who exemplify how a scholar can explicate a song: Gordon

Ball, Adam Bradley, John Paul Hampstead, Jill Jones, Robert P. McParland, Eric Reimer, Jeffrey Roessner, and Ben Yagoda. Finally, it would be an oversight only to feature poets or literature professors without considering so many fine music scholars who, time and time again, call our attention to the great work being recorded. Including the viewpoints of Peter Guralnick, Pat Pattison, and Stephen M. Deusner was necessary as these are writers who have been shaping how the public understands songs. (I should note, however, that many poets and literature professors have been publishing on music as well, including Adam Bradley, David Caplan, Brian Howe, David Kirby, Robert McParland, Jeffrey Roessner, and Tony Tost. Also, Gordon Ball and Peter Guralnick both write creatively.) This wonderful diversity of twelve poets, eight literature scholars, and three music writers is a balance that I sought. I desired a collection driven by those who share the concerns of songwriters, and I wanted a collection that also shows how people with diverse interests could discuss a common topic. While the strategies of explication differ from piece to piece, the nexus of each piece is an unveiling of the poetic history and/or poetic techniques within songs.

One of the many delights in this collection that highlights this exact occurrence are the twin essays by Jeffrey Roessner and Eric Reimer on R.E.M. The essays show how two analyses of the same question can be explored: what is one to make of Michael Stipe's obfuscated lyrics? In and of itself the question is intriguing, because many people might say: "I can't understand the lyrics; what's there to analyze?" Apparently, a lot. Both writers explore the question through the lens of poetry and reach different conclusions. Roessner approaches this question by looking at expectations of the personal "I" in contemporary poems and songs, analyzing in particular Language poetry. Reimer answers this question by looking to the past, particularly the Romantic poets and seeing how R.E.M.'s work is unknowingly influenced by them. The result is an intellectual display of how diverse backgrounds can take a popular subject and mine the depths of it.

Similarly remarkable is how these essays engage in a dialogue, as almost every essay references another writer in the collection or addresses a similar concern. For example, Keith Flynn's essay, "At the Crossroads: The Intersection of Poetry and Blues," discusses a poem by Kevin Young who, in turn, writes on blues' influence on modernism. While discussing the poetic sequence in Magnolia Electric Co.'s *Josephine* album, Jesse Graves references the Pulitzer Prize–winning book *Late Wife* by Claudia Emerson, who writes here on Dylan. Other threads of conversation are shared as well, such as the description of a sonnet's turn in both my essay on the sonnet structure in country songs and in Brian Howe's essay on Leonard Cohen. Other articles such as David Kirby's on Otis Redding and Ben Yagoda's on Bob Dylan engage in discussions of the oral nature of songs that lead to questions such as which version of a song is *the* version. And Tony Tost's essay on Johnny Cash and Robert P. McParland's essay on Bruce Springsteen both engage with the music, emotion, and tone behind the lyrics as a way to understand the songs' artistry. This dialogue between the essays was not planned—which indicates something at work that is much larger than this book, something changing within the current climate of scholarship. The dialogue was already taking place, and this book simply serves as a place—a town square if you will—for many of the leading voices on the subject to come together and analyze songs in a way that moves beyond the expected. These writers concern themselves with the connectivity between craft and effect, between poems and songs, between explication and insight.

"Great work requires great audiences," Walt Whitman said, and we all know that the poetry audience is quite small in comparison to the audience for songs. Part of the problem is that the general public feels that it doesn't "get" poetry, doesn't have the tools, the key code, the answer sheet. This is a fair criticism and relates to something that William Wordsworth expressed two hundred years ago in his preface to *Lyrical Ballads*. He alerted the reader that his poetry should be judged by his own terms and proceeded to explain his choices regarding diction, personification, and subject matter. Basically, he believed, as many contemporary poets still do, that each poet needs to teach his/her audience how to read his/her work. The difficulty with this belief, however, is that the audience may not want to spend the time learning how to read a particular poet's work. And while the burgeoning number of creative writing programs in college is promising, the potential audience for poetry is still limited by relying on academia to be both bullhorn and bully pulpit. Teaching about rhythm or the use of image in songs, for instance, is an effective way to introduce how such techniques operate in poetry, thus cultivating a wider understanding of and appreciation for poetry. The hope is that this collection may increase non-poets' knowledge about poetry through a genre that is popular, familiar, and loved. Songs, not poetry itself, might be the key to increasing poetry's readership.

I suspect that one reason why discussions in English classes on song lyrics tend toward the sociological or historical is that no terminology for close readings of lyrics exists. While the material and tone of this book assume readers' interest in poetry, readers are not expected to know how songs are constructed and evaluated. This collection begins to cultivate a sense of such terminology within the essays, and the glossary provided at the end of the book will help. The glossary, however, also emphasizes the similarities with poetry and stresses that many familiar with poetry already know the terms with which to discuss song lyrics. The collection's intention is to re-energize discussions of poetic form with respect not only to popular song lyrics but also to literary poems. After all, many people are much more familiar with songs; why not access this already cultivated interest and use the opportunity to broaden an appreciation for literary poetry? I would also like to say that, while I have framed this collection in terms of my academic experiences, I think the essays here will find a place outside academia;

in fact, I would say that the readership is like the subject matter—one that straddles a variety of interests and aesthetics.

Within the college classroom, the collection has various applications, including in songwriting courses; American studies courses focused on popular culture; and musicology courses that address the genres of rap, country, pop, and folk. The class I most envision using the book is an introduction to poetry literature course where many students are more familiar with songs than poetry. Beginning with a familiar genre will help students engage with the class, while also teaching them poetic techniques, forms, and history. Readers can learn aspects about rhyme with Caplan's essay, tropes and schemes used by Shakespeare and other Renaissance poets with Jones's essay, sonnet form with my essay, dramatic monologues with Deusner's essay, heroic poetry with Hampstead's essay, and so on. The essays also discuss blues poems, rhythm, modernism, ballads, confessionalism, Language poetry, Keatsian odes, unreliable narrators, personas, poetic sequences, and more. And all of this is discussed in the more approachable context of the song. Also, many essays are excellent models for how to explicate texts, a practice many courses emphasize. Of course, this essay collection was never intended to be the primary text, and one should supplement as necessary. What this essay collection provides is an innovative and interesting start to poetic discussions. In addition to the specific benefits of studying poetry through songs, it is also fitting for songs to be in the literature classroom. To not discuss songs as a form of oral literature—in a serious way rather than a random example or two occasionally trotted out—has been an oversight in literature classrooms for far too long.

One aspect to consider when analyzing song lyrics is to recognize that lyrics cannot be lumped into one genre, since each genre maintains certain conventions based on its market share and audience. Former NEA director Dana Gioia once said in a lecture I attended that a good critic must consider three things when analyzing any work: What is it doing? How well is it doing that? And what is the value of doing that? To approach all song lyrics and wish them to be mini–Bob Dylan songs is a failing not of the song, but of the listener. Simply put, songwriters have different goals considering their genre.

Country, for example, still operates under a division between songwriter and artist that greatly influences the type of song considered "good." Similar to the Tin Pan Alley era, country employs staff songwriters who are hired by publishing companies. They pay a songwriter a yearly salary starting at $12,000 based on his/her past songwriting success, which is solely determined by sales. In exchange for the salary, the songwriter writes songs that the publishing company owns. These songs are then recorded and presented to middlemen known as song pluggers, who then sell the songs to particular recording artists such as Trisha Yearwood. This business process is critical to understanding country music.

For one, the self-expression of the artist, which is valued in other musical genres such as indie rock, is not necessarily the key driving force because the writer is often not the performer. Granted, more and more country artists are writing their own songs and the industry has always had a few artists who are excellent at both writing and performing: Alan Jackson, Brad Paisley, and Dolly Parton are just a few examples. But for the most part, other people are writing songs for the artists, often not knowing at the time of composition which artist will record it. So, what is the criteria in country for "good" if it is not self-expression? The essay in this collection by Jill Jones summarizes some of the expectations of country music: relatability, specificity, clarity, and outright catchiness. As she says, "Certain subjects are conventional: relationships, love of the country life, patriotism, and drinking at honkytonks. Writers also must follow certain expectations about language—colloquial diction, dialectal forms, non-standard grammar, clichés, and simple vocabulary." Her essay is not simply a good essay on what country does, but explains what country is expected to do. This knowledge is critical, as it can guide certain readers who dismiss country based on what they would prefer a song to do. Granted, it is difficult for any one person to know what all musical genres value, but simply being aware that "good" means different things depending on genre is the starting point.

The larger question, however, remains: how can a literature class discuss a song? The process is similar to that of discussing any piece of literature when the goal is to examine what readers/listeners are responding to and how the work is crafted. To begin, one can ask the questions that many close readings often start with: Who is the speaker in the song? Who is the speaker talking to in the song? Who is the audience? What is the context of this song? For example, is the song relating to a current event such as September 11 as does Toby Keith's xenophobic "The Taliban Song"? What is the genre and how does the genre affect the presentation? Which lines grab one's attention and why? Which lines do not and why? How does the music affect the tone of the lyrics? With the exception of the last question, all are questions one would ask of a poem.

Another important question to consider is why some artists are considered worthy of explication and why others are not. The work alone is not the sole issue, but race, gender, and socioeconomic associations all affect how song lyrics are evaluated—or sometimes not evaluated. For instance, Bob Dylan is often heralded as the great songwriter, but how might his generation influence this assumption? It is important to consider that the people who grew up listening to Dylan are now the people who hold positions of power and thus often choose what will be discussed and why. At the same time, many of these same people are lukewarm toward hip hop, perhaps because the content is distasteful or threatening. The result is to dismiss the craft of the lyrics—continuing to ostracize hip hop artists by excluding them from public discourse.

One of the developments regarding the poetics of songs is that when I first proposed this collection, I had to argue for the project's legitimacy. Seven years later, this is not as critical. The last decade has experienced a growing interest in critical reflection on objects of pop culture. And I am happy to say that scholarship on songs within academia is becoming more accepted. Within the hundreds of pages in poetry anthologies, a few songs are now regularly included such as Springsteen's "You're Missing," Dylan's "Tangled Up in Blue," and anonymous ballads such as "Bonny Barbara Allen." Yale University Press's publication of *The Anthology of Rap* (2010), edited by Adam Bradley and Andrew DuBois; Oxford University Press's forthcoming *Rhyme's Challenge* by David Caplan, which analyzes rhyme in hip hop; and this compilation are all indicators of university presses acknowledging the literary viability of songs. When I first conceived of this project, I envisioned writing an introduction that mainly established why lyrics should be explicated in deep ways. But now, nearly ten years later, the point is beginning to seem already made for me. What began as a cause has developed into a collection of some of the best writers we have today who bring a critical appreciation to poetry and songs.

Notes

1. Twenty-seven percent is the enrollment percentage for fall of 2010.

2. Alexander's speech is presented in its entirety in this collection.

3. For example, in *A Boy Named Sue* one finds essay titles that signal this sociology-centered discourse: "Elvis, Country Music, and the Reconstruction of Southern Masculinity" by Michael Mertrand; "Between Riot Grrrl and Quiet Girl: The New Woman's Movement in Country Music" by Beverly Keel; and "Spade Doesn't Look Exactly Starved: Country Music and the Negotiation of Women's Domesticity in Cold War Los Angeles" by Peter la Chapelle.

4. A few titles of comparison are *Poetic Meter and Poetic Form* by Paul Fussell (McGraw-Hill, 1979), *The Poems' Heartbeat: A Manual of Prosody* by Alfred Corn (Story Line Press, 1997), and *How to Read a Poem* by Terry Eagleton (Blackwell, 2006).

5. Bradley, Adam. *Book of Rhymes: The Poetics of Hip Hop.* New York: BasicCivitas Books, 2009, xv.

Part One

POETIC HISTORY AND TECHNIQUES WITHIN POEMS AND SONGS

THE DAY JOHNNY CASH DIED

LAMAR ALEXANDER

*This article is adapted from the remarks of U.S. Sen. Lamar Alexander
(R., Tennessee) on the Senate floor, September 15, 2003.*

*Senator Alexander, who served as Secretary of Education under President George H. W. Bush and as president of the University of Tennessee,
gave a speech on the Senate floor regarding the need for scholars at the
university level to consider song lyrics as a genre worthy of literary criticism. A portion of his talk as reprinted from the* Congressional Record
*of the second session of the 108th Congress is as follows: "When Johnny
Cash died,* The New York Times *streamed the headline: 'Poet of the
Working Poor.' Bob Dylan once said Hank Williams was America's greatest poet. . . . If that is true, why don't we have English professors somewhere criticizing their poetry?"*

Johnny Cash died on Friday in Nashville.

The man whose voice sounded like a big freight train coming is gone.

During the 1980's I once asked him, "Johnny, how many nights a year do you
perform on the road?"

"Oh, about 300," he said.

"Why do you still do that?" I asked.

He looked back at me, puzzled. "That's what I do," he said.

During this past weekend, radio stations have been playing the songs of the
man who performed 300 times a year for all of us—the man in black. Stores all
over Nashville and all over the world were stocking up on Johnny Cash memorabilia. So much has been said in the newspapers and on television that one
wonders what else we Senators might usefully say about Johnny Cash.

What could I say better, for example, than what Steven Greenhouse wrote on
page one of Saturday's *New York Times*:

Beginning in the mid-1950's, when he made his first records for the Sun label, Mr. Cash forged a lean, hard-bitten country-folk music that at its most powerful seemed to erase the lines between singing, storytelling and grueling life experience. Born in poverty in Arkansas at the height of the Depression, he was country music's foremost poet of the working poor. His stripped-down songs described the lives of coal miners and sharecroppers, convicts and cowboys, railroad workers and laborers.

"Foremost poet of the working poor. . . ."
Mr. Greenhouse was not the only one who wrote beautifully about the "foremost poet of the working poor." So did Louie Estrada and David Segal in the *Washington Post*. So did Craig Havighurst and other writers in the Nashville *Tennessean*, as well as Jon Sparks in the *Memphis Commercial Appeal*. I have no doubt that in cities all over this country there were writers extolling the poetry of Johnny Cash.

But, why did we wait until Johnny Cash died to think of him as one of our "foremost poets"?

John R. Cash is not the only overlooked poet who ever lived in Nashville. Bob Dylan, Johnny's friend, once said that Hank Williams was America's greatest poet. At last count, there are several thousand Nashville songwriters struggling to write poetry, some of whom will produce lyrics that one day will be sung and remembered everywhere in the world.

Alice Randall, a songwriter and novelist, once observed that it is odd that there is so little serious literary criticism of the poetry of Johnny Cash and Hank Williams and other country music songwriters. The outpouring of articles that have accompanied Johnny's death suggests that most of the serious criticism of the poetry in country music is being done by pop music critics in our major newspapers.

Why is there not a department or a chair or at least a conference occasionally dedicated to criticism of the poetry in country music? Literary criticism is a fundamental part of departments of English in American universities. Among the most famous of these critics were the "Fugitives" who met during the 1920's at Vanderbilt University in Nashville: Cleanth Brooks, Robert Penn Warren, Allen Tate, Donald Davidson, and Andrew Lytle.

If Vanderbilt University is such a center for literary criticism, then why has Vanderbilt not done more about the literature that is country music? Or why does Belmont University in Nashville or the University of Tennessee or University of Memphis not do it? Why have we waited for outsiders such as the *New York Times* and Bob Dylan to tell us that Johnny Cash and Hank Williams are among the foremost poets in the world? Why didn't some scholar living right among them tell us?

There are hundreds of good English professors in dozens of northeastern universities writing thousands of pages of criticism about average poets, while our Tennessee universities are doing almost nothing to write about poets who others say are among the best in the world. We have had a bad habit in Tennessee of not being willing to look right in front of our own noses to celebrate what is special about us. We will celebrate producing average Chopin, when right down the block lives the best harmonica player in the world.

I am all for Chopin, and for Beethoven, and for Mozart, and for Bach. I have performed their music on the piano with symphonies all across Tennessee. But I have also played with those symphonies some of the most beautiful melodies of the unique American creation we call country music.

The death of our friend Johnny Cash, labeled now by others as "the poet of the working poor," is a good time for our Tennessee universities to consider whether they might want to encourage literary criticism of our songwriters. Our universities might discover what others have suggested, that some of our songwriters are among the best poets in the world.

REDUCED TO RHYME: ON CONTEMPORARY DOGGEREL

DAVID CAPLAN

Doggerel, a term first applied to poetry that was loose or irregular and somewhat burlesque, now is often used derogatorily to mean monotonous in rhythm and clumsy in rhyme. This essay shows how doggerel, in the best sense of the term, is a major form in contemporary hip hop and a minor form in contemporary poetry. Specifically, the essay analyzes the daring effects that hip hop artists achieve with their rhyme.

The Gutenberg era, the era of rhyme, is over.
—Donald Davie[1]

Most intellectuals will only half listen.
—Nas[2]

To hear contemporary rhyme, we must listen carefully and widely. "Every reformation in English poetry has involved shifts in attitudes toward rhyming, in the practices of it, and in the rules for its proper conduct," Anne Ferry notes.[3] Just as rhyming changes across literary eras, it works differently within the same historical period. One kind of writing may rhyme to challenge another or to resist a perceived encroachment. Explaining why she wrote *Muse & Drudge*, Harryette Mullen observed "that rhyme is too powerful a tool to be abandoned to advertising, greeting cards, or even platinum rap recordings. I hope to reclaim it for my poem."[4] More contested than shared, rhyme functions differently in different genres, whether occasional verse, poetry, or songs. Too many literary critics mistake rhyming verse for all rhyme, imagining other kinds as eccentric amusements or, at best, preparation for poetry. The era of rhyme seems over to those who only half-listen. I propose we open our ears and rediscover an amazing rhyming culture.

In September 2001 the Supreme Court of Pennsylvania ruled that Susan Porreco could not void her prenuptial agreement because she had received a cubic zirconium engagement ring. When she met her future husband, Susan Porreco was a seventeen-year-old high school student, living with her parents; he was a forty-five-year-old, previously married millionaire and the owner of a car dealership. After two years of dating, he proposed, presenting her with a ring that she claimed he said was diamond. Though Louis Porreco later insisted that he did not mislead his fiancée about the stone, he listed the ring's value as $21,000 on the prenuptial agreement that his lawyer drafted. When the couple separated after ten years of marriage, she hired a jeweler to appraise the ring. Her lawsuit sought to dissolve the prenuptial agreement based on the misrepresentation.[5]

The court found for Louis Porreco, maintaining that his ex-wife should have obtained "an appraisal of the ring" when it was first given to her and faulted her "failure to do this simple investigation." In a dissenting opinion, Justice Eakin asserted:

> A groom must expect matrimonial pandemonium
> When his spouse finds he's given her a cubic zirconium
> Instead of a diamond in her engagement band,
> The one he said was worth twenty-one grand. (PP 575–76)

Addressing the legal standard of "fraudulent misrepresentation" which requires "justifiable reliance on the misrepresentation," Justice Eakin continued in rhyming couplets:

> Given their history and Pygmalion relation,
> I find her reliance was with justification.
> Given his accomplishment and given her youth,
> Was it unjustifiable for her to think he told the truth?
> Or for every prenuptial, is it now a must
> That you treat your betrothed with presumptive mistrust?
> Do we mean reliance on your beloved's representation
> Is not justifiable, absent third-party verification?
> Love, not suspicion, is the underlying foundation
> Of parties entering the marital relation. (PP 576)

Justice Eakin's opinion distressed his colleagues. In concurring opinions, two of his fellow justices objected specifically to his use of rhyme. Chief Justice Zappala expressed "my grave concern that the filing of an opinion that expresses itself in rhyme reflects poorly on the Supreme Court of Pennsylvania" (PP 572). The chief justice protested on two grounds. First, rhyme diverts attention from the court's true concerns: "the substance of our views that should be the focus of our discussion" (PP 572). For this reason, rhyme's excessive stylization presents a distraction. Second and more disturbingly, its use in a legal document undermines the court's authority. "The dignity of the Supreme Court of Pennsylvania," Chief Justice Zappala observed, "should not be diminished" (*PP* 572). Rhyme, he fears, trivializes the proceedings. The loss of "dignity" endangers the court as an institution because it reduces its credibility and effectiveness. Rhyme encourages the public to see the court itself as frivolous. Agreeing with the chief justice, Justice Cappy focused on the second line of argument: "My concern . . . and the point on which I concur completely with the Chief Justice, lies with the perception that litigants and the public at large might form when an opinion of the court is reduced to rhyme" (*PP* 572).

Justice Cappy's phrase "reduced to rhyme" nicely captures the technique's present status. Contemporary culture delights in rhyme yet devalues the technique's significance. We live in a rhyme-drenched era; rhyme reigns in advertisements, tabloid headlines, aphorisms, and nearly all forms of popular music, including country-and-western, pop, punk, and, most notably, hip hop. Rhymes fill our lives, crowded with idiosyncratic echoes and associations, both intimate and shared. "Attacked daily from all directions by people trying to score political points," as First Lady Hillary Clinton often recalled a favorite quatrain:

> As I was standing in the street,
> As quiet as could be,
> A great big ugly man came up
> And tied his horse to me.[6]

This rhyme sounds strange because it records her obsession, not ours. As with Clinton, rhymes enter our thoughts, seemingly of their own volition. At such moments rhyme finds its occasion. The subject of many scurrilous rhymes, Hillary Clinton also presents an illustrative special case; she enjoys the technique others use to mock her. Rhyme crosses private and public spheres, animating political insults and personal ruminations. It proves irresistible, even when deemed inappropriate.

Two factors complicate this situation. First, English is a rhyme-poor language. As Leslie Fiedler observed, "in a rime-haunted language like Provençal or Italian [. . .] a poem which rejects rime [. . .] seems not a relaxation but an effort of the will."[7] In English, the terms reverse. "Why rhyme?" John Hollander asks before answering, "To make it harder."[8] Hollander's jaunty assessment holds only for a language such as English whose limited rhyme options tests a poet's skill. In English a rhyming poem suggests more an effort of the will than a relaxation. Rhyme challenges the language's given features; it organizes the poem around a relatively meager resource. Second, contemporary songs rhyme to a much greater degree than do poems, a situation that reverses the basic trajectory of English poetry. As the literature developed, the language's poets departed from Greek and Latin authors who typically wrote unrhymed verse composed to be sung. Written to be spoken or read on the page, poetry in English increasingly broke with classical tradition by rhyming. In Renaissance debates about versification, rhyme represents a modern technique, regardless of whether the participant decries rhyme as a "troublesome and modern bondage" or celebrates it as the "the chief life" of "modern [. . .] versifying."[9] By the eighteenth century, many observers declared the argument settled. "Rhyming is what I have ever accounted the very essential of a good poet," Jonathan Swift advised a younger poet, adding, "And in that notion I am not singular." To illustrate this lesson, Swift labored to develop an adequate metaphor for rhyme's extensive powers. "Verse without rhyme is a body without a soul," he wrote, "or a bell without a clapper."[10] Many poets and critics similarly maintained that rhyme defined the language's poetry. "Rhyme," Swinburne observed, building to his own comparison, "is the native condition of lyric verse in English: a rhymeless lyric is a maimed thing."[11] No knowledgeable reader holds this position today.

A change in translation marks this historical shift. Many Renaissance and eighteenth-century translators cast unrhymed classical verse into rhyming couplets; those who did not protested the dominant mode. "It is commonly said that rhyme is to be abandoned in a translation of Homer," Matthew Arnold observed.[12] It seems odd to maintain that a translator of Homer who does not use rhyme has "abandoned" the technique since the original does not rhyme. Instead, Arnold's point makes sense in a specific context. A translator who does not rhyme has "abandoned" the techniques familiar to the English verse tradition. Though Arnold objects to rhymed translations, his telling verb suggests the technique's lingering influence at the time. A different assumption characterizes the contemporary era. Many contemporary translators employ the opposite procedures from Dryden, Pope, and Chapman. Instead of adding rhymes to blank verse, they translate rhyming verse without rhymes. They remove the element, instead of adding it. Asked about translating Borges into English, Norman Thomas di Giovanni minces few words: "Rhyme is hardly poetry, and we found it quite expendable."[13] Pithily, di Giovanni renounces any regret. With a superlative and an intensifier, he characterizes rhyme as irrelevant to the work's artistry and unnecessary: "hardly poetry" and "quite expendable." Other translators cite pragmatic reasons, mentioning the difficulties that rhyme poses. "This is doing it the easy way," Robert Hass self-deprecatingly explains, "which has been typical of late twentieth century translation. I ignored the rhymes."[14] This decision signals the value that translators place on the technique; it presents a problem they need not address.

Observing the contemporary scene, many literary critics view patterned rhyme as frivolous and beside the point, a distraction. "Rhyme these days is in bad repute," observes Hugh Kenner.[15] Referring to "our rhyme-resistant time," J. Paul Hunter notes how even sophisticated contemporary readers struggle to understand the complexity of rhyming verse: "It hardly seems possible, in our rhyme-resistant time, to take the couplet or its contents seriously except as repression—even to avid historical readers and professional critics."[16] A scholar of eighteenth-century literature, Hunter recognizes that this prejudice obscures a major historic form. "Couplets," he notes, "dominated all poetry [. . .] for nearly two hundred years, nearly half the recognizable English tradition" (*SB* 2). As if to confirm Hunter's fears, Marjorie Perloff returns to the same example, untroubled by the situation that Hunter laments. Perloff claims that "today, the very appearance of heroic couplets [. . .] is a signifier of 'light verse,' something fun and parodic, not meant to be taken too seriously."[17] In her first book, *Rhyme and Meaning in the Poetry of Yeats*, Perloff explored the variety of effects that rhyme offers a single great poet.[18] Four decades later, Perloff implies that contemporary poets who write non-comic heroic couplets commit a mistake because the form serves as "a signifier of 'light verse.'" It no longer evokes the wider range of genres including the heroic, dramatic, and amorous modes that previous masters of the couplet have explored. In such arguments, the heroic couplet, the clearest major rhyme scheme, serves as a metonymy for all rhyming poetry; such assertions reduce endstopped rhyme to an essentially comic technique, not a flexible medium capable of expressing a range of attitudes, ideas, and emotions.

But what about non-comic rhyming verse, poetry "meant to be taken seriously"? Lyn Hejinian explains why the presence of rhyme dooms such efforts: "An English poem hammered into position by end-rhymes tends to have a tiresome though sometimes laughable predictability; at best, it suggests only ancient wisdom, age-old truths. It provides familiarity and, through familiarity, consolation. It gives us respite from the hardships of life."[19] Hejinian believes that end rhymes in English make poetry "laughable," regardless of the effect the writer wishes to achieve. If the author aims to express moral seriousness, rhyme allows only bombast. The technique decides the result, condemning the poetry to "familiarity and, through familiarity, consolation," all of which Hejinian sees as undesirable. According to her, all rhyming poems remain essentially the same, whether written in forms as different as the ghazal, the ballad, and villanelle, or by poets of varying artistic temperaments.

Such sweeping dismissals ignore the details of actual practice. Justice Eakin, for instance, favors a specific kind of rhyme: "A rhyme must have in it some slight element of surprise if it is to give pleasure." Ezra Pound observed, "It need not be bizarre or curious, but it must be well used if used at all."[20] Pound's Imagist dictum has achieved the status of a truism, cited in nearly all discussions of the technique. At his most compelling, though, Eakins works from the opposite principle. When his line, "A groom must expect matrimonial pandemonium," sets "pandemonium" as the opening element in rhyme pair, an attentive reader familiar with the case awaits "zirconium." At least two factors draw the reader to this conclusion. Few rhymes exist for "pandemonium"; *Merriam-Webster's Rhym-*

ing Dictionary, for instance, lists only four.[21] Within such narrow range of options, "cubic zirconium" remains a conspicuous possibility, especially since the fake jewel represents a memorable symbol of deceit, the one detail all acquainted with the case will remember. Tacky as the ring it describes, the rhyme confirms the reader's suspicion; it delights as much in its own bad taste as in the bad taste it reports. Instead of building to a surprise, it confirms the reader's expectations. The rhyme gives the pleasure of an unsuppressed groan.

Another bit of legal verse clarifies Eakins's method. In her decision in a 1989 case before the United States Supreme Court, Justice Sandra Day O'Connor cited Shakespeare's lines, "But I'll amerce you with so strong a fine / That you shall all repent the loss of mine," in order to document a historical meaning of "fine."[22] Writing for the majority, Justice Harry Blackmun retorted with his own verse:

> Though Shakespeare, of course,
> Knew the Law of his time,
> He was foremost a poet,
> In search of a rhyme. (*BF* 266, n. 7)

Justice Blackmun's rhyme against rhyme embodies the point it makes. It presents rhyme as an easy trick that gives invention the appearance of truth. Rhyme, it suggests, performs two functions. The technique introduces a potential falsification, as words are chosen less for their meaning than for their sounds. The presence of rhyme discredits Shakespeare's words; it diminishes their evidentiary value since Shakespeare "was foremost a poet / In search of a rhyme." The technique also achieves a second, seemingly incompatible effect. Rhyme gives Justice Blackmun's stanza an air of certitude; "time" and "rhyme" cinch his argument with a certain rhetorical authority. The justice, then, exploits the very technique whose credibility he undermines.

Blackmun and Eakin write doggerel, the rhyming form that suffers from the lowest standing. Often the term doubles as a pejorative, referring to bad or inept poetry. "Tastes shift," a literary historian observes, "and what looks to one generation like 'major poetry' often reads like doggerel to the next."[23] "Major poetry" and "doggerel" represent antonyms, marking literature's extremes. Resembling the term's etymology, the genre itself seems "poor, worthless."[24] A kind of verse to be shunned, not appreciated, doggerel has enjoyed little critical attention.

In two notable exceptions, George Saintsbury and Northrop Frye attempted to understand its origins and distinguish its types. Both attempt to extricate a genre from its disagreeable manifestations; they explore (in Saintsbury's analogy) "a subject as inseparably connected with prosody as vice is with virtue."[25] Each, then, splits doggerel into two types: "a doggerel which is doggerel, and a doggerel which is not." According to Saintsbury, the former is "merely bad verse—verse which attempts a certain form or norm, and fails" (*HEP* 392). When discussing the "good" latter kind, Saintsbury stresses its rarity and the enormous demands it places upon the poet. "It would require," he writes, "a Dantean ingenuity and an ultra-Dantean good-nature to niche it in Paradise" (*HEP* 393). The "doggerel which is not" employs a recognizable verse form and poetic language "with a wilful licentiousness which is excused by the felicitous result" (*HEP* 393). Such poetry violates decorum by employing verse's conventional markers. It registers "a direct though perhaps unconscious *protest* against the inadequacy, against the positive faultiness, of the regular prosody of the time" (*HEP* 394). Saintsbury italicizes "protest" as if to disguise the two words that modify it. Only two paragraphs before, Saintsbury stresses that the good kind of doggerel requires conscious effort: "The poet is not trying to do what he cannot do; he is trying to do something exceptional, outrageous, shocking—and does it to admiration" (*HEP* 393). As the sentence moves from a negative to a positive assertion, Saintsbury insists that the poet achieves his goal; he accomplishes what he "is trying to do." This success distinguishes good doggerel from bad, which simply fails the "form" or "norm" it attempts. The hedging phrase, "perhaps unconscious *protest*," introduces the suggestion that the protest it registers might not be wholly deliberate. The modifier leaves open the possibility that "perhaps" the poem's force derives from other sources.

Frye more confidently returns to this issue, although he does not cite Saintsbury's work. As the terms Frye introduces make clear, "intention" distinguishes "real" and "intentional" doggerel. For Frye, the versions share two similarities; they retain an underlying prose rhythm and "the features of rhyme and meter become grotesque."[26] Doggerel does not fully develop from prose into poetry, yet it employs the visible features of verse, perversely employed. What distinguishes "intentional" doggerel from "real" doggerel is that a greater self-consciousness inspires the better kind, as its author knowingly employs the devices that naïve writers automatically use. For this reason, the writers of "intentional" and "real" doggerel remain adversaries. The more sophisticated doggerel poets turn against the others, using them as objects of ridicule. "What makes intentional doggerel funny," Frye observes, "is its implied parody of real doggerel, or incompetent attempts at verse: the struggle for rhymes, even to the mispronouncing of words, the dragging in of ideas for the sake of a rhyme, the distorting of syntax in squeezing words into meter." (*WTC* 70) "Intentional doggerel" feasts on its unaccomplished twin, reemploying the same grotesque techniques. In particular, the shrewder doggerel poets exploit a generic quirk; in parody and in satire doggerel's vices turn into virtues, an effect Frye celebrates when he categorically observes, "Doggerel in satire is a sign of wit rather than incompetence."[27]

In Frye's terms, both judges write "intentional doggerel." An example of anti-poetry, Blackmun's quatrain mocks poetry as a means of knowledge. Instead of parodying "incompetent attempts at verse," he addresses Shakespeare, the language's most celebrated poet. As if to invoke his predecessor, Blackmun uses the same rhyme group centuries later, turning Shakespeare's sounds against him. To discredit Justice O'Connor's evidence, Blackmun places the law above poetry, presenting a judge's words as truer than the poet's. Eakin's verse rhymes legal terminology ("representation," "third-party verification," "underlying foundation," and "marital relation") as well as some of the case's more salacious details. The verse juxtaposes the law's august abstractions and the case's seedier reality.

In a reversal of Frye's aesthetic standard, the "intentional doggerel" strikes me as more objectionable in a legal context. The verse techniques register a certain attitude to the litigants and their plight; it casts them as the subjects of light comedy. In a sense, the poetry's departure from artistic decorum parallels its departure from legal decorum. In blunt terms, Eakin writes his opinion in doggerel because he finds the case funny.[28]

The two poems provide fairly clear examples of a murky genre in which "intentional" and "real doggerel" are not so easily distinguished. As Saintsbury's hedge suggests, a rhyme precariously marks what the author "is trying to do." Composition blurs the accidental and the intentional; a rhyme introduces unexpected opportunities based in sonic coincidences. "The chain reaction of a rhyme," Seamus Heaney observes, "can proceed happily and as it were autistically, in an area of mental operations cordoned off by and from the critical sense."[29] Following Pound, many poets report that rhymes "surprise" and "astonish" them, diverting the emerging poem from their original intention.[30] Depending on their temperaments, critics and poets have proposed spiritual metaphors for this process or described it as inscrutable.[31] W. H. Auden drew from philosophy to define the composition process as dialectical:

> In the process of composition, as every poet knows, the relation between experience and language is always dialectical, but in the finished product it must always appear to the reader to be a one-way relationship. In serious poetry thought, emotion, event, must always appear to dictate the diction, meter, and rhyme in which they are embodied; vice versa, in comic poetry it is the words, meter, rhyme, which must appear to create the thoughts, emotions, and events they require.[32]

Auden shrewdly distinguishes between the actual process of composition and the appearance the poem gives. A master of the two modes he mentions, Auden realizes that poets cultivate their reader's confidence. To do so, they establish command of their art, albeit differently. Depending on the kind of verse they compose, they project mastery or feign incompetence. Each mode requires an appropriate appearance.

Hip hop, however, does not respect such sensible distinctions between "intentional" and "real" doggerel, comic and serious poetry. Instead of renouncing rhyme, hip hop commits fully and openly to it. Again and again the art reveals the technique's flexibility. A single hip hop song may contain astonishingly different kinds of rhyme, ranging across a number of genres, including doggerel, satire, religious testimony, sexual boasting, social protest, and seduction. Few songs maintain a consistent tone; many artists boast that they do not. "A thousand styles in one verse," brags Rakim.[33] An extremely minor form in contemporary poetry, doggerel abounds in hip hop. Doggerel serves it so well because prosodic satire and parody rely on an established sense of metrical and rhyming decorum, which contemporary print-based poetry notably lacks. To register a "*protest* against the inadequacy, against the positive faultiness, of the regular prosody of the time," the poet needs a "regular prosody" to protest (*HEP* 394).

Lupe Fiasco's "Hip Hop Saved My Life," for instance, depends on the listener identifying the hip hop conventions it evokes. The song's opening describes his current situation:

> He said I write what I see
> Write to make it right
> Don't like where I be

As the title suggests, the song describes a familiar hip hop figure, introduced as "my homie with the dream": an aspiring artist who wants to raise his family out of poverty.

What follows describes how writing is connected with his goals:

> I like to make it like
> The sights on TV
> Quite the great life
> So nice and easy.[34]

Asked to describe his style, Fiasco mentions a "simple complexity. "I always want it to seem simple on the surface," he notes, "but if you listen or try to listen—which most cats don't do—but if you really listen, you'll see . . ."[35] In "Hip Hop Saved My Life," deceptively simple rhymes and a pinched vocabulary describe a deceptively complex situation. The song plays with its monosyllabic language, squeezing thirty-three words into thirty-seven syllables. "He said I write what I see," the unnamed figure advises as if hip-hop requires only unmediated witness. However, the pun "write"/"right" suggests that writing might offer a form of transformation and redress, not merely reportage. The second pun, "I *like* to make it *like* / The sights on TV" (my italics), recovers the longing buried within the trope. Any poetry student can define a simile as the comparison of two unlike things, but in practice readers tend to overlook the unlikeness for the shared property. In other words, we focus on how the two things are similar, neglecting their essential difference. With its understated, punning wordplay, Fiasco's simile recalls what similes generally smooth over: how the tenor differs from the vehicle, and in the song's case, how the speaker's reality remains unlike the "sights" that inspire him.

To succeed, satiric doggerel must perform a contradictory task, mocking techniques both current and outmoded. Later in the stanza, Fiasco describes the song that the aspiring artist records:

> A bass heavy medley with a sample from the 70s
> With a screwed up hook that went
> STACK THAT CHEESE
> Somethin' somethin' somethin'

Like many hip-hop songs, the song within "Hip Hop Saved My Life" presents a hook, a catchy refrain of street slang: in this case, "stack that cheese," meaning to make money.

The verse continues its commentary with these lines:

> Mother sister cousin
> STACK THAT CHEESE
> He couldn't think of nothin'
> STACK THAT CHEESE. *(HH)*

Introducing his hook for the final time in "Jesus Walks," Kanye West boasts, "Next time I'm in the club everybody screaming out [. . .] Jesus walks."[36] In West's song, the crowd's recognition validates his ambition; he crafts a line that fans shout back wherever he goes. In "Hip Hop Saved My Life," Fiasco shows this aspiration's smallness. He criticizes coolness as a goal, detailing the song's success in less glamorous venues: "Eleven hundred friends on his MySpace page / Stack that cheese got seven hundred plays" *(HH)*. Such listeners mistake bad music for good, admiring what they should ignore. To protest against this prevalent bad taste, "Hip Hop Saved My Life" uses a doggerel structure, a song stripped to its most basic, crowd-pleasing element, "a screwed hook," "Somethin' somethin' somethin' / STACK THAT CHEESE." In an evocative rhyme, "somethin'" turns into "nothin'," a lack of artistic invention, since the entire song-within-the-song exists for its hook.

As another song on the same album more bluntly asserts, Fiasco associates the technique of the hook with commercial pandering. In the chorus of "Dumb It Down," the hip-hop artist repeatedly receives the following advice:

> You putting me to sleep nigga (Dumb it down)
> That's why you ain't popping in the streets nigga (Dumb it down)
> You ain't winning no awards nigga (Dumb it down)[3]

Resisting these pressures, Fiasco declares, "I flatly refuse" (*DD*). "Hip Hop Saved My Life" works more slyly. Instead of directly stating its artistic principles, the song achieves "simple complexity." The two hooks resemble each other grammatically; each consists of a three-syllable, three-word command. One hook answers the other. "Stack that cheese" satisfies those who demand he "dumb it down" but does so with a wink and a nod to those who "really listen."

In his doggerel, Fiasco fights bad taste. More commonly, though, doggerel exploits bad taste's powerful appeals. Much doggerel entertains the suspicion that its critics might be right, though for the wrong reasons: that the lurid pleasures the rhymes offer might prove unhealthy, if not destructive. In "Ignorant Shit," Jay-Z rhymes his critics' censure with impressively vulgar street insults from two languages, English and Spanish:

> This is that ignorant shit you like:
> nigga fuck shit ass bitch trick precise.
> I got that ignorant shit you love:
> nigga fuck shit *maricón puta* and drugs.

He continues addressing his critics in this mode and also suggests at the end that the critics are responding to his lines—even if they do admonish them:

> I got that ignorant shit you need:
> nigga fuck shit ass trick plus weed.
> I'm only trying to give you what you want:
> nigga fuck shit ass bitch you like it, don't front![38]

The even lines apparently confirm the most common charges leveled against hip-hop: that it presents nothing more than mindless obscenity, namely, base expressions of misogyny, homophobia, and violent aggression, or, in Jay-Z's terms, "ignorant shit." Entire lines list the roughest vulgarity. As if English lacked the resources necessary to curse with sufficient force, Jay-Z turns to street Spanish, insulting both male and female sexuality. While Fiasco presents hip-hop as an alternative to drug dealing, Jay-Z presents a more traditional figure: the artist as drug dealer. While some songs praise music for its healing force, "when it hits, you feel no pain,"[39] Jay-Z describes it as an illicit drug that turns listeners into addicts: "crack music," as Kanye West similarly calls it.[40]

In "Ignorant Shit," rhyme recasts criticism into celebration. It focuses the furious vulgarity, the nightmare of conventional decorum, into a shapely form. In the song's metaphor, the words resemble a well-cut drug: "precise." To achieve this effect, the rhymes pair desire and fulfillment: "like," "love," "need," and "want" with what the listener seeks: "precise," "drugs," "weed," and "front." In the anomalous final rhyme, "want"/"front," Jay-Z taunts his critics for their hypocrisy: "you like it, don't front." In a more representative gesture, Jay-Z faces the challenge of finding a rhyme for "love," a notoriously difficult task. Bending pronunciation, he rhymes "love" with "drugs." As in this example, the rhymes seek to thrill. Comic and serious, they make "intentional" and "real" doggerel indistinguishable.

In Nas's phrase, both Jay-Z and Lupe Fiasco "carry on tradition"; they claim an artistic lineage, complete with characteristic techniques, canonical figures, and distinctive motifs, a situation in which doggerel thrives.[41] Each performer borrows and transforms. Within the last few decades, hip-hop has achieved great sophistication, growing into the era's defining culture: "an international phenomenon of imitation, reaction, and general influence that in its most common form is obvious to the point of parody."[42] As in Gordon Braden's characterization of Renaissance Petrarchism, hip-hop provides a distinctive period style, including identifiable modes of expression. The ubiquity of hip-hop parodies reinforces the music's influence, able to accommodate Ali G's mock interviews and the Roots' video for "What They Do," a deft parody of hip-hop video conventions. Knowledge of the genre's traditions establishes an artist's credentials; ignorance discredits performer and listener alike. "I got an exam, let's see if y'all pass it," raps Nas, "Let's see who can quote a Daddy Kane line the fastest" (*COT*). In this musical "exam," allusion combines challenge and homage. If the listener cannot swiftly quote a Daddy Kane line, he fails, not Daddy Kane, whose excellence remains undisputed. "I kick it with the OG's / And listen to the oldies," a young rapper boasts in his debut album, recognizing that hip-hop mastery requires historical knowledge.[43] To "carry on tradition," an artist must learn it. His apprenticeship, though, involves a certain irony: the "oldies" he studies date back only a few decades, recorded in hip-hop's "golden age," most commonly defined as the late 1980s and early 1990s.[44] A young art, hip-hop has achieved a startlingly quick maturity, aided by new recording and distribution technologies. Backed by these advances, hip-hop's techniques have grown pyrotechnic and allusive. Following the genre's dazzling development, the current moment offers the richest resources and inspires the greatest accomplishment. We are living in hip-hop's golden age.

Two examples clarify the advantages that hip-hop currently enjoys. In *Cosmopolis*, Don DeLillo eulogizes Brutha Fez, a fictional rapper "born Raymond Gathers in the Bronx."[45] Six times in six pages, DeLillo quotes Fez's songs, "his vocal adaptations of ancient Sufi music, rapping in Punjabi and Urdu and in the black-swagger English of the street." The first example consists of a quatrain with three-stress lines and a terminal rhyme:

> Gettin' shot is easy
> Tried it seven times
> Now I'm just a solo poet
> Workin' on my rhymes (*C* 133)

The lyrics deeply impress Eric Packer, a billionaire asset manager, as he watches Fez's funeral procession from inside his limousine. Humbled by the experience, DeLillo notes of Packer, "Here was a spectacle he could clearly not command" (*C* 136). Fez's music dispirits Packer until he weeps uncontrollably. His sorrow arises from an obscure source. Packer weighs his area of expertise, international capital, against Fez's rhymes, judging the latter to be more vital, expressive, and complex.

The funeral scene evokes two kinds of envy: a character's and a novelist's. While Packer jealously views the "spectacle" Fez can "command," DeLillo, depicting a financier married to a poet, wonders if hip-hop might be the superior art, more capable of addressing the culture's possibilities than the novel, poetry, and financial data. Yet DeLillo also thinks of hip-hop as a kind of artless art, one easily faked. Hip-hop artists typically stress the training they undergo to develop their rhyming skills and the effort each song takes. "I'd be lying if I said it was easy," Eminem observes. "Sometimes I'll spend hours on a single rhyme, or days, or I'll give up and come back to it later. Anyone who says they write a verse in less than twenty minutes is full of shit."[46] Brutha Fez raps about a similar determination to develop his talent. Setting aside his character's insight, DeLillo writes the rhymes that Fez performs, instead of simply describing them or quoting a song.

This strategy is not unique. In Tom Wolfe's *I Am Charlotte Simmons*, college basketball players listen to the music of "Doctor Dis." The novel includes a dozen lines from what it calls "the most rebellious, offensive, vile, obnoxious rap available on CD," lyrics so extreme that one character wonders if "Doctor Dis himself was a cynic who created this stuff as a parody of the genre."[47] Raising this possibility, Wolfe struts for his readers, pleased to show that he, a middle-aged, white dandy, can write lyrics as awful as those the teenagers admire. Wolfe's cynical parody differs from DeLillo's anxious homage by conveying condescension, not ambivalence. A keen observer of contemporary culture, DeLillo wishes to show his mastery of hip-hop technique, to reassert his art against it and reclaim the novel's status. The lyrics, however, lack any animating quality, let alone the trilingual energy that their introduction promises. Their "black-swagger English" sounds more studied than street, more whiny than assertive, casting Fez as a lesser 50 Cent down to the number of wounds he suffered: seven, not nine. They closely resemble Justice Blackmun's verse, employing the plural form of the same rhymes, but without the judge's wit. Presenting hip-hop as easy, DeLillo, a prose stylist, writes charmless, unintentional doggerel.

Of course some highly skilled poets employ patterned rhyme, but typically do so shyly. They favor enjambment, a technique to diminish the rhyme's prominence. A means of concealment, enjambment addresses a potential embarrassment, allowing the rhymes to pass without too much fuss: seen, perhaps, but only faintly heard. Doggerel, though, requires a flamboyance that strains contemporary poetry's resources. When researching *Practical Criticism*, I. A. Richards famously provided his students with poems that lacked a title, author, or date. To consider the predicament that a poet who writes doggerel faces, I briefly will borrow Richards's method. Consider the following poem, which denounces a proposal to expand faith-based education, without the help of the poem's author or title:

> Oh for the pure Intellectual Fever
> Of Halal Madresseh and Kosher Yeshiva
>
> Where every pupil's exactly like you
> And with only one Answer it *has* to be true
>
> Oh for the play of the Disinterested Mind
> The impartial inquiry you're certain to find
>
> Where a Catholic Priest can tell you what's what
> And ensure that you can never encounter a Prot
>
> Where a Protestant Elder can call you to order
> And assure you the Pope should be swimming in ordure
>
> Oh for the stirring sanguinary stories
> That admonish us all with Our Martyrs' past glories
>
> Oh for the splendors of Faith-Based Education
> That spread Fear and Hatred throughout the whole Nation.[48]

It is safe to say that Richards's students would heartily condemn this poem. The students, Richards noticed, disliked off-rhyme, denouncing any examples as "poor rhymes."[49] Richards noted two main reasons for this tendency. Because the students never learned how to rhyme competently, they admired poets who accomplish what they could not and treat with "great severity" those whose verse at least superficially resembles their efforts (*PC* 34). "Success or failure for the neophyte is very largely a question of the control of rhymes," Richards observed. "An exaggerated respect for rhyming ability is the result" (*PC* 33–34). Second, the students criticized off-rhyme because of "the desire for something tangible by which to judge poetic merit":

> Normal sensibilities can decide with considerable certainty whether two sounds rhyme perfectly or not. The task is nearly as simple as that of a carpenter measuring planks. It is a grateful relief to pass from the nebulous world of intellectual and emotional accordances to definite questions of sensory fact. By assuming that the poet intended to rhyme perfectly, we get a clear unambiguous test for his success or failure. (PC 34)

Contemporary literary criticism does not offer "a clear unambiguous test" for "success or failure." Still, the poem's author, Dick Davis, a distinguished translator and writer of metrical verse, safeguards his lines with an excessive scrupulousness, employing the techniques that Richards removed and I briefly set aside. Sharing a strategy with the other recent doggerel, Davis's title, "William McGonagall Welcomes the Initiative for a Greater Role for Faith-Based Education," sets the genre.[50] As the title indicates, Davis openly borrows from Mc-Gonagall, "the King of Doggerel," who, as Davis reports, "has the dubious reputation of being 'the writer of the worst poetry in English'" (TS 53). In the title and the endnote, twice Davis identifies the poem's inspiration as if to protect himself against the accusation that he writes "real" doggerel. Yet the poem lacks the "outrageous, shocking" force that intentional doggerel conveys. Davis borrows the style of a poet dead for more than a century. Addressing current political realities, he longs for a literary culture that would recognize his "rhymes" as "bad." A sad sense of loss infuses the verse. For the purposes of intentional doggerel such as Davis's, a simple method of appreciating rhyme is better than no method at all.

Hip-hop artists of various skill levels proceed with greater confidence. Committed to rhyme, they emphasize the technique so deeply that doggerel almost inevitably results. Just as hip-hop prizes both collaboration and competition, rhyme establishes connections even as an artist asserts his uniqueness. A rhyme echoes and expands; it recalls neighboring sounds and previous uses, and calls for responses. Demonstrating this dynamic, Kanye West's "Gold Digger" starts with a gesture familiar to hip-hop: a nostalgic allusion. Starting the song, Jamie Foxx imitates Ray Charles while Foxx revises lines from "I Got a Woman." "She take my money when I'm in need / Yeah, she's a trifling friend indeed," Foxx sings, borrowing Charles's rhyme but reversing the meaning.[51] Charles sang, "She give me money when I'm in need / Yeah, she's a kind of friend indeed."[52] This allusion marks an affinity based in a contrast; Foxx longs for the subservient loyalty that Charles celebrates. "Never runnin' in the streets and leavin' me alone," Charles praises his lover, "She knows a woman's place is right there now in her home." Yet the song's light tone presents sexual politics as a farce, not a battle, as the unchanged rhyme marks the song's true desire. To borrow Charles's rhyme is to try on his style.

The specific kind of rhyming that the song employs adds to this effects. Midway through "Gold Digger," West introduces a cautionary example, a star pro football player exploited by a gold digger: "You will see him on TV any given Sunday / Win the Super Bowl and drive off in a Hyundai." Instead of the pro football player enjoying his earnings, the following lines provide examples of how the gold digger is spending his money:

> She was supposed to buy ya shorty Tyco with ya money
> She went to the doctor got lipo with ya money
> She walkin' around lookin' like Michael with ya money
> Shoulda got that insured, GEICO for ya money.

In this highly effective doggerel, each rhyme strains to outdo its predecessor. The opening antonym-rhyme, "Sunday" and "Hyundai" ironically counterpoints symbols of professional success and financial failure. The football star drives a Hyundai, not one of the luxury cars ubiquitous in hip-hop songs and videos, though he plays on Sunday, when the National Football League holds its games. The next rhyme group contains four instances, two more than the first, though the rhymes remain trochaic, blurring this division. The second group's opening rhyme connects childhood and adult realms: toys and elective surgery, "Tyco" and "lipo." The next rhyme illustrates this comparison, invoking Michael Jackson, a figure bizarrely caught between childhood and adulthood, as well as genders and race. Like the passage's other primarily visual rhyme, "Hyundai," "Michael" evokes both the image and its contrast: in the case of Jackson, the difference between his peculiarly refashioned body and earlier versions. The rhymes sketch a comic equation: "Tyco" + "lipo" = "Michael." Instead of employing rhyme to maintain distance from contemporary culture, West, like many hip-hop artists, characteristically uses it to evoke the era's distinctive features, including its celebrities, products, surgical procedures, and companies. The rhymes couple new inflections and objects of desire, as well as updated grotesqueries and threats. They mark a sophisticated worldliness, an insider's knowledge of contemporary mores.

The style's availability allows artists to create with breathtaking speed, exploiting the latest technologies. On September 2, 2005, Kanye West appeared on a fundraiser for the victims of Hurricane Katrina, broadcast live. Ignoring the prepared script, he criticized the Bush administration's response to the disaster and the media's portrayal of it. Appearing beside West, Mike Myers looked increasingly helpless: a comedian fated to be the butt of many jokes. Just after West exclaimed, "George Bush doesn't care about black people!" the cameras cut away.[53] Four days after the benefit, a previously uncelebrated Houston hip-hop duo, the Legendary K.O., posted on their website "George Bush Doesn't Care About Black People," their reworking of "Gold Digger" recorded on home computers, and composed through email and instant messaging. "Within the first twenty-four hours, it was downloaded 10,000 times," Legendary K.O. member Damien Randle observed. "It crashed our server."[54] Within days a freelance video producer in New Brunswick, New Jersey, composed an arresting video and circulated it on the internet, attracting more attention.

"George Bush Doesn't Care About Black People" recasts the chorus of "Gold Digger," decrying Bush, not a potential lover: "I ain't saying he a gold digger / but he ain't messing with no broke niggas." Borrowing the "Gold Digger" instrumental, the chorus repeats a more cutting version of West's criticism, asserting again and again, "George Bush don't like black people." In "Gold Digger," West's rhymes display his linguistic and comic inventiveness; they delight in the connections that sound coincidences allow. Setting West's words to his tune, the Legendary K.O. crafts the same device into a gesture of outrage. The first quatrain announces this strategy in suitably forceful language:

> Hurricane came through, fucked us up round here.
> Government acting like it's bad luck down here.
> All I know is that you better bring some trucks round here.
> Wonder why I got my middle finger up 'round here.[55]

The stanza moves from skepticism to defiance. The first end-rhyme pair suggests that more than "bad luck" "fucked us up," that is, caused the speaker's misery. Building on this point, the third line cites logistical needs quite separate from misfortune: "trucks" filled with supplies, ready to transport New Orleans residents from the city. In the fourth line, the rhyme changes both in function and construction, playing with the listener's expectations. Given the rising anger that the lines express, the listener anticipates that the curse, "fuck," will return. Instead, the fourth line repeats the preposition "up" that the first line downplays, raising it to a position of prominence. The rhyme pattern also changes, introducing an approximate vowel-rhyme different from the previous full-rhymes. Both maneuvers recall the anticipated word's absence. It may seem odd to call a doggerel description of an obscene gesture tactful, but the final line draws significant force from the decision not to repeat the swear. Instead, the rhyme itself strikes the formal equivalent of the depicted gesture: "Wonder why I got my middle finger up 'round here." A balance of desperation and dignity, the rhyme surprises with its defiant refusal.

As this example suggests, doggerel listens hard to rhyme, trusting it to direct the song's energies. Rhyme openly generates the possibilities that the song pursues. To many, the result may seem uncontrolled or, rather, controlled by the wrong forces. Yet hip-hop suggests that doggerel achieves a surprising flexibility, ranging from comic to serious, delicate to vulgar. It would be a mistake, though, to say the technique determines the result. Rather, hip-hop hungers for rhymes;

it feeds on nearly whatever it can find. Such doggerel lays bare the machinery of its making, amplifying the process that poetry typically conceals: how an environment of rhyme turns into art.

Notes

1. Davie, Donald. *Collected Poems*. Chicago: University of Chicago Press, 1991. 166.

2. Nas. "Hip Hop is Dead." *Hip Hop is Dead*. Def Jam, 2006.

3. Ferry, Anne. "Love rhymes with of." *Modernism / Modernity* 7:3. 424.

4. "Daniel Kane interviews the poet Harryette Mullen." *Poets on Poetry*. WriteNet, August 2008. www.writenet.org/poetschat/poetschat_h_mullen.html.

5. I take the details of the case from the court opinion, *Porreco v. Porreco*, 811 A.2d 566 (Pa. 2002). LEXIS 2468; hereafter cited in the text as *PP*.

6. Clinton, Hillary Rodham. *It Takes a Village: And Other Lessons Children Teach Us*. New York: Simon and Schuster, 2006. 137; hereafter cited as *ITV*.

7. Fiedler, Leslie A. *No! In Thunder*. New York: Stein and Day, 1972. 25.

8. Quoted in: Van Duyn, Mona. Untitled essay. *Ecstatic Occasions, Expedient Forms*. Ed. David Lehman. Ann Arbor: University of Michigan Press, 1999. 215.

9. Milton, John. *Complete Poems and Major Prose*. Indianapolis, IN: Hacket, 2003. 210; Sidney, Philip. *Sidney's 'The Defence of Poesy' and Selected Renaissance Literary Criticism*. Ed. Gavin Alexander. New York: Penguin, 2004. 52.

10. Swift, Jonathan. *The Works of the Rev. Jonathan Swift, D.D. . . . : With Notes, Historical and Critical, Vol. 8*. Ed. John Nichols. New York: William Durell, 1812. 68.

11. Swinburne, Hugh A. C. Review in *Fortnightly Review*, October 1867, rpt. in *Matthew Arnold: Prose Writings, Volume 2: The Poetry*. Ed. Carl Dawson and John Pfordresher. London: Routledge, 1995. 182.

12. Arnold, Matthew. *On Translating Homer*. London: Smith, Elder, 1896. 15.

13. Borges, Jorge Luis. *Borges on Writing*. Ed. Norman Thomas di Giovanni, Daniel Halpern, and Frank MacShane. New York: Eco Press, 1973. 141.

14. Hass, Robert. *Now and Then: The Poet's Choice Columns, 1997–2000*. New York: Counterpoint, 2007. 256.

15. Kenner, Hugh. *Historical Fictions: Essays*. Athens: University of Georgia Press, 1995. 283.

16. Hunter, J. Paul. "Sleeping Beauties: Are Historical Aesthetics Worth Recovering?" *Eighteenth-Century Studies*, 34:1. 2000. 2; hereafter cited as *SB*.

17. Perloff, Marjorie, and Robert von Hallberg. "Dialogue on Evaluation in Poetry." *Professions: Conversations on the Future of Literary and Cultural Studies*. Ed. Donald Hall. Urbana: University of Illinois Press, 2001. 95.

18. Perloff, Marjorie. *Rhyme and Meaning in the Poetry of Yeats*. De Proprietatibus litterarum, series practica, no. 5. The Hague: Mouton, 1970.

19. Hejinian, Lyn. *The Language of Inquiry*. Berkeley: University of California Press, 2000. 307.

20. Pound, Ezra. *Literary Essays*. Ed. Thomas Stearns Eliot. London: Faber and Faber, 1954. 7.

21. "Pandemonium." *Merriam-Webster's Rhyming Dictionary: A Guide to Creating Lyrical Expressions*. New York: Merriam-Webster, 2001. 263.

22. *Browning-Ferris Industries of Vermont, Inc. et al. v. Kelco Disposal, Inc. et al.*, 492 U.S. 257 (1989 Lexus 3285) 290, B; hereafter cited in the text as *BF*.

23. Parini, Jay. "Introduction." *The Columbia History of American Poetry: Lustra to Mauberley*. Ed. Jay Parini and Brett Candlish Millier. New York: Columbia University Press, 1993. xxv.

24. *The American Heritage Dictionary of the English Language* (Fourth Edition). 2000.

25. See: Saintsbury, George. "Appendix III: The Nature and Phenomena of Doggerel." *A History of English Prosody From the Twelfth Century to the Present Day, Vol I, From the Origins to Spenser*. New York: Macmillan, 1906. 392, 413–16; hereafter cited in the text as *HEP*. For a sensitive consideration of the challenges facing contemporary doggerel, see: Rothman, David. "Ars Doggerel." *Expansive Poetry & Music Online*. Expansive Poetry Online, August 2008. expansivepoetryonline.com/journal/culto297.html.

26. Frye, Northrop. *The Well-Tempered Critic*. Bloomington: Indiana University Press, 1963. 69; hereafter cited in the text as *WTC*.

27. Frye, Northrop. *Fables of Identity: Studies in Poetic Mythology*. New York: Harcourt, Brace & World, 1963. 183.

28. Eakin admitted as much when he told a reporter, "I would never do it in a serious criminal case. The subject of the case has to call for a little grin here or there." Liptak, Adam. "Justices Call on Bench's Bard to Limit His Lyricism." *New York Times*, 15 December 2002.

29. Quoted in: McDonald, Pete. *Serious Poetry: Form and Authority from Yeats to Hill*. New York: Oxford University Press, 2007. 87.

30. For instance, X. J. Kennedy observes: "When you write in rhyme, it's as if you're walking across a series of stepping stones into the darkness, and you can't see what's at the far end of the stepping stones. So you're led onward, often to say things that surprise and astonish you." In *Fourteen on Form: Conversations with Poets*. Ed. William Baer. Jackson: University Press of Mississippi, 2004. 246–47.

For similar reasons, Donald Davie called rhyme "Rhyme, of all the tricks that are / In the Muse's repertoire / The most irrational" (*CP* 224).

31. For instance, Willard Spiegelman observes, "Rhyme may be either discovery or creation, depending on whether it arrives mysteriously and suddenly or striven for and plotted (and who can ever tell?)." In *How Poets See the World: The Art of Description in Contemporary Poetry*. New York: Oxford University Press, 2005. 46.

32. Quoted in: Hecht, Anthony. *Melodies Unheard: Essays on the Mysteries of Poetry*. Baltimore: Johns Hopkins Press, 2003. 49–50. Hecht calls Auden's point "almost indisputable."

33. Rakim. "R.A.K.I.M." *8 Mile: Music from and Inspired by the Motion Picture*. Interscope Records, 2002.

34. Fiasco, Lupe. "Hip Hop Saved My Life." *The Cool*. Written by Wasalu Muhammed Jaco, Nicholle Jean Leary, and Rudolph Loyola Lopez. Atlantic, 2007; hereafter cited in text as *HH*.

35. Fiasco, Lupe. "Almost Famous." Interview with Kenny Rodriguez. Nobody Smiling, August 2008. www.nobodysmiling.com/hiphop/interview/84943.php.

36. West, Kanye. "Jesus Walks." *The College Dropout*. Roc-A-Fella, 2004.

37. Fiasco, Lupe. "Dumb It Down. "Hip Hop Saved My Life." *The Cool*. Written by Demarco Lamonte Castle, Wasalu Muhammed Jaco, and Rudolph Loyola Lopez. Atlantic, 2007; hereafter cited as *DD*.

38. Jay-Z. "Ignorant Shit." *American Gangster*. Written by Shawn C. Carter, Dwight Grant, Ernest Isley, Marvin Isley, O'Kelly Isley, Ronald Isley, Rudolph Bernard Isley, and Christopher H. Jasper. Roc-A-Fella, 2007.

39. Marley, Bob. "Trenchtown Rock." *Trenchtown Rock*. Phantom Sound & Vision, 2004.

40. West, Kanye. "Crack Music." *Late Registration*. Roc-A-Fella, 2005.

41. Nas. "Carry on Tradition." *Hip Hop is Dead*. Def Jam, 2006; hereafter cited as *COT*.

42. Braden, Gordon. *Petrarchan Love and Continental Renaissance*. New Haven: Yale University Press, 1999. 63.

43. Yung Ralph. "I Work Hard." *Most Unexpected*. Universal Republic, 2008.

44. See, for instance: Dyson, Michael Eric. *Know What I Mean?: Reflections on Hip Hop*. New York: BasicCivitas, 2007. 64, who dates "the golden age of hip hop" as "from 1987 to 1993."

45. DeLillo, Don. *Cosmopolis*. New York: Scribner, 2003. 133; hereafter cited in the text as *C*.

46. Smith, Zadie. "The Zen of Eminem." *Vibe*. 28 January 2005. Vibe.com, August 2008. www .vibe.com/news/magazine_features/2005/01/cover_story_zen_eminem/.

47. Wolfe, Tom. *I Am Charlotte Simmons*. New York: Farrar, Straus, and Giroux, 2004. 44–45.

48. From *A Trick of Sunlight* (2006, page 43) by Dick Davis. Reprinted with the permission of Ohio university Press/Swallow Press, Athens, Ohio (www.ohioswallow.com); hereafter cited in the text as *TS*.

49. Richards, I. A. *Practical Criticism: A Study of Literary Judgment*. New York: Harcourt, Brace & World, 1929. 33; hereafter cited in the text as *PC*.

50. See, for instance: Mullen, Harryette. "Jinglejangle." *Sleeping with the Dictionary*. Berkeley: University of California Press, 2002. 35; and Field, Edward. "A Doggerel of Symptoms." *Counting Myself Lucky: Selected Poems 1963–1992*. Boston: Black Sparrow, 1992. 56–59.

51. West, Kanye. "Gold Digger." *Late Registration*. Written by Kanye West, Ray Charles, and Renald Richard. Roc-A-Fella, 2005.

52. Charles, Ray. "I've Got a Woman." *The Very Best of Ray Charles*. Written by Ray Charles and Renald Richard. Rhino, 2000. The song is more commonly referred to as "I Got a Woman," and I follow that convention to minimize confusion.

53. De Moraes, Lisa. "Kanye West's Torrent of Criticism, Live on NBC." *Washington Post*. 3 September 2005; C01. www.washingtonpost.com/wp-dyn/content/article/2005/09/03/AR2005090300165 .html.

54. See: Lenand, John. "Art Born of Outrage in the Internet Age." *New York Times*. 25 September 2005, Sec. 4, p. 1; and "Legendary K.O. Press Release." K-Otix, August 2008. www.k-otix.com/index .php?option=com_content&task=view&id=43&Itemid=2.

55. The Legendary K.O. "George Bush Doesn't Like Black People." Written by Big Mon and Damien, a.k.a. Dem Knock-Out Boyz. August 2008. revver.com/video/71633/george-bush-dont-like-black-people/.

THE SONNET WITHIN THE SONG: COUNTRY LYRICS AND THE SHAKESPEAREAN SONNET STRUCTURE

CHARLOTTE PENCE

The popularity of the sonnet has ebbed and flowed, but one of its popular periods coincided with a time when songwriters and poets experienced a growing separation between their two genres. During the sixteenth century (or perhaps a little earlier), poets and songwriters began to classify their work into separate genres. Simply put, songwriters took to the streets to perform their work whereas poets took to the page to print their work. Since the poem and song were splitting apart more and more during the height of the sonnet's popularity, this essay analyzes how borrowed structures from the sonnet can still be found within some country songs today.

Form is content-as-arranged; content is form-as-deployed.
—Helen Vendler

I was flipping through a poetry anthology and came upon this partial definition for a sonnet: "a form every poet will try." While the definition may not help a beginning poet understand how to write a sonnet, it felt like an inside joke from lexicographer to reader—similar to Samuel Johnson's hidden gems in *A Dictionary of the English Language*, such as his definition of *Monsieur*: "a term of reproach for a Frenchman."[1] What I enjoy about the sonnet being defined as a form every poet will try is how it is correct even while it errs. A sonnet is, of course, a lot more than a form every poet will try—but every poet *will* try it. And every poet will also tell us how "sonnet" means little song (or little sound), implying some marriage between the two genres.

While sonnet does literally mean "little song," there is no evidence that the first sonnets were ever accompanied by music. Giacomo da Lentino did adapt the eight-line *strambotto*, a type of thirteenth-century Sicilian peasant song, to provide the sonnet's base, but otherwise the sonnet represents a shift in poetry away from music (Oppenheimer 176). The lack of musical accompaniment to the sonnet led to profound changes in poetry thereafter. The removal of music from the lyric allowed for a change of focus, tone, and approach; instead of writing on troubadour subjects such as chivalry and courtly love, poets reflected on private matters. Troubadour poetry was meant as performance art, but sonnets were meant as self-reflection. The earliest examples of the sonnet allowed for what Oppenheimer calls the "dialectical resolution of emotional problems," meaning the speaker could explore issues within himself or herself, a notion not found in troubadour poetry to such an extent. This sense of "dialectical resolution" regarding inner struggles remains a feature of contemporary sonnets—and much of contemporary poetry. In this essay, I examine poetry's twin—songs—in relation to this idea of dialectical resolution. Does the ghost of the sonnet exist in contemporary songs? It does indeed. To be clear, however, not every song functions as a sonnet just as not every poem functions as a sonnet. What is interesting is how contemporary songwriters have continued to use and adapt sonnet features.

The popularity of the sonnet has ebbed and flowed, but one of its popular periods coincided with a time when songwriters and poets experienced a growing separation between their two genres. According to *A Dictionary of Literary Terms*, "during the 16th century (or perhaps a little earlier) a kind of fissiparation took place. The poet and composer/musician began to part company and the classifying of literary forms or genres put the song in an individual category" (Cuddon 638). The fact that the poem and song were splitting apart more and more during the height of the sonnet's popularity led me to investigate the sonnet's influence in songs even though I knew the majority of songwriters rarely intended to write a sonnet. I decided to analyze country songs in particular because this is a genre where one can still be solely a songwriter—as opposed to the lead singer, bandmate, or producer; in other words, country music is an industry that emphasizes the lyrics rather than, for example, musical experimentation and innovation. The genre also emphasizes learning traditional forms and employing them.

A little overview of the sonnet is helpful to understand what some songs are doing. While British poets first used the Petrarchan form, Henry Howard, Earl of Surrey adapted the form to create what is now considered the Shakespearean sonnet. Many people might say that a Shakespearean sonnet is a fourteen-line poem that rhymes ABAB, CDCD, EFEF, GG whose meter is iambic pentameter. I would say that those are *not* the distinguishing features of the sonnet—and in fact perhaps the least important. In Helen Vendler's introduction to her excellent analysis on Shakespeare's sonnet sequence, she discusses what is a Shakespearean sonnet—and more importantly what is *not* a Shakespearean sonnet even when all formal poetic concerns are met (i.e., rhyme scheme, iambic pentameter, and length). Vendler even disqualifies some of Shakespeare's own Shakespearean sonnets if the poem does not meet what she considers to be the critical feature of a sonnet: a logical and emotional development. I could not agree more. The sonnet operates on a level that trumps a simple checklist. A true sonnet features a specific rhetorical argument, maintains a large proportion of argument to conclusion, presents a turn, and finally, establishes a change within the speaker. I will explain all of these criteria in more detail through examples from songs.

A look at Randy Travis's song "On the Other Hand" (released in 1985) reveals how a Shakespearean sonnet form can function within a song. Considering that the rhetorical mode is most critical to the sonnet's success, I will begin analyzing in terms of this feature. The Shakespearean sonnet's rhetorical mode allows, in fact, I would say demands, progression of thought, contradiction, dialectical reasoning, and resolution within its three quatrains, and concluding couplet. The first quatrain introduces the issue, the next two quatrains add complications, and the final couplet reaches a hard-fought conclusion. "On the Other Hand" co-written by Don Schlitz and Paul Overstreet organizes itself rhetorically the same way a sonnet does.

This song is written in second form (verse, chorus, verse, chorus). In the first verse (composed of four lines), the issue is introduced when the speaker tells a woman who is present that he would like to spend the night with her: "On one hand I count the reasons, I could stay with you / And hold you close to me, all night long." As this verse ends, the speaker reiterates that he wants to play "lover's games" and that "there's no reason why it's wrong." But the speaker is married, as revealed in the chorus,' which is the next four lines: "But on the other hand, there's a golden band / To remind me of someone who would not understand." Here we have the complication: he is married. We also have a further complication: his wife would not understand nor forgive this act. The second verse, lines nine through twelve, provide more complication as it explains why the speaker would cheat—which is a difficult position to defend and a risky stance for a first-person song. The speaker explains that he has felt dead before this other woman came into his life, and suddenly the adulterer is presented in a more complicated way: "In your arms I feel the passion, I thought had died. / When I looked into your eyes, I found myself" (lines 9–10). Part of the attraction then, and another element to the complication, is that the speaker needs the affair. "I found myself" is not a throwaway line but one that emphasizes why this is not simply cheating out of a loss of self-control; this is cheating due to a sense of self-realization. The rhetorical mode of introduction of issue, followed by complication, another contradiction, then resolution is clear. "On the Other Hand" echoes other features of the sonnet that reveal the extent to which the sonnet form is embedded in this song.

The proportion of argument to conclusion is similar in both Travis's song and the Shakespearean sonnet. For example, typically twelve out of fourteen lines in a sonnet will lead to the conclusion. In Travis's song, eleven of the twelve lines debate what to do until the decision is stated in the last line of the chorus. As Paul Fussell wrote in *Poetic Meter and Poetic Form*, "A poet who understands the sonnet form is the one who has developed an instinct for exploiting the principle of imbalance." Why this "principle of imbalance" is so important relates to the origin of the sonnet; Giacomo da Lentino shaped the sonnet form to aid in the analysis of personal problems. For a sonnet to present a true conundrum, a number of complications need to be present. Therefore, most of the poem will analyze the problem rather than emphasize the conclusion.

This song also features a turn, which helps one to reach the conclusion. The turn in the sonnet, often considered a signature of the form, is the moment where a shift of thinking, a change in perspective, or a movement toward a new direction occurs. Sometimes the turn is implicit in the white space on the page after line twelve in a sonnet or sometimes it is more explicit. (Granted, the sonnet may feature two turns and the turn does not necessarily have to come between lines twelve and thirteen, but it will come near the end of the sonnet.) To understand how the turn works in the Travis song we must first look at the conclusion, because the turn often leads to the conclusion. One can view the turn as providing the critical thought that aids in the solution. The conclusion to Travis's song is "But the reason I must go is on the other hand" (line 8). Here the speaker concludes that he must leave this other woman because of his wedding vows. This conclusion, however, is partly determined by the lines that occur right before it: the turn of the song. A thought development has occurred in the "white space" between the verse and chorus, between lines four and five. Line four tells the listener that the speaker sees no reason why the affair is wrong. But the next spoken phrase says otherwise: "But on the other hand, there's a golden band / to remind me of someone who would not understand" (5–6). What is new in the speaker's development is not that the marriage vows prohibit this love affair; the speaker knew that before the moment at hand. What he determines, however, is to privilege the spouse's perspective above his own.

To be clear, a lyricist would not call those lines a turn, but rather a hook. The hook is the part of the song that grabs the listener's attention and is the "identifiable idea" of the song (Davis 31). Throughout my explication of country songs I often find that the hook, which is usually placed at the beginning or end of the chorus, serves as the equivalent to a sonnet's turn.

Another distinction between a country song and a Shakespearean sonnet is that country lyricists do not wait until the song's end to conclude. Often, the conclusion occurs at the end of the chorus. But the song usually continues after that chorus, presenting another complication in a new verse or bridge so that when the listener hears the chorus a second (or third) time, it takes on another layer of development. The placement of the conclusion within the chorus reflects songwriting tradition, but the added development after the conclusion nods toward the sonnet tradition that insists on continual complications.

The other important criterion in a successful sonnet is that the speaker undergoes an emotional and/or intellectual change, because the fundamental action in a sonnet occurs within the speaker's interior state. Another way to explain it is how Vendler does: the "dynamic reversals of thought and feeling [are] indispensable to the true Shakespearean sonnet" (6). The speaker in "On the Other Hand" has been having an affair for awhile, as indicated by a few details: he mentions the "first" kiss in past tense, he explains how he has changed since he met her, and finally, their physical locale indicates they are in a pre-arranged "safe place" (such as her home or a motel) where they can be together all night. The change is that the speaker no longer can continue emotionally with this affair.

Another country lyric that appropriates the sonnet is "Don't Tell Me What to Do" (released in 1991) sung by Pam Tillis. The song is written in second form (V, C, V, C), and the first verse presents the issue: "We tried and we tried but it's over" (line 1). Not only are they breaking up, but her now ex-boyfriend suggests that she "find another lover," to which she responds "don't tell me what to do" (3–5). At this point in the song, the issue (a breakup) is clear and slightly complicated by the fact that the ex feels so little toward the woman that he would encourage her to see someone else. We think we understand all that we need to in this song—and many a mediocre song would stay at this level of non-development with a simple repetition of "don't tell me what to do." But what follows adds development:

> I'm no longer your concern
> So, don't tell me what to do.
> I'll love you forever if I want to. (lines 8–10)

When the speaker says the first time "don't tell me what to do," she is angry with his suggestion that she find someone else. The prosody of the song with its forceful drum beats supports that sense of direct admonishment. But after line nine, the song alters musically, a pause occurs, and we witness the turn between lines nine and ten: "So don't tell me what to do / I'll love you forever if I want to." With line ten, the speaker reveals how she still loves him and what began as a tell-off song has become a heartbreak song. And when I say the turn occurs between lines nine and ten, I literally mean *between* the lines as in off the page and within the speaker's mind, similar to the Randy Travis song. The speaker experiences a change in perspective, a change from anger to sad acceptance; while the listener is not privy to exactly what triggered the change, the listener hears the result of such a change—which is similar to how the sonnet's turn operates. The turn also leads to the conclusion, again similar to the sonnet's tendency.

Other qualities of this song similar to those of the Shakespearean sonnet include the subject matter of love, the build toward the resolution, the verbal wit and irony present in that resolution, and the explication-to-resolution proportion. Again, not counting the chorus's repetition, the song features twelve lines of explication and complication to the two lines of conclusion, which is exactly the proportion in a Shakespearean sonnet. In sum, the rhetorical mode follows the sonnet's form: issue of the breakup, complicated by the demand for her to see someone else, complicated again by the fact that he is in love with someone else, and concluded by her commitment to unrequited love: she'll continue to love him anyway.

Another interesting comparison between the Shakespearean sonnet and the country song relates to the nature of the conclusions themselves. Fussell contends that in a Shakespearean sonnet, the "solution is more likely to be the fruit of wit, or paradox, or even a quick shaft of sophistry, logical cleverness, or outright comedy" (122). This type of pithy conclusion contrasts with that of the Petrarchan sonnet which provides a meditative sense of resolution due to the fact that the Petrarchan form allows for conclusion within the entire sestet. Country songs' conclusions lean toward the proportion of complication to resolution—and to verbal wit and flex—like that in a Shakespearean sonnet. Some famous examples of these witty or "punny" conclusions are "the only good years we had were on my Chevy"; and "I loved her in a roundabout way, 'round about the time midnight rolled around." Another example of verbal flex is the previously mentioned phrase from the Randy Travis song in which the figurative cliché "on the other hand" is made literal. Similar to country songs, Shakespeare's sonnets sometimes draw criticism for their tightly wrapped conclusions that end with an idiom, proverb, or some folksy platitude. Vendler describes this as *consensus gentium*, but she does not view it as a negative characteristic. She explains that sometimes these pithy conclusions are not really *the* answer but rather a signal of the speaker's despair: "Such a turn toward the proverbial always represents the speaker's despair at solving by himself . . . the conundrum presented by the sonnet" (26). I cannot maintain that some of the too-easy conclusions in country songs are a result of self-delusion and frustration. At times, however, one does sense that the speaker needs to believe in belief to cope with his/her unchangeable situation. The next two songs that I will discuss are examples of this type of conclusion that serves as more coping mechanism than insight.

I have so far enjoyed the benefit of choosing examples that share traits with the Shakespearean sonnet, but I also wanted to see what would happen if I analyzed a random sample. I decided to study the top ten songs on the *Billboard* country chart for the week of April 30th, 2010: "Gimme that Girl" by Joe Nichols, "American Honey" by Lady Antebellum, "Ain't Back Yet" by Kenny Chesney, "The Man I Want to Be" by Chris Young, "Highway 20 Ride" by Zac Brown Band, "I Gotta Get to You" by George Strait, "Keep on Lovin' You" by Steel Magnolia, "Backwoods" by Justin Moore, "The House That Built Me" by Miranda Lambert, and "Unstoppable" by Rascal Flatts. Only one of these met all four of my criteria to be a sonnet. (My requirements are no real indicator of whether a song is good or bad; I am simply trying to find the prevalence, or lack thereof, of the sonnet within songs.) I did notice, however, that three of the ten songs were examples of failed sonnets, often failing by giving too few complications or by the speaker remaining unchanged. One might notice the same failure rate with contemporary poems that try to be sonnets.

The song that most resembles the criteria for a sonnet is "Highway 20 Ride" by the Zac Brown Band, who won a Grammy in 2010 for best new artist. This song reminds me why I ever liked country music to begin with; country (like some rap and hip-hop) is willing to present an unsentimental view of life (although in the last two decades I find country to be trending toward the sentimental). Songs like "The Pill" sung by Loretta Lynn, which celebrates a woman's options because of the birth control pill; "Fancy" sung by Reba McEntire, which tells the story of a girl having to whore herself; or "Walkaway Joe" sung by Trisha Yearwood, about a mother observing how her daughter is dating "the wrong kind of paradise" all share an honest, unsentimental view of life. "Highway 20 Ride" is no exception.

In this song, we have a man who thinks about his estranged son during his trucking route. Throughout the song, the father does not communicate with the son or reach any specific epiphany that will result in a future action; rather, in true lyrical fashion, the father attempts to reconcile his feelings of failure, isolation, and estrangement through reflection. The song begins by the father saying: "I ride east every other Friday / But if I had it my way / A day would not be wasted on this drive" (lines 1–3). Immediately, the speaker presents the issue: he is forced to "waste" his time on this drive. The next three lines explain that he feels he is wasting his time because the father wants "so bad to hold you," the "you" addressing a son who is not present. The direct address is in the style of Horace or Catullus or how Shakespeare sometimes paraphrases other's thoughts, almost as if he is talking to a person who is physically absent.

The chorus that follows continues with the complications on this issue: "I think about my life / And wonder why / that I slowly die inside" (lines 8–10). The speaker does not know why he feels like he is dying—expressed here in a figurative sense. Simply put, we have the first complication in the chorus: the speaker acknowledges a sense of death, but does not understand why. What follows is the speaker's attempt to reconcile this feeling. He counts the days until he returns physically closer to the son: "And I count the days / And the miles back home to you / On that Highway 20 ride." Here we have another complication:

the speaker is counting the days to return, but the truth is that he is returning to nothing. It is already established the son and he do not communicate. The comfort for the speaker is a false one; there is no one waiting for him. All he is left with is the thought of being physically closer to the son. And the third verse presents yet another complication; the father explicitly acknowledges the son might hate him: "And a part of you might hate me / But son please don't mistake me / For a man that didn't care at all."

In this song it is difficult to point to a conclusion and say, "This is it," because the conclusion is not one that actually will change this man's life. The man is experiencing what often occurs in a country song, something that songwriter Alice Randall describes as dynamic stasis.[3] Dynamic stasis, according to Alice Randall, is when characters in a country song are presented with problems—and with a solution. The characters make choices that maintain the status quo. What does change, however, is the character has a mental and emotional acceptance of his/ her situation—and will often frame the "decision" in a positive light. Part of this positivism is a coping mechanism for the fact that the character never had a choice, but merely desires one. What can be perceived as a mawkish, Pollyannaish viewpoint is an extension of Vendler's reasoning for Shakespeare's conclusions sometimes veering toward the *consensus gentium*. In other words, these easy-sounding conclusions are written because the speaker does not know what else to say to improve upon the situation.

The squirmy conclusion to this song begins after the turn, which is marked off with a traditional transition: the word "so."[4] "So when you drive," the father imagines telling his son, "And the years go flying by / I hope you smile." The father then says, "If I ever cross your mind / it was the pleasure of my life." The melody lifts upward triumphantly and the single strumming guitar gives way to a full band accompaniment which includes cymbals and drums, but the lyric is quite anti-climatic and sad. The father does not know if the son will ever think of him, as indicated with the qualifier "if"; he's not even hoping for the unexpected, which is a deep reflection about him. Instead, he will be happy for a stray thought from the son, a simple "crossing of his mind." The "conclusion" then continues with the father saying that the son "was the pleasure" of his life and that he "cherished every time." Nothing syntactically follows that explains what he cherished every time, leaving the listener to fill that in or perhaps leaving the listener to get swept up in the melody and not realize that there is nothing to be filled in here.

The relevant question after identifying similarities and differences is, what is the significance of these? The question itself shifts the focus from viewing popular country lyrics as irrelevant, free-formed, and vapid toward recognizing historical and literary connections. Songs and poetry are not one and the same. They do, however, share a history that transforms contemporary writers' words into art.

Notes

1. Samuel Johnson also defined *sonneteer* as "a small poet, in contempt." And as for the sonnet itself, he describes it as "not very suitable to the English language; and has not been used by any man of eminence since Milton."

2. In each song I mention in this essay, I count the lines of the chorus only the first time they appear, instead of each time the chorus is repeated. This helps to provide a sense of how much new information is given rather than repeated information. Granted, counting the chorus only once is something of a judgment call. I can understand how other writers would not to do that because sometimes when a chorus is repeated, it resonates differently each time because of what comes before it. For this essay, however, I focused on songs without changing choruses and without major shifts of resonance to help alleviate this issue. My main concern is to see the proportion of explication to resolution—new information to old—since that proportion is critical to the sonnet.

3. Novelist and country songwriter Alice Randall shared her thoughts on dynamic stasis in an unpublished interview that Kathryn Alexander and I conducted with her in 2004.

4. Other indicators that a turn is about to occur are words such as "but," "then," "therefore," etc.

Works Cited

Cuddon, J. A. *A Dictionary of Literary Terms*. New York: Penguin, 1976.

Davis, Sheila. *The Craft of Lyric Writing*. New York: Writers Digest, 1984.

Fussell, Paul. *Poetic Meter and Poetic Form*. New York: McGraw Hill, 1979.

Oppenheimer, Paul. *The Birth of the Modern Mind*. Oxford: Oxford University Press, 1989.

Tillis, Pam. "Don't Tell Me What To Do." *Greatest Hits* (CD). Arista, 1997.

Travis, Randy. "On the Other Hand." *Storms of Life* (CD). Warner Brothers, 1985.

Vendler, Helen. *The Art of Shakespeare's Sonnets*. Cambridge: Belknap Press of Harvard University Press, 1997.

Zac Brown Band. "Highway 20 Ride." *The Foundation* (CD). Atlantic, 2008.

RAP POETRY 101

ADAM BRADLEY

"Rap is poetry, but its popularity relies in part on people not recogniz-ing it as such," states Adam Bradley in the introduction to his critically acclaimed Book of Rhymes: The Poetics of Hip Hop. *Reprinted in its entirety here, Bradley's introduction addresses line, rhythm, and tran-scription within rap. In doing so, Bradley not only provides readers and listeners with the skills needed to appreciate the craft of rap, but he also reveals the relation between rap and poetry.*

I start to think and then I sink
into the paper like I was ink.
When I'm writing I'm trapped in between the lines,
I escape when I finish the rhyme . . .
—Eric B. & Rakim, "I Know You Got Soul"

A book of rhymes is where MCs write lyrics. It is the basic tool of the rapper's craft. Nas raps about "writin in my book of rhymes, all the words pass the margin." Mos Def boasts about sketching "lyrics so vi-sual / they rent my rhyme books at your nearest home video." They both know what Rakim knew before them, that the book of rhymes is where rap becomes poetry.

Every rap song is a poem waiting to be performed. Written or freestyled, rap has a poetic structure that can be reproduced, a deliberate form an MC creates for each rhyme that differentiates it, if only in small ways, from every other rhyme ever conceived. Like all poetry, rap is defined by the art of the line. Metri-cal poets choose the length of their lines to correspond to particular rhythms—they write in iambic pentameter or whatever other meter suits their desires. Free verse poets employ conscious line breaks to govern the reader's pace, to emphasize particular words, or to accomplish any one of a host of other poetic objectives. In a successful poem, line breaks are never casual or accidental. Re-

35

write a poem in prose and you'll see it deflate like a punctured lung, expelling life like so much air.

Line breaks are the skeletal system of lyric poetry. They give poems their shape and distinguish them from all other forms of literature. While prose writers usually break their lines wherever the page demands—when they reach the margin, when the computer drops their word to the next line—poets claim that power for themselves, ending lines in ways that underscore the specific design of their verse. Rap poets are no different.

Rap is poetry, but its popularity relies in part on people not recognizing it as such. After all, rap is for good times; we play it in our cars, hear it at parties and at clubs. By contrast, most people associate poetry with hard work; it is something to be studied in school or puzzled over for hidden insights. Poetry stands at an almost unfathomable distance from our daily lives, or at least so it seems given how infrequently we seek it out.

This has not always been the case; poetry once had a prized place in both public and private affairs. At births and deaths, weddings and funerals, festivals and family gatherings, people would recite poetry to give shape to their feelings. Its relative absence today says something about us—our culture's short attention span, perhaps, or the dominance of other forms of entertainment— but also about poetry itself. While the last century saw an explosion of poetic productivity, it also marked a decided shift toward abstraction. As the poet Adrian Mitchell observed, "Most people ignore poetry because most poetry ignores most people."

Rap never ignores its listeners. Quite the contrary, it aggressively asserts itself, often without invitation, upon our consciousness. Whether boomed out of a passing car, played at a sports stadium, or piped into a mall while we shop, rap is all around us. Most often, it expresses its meaning quite plainly. No expertise is required to listen. You don't need to take an introductory course or read a handbook; you don't need to watch an instructional video or follow an online tutorial. But, as with most things in life, the pleasure to be gained from rap increases exponentially with just a little studied attention.

Rap is public art, and rappers are perhaps our greatest public poets, extending a tradition of lyricism that spans continents and stretches back thousands of years. Thanks to the engines of global commerce, rap is now the most widely disseminated poetry in the history of the world. Of course, not all rap is great poetry, but collectively it has revolutionized the way our culture relates to the spoken word. Rappers at their best make the familiar unfamiliar through rhythm, rhyme, and wordplay. They refresh the language by fashioning patterned and heightened variations of everyday speech. They expand our understanding of human experience by telling stories we otherwise might not hear. The best MCs—like Rakim, Jay-Z, Tupac, and many others—deserve consideration alongside the giants of American poetry. We ignore them at our own expense.

Hip hop emerged out of urban poverty to become one of the most vital cultural forces of the past century. The South Bronx may seem like an unlikely place to have birthed a new movement in poetry. But in defiance of inferior educational opportunities and poor housing standards, a generation of young people—mostly black and brown—conceived innovations in rhythm, rhyme, and wordplay that would change the English language itself. In *Can't Stop, Won't Stop: A History of the Hip-Hop Generation*, Jeff Chang vividly describes how rap's rise from the 1970s through the early 1980s was accompanied by a host of social and economic forces that would seem to stifle creative expression under the weight of despair. "[A]n enormous amount of creative energy was now ready to be released from the bottom of American society," he writes, "and the staggering implications of this moment eventually would echo around the world."[1] As one of the South Bronx's own, rap legend KRS-One, explains, "Rap was the final conclusion of a generation of creative people oppressed with the reality of lack."[2]

Hip-hop's first generation fashioned an art form that draws not only from the legacy of Western verse, but from the folk idioms of the African Diaspora; the musical legacy of jazz, blues, and funk; and the creative capacities conditioned by the often harsh realties of people's everyday surroundings. These artists commandeered the English language, the forms of William Shakespeare and Emily Dickinson, as well as those of Sonia Sanchez and Amiri Baraka, to serve their own expressive and imaginative purposes. Rap gave voice to a group hardly heard before by America at large, certainly never heard in their often profane, always assertive words. Over time the poetry and music they made would command the ears of their block, their borough, the nation, and the world.

Though rap may be new school music, it is old school poetry. Rather than resembling the dominant contemporary form of free verse—or even the free-form structure of its hip-hop cousin, spoken word, or slam poetry—rap bears a stronger affinity to some of poetry's oldest forms, such as the strong-stress meter of *Beowulf* and the ballad stanzas of the bardic past. As in metrical verse, the lengths of rap's lines are governed by established rhythms—in rap's case, the rhythm of the beat itself. The beat in rap is poetic meter rendered audible. Rap follows a dual rhythmic relationship whereby the MC is liberated to pursue innovations of syncopation and stress that would sound chaotic without the regularity of the musical rhythm. The beat and the MC's flow, or rhythm cadence, work together to satisfy the audience's musical and poetic expectations—most notably, that rap establish and maintain rhythmic patterns while creatively disrupting those patterns, through syncopation and other pleasing forms of rhythmic surprise.

Simply put, a rap verse is the product of one type of rhythm (that of language) being fitted to another (that of music). Great pop lyricists, Irving Berlin or John Lennon or Stevie Wonder, match their words not only to the rhythm of the music but to melodies and harmonies as well. For the most part, MCs need concern themselves only with the beat. This fundamental difference means that

MCs resemble literary poets in ways that most other songwriters do not. Like all poets, rappers write primarily with a beat in mind. Rap's reliance on spare, beat-driven accompaniment foregrounds the poetic identity of the language.

Divorced from most considerations of melody and harmony, rap lyrics are liberated to live their lives as pure expressions of poetic and musical rhythm. Even when rap employs rich melodies and harmonies—as is often the case, for instance, in the music of Kanye West—rhythm remains the central element of sound. This puts rap's dual rhythms in even closer proximity to one another than they might usually be in other musical genres. Skilled MCs underscore the rhythm of the track in the rhythm of their flows and the patterns of their rhymes. As a consequence, the lyrics rappers write are more readily separated from their specific musical contexts and presented in written form as poetry. The rhythm comes alive on the page because it is embedded in the language itself.

Many of the reasonable arguments critics offer to distinguish musical lyrics from literary poetry do not apply to rap. One of the most common objections, voiced best by the critic Simon Frith, is that musical lyrics do not need to generate the highly sophisticated poetic effects that create the "music" of verse written for the page. Indeed, the argument goes, if a lyric is too poetically developed it likely will distract from the music itself. A good poem makes for a lousy lyric, and a great lyric for a second-rate poem. Rap defies such conventional wisdom. The heavily rhythmic but sonically spare instrumentals so common to rap create an ideal space for the lyricist to flourish. Unburdened of expectations of melody and harmony, rappers have unparalleled freedom to generate poetic textures in the language itself.

Another objection is that popular lyric lacks much of the formal structure of literary verse. Rap challenges this objection as well by crafting intricate structures of sound and rhyme, creating some of the most scrupulously formal poetry composed today. Rap can usefully be approached as poetry while still recognizing its essential identity as music. There is no need to disparage one to respect the other. In fact, perhaps more than any other lyrical form, rap demands that we acknowledge song lyrics' dual identity as word and music.

The ancient Greeks called their lyric poetry *ta mele*, which means "poems to be sung." For them and for later generations, poetry, in the words of Walter Pater, "aspires towards the condition of music."[3] It has only been since the early twentieth century that music has taken a backseat to meaning in poetry. As the poet Edward Hirsch writes, "The lyric poem always walks the line between speaking and singing. . . . Poetry is not speech exactly—verbal art is deliberately different than the way that people actually talk—and yet it is always in relationship to speech, to the spoken word."[4]

Like all poetry, rap is not speech exactly, nor is it precisely song, yet it employs elements of both. Rap's earliest performers understood this. On "Adventures of Super Rhymes (Rap)" from 1980, just months after rap's emergence on mainstream radio, Jimmy Spicer attempted to define this new form:

> It's the new thing, makes you wanna swing
> While us MCs rap, doin' our thing
> It's not singin' like it used to be
> No, it's rappin' to the rhythm of the sure-shot beat

Rap is an oral poetry, so it naturally relies more heavily than literary poetry on devices of sound. The MC's poetic toolbox shares many of the same basic instruments as the literary poet's, but features others specifically suited to the demands of oral expression. These include copious use of rhyme, both as a mnemonic device and as a form of rhythmic pleasure; as well as poetic tropes that rely upon sonic identity, like homonyms and puns. Add to this those elements the MC draws from music—tonal quality, vocal inflection, and so forth—and rap reveals itself as a poetry uniquely fitted to oral performance.

Earlier pop lyricists like Cole Porter or Lorenz Hart labored over their lyrics; they were not simply popular entertainers, they were poets. Great MCs represent a continuation and an amplification of this vital tradition of lyrical craft. The lyrics to Porter's "I've Got You Under My Skin" are engaging when read on the page without their melodic accompaniment; the best rap lyrics are equally engrossing, even without the specific context of their performance. Rap has no sheet music because it does not need it—it has no harmonies and melodies to transcribe—but it *does* have a written form worth reconstructing, one that testifies to its value, both as music and as poetry. That form begins with a faithful transcription of lyrics.

Rap lyrics are routinely mis-transcribed, not simply on the numerous websites offering lyrics-to-go, but even on an artist's own liner notes, and in hip-hop books and periodicals. The same rhyme might be written dozens of different ways—different line breaks, different punctuation, even different words. The goal should be to transcribe rap verses in such a way that they represent on the page as closely as possible what we hear with our ears.

The standardized transcription method proposed here may differ from those used by MCs in their own rhyme books. Tupac, for instance, counted his bars by couplets. Rappers compose their verses in any number of ways; what they write need only make sense to them. But an audience requires a standardized form organized around objective principles rather than subjective habits. Serious readers need a shared way of transcribing rap lyrics so that they can discuss rap's formal attributes with one another without confusion.

In transcribing rap lyrics, we must have a way of representing the beat on the page. The MC's basic challenge is this: when given a beat, what do you do? The beat is rap's beginning. Whether the hiccups and burps of a Timbaland track, the percussive assault of a Just Blaze beat, knuckles knocking on a lunchroom table, a human beat box, or simply the metronomic rhythm in an MC's head as he spits a cappella rhymes, the beat defines the limits of lyrical possibility.

Transcribing lyrics to the beat is an intuitive way of translating the lyricism we hear into poetry we can read without sacrificing the specific relationship of words to music laid down by the MC's performance. Each bar (or measure) in a typical rap song consists of four beats; a poetic line consists of the words one can deliver in the space of that bar. Therefore, one musical bar is equal to one line of verse. This description fits the way that rappers themselves most often talk about their lyrics. "I used to get the legal pad . . ." Crooked I recalls, "and I used to write each bar as one line, so at the end, 16 lines, 16 bars."[5] By respecting the integrity of each line in relation to the beat, we preserve the dual rhythmic relation between beat and lyric.

To demonstrate this method of lyric transcription, consider a fairly straightforward example: Melle Mel's first verse on Grandmaster Flash and the Furious Five's classic "The Message."

One	TWO	Three	FOUR

Standing on the front stoop, hangin' out the window,
watching all the cars go by, roaring as the breezes blow.

Notice how the naturally emphasized words ("standing," "front," "hangin'," "window," etc.) fall on the strong beats. These are two fairly regular lines, hence the near uniformity of the pair and the strong-beat accents on particular words. The words are in lockstep with the beat. Mark the beginning of each poetic line on the one and the end of the line on the four.

Not all lines, however, are so easily transcribed; many complications can occur in the process of transcription. Consider the famous opening lines from this very same song:

One	TWO	Three	FOUR

Broken   glass   everywhere,
people pissin' on the stairs, you know they just don't care.

Looking at the two lines on the page, one might think that they had been incorrectly transcribed. The only thing that suggests they belong together is the end rhyme. How can each of these lines—the first half as long as the second, and with fewer than half the total syllables—take up the same four-beat measure? The answer has everything to do with performance. Melle Mel delivers the first line with a combination of dramatic pause and exaggerated emphasis. He begins rhyming a little behind the beat, includes a caesura (a strong phrasal pause within the line) between "glass" and "everywhere," and dramatically extenuates the pronunciation of "everywhere." Were it not for an accurate transcription, these poetic effects would be lost.

Sometimes rap poets devise intricate structures that give logical shape to their creations. Using patterns of rhyme, rhythm, and line, these structures reinforce an individual verse's fusion of form and meaning. While literary poetry often follows highly regularized forms—a sonnet, a villanelle, a ballad stanza—rap is rarely so formally explicit, favoring instead those structures drawn naturally from oral expression. Upon occasion, however, rap takes on more formal structures, either by happenstance or by conscious design. Consider these two verses: on the top is Langston Hughes's "Sylvester's Dying Bed," written in 1931; below it is a transcription of Ice-T's "6 'N The Mornin'," released in 1987. Though distanced by time, these lyrics are joined by form.

> I woke up this mornin' 'bout half past three.
> All the womens in town was gathered round me.
> Sweet gals was a-moanin', "Sylvester's gonna die!"
> And a hundred pretty mamas bowed their heads to cry.

> Six in the mornin', police at my door.
> Fresh Adidas squeak across my bathroom floor.
> Out my back window I make my escape.
> Didn't even get a chance to grab my old school tape.

Hughes's form relies upon splitting the conventional four-beat line in half; here, for the purposes of comparison, I have rendered it as a pair of four-beat rhyming couplets. I might just as easily have rewritten Ice-T's lines as eight two-beat lines. This adjustment aside, the two lyrics are nearly identical in form. Both employ an aabb rhyme pattern with each line resolving in a natural syntactical unit. Both draw upon the rhythms of the vernacular, the language as actually spoken. This formal echo, reaching across more than a half century of black poetic expression, suggests a natural affinity of forms.

Rap lyrics properly transcribed reveal themselves in ways not possible when listening to rap alone. Seeing rap on the page, we understand it for what it is: a small machine of words. We distinguish end rhymes from internal rhymes, end-stopped lines from enjambed ones, patterns from disruptions. Of course, nothing can replace the listening experience, whether in your headphones or at a show. Rather than replacing the music, reading rap as poetry heightens both enjoyment and understanding. Looking at rhymes on the page slows things down, allowing listeners—now readers—to discover familiar rhymes as if for the first time.

Notes

1. Jeff Chang, *Can't Stop, Won't Stop: A History of the Hip-Hop Generation* (New York: St. Martin's, 2005), 82–83.

2. KRS-One, *Ruminations* (New York: Welcome Rain, 2003), 217.

3. Walter Pater, "The School of Giorgione" (1877), reprinted in *Selected Writings of Walter Pater*, ed. Harold Bloom (New York: Columbia University Press, 1974), 55.

4. "The lyric poem always walks the line": Edward Hirsch, *How to Read a Poem and Fall in Love with Poetry* (New York: Harcourt, 1999), 10.

5. Paul Edwards. *How to Rap: The Art and Science of the Hip-Hop MC* (Chicago: Chicago Review Press, 2009), 69.

IT DON'T MEAN A THING: THE BLUES MASK OF MODERNISM

KEVIN YOUNG

Kevin Young's essay is a chapter from The Grey Album, *a book of essays on race, music, and literature that received the Graywolf Nonfiction Prize and will be published in 2012. In this essay, Young analyzes the influence of blues music on modernism. As he explains, "While the era and movement has been greatly explored in recent years, the Harlem or New Negro Renaissance's importance, intricacies, and intimacies cannot be overstated—if only to reemphasize how the achievement of these African American writers (and sculptors and artists) should be thought of as one of the heights of modernism."*

The blues contain multitudes. Among the last mysteries, blues music resists not only sentimentality but also easy summary: just when you say the blues are about one thing—lost love, say—here comes a song about death, or about work, about canned heat or loose women, hard men or harder times, to challenge your definitions. Urban and rural, tragic and comic, modern as African America and primal as America, the blues are as innovative in structure as they are in mood—they resurrect old feelings even as they describe them in new ways. They are the definitive statement of that new invention, the African American, though when Langston Hughes first wrote on them and through them in the 1920s, he felt as much resistance from black folks as white. Known by black churchgoers as "devil's music," the blues are defiant and existential and necessary. Blues singers describe walking with the devil, or "Preachin' the Blues" as Son House did—

Yes I'ma get me religion
I'ma join the Baptist church

Yes I'ma get me religion
I say I'ma join the Baptist church

You know I want to be a Baptist preacher
So I won't have to work

—then turn round and sing of "John the Revelator." Both the bluesman and the preacher, whose own story often includes being called to the pulpit after a life of sin, know full well that most folks choose both Saturday night and Sunday morning: one, after all, turns into the other.

Perhaps the best way to describe the blues is that they reveal and revel in all our holy and humane contradictions—and that this revelatory quality announces itself not with the book of the seven seals, but rather the broken seal on a bottle of whisky. The same bottle that, poisoned one way or another, will leave you barking at the moon. The same bottle that, broken, you can smooth down to slide over the neck of your guitar.

The blues will surely get you, but offer "Good Morning" when they do.

What Did I Do (To Be So Black and Blue)?

The rise of modernism parallels the rise and reach of the blues. This is no coincidence—after all, what critic Frederic Jameson identifies as "the great modernist thematics of alienation, anomie, solitude, social fragmentation, and isolation"[1] could be summed up as simply having them blues.

But, as I have said elsewhere, the blues means both a form and a feeling, the one a cure for the other.[2] The blues are good-time music after all, meant to make you tap your feet and feel, if not better, then at least comforted by the fact that you are in good (or deliciously bad) hands. The blues offer company, even if only misery's.

It is in the face of alienation and anomie that the mask, modern and often racial, becomes necessary. This is why the dominant mode of the modernist era is the *persona*—the mask both as metaphor and means of production. But the mask is not just T. S. Eliot's blackface, Ezra Pound's love of Noh drama, or Edvard Munch's iconic rictus of despair in *The Scream*, but also the Janus mask of the blues, which laughs and cries at the same time.

The blues then are both an approach and a feeling—one that had to wait for former slaves to name. Virginia Woolf tried, declaring "On or about December 1910 human character changed."[3] Woolf's dating, even in hindsight, what may be called the advent of modernism has become more true after it was said—just as when asked about why his portrait of Gertrude Stein didn't look like her, Picasso reportedly answered: "It will." Such history as a form of fortune-telling was reflected and refracted in the first published blues, W. C. Handy's "St. Louis Blues" (1914), and in the first recorded blues, Mamie Smith's "The Crazy Blues" (1920), whose very title indicates the vector of this change of "human character" ten years after the fact. Alongside Louis Armstrong's "West End Blues," which reinvented the jazz solo, forever changing music, ultimately history itself was reinvented by those too often seen as victims of it. From New Orleans on north up the Mississippi, the blues and their offspring, jazz, mark the modern moment as well as anything.

For the "St. Louis Blues" weren't just St. Louis–born T. S. Eliot's or Josephine Baker's; they were everyone's. When Handy wrote down the first blues lyrics, he was capturing the common oral culture of African Americans, the "floating verses" that amounted to a shared store of imagery, one as allusive and elusive as *The Waste Land*, published years later. "I hate to see de ev'nin' sun go down": even the iconic first line of the song looks west, and ahead to the "The Love Song of J. Alfred Prufrock" with its evening sky "like a patient etherized on a table." Could hindsight as second sight help us recognize that the love song Prufrock proffers might indeed be a blues? Well before "Ash Wednesday" the "St. Louis Blues" announced

Oh ashes to ashes and dust to dust,
I said ashes to ashes and dust to dust
If my blues don't get you my jazzing must.

Years later when Eliot placed black song in his *Waste Land*, "sampling" James Weldon Johnson, the emergence and merging of modernism—our Shakespearian rag—was complete.

However we date its start, by the early 1920s the modernism that before and during World War I once proved strange and unsettling seemed to culminate in the high modernist moment: in literature alone, the publication of William Carlos Williams's *Spring and All* (1923), H. D.'s *Palimpsest* (1921), Eliot's *The Waste Land* (1922), Marianne Moore's *Observations* (1923), James Joyce's *Ulysses* (1922), and Wallace Stevens's *Harmonium* (1923) all signaled not just a new sheriff in town, but that all the "low modernists" and populists who had begun the deputizing of modernism a decade or more before, now had till sunset to get out of town. As the twenties roared, high modernism was in full swing.

Swing would seem to be the operative word, not just describing the music that propelled the Jazz Age, but also the quality of change in attitudes and culture that accompanied the advent of the New Negro—who had been agitating for change since at least the century's turn, and whose rise almost exactly parallels modernism's. What is commonly called the Harlem Renaissance had begun by the early 1920s, inaugurated by Claude McKay's *Harlem Shadows* (1922), Georgia Douglas Johnson's *Bronze* (1922), Jean Toomer's *Cane* (1923), and James Weldon Johnson's *The Book of American Negro Poetry* (1922); by the time of the second of *Opportunity*'s award dinners in 1925 (from the first had come the anthology *The New Negro*), the younger generation had been duly anointed.⁴ This younger group, affiliated with heiress A'Lelia Walker's Dark Tower Salon—the house that Hurston, Wallace Thurman, and others jokingly termed "Niggerati Manor"—simultaneously continued and rebelled against the strict desire for a "positive" image set forth by the older generation.⁵ While the era and movement has been greatly explored in recent years, the Harlem or New Negro Renaissance's importance, intricacies, and intimacies cannot be overstated—if only to reemphasize how the achievement of these African American writers (and artists) should be thought of as one of the heights of modernism.

So, too, should the release of the first blues record in 1920. The popularity and passion of "Crazy Blues" by Mamie Smith (which, in its first year, sold over a million copies) provides the first full expression, still overlooked, of a black modernist presence previously hinted at by the dialect of Dunbar and realized in the 1910s by the work of Fenton Johnson, a poet equally worthy of further study. You could even say that what I call the storying tradition serves as a true vernacular to the standard borne by modernism, however avant-garde modernism self-consciously (and -congratulatorily) thought itself. For now, it seems to me that, alongside Modernism & All, we should place Blues & Thangs, in order to fully appreciate the new, modern consciousness—one urban and urbane, ironic and genuine, cosmopolitan and American, black and white. Mine is an attempt to unmask the blues, and see in them a useful rootlessness—and the roots of modernism more generally.

Sitting on Top of the World

This idea of blackness containing modernism, and vice versa, has been increasingly recognized by critics detailing Harlem's role in New York's emergence as a literary capital. But despite Houston Baker's *Modernism and the Harlem Renaissance* (1987), Ann Douglas's *Terrible Honesty* (1996), Susan Gubar's *Racechanges* (2000), Brent Edwards's *The Practice of Diaspora* (2003), and many other efforts to reveal the racial and international underpinnings of what Ann Douglas calls a "mongrel modernism," the whites-only view of modernism persists.

Perhaps then we should not be surprised when Peter Gay's otherwise thoughtful, large-scale study *Modernism* (2008)—completed after all the other above studies—fails to mention African Americans at all in its 610 pages. (That is, except for Baudelaire's "mulatto mistress.") It is a dizzying, disheartening thing to register such an absence, particularly when critic Christopher Miller's *Blank Darkness* has so endlessly detailed the "Africanist" presence in the array of early modernists Gay does consider, from Baudelaire to Rimbaud and beyond. *Vous êtes des faux nègres.*

Which leads us to the question: Is it better to be misread, as in Africanist, racist white texts? Or unread, as in Gay's study?

Such separate but unequal—and more or less invisible—divisions continue even in an influential anthology like *Modernism/Postmodernism*, which starts by declaring "Both modernism and postmodernism are phenomena, primarily, of twentieth-century Anglo-American and European culture, though with a changing relation to that culture."[6] While there is some debate over terms—to some Anglo means "British," to others "white"—there is no doubt that for many the true locus of modernism remains far from the juke joint or coldwater flat where blues records spin, or far beyond Langston Hughes circulating the Black Atlantic, writing poems about the Negro and "his rivers." Though some have explored the interactions and interracialism of modernism, often in terms of racism, I want to go further—locating modernism's origins specifically in black culture. The change, the roar, the very swing in the "Anglo" culture, might well be said to be exactly this too-often invisible African American influence.

What's at stake is not just a representation of reality, but also one of the counterfeit's chief aims: to give credit where credit is overdue.

The whites-only view of modernism cuts both ways, obscuring its origins while also leaving modernism open for critique as just another form of imperialism. Take this definition of modernism by art critic Thomas McEvilley:

> Modernism—here, let's describe it loosely as the ideology behind European colonialism and imperialism—involved a conviction that all cultures would ultimately be united, because they would all be Westernized. Their differences would be ironed out through assimilation to Europe. Post-Modernism has a different vision of the relation between sameness and difference: the hope that instead of difference being submerged in sameness, sameness and difference can somehow contain and maintain one another—that some state which might be described as a global unity can be attained without destroying the individuals of the various cultures within it.[7]

Critics like McEvilley see a dictum like "It is necessary to be completely modern" as akin to European colonialism. To him, "Make It New" might as well be American Western expansionism's "Go West, young man"—with the same devastating consequences. This anti-imperialist view sees the impulse to modernize in literature not as a response to industrialization, but a colonial desire to update art like just another export or exploit. Oppression is the real reason, or effect, of such an urge to "modernize," the result not so much fated as fatal.[8]

Yet if the nineteenth century sought either to cure or kill the native, however noble, one crucial way the modern era consistently defines itself is in embracing primitivism. The Freudian modernists, both "high" and "low," went native precisely (and messily) to avoid being Victorian, separating themselves from the staid past or the chaotic present. Not only was modernism a reaction to the Victorian era and its distanced, defanged Romanticism, it conducted much of this reaction in terms of black culture. In the case of an American modernism interested in an everyday language separate from a foreign, European past, the modern artist often turned to the Negro as both symbol and sustaining force.

This occurs not just in the work of high modernists but in that of the "low" or what I call "domestic" modernists quite popular at the time. Witness Pulitzer Prize–winner Stephen Vincent Benét, whose epic *John Brown's Body* (1928) considers the Civil War, its very title a black spiritual; we may discern the telling mix of modernism and nativism in his poem "American Names," which ends with the famous line, "Bury my heart at Wounded Knee." Beginning with the declaration, "I have fallen in love with American names," the speaker celebrates the "snakeskin-titles of mining-claims, / The plumed war-bonnet of Medicine Hat, / Tucson and Deadwood and Lost Mule Flat." Concluding that he is "tired of loving a foreign muse," he pledges to "get me a bottle of Boston sea / And a blue-gum nigger to sing me blues."[9] Putting aside the ways in which "American Names" calls black folks out of theirs, for Benét the surefire antidote to a "foreign muse," in rhyme and source and sound, not accidentally turns out to be the blues.

Might the "it" being made new in Pound's "Make it new" dictum not be tradition, but the Negro?

Concrete Jungle

By the second decade of the twentieth century, race had already become a metaphor for the modern era, much as Du Bois predicted—one in which black folks functioned as both signs of the changing times (how fresh and lively their music!), and signs of a primal, unchanging past in which history plays no part (how freeing to not be burdened by thought or history!). There is, indeed, a strangely contradictory notion at play whereby blacks are simultaneously modern and primitive.

The double mask of this conception of blackness is revealed not just in "more literary" high modernists or in the domestic modernists, but in the popular literature of the time. Take *Black Sadie*, an attractive, Art Deco–covered 1928 volume I found in a used bookstore; the troubling inside flap copy remains all too typical of the time:

'Black Sadie' is a dusky imp who was borne in on the crest of the 'negro fad' just before the War. Gradually she learned to speak like the whites, forsake her low-born Southern friends for high-class Harlem 'yallers,' pose as a model, and dance at a famous night-club named in her honor.

Skin of soft ebony, eyes like coals, delicately poised head, she dominates this book as completely as she dominated the Black Sadie night-club. Her story is modern, elemental, compelling. The author, who was brought up on a Southern plantation, has flavored it with moments of humor and sharp irony. He has achieved an astounding *tour de force* which deserves to stand with the very best of the negro novels.[10]

The lowercase "negro" is here in full swing—low-born but high-class, black in name but "yaller" in appearance, simultaneously "elemental" and "modern." Such inherent, paradoxical features coexist with each other, separate but not equal. Sadie is not born, but "borne in on the crest of the 'negro fad' just before the War." (In this she seems a bit premature, and in her infancy to have somehow missed the Red Summer of 1919. You could say she Jes Grew.) Indeed, the flap conflates not just modern and primitive, but Sadie the character, *Black Sadie* the novel, and Black Sadie the uptown club. The slippage between the three is only part of its pleasure—one presumes when one is in Black Sadie, who's to care! Same difference!

Of course, Sadie's novel's similarities to Josephine Baker's own story (and storying) should not be overlooked—though we should recall Baker's fame required, if not exile, then the willed self-exile of expatriatism. Exile, all too familiar to the Negro, is to become arguably the chief condition of modernism. *La Bakair* both embodied this and disrobed it—her *La Revue Négre* show managed to be at once au courant, exhibitionistic, and coy. For amidst and in lieu of the ubiquitous, symbolic, and literal Waste Land that the Lost Generation found after the war, Baker offered a Dark Africa—or rather, a brown-skinned one—that you could visit, safely, tantalizingly close. A sexual safari of sorts, a *danse banane*. But even as she participated in the show, Baker seemed to mock it—dancing on the tightrope of race in ways that echo or anticipate black artists from Bert Williams to Jean-Michel Basquiat.

A word here on the Jungle. Just as the idea of Ole Virginny provided a needed "once upon a time" for white Americans before and even long after the Civil War, the Jungle proved a place of refuge, refusal, and rejection of all things modern, while also providing a handy, if static, metaphor for the modern age itself. Eliot himself uses the jungle this way: while *The Waste Land* as book and place was one conception of the modern landscape, his notion in *Sweeney Agonistes* is intimately tied to a foreign shore, or rather, an outlying place of foreignness, "a cannibal isle" that is Jungle for all intents and purposes.[11] Whether in a Tarzan matinee or "reality television,"[12] the Jungle remains a dangerous, alluring Eden that might swallow us up if we are not careful.

This Never Never Land, lying in a direction almost opposite a slave-conjured Canaan, is a place rich in contraband. In the endpages of my copy of Michael

North's *The Dialect of Modernism*, where he discusses Eliot and McKay and others in relation to race and representation, are notes I made a number of years back about the idea of contraband, scrawled in pencil:

> Some contraband: Berryman, some swing, Cotton Club, minstrelsy, Elvis, Rolling Stones, *Melanctha*, Moynihan report, "voguing," Beat writing.

Below this, there is a quick definition of contraband: *not just stealing culture or stealing an image, but mistaking an image for reality i.e. not realizing that many of these are parodies, taken at face value.* The problem here is not the "negative typing" of these works by whites, but rather their adopting of black masks and then mistaking them for a face.

The Western fascination with the Jungle can be seen in some of the most famous titles of the modern era, from Upton Sinclair's *The Jungle* to Rudyard Kipling's *The Jungle Book*, with its tabloid-like story of a boy raised by wolves (not to mention the Disney movie's wolf-ticket jazz). The Jungle was either symbolic of the unruliness of the city itself or indicative of what innocence the city had lost. French "outsider artist" (okay, let's call him *primitif*) Le Douanier's renderings of the Jungle are clearly imaginary, yet no less filled with a fertile danger (later to be wrested from the modernists—or should I say the colonists—by the postcolonial, Asian-black Cuban artist Wilfredo Lam). Just as he had celebrated the workers with drinking ballads, Kipling's *Jungle Book*, its very title a kind of paradox, was one response to a disappearing "Genteel Tradition" and the worried "White Man's Burden" he named in its wake.

We see this burden at large in the nostalgia found in the plantation tradition that preceded the modern era—too rarely discussed in terms of the Genteel Tradition which follows and is in large part subsumed by it. It is this Plantation America to which Pound and Eliot turned, as Michael North notes in *The Dialect of Modernism*, when writing to each other in the voices of Uncle Remus; as "Possum" and "Uncle Ez" they are undergoing a deliberate if subconscious racial masquerade to get beyond the social masquerades and mores of their time. We might even say that, in looking back at the Genteel tradition and trying to rebel against it, the two architects of modernism required the somewhat rebellious energy that the plantation tradition, and the blackface of Uncle Remus in particular, provided. The "Jazz Age" as a whole could be said to be responding to this rebellious blackness.

Is it any wonder that—among the challenges and swift changes brought about by modernity—the mask was turned to as a means of resolution? And that the mask was so often black—as a reflection of change even as it was a refuge from that change and a retreat into a primal past?

Jungle Boogie

It is a short trip from the perfect plantation past to the scary, or symbolic, jungle-filled one. In venues such as Paris's *La Revue Négre* or Harlem's Cotton Club, the two were, if not directly conflated, then suggestively interchangeable. But what does the Jungle mean for African Americans, who have sometimes played into it, donning the mask of the primitive?

In part it may mean liberation.

Urban in origin, and often conflating the verticality of the skyscraper with that of the Jungle setting (as visualized, say, in the work of Aaron Douglass[13]), this idea of the Jungle, if not entirely accurate, is black-made and -masked not to express a real self or an imagined other but *to conjure an imagined self*. This Jungle self is not so much savage as freed; is not the paradoxical noble savage but a transport back to a lost heritage—the more aggressively or laughably artificial, the better. If not quite the Elsewhere of the Negro spirituals, this transformative Jungle recognizes that the mask is not a cover, but a vehicle, a way for its spirit—let's call it swing—to enter you and your art or music or movement.

Much like its seeming opposite, the biblical desert, the Jungle is a place not of lifelessness but renewal. The Jungle is an oasis in a modern world come to resemble a less transcendent sort of desert, a virtual Waste Land; yet the Jungle also provides a metaphor for that same, out of control world. *Down in the jungle, way down by a creek, the Signifying Monkey hadn't eaten in a week.* We might not be surprised to learn that the word "jungle" in fact derives from "waste land": "[Ult. < Skt. *jangalam*, desert, wasteland, uncultivated area < *jangala-*, desert, waste.]"[14]

But don't take my word for it: the Jungle's regenerative power is trumpeted by later black artists, from Kool & the Gang's "Jungle Boogie" to James Brown's album *In the Jungle Groove*, which introduced the world to the break on "Funky Drummer," and thus to hip-hop. Which in turn gave us the Jungle Brothers. Not to mention the form of drum-and-bass music known as jungle (often based on a sample of a drum solo fittingly known as "The Amen Break"). These be the jungle as funk-filled forest—*funk* being another name for the blues in both senses of the term. The persistence of the Jungle into black-made art forms, a half-century or century later, indicates its defiant appeal. And usefulness.

White readers often brought to the Jungle the image of the Forest, found in European fairy tales as a site of danger, of wolves and lost children, while the black audience and artist seems almost always to have found in Jungle the liberating notion of "going wild." (Though of course, by accepting the Jungle, or going "Wild about Harry," some whites in the 1920s would do the same.) Wilderness for the African American had, during slavery, long meant a place preferable to the plantation and its ornate garden: "Slaves knew that as chattel they were considered part of the property and wilds of nature, which a smoothly functioning plantation could restrain. The nearby woods contained enough birds and roaming animals to provide slaves with geographical and naturalistic references for freedom. . . . Thus it was hardly a difficult choice for slaves to forsake the pastoral Eden for the unpredictable wilderness."[15] If the garden meant order, and order meant slavery, I'd take wilderness and its freedom too.

For the slave wilderness also meant praise. The slave songs—or should we say freedom songs—were often performed in the wilderness, in what has been termed "the invisible church": those services and worship that the slaves conducted in secret. You might call it "the Amen break." "A common practice was to meet in the deep woods, in remote ravines or gullies, or in secluded thickets (called 'brush arbors'). The preachers and exhorters would speak over a kettle of water in order to drown the sound, or the group would turn a kettle upside down in the center of the gathering so that the kettle would absorb the sound of the singing."[16]

> My name it is poor Pilgrim
> To Canaan I am bound
> Travellin' through this wilderness
> On-a this enchanted ground.

This remapping of the wilderness by African Americans, both in praise and in practice, was in direct rebuke of the ways white settlers saw the New World. From the start the colonists, bringing the Forest with them, had pitched their destiny upon the most primal of pasts, invoking either Eden or Wilderness as an originating force. In his *Blacks in Eden*, critic J. Lee Greene notes that for the Puritans America was wilderness, a "devil's land" they were sent to tame. In contrast, white Southerners saw the country as Eden, themselves as descendants of Adam and Eve (with blacks a sign of original sin). If one group saw the New World as after the fall, the other before it, both worldviews required the conversion or ignoring of Native Americans and African slaves to continue.[17] Such a dichotomy—Eden or Wilderness—found its way into the contradictions of western expansionism and the frontier. No wonder the West needed conquering.

In contrast, for African Americans the Jungle means both Eden blackened and Wilderness redeemed—or better yet, wilderness proved an "enchanted ground," a form of home.

If the redemptive black view of Jungle persisted, so did the racialized, racist, modern one, from at least the time "Mistah Kurtz—he's dead" struck fear into *Heart of Darkness* to later become used as a sign of phonetic and other decay as an epigraph to Eliot's "Hollow Men" (1925). Years later, in *Jungle Fever*, artist and photographer Jean-Paul Goude accounts for his fascination with blacks (and before that Indians) growing up in Josephine Baker's Paris:

I have been in love with Indians since before I could read or write. I had seen them first in comic books like *Tin-Tin* and later in Westerns. . . . I loved the brown color of their skin. Their teeth looked so white by comparison. This is true not only of Indians but also of blacks—of anyone with a color of skin darker than pink. . . . I'd have an army of Indians and an army of cowboys. To help you understand that the cowboys were crummy guys, I made them all look alike. The good guys, the Indians, were all different. They had nice ornaments. I made one drawing of Womba which is completely black, a black-faced Indian with white tribal marks . . . Indians were the first brown people I liked. Black people came later.[18]

Even his beloved blacks are ornaments, racial profiles of a literal sort. Goude's entire book traces the way that not just Americans but Europeans spend their childhood as Imaginary Indians, and their adolescence, however extended, as Imaginary Negroes (or wishing to be with them). Goude's art book is less a personal history than a racial one: images depict not just Womba (drawn in 1947 when Goude was seven, a fascinating picture) but also Goude's mom, a dancer, photographed among whites in blackface in 1927; and seven years later as part of the chorus surrounding a wide-mouthed Ethel Waters. As his title indicates, Goude's often erotic drawings and photographs are "Wishful thinking," as he terms one 1965 explicit depiction of interracial oral sex; he even goes so far as to include photographs he terms "from memory," made years later in the 1970s, that depict past visions of racial contact such as an Alvin Ailey dancer not so much eroticized as abstracted, literally manipulated, extended, blurred.

All this, no doubt, is meant as praise. So too is his description of his and fellow audience's mix of horror and lust watching a black performer: ". . . she was performing wearing just a prom skirt and nothing else. Her tits were bare. The strength of her image, then as now, is that it swings constantly from the near grotesque—from the organ grinder's monkey—to the great African beauty. You are constantly looking at her and wondering if she's beautiful or grotesque, or both, and how can she be one if she's the other?"[19] Same difference. The fact that he here is describing Grace Jones, not only one of Josephine Baker's clear inheritors but Goude's future common-law wife, should give us pause.

Are we again in the presence of the fetish? Goude's manipulation of Grace Jones's literal image—"I cut her legs apart, lengthened them, turned her body completely to face the audience like an Egyptian painting, and of course, once it was all done, I had a print made which I used as my preliminary drawing. Then I started painting, joining up all those pieces to give the illusion that Grace Jones actually posed for the photograph and that only she was capable of assuming such a position"—certainly is contraband that views the mask as reality, strains to convince us it is. Certainly Grace Jones herself played with her own image in fascinating ways, and was as interested in artifice as anything else. But Goude goes further, rendering not just his own memories false, but hers: "The first picture you'll see of Grace is of her as a child exposing herself. Why not? I show her as the natural exhibitionist she probably was."[20]

It is not enough for Jones or Goude's other blacks (and Indians, and Puerto Ricans, and gays, and Vietnamese who also appear) to be wild in the present, he must also imagine their wildness as primal, prima facie, and a "natural" part of their past. "Wild Things" he calls a photo shoot from 2009 for *Harper's Bazaar*, with black supermodel Naomi Campbell depicted in jungle garb, racing alongside a cheetah (her weave flying) and even jumping rope spun by two monkeys.[21] *Me Tarzan, You Cheetah:* the fetishized white-placed Jungle persists to this day.

This is tricky terrain. In the wrong hands Jungle is reminiscent of Ole Virginny as a site of pernicious nostalgia; in others, it is a call to Africa.

The recent disregard heaped upon the notion of Africa as a popular theme in the Harlem Renaissance, in what's called "literary Garveyism"—not to mention actual Garveyism, the empowering of those of African descent to look literally to Africa—denies the power of place in the black imagination. Indeed, it ignores the use of remapping as a strategy of the African in the Americas, both as an escape route and as an escape hatch, that we have discussed and should take care to remember. This is, as a stock certificate of Garvey's UNIA says: "Africa: The Country of Possibility."[22]

Such a "country" is aligned not with the past, but also the future. Garvey himself is said to have recognized this: "In one of his Liberty Hall speeches, the indefatigable leader of the 1920s warned opponents that he could not be tampered with or harmed because, as he said, 'I am a *modern*.'"[23]

Liberty Hall

Just as the idea of Canaan proved a necessary part of the slave's liberation, an Elsewhere present in the spirituals, Africa persists in the freedperson's collective memory, and as part of the slave's ever-present past. The danger of course is that Africa is a real place—not a mere country, as some still seem to think (and even Garvey advertised), but a diverse, populous continent. At its best, Garveyism of any stripe does not make this mistake: instead of a physical place, both literary and political Garveyism argues over the image of Africa, redeeming it from centuries of its dismissal (and fascination—or should I say, fetishizing) as The Dark Continent.

The main idea behind the Jungle is that of home. The home the blues have left behind, the rootlessness that jazz embodies: both take not just aspects of technique from African music, but also solace from the very idea of Africa. *I sought my Lord in de wilderness, For I'm a-going home.* Basquiat put it this way: "I've never been to Africa. I'm an artist who has been influenced by his New York environment. But I have a cultural memory. I don't need to look for it; it exists. It's over there, in Africa. That doesn't mean that I have to go live there. Our cultural memory follows us everywhere, wherever you live."[24]

The remapping performed by the enslaved African and the freed artist—turning an Africa of memory, and even of recent experience, into utopia—was pitched against the notion of Africa as "no place" in the European imagination. In their more modern remappings—of Africa, of the Jungle—African Americans such as Baker or Duke Ellington or Hughes sought to fight the "colonial memory," as Delueze and Guattari termed it, and the rampant "phantasy" found in Eliot's and other modernists' encounters with imaginary blackness. Given that the imagination is where the Negro was first questioned and dismissed, why wouldn't black folks also choose the imagination as the site of this struggle and reclamation?

And why not Harlem? While certainly Harlem does not include all the wings of what might best be called the New Negro renaissance—which took place in Washington, D.C., Philadelphia, Paris, and other outposts as early as the 1890s—Harlem had by the end of the 1920s come to stand as a mythic as well as literal home for those in the African Diaspora. Perhaps the Jungle is not actually found in Africa, then, but America. Or, is Jungle just another word for heaven: as Arna Bontemps put it, "in some places the autumn of 1924 may have been an unremarkable season. In Harlem it was like a foretaste of paradise."[25]

Home to Harlem

Paradise had been promised by the spirituals: *I am going to make heaven my home.* But the culture black folks made promised a kind of belonging in the idea of nativeness, even in the midst of exile. For black culture, going "native" was less a dangerous excursion than a reclaiming of the home they found themselves in. *Native Son*, *Notes of a Native Son*, Natasha Trethewey's *Native Guard*, the Native Tongues hip hop collective: African American conceptions of nativeness mean belonging, a nativity.

Or taking the A Train to bring you home, to Harlem, again. As Cheryl Wall's *Women of the Harlem Renaissance* eloquently notes:

> The idea of "home" has a particular resonance in African-American expressive tradition, a resonance that reflects the experience of dispossession that initiates it. In the spirituals, blacks had sung of themselves as motherless children "a long way from home." Images of homelessness—souls lost in the storm or the wilderness—abound. In the absence of an earthly home, the slaves envisioned a spiritual one, a home over Jordan, for example; or they laid claim defiantly to "a home in dat rock." . . . The efforts to claim Harlem as home found voice in texts such as James

Weldon Johnson's *Black Manhattan* and McKay's *Harlem: Negro Metropolis*. In the political realm, Marcus Garvey sought through his visionary rhetoric to inspire a New Negro who would fight to redeem Africa, the ancestral home.[26]

While Wall mentions both McKay's study, *Harlem*, and his memoir *Long Way from Home*, she does not mention here his *Home to Harlem* (1928), McKay's first novel and the first bestseller by an African American. Certainly the book's popularity stemmed in part from its tapping the "Harlem vogue." Such a vogue, though seen as a misnomer by some, is represented at least by the publisher on the cover of my first edition (with its lovely Aaron Douglas illustration) by a sticker advertising "A negro's own novel—for those who enjoyed NIGGER HEAVEN, PORGY and BLACK APRIL." As with *Black Sadie*, the selling point (though not necessarily the novel's) is the accessibility of Harlem, presumably not just for black folks, to cash in on and enjoy. "For those white Americans with the time, money, and sophistication to make the trip, Harlem at night seemed a world apart. In contrast to their own world, discipline, hard work, and frugality were counterfeit coin in the realm of imaginary Harlem. Nothing symbolized its otherness more than the cabaret."[27]

Yet Harlem was imaginary, too, at least in part, for the black folks who lived, loved, and visited there—who thought of it as a, if not *the*, "black mecca." For them it was counterfeit coin in the best, storying sense: Harlem meant being free both spiritually and economically. However temporary, the power of the migrant and the exoduster's ennobling dream of homesteading cannot be overstated. For black folks, Harlem/home remains expressive of a black self, however fictive: a place where Hurston could feel her color coming on like a mythic tribesman; or where Ellington could play "jungle music" that was jazz by another name. What the cabaret provides—like the Southern juke joint, or the Harlem drag ball—is not mere tourism, but also black agency, no matter how mediated.

In a way, Harlem itself represents a *recolonization* of Manhattan. Instead of merely breaking from the British Isles, as many American modernists sought to do culturally, black folks recaptured the Isle of Manhattan, and on their own terms. Traveling from the South and the Caribbean, black migrants came north and east to reclaim the island the Indians were low-balled for centuries before—to rewrite the song Manhattan was sold for—recapturing a Harlem named by the Dutch who once lived there too. Recolonization meant a kind of coming home—keeping in mind that, especially for those of African descent in exile in the West, the exile finds home wherever she can.

Might we also say that the Great Migration, with its satisfying notion of "feeling at home" in a brand new, cosmopolitan place, not only counters modernist exile, but exemplifies it? Such exile provided less a sense of loss than a vantage point. "The maroon community of 'Harlem,'" Houston Baker reminds us, "conceived as the *modern* capital of those 'capable of speaking' for themselves, is thus source (of insubordination)—haven (for fugitives)—base (for marauding expedition)—and nucleus (of leadership for planned uprisings)."[28]

Just as Josephine Baker and jazz overtook Paris, after taking Harlem by storm, the Jungle always threatened to spread. (Not that Jean-Paul Goude would mind a generation later.) Such recolonization follows the remapping of the American landscape, and the reclaiming of black dialect from the jaws of the blackfaced, white-wide mouth by Dunbar and his Harlem Renaissance descendants. The transformation of the Island-English of Britain into the "nation language" of McKay and company on the northern tip of the island of Manhattan could be said to be another part of this recolonization. Such recolonization may even result in or make use of what Susan Gubar calls "recoloring," black artists taking over often restrictive roles that white artists had invented as black.

For now, let's say that in the hands of the author of *Black Sadie*, the real Josephine Baker's hard-won autonomy—indeed any notion of Negro authority or autonomy—is quickly displaced by the notion of the "negro novel" as a blackface, "whites-only" form.[29] In this, *Sadie* contrasts only slightly with the *Home to Harlem* sticker's citing *Nigger Heaven*, *Porgy*, and *Black April* as examples of similar, blackface writing. In such a context, *Home to Harlem* being the "A negro's own novel" is indeed quite novel.

We need only think for a moment of the contemporary young black writer, whether McKay or Hurston or Langston Hughes, wanting to write about "common" folk and about subjects less than pretty and stepping into the minefield of assumptions created by books such as *Sadie*. Reading the back flap of Hughes's *Fine Clothes to the Jew* (1927), for example, and seeing that "These poems, for the most part, interpret the more primitive types of American Negro, the bell-boys, the cabaret girls, the migratory workers, the singers of Blues and Spirituals, and the makers of folk-songs," one might better understand the flap the book caused upon publication, by black as well as white reviewers, who mistakenly saw it in *Sadie*'s same dusky, "primitive typed" blackface light. It was a similar view that prompted many, most famously Du Bois, to be angry at Carl Van Vechten's *Nigger Heaven*—a book Hughes and other younger writers defended liking as a part of their artistic freedom and resistance to the burden of a narrowly positive, New Negro representation. Given the importance of heaven = home = Harlem in the black imagination, no wonder the outrage over the reductiveness of *Nigger Heaven*, a flip phrase that implied settling for far less.

It is in the context of all the Black Sadies that Hughes's cry for unfettered expression in "The Negro Artist and the Racial Mountain" becomes important, and its perils (especially as seen by the older generation) more clear: for those dedicated to the New Negro, low-class meant lowercase. For Du Bois, all art is propaganda, and artistic freedom a luxury the uppercase and uplifting Negro could ill afford.

For Hughes, the New Negro also meant the Newness of modernism, a freedom to write about whatever he wished. This also meant a resistance—a poetics of refusal—that characterized Hughes's complex lifework.

Cross Road Blues

Not coincidentally, much like the people who made them did, the blues see the city as a place teeming with possibility. If in Harlem, black folks sensed "a foretaste of paradise," in this they were thoroughly modern, American style—taking delight, even romance, in the challenges of city life. The blues also foresaw the postmodern reaction to the urban environs: the City that seems a "Waste Land" to Eliot becomes the heroic "Paterson" of William Carlos Williams after the war (or his "Pastoral" written before it); for Hughes, while the city would become a "dream deferred," it remained still a dream, not yet a nightmare. And when, in his long poem *Montage of a Dream Deferred* (1951), Hughes goes on experience nightmare it is a "Nightmare Boogie," art made from pain in the blues tradition.

Even in the 1920s the blues enact a citified two-step between acceptance and despair. As Hughes noted:

> The Spirituals are group songs, but the Blues are songs you sing alone. The Spirituals are religious songs, born in camp meetings and remote plantation districts. But the Blues are *city* songs rising from the crowded streets of big towns, or beating against the lonely walls of hall bed-rooms where you can't sleep at night. The Spirituals are escape songs, looking toward heaven, tomorrow, and God. But the Blues are *today* songs, here and now, broke and broken-hearted, when you're troubled in mind and don't know what to do, and nobody cares.[30]

If at times, like Williams did, the blues find beauty in the city, the music also knows heartache can follow you wherever you go. As such, the blues are about the crossroads—between good and evil, tragedy and comedy—and also *are* the crossroads, the exact place where north meets south, city meets country. As befitting a crossroads, the blues shift between two sets of dueling impulses: first, seeing the city as a place of both welcome and betrayal—its landscape as haunted, even helpless—and, second, seeing modern life as exile and black life in particular as a delightful survival.

"Poor man's heart disease," the blues also describes a particular American— or should I say African American—rootlessness. Where the spirituals used Elsewhere as a comfort, for the blues the very possibility of Elsewhere causes both pain and pleasure. As Hughes says, the blues are "sadder even than the spirituals because their sadness is not softened with tears but hardened with laughter, the absurd, incongruous laughter of a sadness without even a god to appeal to."[31] Even as what Hughes calls "songs of escape," the spirituals reiterate their own surety: *I've Got a Home in Dat Rock, Don't You See?* But the blues offer an Elsewhere that may never be; even the escape of migration, one of the key subjects of the blues, is not always fully realized.

Indeed, the difference between migration and exile can be slim. Think of Bessie Smith's "Backwater Blues," here transcribed by Angela Davis. It begins:

> Then I went and stood upon some high old lonesome hill
> Then I went and stood upon some high old lonesome hill
> Then looked down on the house where I used to live.

The song, written by Bessie Smith, alludes to the disastrous 1927 flood of the Mississippi:

> Backwater blues done caused me to pack my things and go
> Backwater blues done caused me to pack my things and go
> 'Cause my house fell down and I can't live there no mo'.

The conflation between migration and exile is rendered with these final lines:

> Mmmmmmmmmm, I can't move no mo'
> Mmmmmmmmmm, I can't move no mo'
> There ain't no place for a poor old girl to go.[32]

Not only does the song describe a larger African American condition, but it could apply today to the displaced people from Hurricane Katrina and the Bush administration's failed infrastructures and sympathy. One hopes it is not still relevant in the wake of the recent toxic Gulf oil spill.

Rather than that creeping black, it is the structure of the blues that interests me here: the rootlessness of blues feeling is both mirrored and fought by the restlessness of the form; the form's constant recasting parallels the singer's search for meaning, and for home. In the blues the feeling of being displaced— also found in the spirituals—becomes a search for a safe haven rather than its guarantee. Whether "Sweet Home Chicago" or "Kansas City Here I Come," the blues seek an earthbound Elsewhere, extending the hope of the spirituals while arguing against such hope, foregrounding the here and now. The result is a sustained argument over existence.

Needless to say "the poor girl" in Bessie Smith and other singers' blues also offers a protest, however indirect, against both class and gender oppression in a city or country that does not have much of a place for black women at all. Angela Davis's and Hazel Carby's studies of blues women prove indispensable in understanding this.[33] As Carby points out, different, gendered reactions to oppression are revealed by the famous blues lyric:

> When a woman gets the blues she goes to her room and hides,
> When a woman gets the blues she goes to her room and hides,
> When a man gets the blues he catch the freight train and rides.

Riding and hiding: these not only gendered options, but two crucial ways the blues make meaning. For, alongside their almost exact contemporary the cinema, the blues provide a shifting space of identity. They provide not just a metaphor for migration but also—through the kicker and its series of reversals, with often last line inverting or ironically calling on all that goes before—a migration of meanings.

In a way, this floating lyric about hiding and riding is echoed by the often quoted opening of Hurston's *Their Eyes Are Watching God* (1937):

> Ships at a distance have every man's wish on board. For some they come in with the tide. For others they sail forever on the horizon, never out of sight, never landing until the Watcher turns his eyes away in resignation, his dreams mocked to death by Time. That is the life of men.
> Now, women forget all those things they don't want to remember, and remember everything they don't want to forget. The dream is the truth. Then they act and do things accordingly.[34]

This recasts the blues trope of the train in terms of the ship—heading where, I wonder? (But then again, I am a man.) Adrift, mocking, the dream as the truth: these are things the storying tradition knows well, and perhaps speaks of best in the blues.

Besides the revelatory quality of the songs and lives—the storying—of blueswomen charted by Davis and Carby, the blues also reveal shifting meanings of maleness. Many have written of Langston Hughes's writing in the voices of black women, but we can see such polyvocal expression even in bluesman Robert Johnson, the bad man of the blues. Despite the overemphasis on his short life and death by certain critics, Johnson may best be defined by double entendre as by direct autobiography. For him, double consciousness may be the true hellhound on his trail: "two warring ideals in one dark body, whose dogged strength alone keeps it from being torn asunder."[35]

The bad man, as Johnson sings and Hughes points out, is but one side of a double consciousness in which "sad boy" or "poor girl" is its tragicomic counterpart. This sad, less braggadocious side of manhood is clearly seen in Johnson's remarkable "Come On in My Kitchen": Johnson's plea is for a lover to come in the singer's "kitchen"—a place of warmth and comfort, a site of nurturing and socializing. Johnson's remapping is personal and metaphoric: in the blues, where cookin' is usually a metaphor for much more, the kitchen is never only literal place; here the kitchen is welcoming and even sexual, the base of happiness and the hair's nappiness. *If today was Christmas Eve, If Today was Christmas Eve, and tomorrow was Christmas Day*: Johnson's lines sing of possibility and pain.

The fact that the blues sing of pain at all helps them resist the sentimentality of the pop music of the times—not to mention the blackface crooners and plain-faced white contemporaries who would attempt to coopt the blues. "Blues music . . . is neither negative nor sentimental. It counterstates the torch singer's sob story, sometimes as if with the snap of two fingers!"[36] In short, blues do resist the popular, even as they represent the first modern popular black culture.

The blues as popular culture, it should be said, has not proved a very popular notion, largely because the blues are also an important folk tradition. It has proved irresistible for experts (as distinct from music lovers) to dismiss the "classic blues" in favor of "country blues," to reify the bad-ass bluesman over the Empresses, Queens, and host of Smiths who first broadened the blues' appeal. Such a narrow view, however, ignores the fact that the blues mark exactly the transition between the folk and the popular—not to mention that even the country blues reject the pastoral mode with its idealized South. The blues care little for purity, except when drinking canned heat.

As with modernism, the popular is something the blues resists even as it reforms it. Hughes, for instance, engages with the popular—fabricating folk songs at the last minute when Van Vechten could not obtain permission for reprinting the blues songs he wanted for *Nigger Heaven*. (Which begs a kind of question—is *Nigger Heaven* a further kind of contraband, not for its stolen images, but for the presence of Hughes's counterfeit blues? Why haven't we seen enough written about the ways, in jazz fashion, Hughes performed a sort of collaboration with Van Vechten?) Along with Williams's wheelbarrow and Lorca's deep song, Hughes's blues rebuff the purist, international notion of high modernism that soon came to be seen as the only forum for great art.

Certainly Hughes was drawn to blues because of its form: the unique ability of the blues to tell a single story (losing love, coming north, loneliness and mistresses and misters and mistrust) while making that story resonant and plural; to tell a simple story (my man left me, the flood took everything) and make it complex (referencing displacement, protesting conditions, echoing biblical undertones); the making of a fruitful music from loss; and in the end, often abandoning story altogether for sound. From their blurred notes to their tension between word and deed, between meaning and moaning, between the backing bottleneck sound and the up-front voice—in a word, irony—the blues recognize that even blurring posits its own claim to meaning, storying all the way home.

In Hughes, not to mention Bessie and Robert, we can see how the blues continues a movement from the "we" of the spirituals to the modern "I"—the blues, as Hughes reminds us, are to be sung alone. The blues are songs about loneliness that somehow, in our listening, turn their "I" into a form of "we": we listen to the blues so as not to feel alone. In this "I," the blues are Whitmanesque and profound, doing what Helen Vendler says the lyric poem does—for a moment, the duration of the lyric at least, we experience what the "I" experiences. You could say both lyric poetry and the blues turn us into a city of one.

The blues do offer comfort, no matter how cold.

A Strong Brown God

As plain talk and local metaphor, the blues would go on to influence much of modern literature—if only as a useful example of, or contrast with, such a literature's own making and masking. While some might argue about the entertainment or popular value of *The Waste Land*, Eliot's poem, like the blues from the Smiths to Robert Johnson, relies on an implied protest about the modern human condition. If we say one does so by collage, the other by refrain, we are apt to confuse which is which: "HURRY UP PLEASE IT'S TIME" quickly can seem like a blues lyric, while "I've got a kindhearted woman, she studies evil all the time" fits somewhere between the gossip of the old ladies and the quake of thunder.

As such, the chief difference between high and low modernism may be the mere borrowing of black material by the popular, domestic modernists, versus its outright theft by the more skilled, "high modernists." Originally called "He Do the Police in Different Voices," Eliot's *Waste Land* used the multiple voices found in the minstrel show, America's first popular entertainment.[37] But while Eliot was burying the blackface origins (as well as the autobiographical ones) of *The Waste Land*, they resurfaced as part of *Sweeney Agonistes*, not only in its characters Tambo and Bones, but in its being labeled as "melodrama"—which originally meant a drama "with music."

Not just black, this music was also jazz. Indeed, despite his brilliant critique of Eliot's use of race, Michael North neglects to note how the multifaceted, multi-voiced structure of *The Waste Land*—and by extension the poets whose accolades, criticism, and own poetry cemented its place as the prototypical and certainly most influential modernist poem—could be said to mirror the multiplicity of jazz. Ralph Ellison certainly saw a correlation between Eliot's collage and the concerted *storying* of Satchmo: "Consider that at least as early as T. S. Eliot's creation of a new aesthetic for poetry through the artful juxtapositioning of earlier style, Louis Armstrong, way down the river in New Orleans, was working out a similar technique for jazz."[38] Satchmo would also use collage not just in his music, but on the road, as anyone viewing his recently published collages—not to mention his own collage-like letters—may discover.

In further observing Eliot's upriver technique, Ralph Ellison describes finding Eliot's transcription inclusion of a song written by James Weldon Johnson as transcendent:

Somehow music was transcending the racial divisions. Listening to songs such as "I'm Just Wild About Harry" and knowing that it was the work of Negroes didn't change all our attitudes but it helped all kinds of people identify with American-ness or American music. Among all the allusions to earlier poetry that you find in Eliot's *The Waste Land* he still found a place to quote from "Under the Bamboo Tree," a lyric from a song by James Weldon Johnson, Bob Cole, and Rosamond Johnson. During the twenties when *The Waste Land* was published many readers made the connection.[39]

Others such as Kamau Brathwaite have noted such connections: "What Eliot did for Caribbean poetry and Caribbean literature was to introduce the notion of the speaking voice, the conversational tone." For Brathwaite and others, Eliot's deformation of language was not a sign of the modern world's flaws, but of a lib-erating step toward fully acknowledging an English influenced by blacks brought to the Americas—a "nation language" now emergent and pervasive.[40] For many black writers, not just Eliot's poetry but his birth in St. Louis—home to Scott Joplin, Staggerlee, and likely the Bamboo Tree—and his invoking of the "strong brown god" of the Mississippi, link him and his voice to a long history of race and music in the Americas. As Brathwaite notes, "For those who really made the breakthrough, it was Eliot's actual voice—or rather his recorded voice, property of the British Council—reading 'Preludes,' 'The love song of J. Alfred Prufrock,' *The Waste Land* and the *Four Quartets*—not the texts—which turned us on. In that dry deadpan delivery, the riddims of St. Louis (though we didn't know the source then) were stark and clear for those of us who at the same time were lis-tening to the dislocations of Bird, Dizzy and Klook. And it is interesting that on the whole, the Establishment couldn't stand Eliot's voice—far less jazz!"[41]

Yet why do Ellison, Brathwaite, and those "many readers" in "our segregated schools" see a connection between blackness and modernism, while for some critics, and, no doubt, the popular imagination, there is little to none to speak of? More importantly, why does what, for Ellison, seems like love, feel at times to me like theft?

Crazy Blues

You say *Waste Land*, I say "Crazy Blues": both declare the madness of the modern moment, with Eliot disguising his personal breakdown as society's, while Mamie Smith breaks down a song into a breakthrough of black voice, echoing across the land.

We may measure modernism not just by the journey from the domestic mod-ernism to high modernism to New Criticism, or from Handy's "St. Louis Blues" to Eliot's "The river is a strong brown god," but from "St. Louis Blues" to Louis Armstrong's "West End Blues," with its redefinition and virtual invention of the jazz solo. For the journey from collective folk vision, recorded by Handy, to individual excellence and promise found and reformed in Satchmo—backer to Bessie Smith on her "St. Louis Blues"—is no less powerful than Eliot's notion that the modern era meant the disintegration of not just society but the self. Not to mention his startlingly corresponding view that any effective individual talent must function like a catalyst, as an escape from personality, changed by but changing tradition.

Mamie Smith solidified and started a new tradition, one that insists on if not personality, then swing. When she stepped in to a recording studio in 1920, the "Crazy Blues" she recorded would be the very first blues committed to wax, selling thousands in one month, and over a million in its first year. Incredible numbers. The recording was in many ways a "recoding": Smith changes not only the chords, blurring them with the music as provided by her Jazz Hounds, but also inventing, if only for the studio, the new form of a recorded blues. (Is this another kind of recolonizing?) Those who object to her "vaudeville voice," or deny the song because it doesn't fit the purity of the blues, seem unaware of the blues' always syncretic nature. They almost certainly fail to hear the coded meanings and implied protest in the song, written by black songwriter Perry Bradford.

> Now I've got the crazy blues
> Since my baby went away
> I ain't got no time to lose
> I must find him today
> Now the doctor's gonna do all . . . that he can
> But what you gonna need is a undertaker man
> I ain't had nothin' but bad news
> Now I've got the crazy blues

Smith's high-pitched voice seems to me not a fault but a conduit. For with it she manages to convey simultaneous identification with both victim and perpetrator; its very eerieness evokes "crazy."

There is a technology at work here, black as wax, a virtual voice speaking for and to the masses who bought and borrowed it. "Crazy Blues" sings of disembodiment, a synthesis of folk and machine found not just in the recording but in Smith's warbling. Behind her, Her Jazz Hounds echo and engulf the singer (and listener) with a clarinet accompanying her almost phrase for phrase, the trombone practically looping and swooping behind her. These are the foundational, key instruments in jazz (before the trumpet and then the saxophone took over) singing their swan song as "Crazy Blues" gestures toward a new one. Much of it is in her tremulous tone:[42] *I don't have any time to lose,* she sings, and we believe her. The urgency is palpable, an analogue to diasporic yearning.

Smith's narrator must find her lover "today" and the doctor's been called, either for her presumed heartache or for the violence implied against her "baby." In a way, her "baby" is the selfsame the undertaker man "[she] gonna need": a man the narrator also can't help but desire, but who may send her to the grave; or who, by mistreating her, unwittingly dooms himself. Not just a description of our heroine's feelings, the "Crazy Blues" is metaphor for modern life as vibrant as the notion of Jungle or Waste Land. Or home.

Critic Adam Gussow focuses most interestingly on the last stanzas of the song, the first few lines of which incorporates a floating verse perhaps made most familiar in the song "Trouble in Mind":

> I went to the railroad
> Hang my head on the track
> Thought about my daddy
> I gladly snatched it back
> Now my babe's gone
> And gave me the sack
>
> Now I've got the crazy blues
> Since my baby went away
> I ain't had no time to lose
> I must find him today
> I'm gonna do like a Chinaman . . . go and get some hop
> Get myself a gun . . . and shoot myself a cop
> I ain't had nothin' but bad news
> Now I've got the crazy blues
> Those blues[43]

Where Eliot once wanted to "Do the Police in Different Voices," the Crazy Blues would have you "do like a Chinaman," putting on yet another racial mask, and then shoot a cop. Gussow reads the floating verse "snatch my head back" as a reference to the practice of lynching or mutilation by train, and the ending of the song as a protest against police violence, however veiled.

I myself am interested here in several things: not only the way that "Crazy Blues" tapped into an underground set of meanings, but the way it tapped into an underground economy. The two were no coincidence. Many reports have it that the record was distributed informally by black Pullman porters who bought the record in the north for $1 and sold it along their routes south and west for $2 or even $3. Certainly each copy was listened to by more than just the purchaser, and like any underground classic, got passed around like gossip.

If it might be a protest about lynching, the song is certainly a symbol of the railroad as empowering the porters; as a symbolic means of escaping the South (and distributing the blues, quite literally); and also as an implied protest of working conditions where a railroad like a lover could up and "give you the sack," especially if you were a black worker unlucky enough to be hurt on the job.

The train needless to say courses through black and folk expression, where it occupies many stations of meaning. Chief among them for black culture may be the locomotive as a sign of motion and freedom; the underground railroad is itself an elegant metaphor for escape. Call it the *blues correlative*: when De Ford Bailey, or Robert Johnson, or Bessie Smith refers to the train through lyrics or music, they need not explain the history of railroad imagery, from the underground railroad to John Henry's hammer, in order to embody locomotive's crucial complexities as a metaphor for leaving and for life itself. *The blue light was my blues, the red light was my mind.* Even a song like "The Midnight Special" was originally not the defanged bar-band singalong it has become, but rather the words of a prisoner from his cell watching the light of the midnight train go by, and wishing it carried him—and his very wishes—along with it.

Where modernism sought an objective correlative to describe one's emotions through the apt symbol, the blues artist sought a subjective, blues correlative from the store of shared imagery inherited, changed, and reinvigorated by the latest artist in the tradition. Much the way an abstract artist drawing a horizontal line calls up centuries of landscape painting, the black and blues artist invoking a train—or river, or valley, or other remapped landscape—conjured a host and history of meanings.

The railroad links not just the country blues to the city blues, but also black struggle to the "Chinaman's chance." For the railroad, symbol of modernization and the East meeting West, was also the site of cultural connection, with black railroad workers literally connecting Asian American ones. While troubling in the way "Chinamen" here represent being "hopped up," "Crazy Blues" borrows Asian-ness not merely to signify "crazy" but to help transform the narrator into a "crazy nigger" who would shoot a cop. Smith's song then, suggests the shifting identities of the modern era—and of a patently racialized, if masked, rebellion. From the Boston Tea Party onward, American rebellion and rewriting tradition requires not reality but such a mask.

For crazy, as everyone from Gussow to Richard Pryor knows, may not necessarily mean insanity so much as a fierce recognition of the craziness of the world. The "Crazy Blues" of the title may indeed not be the narrator's view, but the view of authorities for whom any uncompromising black (or Asian) response left the colored folks deemed crazy and killable. "Crazy" is another outlaw identity black folks have championed—along with the bootlegger, the numbers runner, and the graffiti writer—because when "normal" means kowtowing to figures of power, "crazy" may not be insane in the least. *Where I come from*, as I recently said in an "Ode to Homemade Wine," *crazy is a compliment.*[44] Crazy is the tonic in which misbehavior mixes with outright rebellion; the blues ain't nothin' but a bad woman feeling good.

In an important sense, Mamie Smith's achievement mirrors Langston Hughes's much-remarked-upon innovation in his *Fine Clothes*—that is, removing the framing device so that instead of being listened to by a narrator ("I heard a Negro play" in his "Weary Blues"), the bell-boys, bad men, and sad girls speak or sing directly to us. Smith, as it happens, stepped in to replace a "popular" white singer to sing another song, which then prompted black songwriter Perry Bradford to convince OKeh records to let him record "Crazy Blues" at the session. The recording went on to reveal to record companies a black audience hungry for the blues, and for black song.

Without the removal of the white star's frame Smith might never have sung Bradford's blues as the blues, instead keeping it mere novelty. For Smith's rendition not only begat "race records"—and the promotion of records for a black audience—it also cemented a blues craze. Such a craze can be seen in sheet music of the time; from ragtime to cakewalks to boogie woogie to "Ethiopian Airs" to the blues, sheet music traces the ways in which whites used black forms not just for profit, but pleasure.[45] And reveals that this often required, at least on the covers, erasure of their black origins—or a highlighting of blackface ones in the "coon songs," images that are not people, but a degraded image. In turn, many a white person graces the covers of songs called "blues" in a way later familiar to rhythm and blues and even jazz albums—defacing those origins enough that they are no longer recognizable. The white and blackface masks the blues and jazz were made to wear also appear among much of the literature of the time. The real framing device that Mamie Smith and Langston Hughes cast off was not only black mores, but white pleasure.

Black and Tan Fantasy

Such pleasure often masked a form of anxiety. Rather than a comfort with progress—that American ideal—modernism itself may represent an anxiety over precisely that progress. Part of the blues' brood, jazz was and remains for many a site of this anxiety. While the music is seen as hectic, anxious, symptomatic, jazz is actually the diagnosis: we've all come down with a serious case of modernism. In its self-consciousness jazz mirrors modernism; in its willingness to refer to itself (especially later, in bebop), jazz foreshadows the growing self-reflexivity found in the postmodern and the art over the course of the last century.

One example of jazz anxiety—and by extension, modernism's—is mentioned by Toni Morrison in her *Playing in the Dark*. Morrison quotes at length from Marie Cardinal's interestingly titled *The Words to Say It*; this "autobiographical novel" describes Cardinal's lifelong bouts of depression and nervous breakdowns—what she calls "the Thing"—a condition first precipitated by hearing Louis Armstrong play live:

> My first anxiety attack occurred during a Louis Armstrong concert. I was nineteen or twenty. Armstrong was going to improvise with his trumpet, to build a whole composition in which each note would be important and would contain within itself the essence of the whole. I was not disappointed: the atmosphere warmed up very fast. The scaffolding and flying buttresses of the jazz instruments supported Armstrong's trumpet, creating spaces which were adequate enough for it to climb higher, establish itself, and take off again. The sounds of the trumpet sometimes piled up together, fusing a new musical base, a sort of matrix which gave birth to one precise, unique note, tracing a sound whose path was almost painful, so absolutely necessary had its equilibrium and duration become; it tore at the nerves of those who followed it. . . . Gripped by panic at the idea of dying there in the middle of spasms, stomping feet, and the crowd howling, I ran into the street like someone possessed.[46]

It would seem the Thing is not just the author's own anxiety, but the modern world's—the threat of possession tearing at the nerves till fleeing is the only response worth having. (Where for someone like Vachel Lindsay, mislabeled "The Jazz Poet," the only impulse was to fight.) There's that Thing, an uneasy "It" again: black and modern and possessed; or should we say dispossessed.

Morrison goes on to read this passage in different directions, but I want to note the ways the passage describes Armstrong's ability so wonderfully, even fetishizing it—but where I see achievement, remapping, a storying tradition, Armstrong's flights of sound lead the protagonist merely to flee. Faced with such freedom, could she be said to have another choice?

A similar, fetishized feeling courses through the opening of Blair Niles's 1931 novel, *Strange Brother*, an important early novel concerning a gay white man exploring Harlem. In its opening paragraphs we find a cabaret that perhaps not surprisingly echoes the other views of the cabaret we have seen, capturing the venue's unsettling of the white viewer through a jazz song's suggestiveness:

> Colored lights hung under the low ceiling—red, blue, and yellow lights. There was a dance floor in the center of the room, with tables surrounding it on three sides, and on the fourth side an orchestra. There were saxophones, trombones, trumpets and fiddles, banjos and flutes and drums—a great jazz orchestra. At the tables there were white men and women; and alone on the dance floor there was Glory, standing straight and slender, with the spotlight full upon her, Glory singing the Creole Love Call.
>
> There were no words in Glory's song. Glory seemed simply to open her mouth

and let her heart find expression in wordless sounds which fluttered up from the dark column of her throat and floated through the thick smoke-blue air of the crowded night club.

It was said in Harlem that Glory was the sort of girl who can make a man "see the City," make a man know joy.

But to June Westbrook, Glory's voice brought unrest.[47]

While we do not have the space to fully consider Glory or the "unrest" she and the "colored lights" calls forth in the white viewer, for now we might recall Black Sadie—and her other incarnations—the scene evokes. *Knowing joy, bringing unrest:* these seem the typical, if here well put, poles of jazz for the white viewer.

Actually an Ellington composition, the "Creole Love Call" is not literal, but a blend of language (and love) that is overwhelmingly suggestive, and that little else can name. Unlike the French my grandparents and their generation spoke in southern Louisiana, "Creole" in the original is not necessarily a language but a stand-in for a high-pitched, unsettling, dare I say primitive, wail. *Strange Brother's* all-too-familiar witnessing of such wordlessness echoes other instances of a white audience used to viewing black productions through the noise of racism—whose extreme took place in minstrelsy's *nonsense*, which as Houston Baker recounts, is not just linguistic. And yet, the nonsense of minstrelsy did provide meaning, even if it was only to demean.

With Ellington's "jungle music" (a name reportedly first given by George Gershwin) the meaning is far more irreducible and fluid—not nonsense, but exactly the unease these white accounts record. Standing as it does between gossip and thunder, jazz offers not just freedom, but another, radical tradition—instead of progress, jazz emphasizes *process*. Most interested in the past only as a way of riffing toward the future, jazz seems to say we "make it new" only when we make it our own. Negotiating between modern individuality and community, in both its actual form and its ongoing history, jazz and its birth mother the blues are in many ways the collective unconscious of African America, and by extension America—offering a firsthand account of risk, redemption, and yearning. No wonder, then, with its sound alone, jazz provided both a cure and a cause for anxiety.

If the blues don't get you, my jazzing must: the conclusion of the "St. Louis Blues" proved less a threat than a promise, the black seduction of modern culture coming true just as did Virginia Woolf's declaration or Picasso's portrait of Stein. Still, despite their inventions and predictions—or perhaps because of them—African Americans were often reduced to "It," a Thing. Such forms of objectification black music would playfully and subversively contest in the very title of one of Duke Ellington's key numbers, "It Don't Mean a Thing (If It Ain't Got That Swing)." The song, which would name swing music, in its very title wrested African American music away from the nonsense that threatened it by a title in which "It" had no antecedent. Both the "It" and the music, the song insisted, were *sui generis*. It was not a love call, but a battle cry about the direction of the art.

The "it" here I like to think of as the same "it" in "Make it new"—which I take to mean the tradition—but also further, and funkier, a black body, which, for the black storyteller or author, became a body of work. This "It" also happens to be the slippery pronoun Smith recorded as the other side of "Crazy Blues": "It's Right Here For You, If You Don't Get It, 'Tain't No Fault of Mine." At once plainly sexual and more elusively suggestive, the taint is faultless, and right here for you to engage, as tradition. And to make, like the Negro, new.

Notes

1. Frederic Jameson. "The Cultural Logic of Late Capitalism." *Postmodernism*. 11.

2. See my introduction to *Blues Poems*, New York: Everyman's Pocket Poets, 2003. Kevin Young, ed.

3. Taken from Woolf's essay "Mr. Bennett and Mrs. Brown" in 1924. Questions of proper dating and periodicization swirl around the Harlem Renaissance modernism, usually with political implications, both large and small. In her terrific *Women of the Harlem Renaissance* (1995), Cheryl Wall effectively argues that ending the Renaissance in 1932 is not just a question of accuracy, but bias: if we do not expand either the start or end, we leave out many of the important works by Hurston and other women writers. Others would say by not dating the Renaissance earlier than the 1920s, we avoid the connectedness to what might be called the New Negro movement that can be seen even before the turn of the century. In his *Modernism and the Harlem Renaissance*, Houston Baker opens with a discussion of Woolf's quote, countering it by establishing the commencement of "Afro-American modernism" to September 18, 1895, and "Washington's delivery of the opening address at the Negro exhibit of the Atlanta Cotton States and International Exposition." Baker, *Modernism*, 15.

4. Just as I have not provided here an endpoint of modernism, I do not provide one for the Harlem Renaissance—in part to provide for a broader inclusiveness and avoid problems of periodicization (see footnote 3, above). For a description of the *Opportunity* parties (and a good gossipy overview), consult Steven Watson, *The Harlem Renaissance: Hub of African American Culture, 1920–1930*. Pantheon, 1995. 1995 was a banner year for Renaissance studies!

5. For a look at some of the Harlem or New Negro Renaissance's publishing history and visual impact, consult the catalog I curated, *"Democratic Vistas": Exploring the Raymond Danowski Poetry Library*.

6. Peter Brooker, ed. *Modernism/Postmodernism*. Editor's Preface. xi. London, New York: Longman, 1992. I have had some debates over whether the "Anglo" here means "white, English speaking" (as the dictionary, and current usage, would have it) or merely British, but at best this is badly worded, at worst poorly considered. Why not say "British"? Perhaps unsurprisingly, it seems white critics often refer to "Anglo" to mean "British"; African American and Afro-British writers often use it to indicate "white" or "white American."

7. Thomas McEvilley. *FUSION: West African Artists at the Venice Biennale*. The Museum for African Art (New York). Munich: Prestel-Verlag, 1993. 10–11. The catalog goes on to view history in four phases of identity: "the pre-Modern period"; "the colonial or modernist period, [where] the idea of cultural identity became a weapon or strategy used by the colonizers both to buttress their own power and to undermine the will and self-confidence of the colonized"; a third stage in which "the colonized not only negated the identity of the colonizers, but also redirected their attention to their own perhaps abandoned, certainly altered identity. This is the phase of resistance, which leads to the end of colonialism. In Africa it is reflected in the *Négritude* movement"; and lastly a fourth stage whose artists are "Secure in their sense of identity, formed by whatever blends of African and European influences, they want to get beyond questions of identity and difference and to move into the future" (11). Such a development has interesting if too simple contrasts to the four sections and phases of this study.

8. This, ironically, shares certain commonalities of vision expressed with those who recently formed a view termed Occidentalism, critiquing the hatred of the West. See *Occidentalism*, whose first chapter summarizes and historicizes this view of modern equaling Western in postwar Japan. The book fails to indicate the ways in which the West, even not in relation to "the East," did make the imperial-modern-progress connection on its own—in Manifest Destiny, say, in the American West—and how the modernists continued this.

9. Stephen Vincent Benét. "American Names." *American Poetry. The Twentieth Century. Volume Two: E.E. Cummings to May Swenson*. New York: Library of America, 2000. 154–55. Originally gathered in *Poems and Ballads 1915–1930* (Garden City, NY: Doubleday, Doran, 1931).

10. T. Bowyer Campbell. *Black Sadie*. Boston: Houghton-Mifflin, 1928. Front inside flap. A very deco, if clumsy and stereotypical cover, by Jack Perkins. I must confess the text seems more of the same; the book starts: "Black Sadie's father was hanged several months before she was born. Lightfoot Mose died on the gallows for raping an old white woman. He descried her one evening in her cowshed milking her cow." Downhill from there.

11. Michael North notes the ways Eliot, in *Sweeney* and in other poems, uses the Negro image. See *The Dialect of Modernism*. Such a placelessness is different from the rootlessness found in the blues; where the blues provide a grim hope, a stoic yet funny resistance, Eliot provides us with a mask where death and despair meet, blackface meeting a death mask, a literal cenotaph that is our and his modern hero's fate.

12. Recently an advertisement for TV's reality show *Survivor Gambon* advertised "In Exotic Africa—Earth's Last Eden—Temptation is Everywhere." Only in the West would televised starvation be part of entertainment, and living in Africa be about mere "survival" that provides a path to riches.

13. With Douglas, his silhouettes form a kind of mask, a visual ritual often literally perched between Jungle and skyscraper, nature and modernity. Caroline Goeser describes Douglas's "in-betweenist" strategy, saying:

> Douglas developed a new American primitivism, which became his multifaceted strategy to complicate the ways in which Euro-Americans had codified such categories as civilization to exclude black America. By collapsing the Western polarity between the civilized primitivist and the "savage" primitive, he subversively held a role as both primitivist and primitive. In his graphic art, primitivism no longer constituted a longing for what was outside civilization or what had been lost. It connoted instead that black Americans could

contribute to modern American culture by reconnecting the primitive and civilized, the past and present, from a strategically intersititial position as a welcome "compound of the old and new."
Goeser, *Picturing the New Negro*, 25.

14. *American Heritage College Dictionary*, Third Edition. Houghton Mifflin, 1993. 736.

15. Dixon, 17–18.

16. Eileen Southern, 166.

17. Black thought contested such notions by seeing the States, chiefly southern, as Eden *after* the Fall, Greene notes. J. Lee Greene, *Blacks in Eden*, University Press of Virginia, 1995. The first chapter is particularly useful for the history of the Garden and Wilderness concepts. For a contrast and deepening with the black notion of wilderness, consult Melvin Dixon, above.

18. Jean-Paul Goude. *Jungle Fever.* New York: Xavier Moreau, 1982. 4–5.

19. Goude, 102.

20. Goude, 105. One thinks of Deleuze and Guattari writing on "becoming," but they could be talking about Goude's view of Jones:

> Of course, the child, the woman, the black have memories; but the Memory that collects those memories is still a virile majoritarian agency treating them as "childhood memories," as conjugal, or colonial memories. It is possible to operate by establishing a conjunction or collocation of contiguous points rather than a relation between distant points: you would then have phantasies rather than memories. For example, a woman can have a female point alongside a male point, and a man a male point alongside a female one. The constitution of these hybrids, however, does not take us very far in the direction of a true becoming (for example, bisexuality, as the psychoanalysts note, in no way precludes the prevalence of the masculine or the majority of the "phallus").

Deleuze and Guattari, 293. This conjugation continues in Goude's imagined photos of Jones's "brother," a twin identical except for a giant phallus.

21. "Wild Things" series was accessed on Goude's website: http://www.jeanpaulgoude.com/ on 4 August 2010. It apparently also ran in *Harper's Bazaar* in 2009.

22. *African Americana.* Swann Gallery auction catalog. February 2009.

23. Houston Baker, quoting Professor Robert Hill. *Modernism*, 95. Dixon too helps us see Harlem as part of "The Black Writer's Use of Memory": "By calling themselves to remember Africa and/or the racial past, black Americans are actually re-membering, as in repopulating broad continuities within the African diaspora. This movement is nonlinear, and it disrupts our notions of chronology. If history were mere chronology, some might see Africa as the beginning of race consciousness—and racial origin—rather than the culmination or fulfillment of ancestry." Dixon, "The Black Writer's Use of Memory." *A Melvin Dixon Critical Reader.* Jackson: University Press of Mississippi, 2006. 9.

24. Jean-Michel Basquiat. "Interview." Conducted by Demosthenes Davvetas. Originally appeared in *New Art International*, no. 3, October-November 1988. Reprinted in *Basquiat*, Edizioni Charta, 1999. Lxiii. I love the switch of pronouns from "we" to "you" here, indicative of community and memory's shifts and acceptances.

25. Watson, 66.

26. Cheryl Wall, *Women of the Harlem Renaissance*, 31.

27. *Ibid.*, 28.

28. Houston Baker, *Modernism*, 89.

29. With *Black Sadie* we do see modernity's fetishization of blackness—and that this fetishization is crucial part of modernism ("Her story is modern, elemental, compelling") and to history (despite the story being called "hers"). More importantly, notice how the fetish is used to establish white authenticity, and in turn, authority: the author was "brought up on a Southern plantation" so knows what he's talking about. The power of his authority comes from his proximity to blackness. The fetishization, then, of an elemental blackness has a purpose: to make the whiteness both clearer and the blackness more containable. Keep 'em down on the plantation where he was raised! But also, to empower the white writer himself, to make his "negro novel" part of the Harlem vogue, both in publicity and plausibility.

30. Langston Hughes. "Songs Called the Blues." *Write Me a Few of Your Lines: A Blues Reader*. Ed. Steven C. Tracy. Amherst: University of Massachusetts Press, 1999. 391–93.

31. Langston Hughes to Carl Van Vechten. 17 May 1925. *Remember Me to Harlem: The Letters of Langston Hughes and Carl Van Vechten*. Emily Bernard, ed. Vintage, 2001. 12.

32. Bessie Smith, composer and singer. "Backwater Blues." Transcribed by Angela Davis. *Blues Women and Black Feminism*. Reprinted in Kevin Young, ed., *Blues Poems*, 72–73.

33. See Hazel Carby, "It Jus Be's Dat Way Sometime: The Sexual Politics of Women's Blues." *The Jazz Cadence of American Culture*. New York: Columbia, 1998. 474. Originally published 1986.

34. Hurston, *Their Eyes Were Watching God*, 1. Originally 1937. We may also read this alongside Gilroy's *Black Atlantic*.

35. W. E. B. Du Bois. *The Souls of Black Folk*. 1903. *The Norton Anthology of African American Literature*. Henry Louis Gates and Nellie Y. McKay, eds. Norton, 1997. 615.

36. Albert Murray, *Stomping the Blues*, 254.

37. This is in contrast to the United States' first music—after Native American music—in the Negro-made spirituals. One recent critic, noting the relation of the minstrel show to *The Waste Land*, amazingly manages to discuss it while avoiding race altogether.

38. Ralph Ellison. "On Bird, Bird-Watching, and Jazz." *Living with Music*. Originally published in *Saturday Review*, 18 July 1962, and collected in *Shadow and Act*.

39. For Ellison, this connection continues in recognizing that "the poetry of Countee Cullen and Langston Hughes had a connection with the larger body of American poetry. . . . Given the racial stereotypes Negroes must learn to recognize the elements of their own cultural contribution as they appear in elements of the larger American culture." "Ralph Ellison's Territorial Vantage." *Living with Music: Ralph Ellison's Jazz Writings*. Robert G. O'Meally, ed. New York: Modern Library, 2001. 29. Interview originally conducted by Ron Welburn in 1976.

In another essay, "Hidden Name and Complex Fate," Ellison describes how "*Wuthering Heights* had caused me an agony of unexpressible emotion, and the same was true of *Jude the Obscure*, but *The Waste Land* seized my mind. I was intrigued by its power to move me while eluding my understanding. Somehow its rhythms were often closer to those of jazz than were those of the Negro poets, and even though I could not understand then, its range of allusion was as mixed and as varied as that of Louis Armstrong." *Collected Essays*, 203. It would seem fitting, given Eliot's birth there, that the "St. Louis Blues" was the first blues written down, by W. C. Handy. The song's sense of the sea's despair might mirror that of Eliot's "Prufrock" and has proved just as lasting.

40. Edward Kamau Brathwaite. *History of the Voice: The development of nation language in Anglophone Caribbean poetry.* New Beacon, 1984. 30.

41. Brathwaite, 30–31. This terrific point appears in a footnote to the sentence cited above.

42. "Only when the voice is tied to timbre does it reveal a tessitura that renders it heterogeneous to itself and gives it a power of continuous variation: it is then no longer accompanied, but truly 'machined,' it belongs to a musical machine that prolongs or superposes on a single plane parts that are spoken, sung, achieved by special effects, instrumental, or perhaps electronically generated." Deleuze and Guattari, 96.

43. This transcription, done by Adam Gussow, can be found with others of the songs, in my *Blues Poems*.

44. Richard Pryor has an ironic reading on the idea of "crazy," not only through his own album *That Nigger's Crazy*, but through a monologue as recorded in a painting by Glenn Ligon, *Beautiful Black Men* (1995):

> In my neighborhood there used to be some beautiful black men that would come through the neighborhood dressed in African shit you know, really nice shit, you know, and they'd be "Peace. Love. Black is beautiful. Remember the essence of life. We are people of the universe. Life is beautiful."
>
> My parents go "That nigger's crazy."

Glenn Ligon—Some Changes. Curated by Wayne Baerwaldt and Thelma Golden. Toronto, Ontario, Canada: The Power Plant Contemporary Art Gallery at Harbourfront Centre, 2005.

45. These can be seen in my own small collection, and the large collections at Indiana University's Lilly Library; some of the "blues" sheet music graced the printed hardcover case of my third book *Jelly Roll: A Blues* (2003). Such borrowed blues may be symbolized by "High Society Blues" (1930), lyric by Joseph McCarthy and music by James F. Hanley, that I have the sheet music for—it apparently was also a "William Fox Musical Movietone." The song's chorus seems unintentionally telling of the larger "society" and its attitude toward the cover:

> I guess we've got what they can't use
>
> We've sort o' got those high society blues.

46. Quoted in Toni Morrison, *Playing in the Dark.* A contemporary novel *Strange Brother* by Blair Niles (New York: Horace Liveright, 1931) starts with a description of a singer doing "Creole Love Call"—its title rendered without quotes, as if it less a song than a state of being. This book, which explores a white male (which the flap copy calls "an intermediate man") attracted to Harlem and the black men there, is an important and interesting novel worthy of further study. Thanks to Schwarz's *Gay Voices of the Harlem Renaissance* for calling attention to the novel.

47. Blair Niles. *Strange Brother.* New York: Horace Liveright, 1931. 9–10.

GANGSTA RAP'S HEROIC SUBSTRATA: A SURVEY OF THE EVIDENCE

JOHN PAUL HAMPSTEAD

This essay neither attacks gangsta rap for its sins nor celebrates its politics of resistance, but rather places some of its most visible features in a new context—alongside ancient and medieval heroic poetry, chiefly Homer, Virgil, and Anglo-Saxon material. Hampstead organizes his argument around five threads that run through both gangsta rap and heroic poetry—feasting, raiding, treasure, misogyny, and fatalism—in order to comprehend gangsta rap's excesses as part of a larger sociocultural pattern with a long history. Thus, John Paul Hampstead's essay illustrates gangsta rap's significant continuities with the traditional canon of Western literature.

angsta rap emerged from hip-hop as a self-consciously controversial, provocative subgenre in southern California in the late 1980s with the work of Ice-T and N.W.A, before finding a foothold in New York City with hard-hitting rappers Run-DMC and Kool G Rap. While gangsta rap's aggressive, percussive delivery and focus on social problems had been inspired by "conscious" acts like Public Enemy and Rakim, it was the noirish intrigue of the inner-city criminal underworld gangsta rap depicted that guaranteed both commercial success and moral panic.[1] From its very beginning, gangsta rap was publicly criticized for its materialism, violence, and misogyny by journalists (the editorial page of the *Wall Street Journal*, for example) and politicians (notably Dan Quayle and Tipper Gore). Later, as academic hip-hop studies matured, cultural critics interested in identity politics produced a spate of books analyzing gangsta rap's subversive lyrics, while at the same time interrogating its ideological assumptions.[2]

My project in this essay is neither to attack gangsta rap for its sins nor to celebrate its politics of resistance, but rather to place some of its most visible features in a new context, alongside ancient and medieval heroic poetry, chiefly

Homer (eighth century BC), Virgil (first century BC), and Anglo-Saxon material (ninth and tenth centuries AD). My argument is organized around five threads that run through both gangsta rap and heroic poetry—feasting, raiding, treasure, misogyny, and fatalism—in order to comprehend gangsta rap's excesses as part of a larger sociocultural pattern with a long history and wide dispersal. In doing so, I hope to illustrate gangsta rap's significant continuities with the traditional canon of Western literature. For me, these parallel structures and behaviors simultaneously ennoble gangsta rap and cast the "heroic" poetry of ages past in a more skeptical, less romantic light.[3]

While contemporary sociologists recognize gang culture as a global phenomenon, a never-ending attempt by groups of armed young men to assert authority over uncontrolled slums created by immigration, poverty, and weakened states,[4] gangsta rap is specifically a product of America's inner cities, which were gutted by deindustrialization in the 1970s and then poisoned by the influx of crack cocaine in the 1980s and 1990s. Gangs came to dominate the hollowed-out urban cores, often becoming the principal economic, political, and social organizations of these neglected spaces. Early gangsta rap professed to realistically document that environment, and authenticity and veracity remain central values in gangsta rap, as in hip-hop generally. After Jay-Z was criticized for celebrating crime and materialism, he spat back: "See I'm influenced by the ghetto you ruined."[5]

All this is not to say that we can take rappers' accounts at face value. First and foremost, they are postmodern recording artists, inflected by celebrity culture and entrepreneurialism, and they borrow freely from Hollywood and Chinese movies, comic books, and pop culture in general. The relationship between the rapper's persona and an underlying reality is complex: Lil Wayne has been warped by child stardom as much as Britney Spears (and sold more records than her in 2008), but he went to prison in 2010 for drug and gun charges. Rick Ross, on the other hand, claims to be a helicopter-piloting, speedboat-riding *Miami Vice*–style kingpin, but is actually a former security guard. Not every rapper I cite participates in all five of the behaviors that I say characterize gangsta rap's heroic substrata, either: Kanye West rarely if ever threatens violence, but certainly exemplifies the other categories; Eminem's destructiveness is rooted in psychological turmoil rather than male-to-male competition (he might be properly labeled a Byronic hero, a brooding, troubled genius alienated from his society). Gangsta rap, then, is certainly an autonomous artistic medium rather than a mimetic reproduction of a culture, just as, perhaps, heroic poetry idealizes what must have been a more chaotic, meaningless existence.

As in heroic poetry and all artistic traditions, the literary history of gangsta rap can be characterized by cycles of convention and innovation. Some of the more clumsily constructed verses in gangsta rap are no more than collages of formulaic phrases and clichés, like second-rate Petrarchan sonnets, while the best rappers have instantly recognizable deliveries, vocabularies, and ways of thinking. Students of heroic poetry may especially relish gangsta rap's bridging of orality and literacy. Many verses, which are conventionally sixteen measures or "bars," are composed orally and rely on the types of metrical formula long familiar to Homeric scholars; however, the fact that these songs are permanently recorded allows for the construction of a canon of artists and themes, as well as specific verbal allusions. The recording process abstracts the rapper from his verse just as the act of writing separates a literate poet from his text, but there remains in gangsta rap, like heroic poetry, a myth of divine origins. Plato said that poetry came from something like a "divine frenzy"; Greek, Roman, and English epic poets invoked muses, pagan and Christian; in Bede, Cædmon's miraculous oral poems arrived to him fully formed from a divine source; and much later, Romantic poets had their own mythologies of inspiration and genius.

So, too, when gangsta rap speaks of compositional technique, it mythologizes its own origin, blurring the line between spontaneous oral "freestyling" and meticulously revised literate writing. The Notorious B.I.G., Jay-Z, and Lil Wayne insist that they do not write out any of their elaborately patterned verses (though their recording processes are very involved); Nas and The Game, on the other hand, are anxious about writing itself and the weight of the received canon it has created.[6] The myth of spontaneous, inspired composition has now become something of an ossified convention, merely an opportunity for another one-liner, instead of a sincere statement about artistic production. Wayne, an avid ESPN watcher, used the convention of spontaneity as an occasion to compare himself to a professional football quarterback—"Peyton Manning flow; I just go, no huddle"[7]—and one of his more obscure protégés, Short Dawg, smirked, "My rhymes are ambidextrous, so I don't have to right [write]."[8]

The survey of feasting, raiding, treasure, misogyny, and fatalism in gangsta rap that follows is colored by my own taste and the limitations of my expertise; readers steeped in the hip-hop canon might expect more citations from the 1980s, but the gangsta rap aesthetic crystallized in the last years of that decade. I have cast my net widely, citing dozens of albums to give the reader a sense of gangsta rap's scope, and though I have tried to mention most of the canonical gangsta rappers, the emphasis is on contemporary artists still actively producing work. For the most part, I have focused on highly visible (and thus highly influential) hit-making artists, rather than underground rappers, but have included bootleg releases like mix tapes, widely available on the Internet, in addition to major label albums and radio singles.

Feasting

In heroic societies, ritualized communal feeding strengthens social bonds between men by rewarding the retainers' loyalty and demonstrating the lord's beneficence, and heroic poetry abounds with examples of such feasting. The social importance of feasting to antique Greek society, for example, is attested by the presence of kraters, tripods, and other specialized equipment in the archaeological record. In the Homeric poems, apart from battle, formulaic feasting is the single most frequent activity, sometimes occurring more than once a day; Homeric feasting is multipurpose and used for mourning and reconciliation as well as celebration (not to mention those occasions when the bulk of the meat is sacrificed to the gods). While the Homeric poems present feasting episodes at an unrealistic frequency, they also exaggerate the scale of feasts: The gods' favorite sacrifice is a hecatomb, the slaughter and consumption of one hundred bulls, an event that must have been exceedingly rare in reality, but is almost routine in Homer.[9] Just like the aristocratic warriors of Homeric epic, gangsta rappers even pour out libations for the dead: "For the brothers who ain't here, pour a little on the floor, son."[10]

Gangsta rappers also feast frequently and splendidly, for many of the same reasons. Before rappers' feasts can attract underlings and women, though, they have to upgrade their eating habits. The Notorious B.I.G., whose spectacular girth evidenced his prodigious ability to feed himself, wanted "a T-Bone steak, cheese eggs, and Welch's Grape" in his 1994 ode to the high life, "Big Poppa,"[11] but by 1999, Texas-based rapper-producer Pimp C would boast, "I eat so many shrimp, I got iodine poisonin'."[12] Rick Ross, a flamboyant, even buffoonish coke-rapper from Miami, apparently associated high-status feeding with healthy eating, rhyming "Caesar's salad" with "Caesar's Palace,"[13] while the Wu-Tang Clan's Inspectah Deck used fancy food to evoke a cinematic, Mafioso atmosphere: "I pop off like a mobster boss—Angel Hair with the lobster sauce."[14]

Gangsta rap's most familiar feasting-as-conspicuous-consumption trope is, of course, its unquenchable thirst for top-shelf liquors and champagnes, notably Hennessey, Remy Martin, Dom Perignon, and Cristal. In their famous duet "Brooklyn's Finest" on Jay-Z's debut album, The Notorious B.I.G. proclaimed "Cristal forever" right after Jay-Z laid out his own discriminating tastes: "Time to separate the pros from the cons / The platinum from the bronze . . . / A Cham. Dom. sipper from a Rosé nigger."[15] Nas, another formally ambitious New York City rapper, imbibed while preparing to compose his verses: "I sip the Dom P., watchin' *Gandhi* till I'm charged, then / Writin' in my book of rhymes; all the words pass the margins."[16] Rappers deploy these luxury brand names to accumulate social capital and broadcast their wealth to potential allies and mates.

In recent years, numerous rappers have so exploited the fortuitous bottles/models rhyme—just in case their audiences missed the point—that the phrase is now completely formulaic. Kanye West put it most succinctly on a guest verse for a Jadakiss track—"pop bottles, fuck models"[17]—but offered a variation on his theme three years later when he welcomed his audience to the "Good Life": "Where we like the girls who ain't on TV / Cuz they got more ass than the models / The good life, so keep it comin' with the bottles . . ."[18] In the chorus of his single

"Pop Bottles," Birdman trotted out a predictable double entendre to create the multisyllabic rhyme "Chopper straight shots and then pop bottles / Flirt with the hood rats then pop models,"[19] and by the time a *Relapse*-ing Eminem brayed, "So crack a bottle, let your body waddle / Don't act like a snobby model—you just hit the lotto!" in 2009, the bottles/models rhyme was a firmly established cliché.[20]

Feasting in gangsta rap, as in traditional heroic poetry, cannot simply be reduced to flaunting wealth; it also represents a communal activity crucial to the maintenance of social bonds threatened by violence and privation. Rappers need time to relax and relieve the stress caused by their hectic outlaw lifestyles, just as Odysseus sat down with Achilles to sip wine diluted with water and warriors in Anglo-Saxon poetry retired to their mead-halls to feast and swear vows.[21] The Notorious B.I.G.'s rags-to-riches chronicle "Juicy" emphasized the alpha male's generosity toward his underlings while celebrating the plenitude that accompanies fame: "And I'm far from cheap, I smoke skunk with my peeps all day / Spread love, it's the Brooklyn way." Later in the track, Biggie again points out how his wealth flows downward and outward to his dependents, pleased that ". . . my whole crew is loungin' / Celebratin' every day, no more public housin'."[22]

If the communal, ritualized consumption of alcoholic libations solidified alliances in traditional heroic poetry, the most important social intoxicant in gangsta rap is cannabis: While brief references to cannabis abound in gangsta rap, anthems wholly concerned with smoking marijuana in rolled cigars ("blunts") constitute one of gangsta rap's most popular and enduring genres. Dr. Dre named his seminal G-funk album *The Chronic* (1992) after a potent variety of the plant; gangsta rap collectives Three 6 Mafia and Bone Thugs-n-Harmony as well as solo artists Snoop Dogg, Redman, and Lil Wayne have devoted significant portions of their careers to rhapsodizing cannabis. Although cannabis is ubiquitous and generic in gangsta rap, individual artists approach weed from a diversity of aesthetic and ideological perspectives. The consummate entertainment-industry professional Dr. Dre refers to his musical output as an intoxicating "product"; Three 6 Mafia's dark, paranoiac tracks about smoking cannabis are complemented by their verses' eerie, hypnotic cadences; Snoop Dogg generally presents himself as an affable, sometimes goofy hedonist content with low-riders and blunts; Nas's introspective "street prophet" persona lends a spiritual quality to smoking cannabis—he raps about being "blessed by the herb's essence," and his weed anthem "Smokin'" begins with a prayer in Arabic.[23]

Raiding

In many human societies across time and space, young men have sought wealth and fame through battlefield prowess. Some of the more violent of these cultures include ancient patrician Rome, the Norsemen of the ninth and tenth centuries, and the isolated Yanomamo in the present-day Amazon basin, one-third of whose males die in war. Typically, warriors organize themselves under a charismatic leader and raid nearby groups for livestock, slaves, women, and reputation.[24] In ancient Greek heroic poetry, as in the Indo-European tradition generally, the cattle-raid took on particular importance. The gnarled old warrior Nestor, for instance, after complaining that Achilles has done nothing to aid the wounded Greeks, boasts of a cattle raid he conducted in his youth against the Eleians in *Iliad* 11:

> I was driving cattle in reprisal, and he, as he was defending his oxen, was struck among the foremost by a spear thrown from my hand and fell, and his people who live in the wild fled in terror about him. And we got and drove off together much spoil from this pastureland: fifty herds of oxen, as many sheepflocks, as many droves of pigs, and again as many wide-ranging goatflocks, and a hundred and fifty brown horses, mares all of them and with many foals following underneath.[25]

The comparative religions scholar Bruce Lincoln has identified what he calls a "cattle cycle" in which sacred cattle are given by the gods, stolen by enemies, reclaimed by warriors, and given back to the gods in sacrificial rituals conducted by priests. This common premodern religious structure emerged in many ecosystems where pastoralists survived by creating and protecting flocks of livestock.[26]

Heroic poetry often pairs the rape or abduction of women with livestock raids; recall that the Trojan War results from a famous incident of bride-theft, the abduction of Helen, and that Achilles refuses to fight because Agamemnon dishonored him by taking his war-bride for himself. Jonathan Gottschall has gone so far as to identify rape, harem-building, and reproductive competition between males as the central motive for ancient Greek violence.[27] The ecology of post-industrial inner-city America has brought other valuable commodities into play, however, namely cash, drugs, and drug-market territory, which are the objects of the local raids that gangsta rappers describe. As Young Buck puts it, "You gon' make me crawl through your backyard and cut off your light switch / Kick in your back door and take all that white shit."[28]

Before delving deeply into the poetry of gangsta rap raiding, though, I want to point out an intriguing, if apparently superficial similarity between traditional heroic poetry and gangsta rap: the careful attention given to the description of weapons. In Homeric poetry, arming scenes where warriors prepare for battle are formulaic, but unique arms such as Ajax's shield are afforded special treatment (*Iliad* 7.219–25). In the Old English epic *Beowulf*, a young Heathobard's "polysemous" sword functions alternately as "treasure, heirloom, trophy, taunt, and weapon,"[29] and the heroic-tragic "Battle of Maldon," an account of a Viking raid in 991, provides multiple terms for spear: "point," "ash," "ash-spear," "hand-dart," and "grim one." Extended descriptions of particular weapons emphasize their special significance, sometimes stemming from their divine origin (as in the ekphrasis of Aeneas's shield in *Aeneid* 8); euphemisms and synonyms proliferate in oral poetry for the purposes of metrical scansion and in literate poetry to avoid tedious repetition.

Firearms in gangsta rap occupy pride of place; typically the characters in gangsta rap narratives carry pistols (Glocks, Smith and Wessons, Colts) for personal protection and automatic weapons (TEC-9s, AK-47s, MAC-10s) for more vigorous clashes like drive-by shootings. The nomenclature for weapons in gangsta rap is so expansive that an exhaustive catalogue is impossible here; instead, I will limit myself to some very common epithets and general features of firearms slang. A generic handgun can be a "gat," a "tool," or a "burner," and specific types have their own terms: a nine-millimeter pistol is a "nine," "nina," or "nine milli"; The Notorious B.I.G. memorably referred to a .45 caliber pistol as a "quatro-cin-co."[30] Lil Wayne, for example, frequently plays on "nina" for "nine millimeter" to personify his handgun as a female companion; "I got a bitch named Nina, and Nina's so slutty / Cuz she'll do him and every one of his buddies," he jokes on the aptly titled freestyle "Nina."[31] While taunting rappers who pose as gangsters on his breakthrough hit "Wanksta," 50 Cent, an indisputable master of gun rap, tends toward Hollywood-inspired hyperbole, asking "Niggas sayin' they gon' merc [murder] 50—how? / We ridin' 'round with guns the size of Lil Bow Wow" (a teenaged rapper). He goes on to catalogue his own military-grade firepower: "What you know about AKs and AR-15s? / Equipped with night vision, shell catchers, and infrared beams?"[32]

Apart from the one-liners and puns that account for much of gangsta rap's gun-talk, drive-by and robbery narratives shed light on the risk and rewards of raiding. "Shakey Dog," from Ghostface Killah's baroque crime epic *Fishscale*, is a hitman's stream-of-consciousness narrative that moves from jittery, crack-smoking preparation to paranoid, panicked aftermath: "Made my usual gun check, safety off, 'Come on Frank / The moment is here, take your fuckin' hood off and tell the driver to stay put!'"[33] The Notorious B.I.G. plays the ventriloquist when he raps the parts of both perpetrators during a two-man armed robbery job in "Gimme the Loot," his classic entry in the "stick-up kid" subgenre.[34] The title track of Project Pat's 1999 album *Ghetty Green* tells his audience the lengths he will go to in the pursuit of "dat cheese, dat fetty, dat loot"; when a man breaks an agreement by bringing a companion with him to deliver cash for drugs, Pat responds by murdering them both and fleeing with the money.[35] In 1994, Nas imagined what it would be like to be the victim of an ambush; Nas and his associates are surprised by a rival crew, but he picks up a MAC-10 hidden in the grass and begins firing, turning the tide of the skirmish until his weapon jams: "Tried to cock it, it wouldn't shoot now I'm in danger / Finally pulled it back and saw three bullets caught up in the chamber."[36] 2Pac's choleric persona and staccato cadences enhance his threats in a drive-by battle-cry penned at the height of Los

Angeles's gang wars: "When it's time to ride, I'm the first off this side, give me the nine!"[37]

Treasure

The word *treasure* brings to mind a pile of gold coins waiting for a hero at the end of a quest, as in Beowulf's fatal encounter with the dragon, but this is misleading. Rather than liquid cash, treasure should be understood to include the whole range of goods that elites use to signify social status, from jewelry to shining vehicles and fine clothing. These luxury items are circulated horizontally among elites in gift exchanges and vertically when given as rewards to underlings; their accumulation in the archaeological record as grave goods on the Roman imperial frontiers, for instance, signals the increasing centralization of barbarian political organization.[38] The exiled narrator of the Old English elegy "The Wanderer" uses a euphemism for his lord that speaks to this socioeconomic function when he asks, "Where has gone the giver of treasure [maPPumgyfa]?"

Gangsta rap's fascination with treasure can perhaps best be represented by the wide dissemination of the term "bling" for ostentatious jewelry since its coining in 1999. While it is true that gangsta rap in the late 1990s especially emphasized diamonds and gold, treasure had always been crucial in delineating the hierarchies of America's inner-city underworld. As early as 1988, Ice Cube noticed that "a little bit of gold and a pager" was enough to arouse the suspicion of the Compton police.[39] In the "bling" era, gangsta rappers adorned their watches, bracelets, necklaces, belt buckles, cups, and teeth with precious stones and metals, and still felt they needed to point it out in song: "All I wanna do is ride around shining while I can afford it / Plenty ice on my neck so I don't get nauseous."[40] A specialized sector of the jewelry industry rose to meet gangsta rap's demand for diamonds, and name-checking Jacob Arabo, a high-end New York City jeweler, became shorthand for participation in rap's diamond-encrusted lifestyle. Young Jeezy spent "eighty grand just to see the Jacob go tick tock";[41] after West Coast rapper The Game was recruited by 50 Cent's collective G-Unit, based in New York, he crowed, "Now I'm goin' back to Cali with my Jacob on";[42] Fabolous bragged, "I see things clear through these Marc Jacobs shades / Like the clarity in these jewels that Jacob made."[43] As of January 2010, Jacob Arabo's Wikipedia entry lists roughly sixty rap songs that mention his name.

The positions and attitudes projected by a rapper's fine clothing are more subtle than diamonds because the potential styles are more varied. A New York City subculture emerged in the late 1980s devoted to wearing—only—Ralph Lauren Polo clothing or "gear"; these devotees are known as "Lo Heads." The Wu-Tang Clan's apparel choices, along with their technical, virtuosic rapping and old-fashioned drum machines, are meant to signify a fidelity to the aesthetics of early 1990s New York City hip-hop culture, especially that of Staten Island's housing projects. A typical Wu-Tang outfit would include a Ralph Lauren Polo goosedown jacket, Timberland boots, and baggy Tommy Hilfiger jeans, while a Californian rapper might wear a plaid short-sleeve button-down shirt, an NFL Raiders hat, baggy khakis, and Chuck Taylor sneakers. Jay-Z's Mafioso aspirations are apparent on the cover of his first album, *Reasonable Doubt*, which depicts him in a fedora, scarf, and pinky ring. More recently, gangsta rappers have embraced European haute couture. Pusha T buys French shoes for his lady friends: "Now let's go shoppin', let's go chill / Let's go buy them new Louis Vuitton heels";[44] likewise Kanye West, probably the most fashion-conscious rapper, is no longer impressed by sneakers: "Reebok—baby, you need to try some new things / Have you ever had shoes without shoe strings? / 'What's that 'Ye?' Baby these heels . . .";[45] an Atlanta rapper even named himself Gucci Mane.

Transportation is similar to clothing: a diverse field of aesthetics serves various ends. A rapper may want to use a Lincoln Navigator with tinted windows to transport his associates, drugs, and weapons, but he would prefer a sleeker Porsche to entertain women; spacious older Cadillacs are perfect for aimless cruising ("Canary yellow '79 Seville is on display"),[46] and the classic Californian gangland cars are lowered vintage Chevrolets, especially Impalas. Customized options like wood-grain steering wheels, large hubcaps, vertically opening Lamborghini-style doors ("when the doors open up, they open up!"),[47] specialized paint jobs, heavy-duty speaker systems, and even televisions transform mass-produced vehicles into unique, fetishized, complex signifiers of status and taste. Lil Wayne, a convertible aficionado—"Sittin' in the coupe, lookin' like a racer / Top peeled back like the skin of a potato"[48]—titled a recent mix tape *No Ceilings*.

Misogyny

Women do not usually appear as active protagonists in traditional heroic poetry, though they drive much of the plots' action and determine the relations between men. Ancient Greek society was perhaps even more repressive than what we think of as contemporary gangsta culture. Women were confined to specific sections of the house, not permitted to leave while unattended, and were traded back and forth between powerful men as gifts to seal alliances. In a striking simile from Book 8 of the *Odyssey*, Odysseus, having been moved to tears by Demodocus's account of the fall of Troy, is compared to a woman about to be dragged away into captivity after her husband has fallen in battle:

> And as a woman wails and throws herself upon her dear husband, who has fallen in front of his city and his people, seeking to ward off from his city and his children the pitiless day; and as she beholds him dying and gasping for breath, she clings to him and shrieks aloud, while the foe behind her beat her back and shoulders with their spears, and lead away to captivity to bear toil and woe . . .[4]

Roman women had more rights and freedoms than Greek women, but remember that the rape of the Sabine women is one of Rome's founding myths, and that in Virgil's *Aeneid*, Dido of Carthage commits suicide when Aeneas abandons her. Speaking in general terms, in premodern heroic poetry, men fight men over women, among other things, with little room for autonomous female speech and action.

In much of gangsta rap, women are also mute status objects used for pleasure and for mediating the relations between men. Gangsta rappers are promiscuous harem-builders who have "baby mamas" rather than wives; they seduce each other's women in order to demonstrate their dominance over a man rather than their love of a woman. During the feud between Jay-Z and Nas that consumed the rap scene in New York in the early 2000s, the women in the rappers' lives became sites of conflict. Nas released *Stillmatic* (2001), an album with several "diss tracks" impugning Jay-Z's character and talent, the most famous of which was "Ether," which remains a touchstone for the genre. But "Got Yourself a Gun" contained some not-so-subtle insults aimed at Jay-Z; a few days after the album's release, Jay-Z put out a freestyle over the instrumentation from "Got Yourself a Gun" and claimed to have slept with the mother of Nas's daughter Destiny, Carmen Bryan, in Nas's cars, and added that Allen Iverson did the same thing.[50] The moral outrage over gangsta rap's misogyny is well documented and repeating it here is unnecessary. A number of female rappers have challenged gangsta rap's self-conception as a male enclave, including Eve, Lil' Kim, Queen Latifah, Gangsta Boo, and, more recently, Nicki Minaj. Of these, academics have given Lil' Kim's provocative, sexually aggressive lyrics the most attention, which sometimes seem to articulate an empowered feminist politics and at other times readily participate in what can be little more than pornography.[51] Instead of entering the debate over the possibility of a feminist challenge to gangsta rap from within, I will merely review general patterns in gangsta rap's misogyny and identify similarities in premodern heroic poetry.

Gangsta rap's archetypal "ho" (whore) is a self-possessed, crafty woman well-adapted to life in a brutal patriarchy. She uses her cunning and physical charms to convince rappers to divert their resources to her, but she maintains no loyalties, double-crossing her patrons when it seems advantageous. As a result, the ho is the object of much suspicion and mistrust, and she suffers violence when she refuses to cooperate and has no protectors left. Three 6 Mafia's disturbing hookup dirge "Late Nite Tip" depicts Lord Infamous seducing a woman with alcohol, marijuana, and pornography, gradually breaking down her inhibitions so that he can have his way with her. Later in the song, Gangsta Boo grimly narrates the ho's progress: "Feelin' kind of whorish, I call and all I want is sex / Slip on Victoria's Secret, hit the liquor store before it close / Call Chris so I can get somethin' white to go up in my nose."[52] When Method Man thinks of hoes, "Ice Cream" comes to mind, not human beings: "Watch these rap niggas get all up in your guts / French-vanilla, butter pecan, chocolate deluxe."[53] On a lighter note, OutKast, a critically acclaimed duo from Atlanta not usually associated with gangsta culture, seem to revel in the ho's artifices, cackling, "From the weave to the fake eyes / To the fake nails down to the toes / Ha ha ha ha! We love these hoes!"[54]

Violence against hoes occurs when paranoid, easily offended rappers lose control of their anger and when hoes overestimate their own positions and make inappropriate demands: "Talkin' smart to a pimp, you done broke the first rule," Pimp C sneered at a young woman unfortunate enough to find herself under his wing.[55] Willie D taunted other rappers who refused to beat and kill women willing to betray them: "Are you the type who won't put a ho in front of a trigger?"[56] Big L bragged about his merciless power over the women in his life: "Yeah, cuz I got all of 'em sprung, Jack / My girls are like boomerangs / No matter how far I throw 'em, they come back!"[57] Gangsta rap's sexual language, too, is laced with violent metaphors and imagery; we frequently hear of "breaking," "pounding," and "beating" in reference to sex, and on his hookup track "I'm Not a Player," Big Punisher rhymes, "I bang a stranger in my torture chamber," then proceeds to deconstruct his partner into a mass of anatomical parts, recalling de Sade and the Earl of Rochester.[58] Kool Keith's album *Sex Style* is a scurrilous sendup of rap's sexual perversity: "You want freestyle? That's right, the style is free / Niggas suck my dick and they girls drink my pee."[59]

Fatalism

When roving war-bands and enemy ships lurk over every horizon, fatalism toward life and death takes hold. Personal agency and individual autonomy are subject to the whims of the gods and the mysteries of fate; the best a man can do is meet his destiny with dignity. Achilles, for instance, knows that he must choose between an undistinguished long life, or death at a young age and everlasting fame. That Oedipus will murder his father and marry his mother is unavoidable, regardless of human attempts to intervene.[60] Anglo-Saxon heroic poetry's *wyrd* (fate) seems more mysterious and less directive than the machinations of the Greek pantheon, which can be divined by oracles, but human action is again limited and relatively ineffectual. The Old English elegy "The Wanderer" puts it this way: *"Wyrd bi∂ ful aræd"* (Fate is wholly inexorable). Indeed, Anglo-Saxonist Stanley Greenfield, following Coleridge, thought that fate's supremacy was the defining feature of epic poetry.[61]

Centuries of oppression under slavery and Jim Crow have produced in African American culture two competing but clearly related philosophical strands: The world-weary fatalism in work songs, blues, and jazz that has seen too much pain to put stock in human endeavor; and, on the other hand, the striving, utopian Messianism of African American Christianity, the rhetoric of the civil rights movement, the Nation of Islam, and other assertions of black power. The influence of the former is obvious in gangsta rap's continuation of the legacy of African American music, its bittersweet balance of sensuality and despair. In closing, we will turn to examples of gangsta rap's spiritual and political fatalisms.

Chillingly casual references to physical death scattered throughout gangsta rap's corpus are the first sign of its fatalism: "Niggas get capped and wrapped in plastic / And zipped up in bags; when it happens, that's it," warns Dr. Dre.[62] After Be-Real startles a would-be burglar and the intruder faints, the rapper still shoots him: "Didn't have to blast him, but I did anyway / Ha ha ha . . . that young punk had to pay."[63] Young Buck suggests that anyone who participates in gangsta culture's economy of competition and patronage should be prepared to face a violent death: "Don't nobody wanna die, but e'erbody wanna ball / Somebody gotta go when them killers call."[64]

This chaotic, murderous environment prompts more reflective rappers to lament the harsh, cold world in which they live and the powerlessness of human existence. The Wu-Tang Clan's oft-quoted anthem "C.R.E.A.M.," i.e., "Cash Rules Everything Around Me," offers two perspectives on living inside "the game": Raekwon's verse describes his childhood in a broken home and petty larceny, impoverished and miserable, before celebrating his newfound narco-riches, but Inspectah Deck recognizes the ultimate futility of the paper chase: "But as the world turns, I learned life is hell / Livin' in the world [is] no different from a cell."[65] UGK's "How Long Can It Last" exemplifies a staple of Southern rap, the mournful, pseudo-religious "hood elegy": Pimp C wails, "Tonight if I get down on my knees and ask the Lord to forgive me please / You think he gon' hear me? Cuz tomorrow I'm still gon' be slangin' keeeeys [kilograms]," and Bun B gives a deterministic rationalization for gangsta culture: "They wish their daddy was home, mama wasn't on drugs / And they didn't have to grow up to be dealers and thugs."[66]

One perennial aspect of gangsta rap's fatalism is a profound cynicism toward government and politics, present at least since N.W.A's "Fuck tha Police" (1988)[67] and Public Enemy's "911 is a Joke" (1990).[68] Other entries in this genre include Lil Wayne's rant against the Bush Administration in the wake of Hurricane Katrina "Georgia . . . Bush,"[69] and even the Beastie Boys' "Fight for Your Right (To Party)," though not a gangsta rap track, accuses the police of hypocrisy.[70] Kanye West's televised, unscripted outburst—"George Bush doesn't care about black people"—belongs to this cynicism, as do rumors that the CIA created the HIV virus, the anti-Semitic remarks of N.W.A's Professor Griff, etc.

I want to close this survey of fatalistic rappers by remarking on a recent trend in gangsta rap: Expressing fatalism by consciously committing oneself to a ceaseless, pitiless work ethic, a quest for money, termed "the grind." Lil Wayne's verses on "Leather So Soft" epitomize, for me, the resignation with which heroes

12. Jay-Z feat. UGK. "Big Pimpin'." *Vol. 3 . . . Life and Times of S. Carter.* Roc-A-Fella, 2000.

13. Rick Ross feat. R. Kelly. "Speedin'." *Trilla.* Def Jam, 2008.

14. Raekwon feat. Inspectah Deck, Ghostface Killah, Method Man, GZA. "House of Flying Daggers." *Only Built 4 Cuban Linx . . . Pt. II.* EMI, 2009.

15. Jay-Z feat. The Notorious B.I.G. "Brooklyn's Finest." *Reasonable Doubt.* Roc-A-Fella, 1996.

16. Nas. "The World is Yours." *Illmatic.* Columbia, 1994.

17. Jadakiss feat. Kanye West. "Gettin' It In." *Kiss of Death.* Interscope, 2004.

18. Kanye West feat. T-Pain. "Good Life." *Graduation.* Roc-A-Fella, 2007.

19. Birdman feat. Lil Wayne. "Pop Bottles." *5 * Stunna.* Cash Money, 2007.

20. Eminem feat. Dr. Dre, 50 Cent. "Crack a Bottle." *Relapse.* Interscope, 2009.

21. As Brooklyn rapper AZ put it, "Life's a bitch and then you die—that's why we get high" (Nas feat. AZ. "Life's a Bitch." *Illmatic.* Columbia, 1994).

22. The Notorious B.I.G. "Juicy." *Ready to Die.* Bad Boy, 1994.

23. Nas. "Smokin'." *Stillmatic.* Columbia, 2001.

24. The Roman historian Tacitus made a perceptive observation of the raiding mentality in his first-century A.D. ethnographic treatise *Germania* that is worth quoting in full: "You cannot keep up a great retinue except by war and violence, for it is from their leader's bounty that they demand that glorious warhorse, and that murderous and masterful spear: banquetings and a certain rude but lavish outfit are equivalent to salary" (14).

25. Lattimore, Richmond. *Iliad of Homer.* Chicago: University of Chicago Press, 1951. 252.

26. *Priests, Warriors, and Cattle: A Study in the Ecology of Religions.* Berkeley: University of California Press, 1981.

27. *The Rape of Troy: Evolution, Violence, and the World of Homer.* New York: Cambridge University Press, 2008.

28. Young Buck feat. 50 Cent. "I'm a Soldier." *Straight Outta Cashville.* Interscope, 2004.

29. Clark, George. "Beowulf's Armor." *English Literary History* 32.4 (December 1965), pp. 409–41.

30. See *supra* note 14.

31. Lil Wayne. "Nina." *Da Drought Is Over Pt. 6.* [Bootleg], c. 2008.

32. 50 Cent. "Wanksta." *Music from and Inspired by the Motion Picture 8 Mile.* Interscope, 2002.

33. Ghostface Killah. "Shakey Dog." *Fishscale.* Def Jam, 2006.

34. The Notorious B.I.G. "Gimme the Loot." *Ready to Die.* Bad Boy, 1994.

35. Project Pat. "Ghetty Green." *Ghetty Green.* Hypnotize Minds, 1999.

36. Nas. "N.Y. State of Mind." *Illmatic.* Columbia, 1994.

2Pac. "Ambitionz Az a Ridah." *All Eyez On Me.* Interscope, 1996.

Cunliffe, Barry. *Greeks, Romans & Barbarians: Spheres of Interaction.* New York: Methuen, 1988.

N.W.A. "Fuck tha Police." *Straight Outta Compton.* EMI, 1988.

Clipse. "Ride Around Shining." *Hell Hath No Fury.* Jive, 2006.

Young Jeezy. "Trap Star." *Let's Get It: Thug Motivation 101.* Def Jam, 2005.

The Game feat. 50 Cent. "Hate It or Love It." *The Documentary.* Interscope, 2005.

Fabolous feat. Lloyd. "Real Playa Like." *From Nothin' to Somethin'.* Def Jam, 2007.

Clipse. "Dirty Money." *Hell Hath No Fury.* Jive, 2006.

must face their fate. "My leather so soft . . . bitch I go so hard," Wayne
the song's hook, setting up a dichotomy between the luxury ("softne;
joys and his unwavering commitment to an empty, lonely lifestyle ("I
Of course the terms are mutually interdependent: Lil Wayne's hardn(
es his soft luxury and keeps him "sharp" amidst all the material comf
can buy; the sensual, but fleetingly material pleasures of soft leath
his hardness. Wayne's second verse recalls his birth in a charity hos;
Orleans in 1982, before finally closing with a fatalistic vision of s
forces: "They dropped us in the game and everybody's tryna ball / A
hand'll touch ya, the large hand'll cut ya / But until that day, I'm a n
stunna."[71]

Notes

1. Gangsta rap's ken is the lyric and narrative description of urban crime, wh
less organized, but for the purposes of this essay, I also consider songs about gold
largely conform to the gangsta "ethos" but may be only peripherally concerned (
bery, or murder.

2. See especially Chang, Jeff. *Can't Stop, Won't Stop: A History of the Hip-F*
York: St. Martin's, 2005; Dyson, Eric Michael. *Between God and Gangsta Rap: Bec*
Culture. New York: Oxford University Press, 1997; Forman, Murray, and Marl
That's the Joint: The Hip-Hop Studies Reader. New York: Routledge, 2004; hooks,
New York: Routledge, 1994; Rose, Tricia. *Black Noise: Rap Music and Black Cu*
America. Hanover, CT: Wesleyan University Press, 1994; Watkins, S. Craig. *Hi*
Pop Culture, and the Struggle for the Soul of a Movement. Boston: Beacon Street

3. In fact, it was bell hooks who said that gangsta rap, rather than origina(
"other," expresses "the logic of white supremacist capitalist patriarchy" in its
dividualism. Thus gangsta rap does not operate from the periphery of Americ
center (see *supra* note 1, p. 137).

4. Hagedorn, John M. *A World of Gangs: Armed Young Men and Gangs)*
University of Minnesota Press, 2008.

5. Jay-Z feat. Eminem. "Renegade." *The Blueprint*. Roc-A-Fella, 2001.

6. The Game contradicts himself on this matter: in "Dreams," he "watcl
bleed," but later on the same album, in "We Ain't," he cites Jay-Z's oral com;
rap shit is basic—I followed that Jay shit / Think of what I wanna say, st
take' it" (*The Documentary*. Interscope, 2005).

7. Lil Wayne. "Put Some Keys on That." *Da Drought 3*. [Bootleg], 2007.

8. Lil Wayne feat. Short Dawg, Gudda Gudda. "Break Up." *No Ceilings*

9. Sherratt, Susan. "Feasting in Homeric Epic." *Hesperia* 73.2 (April-J(

10. Mobb Deep feat. Q-Tip. "Drink Away the Pain." *The Infamous*. BM

11. The Notorious B.I.G. "Big Poppa." *Ready to Die*. Bad Boy, 1994.

45. Jay-Z feat. Rihanna, Kanye West. "Run This Town." *The Blueprint 3*. Def Jam, 2009.

46. OutKast. "So Fresh, So Clean." *Stankonia*. Arista, 2000.

47. Baby Boy Da Prince. "The Way I Live." *Across the Water*. Republic, 2007.

48. Lil Wayne. "Upgrade U." *Da Drought 3*. [Bootleg], 2007.

49. Murray, A. T. *Odyssey*, vol. 1. Cambridge, MA: Harvard University Press, 1995. 311.

50. This freestyle is widely available on the Internet, but Carmen Bryan also gives her account of the incident, depicting Jay-Z's claims (she calls him "S.C." for "Sean Carter") as desperate, baseless attacks in her tell-all memoir *It's No Secret* (New York: Simon and Schuster, 2006), pp. 224–25.

51. See Gwendolyn Pough's *Check It While I Wreck It: Black Womanhood, Hip-hop Culture, and the Public Sphere* (Lebanon, NH: Northeastern University Press, 2004) for an account of Lil' Kim as a transgressive feminist challenge to rap's patriarchy; on the other hand, see Imani Perry's *Prophets of the Hood: Politics and Poetics in Hip-hop* (Durham, NC: Duke University Press, 2004) for an indictment of Lil' Kim's pornographic aesthetic.

52. Three Six Mafia. "Late Nite Tip." *Chapter 1: The End*. Hypnotize Minds, 1996.

53. Raekwon feat. Ghostface Killah, Cappachino, Method Man. "Ice Cream." *Only Built 4 Cuban Linx . . .* BMG, 1995.

54. OutKast. "We Luv Deez Hoez." *Stankonia*. Arista, 2000.

55. Project Pat feat. Pimp C. "Talkin' Smart." *Walkin' Bank Roll*. Hypnotize Minds, 2007.

56. Geto Boys. "Let a Ho Be a Ho." *The Geto Boys*. Warner Brothers, 1990.

57. Big L. "M.V.P." *Lifestylez Ov Da Poor & Dangerous*. Columbia, 1995.

58. Big Punisher. "I'm Not a Player." *Capital Punishment*. Loud, 1998.

59. Kool Keith. "Sex Style." *Sex Style*. Funky Ass Records, 1997.

60. For a thorough overview of cause, effect, fate, determinism, and free will in ancient Greek philosophy and literature, from the pre-Socratics to the neo-Platonists, see R. J. Hankinson's *Cause and Explanation in Ancient Greek Thought* (New York: Oxford University Press, 1998).

61. *Hero and Exile: The Art of Old English Poetry*. London: Hambledon, 1989. 25.

62. Dr. Dre. "The Watcher." *2001*. Interscope, 1999.

63. Cypress Hill. "How I Could Just Kill a Man." *Cypress Hill*. Columbia, 1991.

64. Young Buck. "Bang Bang." *Straight Outta Cashville*. Interscope, 2004.

65. Wu-Tang Clan. "C.R.E.A.M." *Enter the Wu-Tang (36 Chambers)*. Loud, 1993.

66. UGK feat. Charlie Wilson. "How Long Can It Last." *Underground Kingz*. Jive, 2007.

67. *Ibid*.

68. Public Enemy. "911 Is a Joke." *Fear of a Black Planet*. Def Jam, 1990.

69. Lil Wayne. "Georgia . . . Bush." *Dedication 2*. [Bootleg], 2006.

70. Beastie Boys. "Fight for Your Right (To Party)." *Licensed to Ill*. Columbia, 1986.

71. Birdman, Lil Wayne. "Leather So Soft." *Like Father, Like Son*. Cash Money, 2006.

AT THE CROSSROADS: THE INTERSECTION OF POETRY AND THE BLUES

KEITH FLYNN

Musician and poet Keith Flynn reminds us how poets and musicians have long fostered a symbiotic relationship. In this essay, he takes a look at the relationship between blues music and the blues poem. He writes: "A blues song has life only as long as the musician is playing it, but it changes the player. Words are music; the poem and its sound have always walked together, or one inside the other, for the poet wears his music like a skin. The poem is the force the music exerts. 'Sound brings us to our senses,' said Thoreau. 'I am the blues,' said Willie Dixon."

"The power of music that poetry lacks is the ability to persuade without argument," William Matthews has written, but the best poems hide their argument, as well as the seams in their form. The style is the mysterious bond between the audience and the poem's mechanics, slipping in and out of the reader, inviting him or her back to read it again and again, coaxing the imagination out like energy in a spring. We all have a sound blueprint within us, a voice we would like to inhabit. I would love to be a being of pure sound. To make an orchestra of a single man. To take everything I hear and return it as poetry. Even when we are asleep, our ears are wide open, gathering sounds into the body. "Art is the path of the creator to his work," said Emerson, "and we hear so that we may speak." Poetry changes by touching other poetry. In this manner, the composition of poetry is like the blues tradition. A constant borrowing takes place where ideas and lyrics overlap, and are passed down or shared from artist to artist, or one generation to the next, in seemingly different contexts. A blues song has life only as long as the musician is playing it, but it changes the player. Words are music; the poem and its sound have always walked together, or one inside the other, for the poet wears his music like a skin. The poem is the force the music exerts. "Sound brings us to our senses," said Thoreau. "I am the blues," said Willie Dixon.

To make a perfect sound, one has to abandon oneself to the making of it. In other words, to surrender to a sound, you must become pure sound. Poetry is made from music, but is not the same thing. Poetry stops time, and music depends upon its movement. Also, poetry and music are mongrels; when properly fed they gather things to them and are comprised of the things they gather. A poem has "a fictive covering," but a song and its singer are naked, and must be so. But the radiation of sound guarantees we are not alone, and we call the others to us, by repeating our favorite sounds. A million folks would say they can write a poem; considerably less would profess to being able to squeeze jazz from a horn.

Poets and musicians have fostered a symbiotic relationship in America, especially in the last fifty years, when they have begun to morph into the same thing. And the list of poets who have been influenced by the blues they have heard is constantly growing. Amiri Baraka, Carl Sandburg, Jayne Cortez, Lucille Clifton, Marvin Bell, Sterling Brown, Michael Harper, John Berryman, Joy Harjo, Vachel Lindsay, Langston Hughes, Gwendolyn Brooks, Hayden Carruth, Jack Kerouac, William Matthews, Yusef Komunyakaa, Horace Coleman, Mina Loy, Kenneth Rexroth, Sonia Sanchez, Quincy Troupe, Leonard Cohen, Patti Smith, Bob Kaufman, Saul Williams, and Kevin Young are just a few of the poets whose work would be impossible to imagine without a prolonged exposure to the blues. Improvisation is the art of presence and what did not exist a moment before is the testament the next performer is building his instant upon. Communication (and history) requires two. Maybe music does, too. Rhythm forces everyone to join it, like birds overwhelmed by the sound of beating wings, compelled to take to the air. The first blues songs were sung in the fields, and the lyrics formed a code that all the workers understood, a call to meeting, or a piece of news that the foreman did not need to know about, a smoke signal tuning in the wavelength of the tribe.

In the first two or three decades of the twentieth century, the prized possession in most homes was the wind-up Victrola, playing a vast array of music, emanating through the needle and out of the horn from the early records' deep wax grooves. And every time the machine wound down, the listener had to wind it back up, using a crank on the side, singing back the music they had just listened to as they turned the crank. By 1920, Americans were buying twenty-five million records a year, and the most popular recordings were ragtime and jazz. But the music that jazz was based on, the blues, began to emerge in popularity during the 1920s. The first blues recording, "Crazy Blues," was released by Mamie Smith to wide acclaim. A trio of women followed, each with their own distinctive charm: Bessie Smith, Ida Cox, and the sly and slinky Ma Rainey. Bessie Smith combined gospel chops with a weary blues tone and a vivacious vibrato to become one of the biggest recording stars of the decade, influencing a whole generation of singers, most notably Billie Holiday.

Classic blues is called "classic" because it was the music that seemed to contain all the diverse and conflicting elements of Negro music, plus the smoother emotional appeal of the performance. It was the first Negro music that appeared in a formal context as entertainment, though it still contained the harsh, uncompromising reality of the earlier blues forms. It was, in effect, the perfect balance between the two worlds, and as such, it represented a clearly definable step by the Negro into the mainstream of American society. All of the great classic blues singers were women. Ma Rainey, Bessie Smith, and the others became professionals at early ages; Ma Rainey started when she was fourteen, Bessie Smith before she was twenty. The majority of all the formal blues in the 1920s were sung from the point of view of women. The great country blues singers, however, were almost always men. They were wanderers, migratory farm workers, or men who were street performers going from joint to joint in search of work. And the country blues singers were not recorded until much later, during the great swell of blues and "race" recordings when the companies were willing to try almost any black singer because of their newfound market. But the first recordings were classic blues and they (the ladies) brought the blues into every living room in America.

Mamie Smith's initial recording of "Crazy Blues" on February 14, 1920, was not expected to be a success, but from the outset it sold 8,000 copies a week for almost three years. Classic blues became big business and the lyrics were saturated with sex, like Ida Cox singing, "When your man comes home evil, tells you, you are getting old, / that's a true sign he's got someone else baking his jelly roll." Or Sippie Wallace telling the girls, "Don't advertise your man." Hoodoo, too, is a big part of the blues. Ma Rainey's "Black Dust Blues," for instance, tells about a woman who is angry because Ma took her man. "Lord, I was out one morning, found black dust all 'round my door," the song begins, but the speaker starts to get thin, and develops trouble with her feet: "Black dust in my window, black dust on my porch mat . . . / Black dust's got me walking on all fours like a cat." The subject here is "throwin' down" on someone; in African magic, the feet are considered to be a specifically vulnerable entry point for evil. Magical powder sprinkled in socks or shoes might bind the evil spell; in love spells, socks might be tied together.

Ma Rainey was the link between the harsher, more spontaneous country or primitive styles and the smoother, more theatrical style that conquered radio. Rainey toured for years with the Rabbit Foot Minstrels, and her vaudeville skills were honed to a razor-sharp edge. She passed her knowledge along to the first superstar black performer of her time, one who would be the highest paid singer in America—Bessie Smith. Long before microphones and amps and digital equipment, in 1923, Bessie made her first recording with the Columbia Gramophone Company. She hollered her vocals into a funnel, and sheer sonic vibrations were converted into grooves on soft black wax. The record was "Down Hearted Blues," and would be an immediate smash.

Born dirt poor in Tennessee with seven siblings, her father, a Baptist preacher, died when she was an infant. Her mother died when she was eight. Slavery had ended just thirty-one years before she was born, and it still stained everyone and everything. Bessie's first recording sold 800,000 copies in six months, and she was instantly known as the "Empress of the Blues." She would go on to make 200 more records for Columbia, and when she died, she had been paid a total of $28,575. She was nearly six feet tall, weighed over two hundred pounds, and walked around with her money stuffed in her clothes. But Bessie was not to be trifled with. One man who tried to rob her stabbed her in the stomach, but she chased him down and tackled him, holding him until help arrived, and only then she collapsed. Once, to convince her husband she had been hit by a car (and not on a two-day tryst with another man), she threw herself down two flights of stairs. The chorus girl who slept with her husband? The dancer exited the train in the middle of nowhere, at full speed, with Bessie's foot firmly planted on her behind. Bessie met her demise on the mythic Highway 61 near Clarksdale, Mississippi, not far from the devil's crossroads. The car her husband was driving plowed into a truck parked in the dark beside the road. Bessie's arm came out of its socket at the shoulder. A white doctor drove by and stopped, but instead called for an ambulance, supposedly to keep from bloodying his white car. Rumors spread thick as mosquitoes in the scorching heat of the Delta. With Bessie gone, so too died the era of classic blues; it simmered and stopped. Jazz was hot, and the new sound washed over the old like a white wave on the sand.

The poet, listening to music, listens to himself as part of the expressive act, and that listening itself becomes an essential part of the poem. Boris Pasternak believed that "poetry searches for music amidst the tumult of the dictionary." Poets like Carl Sandburg wrote in a free-verse style that searched within the tumult of his tone for an expressive story shifting and twisting to the onslaught of mood changes, and pinned to the consistent beat of the drum. At times, instead of words, the bluesman scats, singing sounds (or notes) instead of words. He is following the music, just as the poet, carried along by the rhythm, follows the poem—and the reader follows both, listening as the poem is spoken, translating it as it is read. "In the world of imagination," wrote Richard Hugo, "all things belong. If you take that on faith, you may be foolish, but foolish like a trout."

The success of "race" and "hillbilly" records in the 1920s and 1930s led record producers into the Mississippi Delta where, among the last vestiges of slavery, the sharecropper cotton shacks, and deep poverty, a distinctly American music was being perfected in the juke joints and shanties. The blues's simple structure belies its hypnotic effect, and in the hands of masters like Charlie Patton, Son House, Willie Brown, and Robert Johnson, it is perhaps the most moving art form in our cultural history. Once every twelve-bar song could be called blues, but as the players became more sophisticated, the forms began to change as well. More instrumentation was needed, bridge and solo sections were added. Brass instruments lent greater range to the sonic architecture. Many jazz players, such as Louis Armstrong or Jelly Roll Morton, were exceptional blues singers. The call and response of the early a cappella blues lent itself to the three-line verse structure, each line about four bars long. The words of the song occupy about half of each line, leaving a space of two bars for either a sung answer or an instrumental response. The rise of the tercet in the American poetic vernacular, spearheaded by William Carlos Williams in the thirties, was a way of wresting American speech patterns and colloquialisms from the straitjacket of European poetic forms almost as old as the language. Out of this broken vessel, new forms coalesced, and the wilder, more untamed American South and its literary and musical voices began to take center stage.

A howling wilderness only 150 years ago, the Delta, convoluted by cypress swamps and forbidden dunes, was carved with great effort and human blood into cotton, peanut, and tobacco fields, oppressing the working man, black and white alike. Out of these extreme working conditions, vivid narratives—of love, loss, death, and voodoo—bubbled up into the blues, a desperate endurance in response to a unique human experience. If Son House was the plaintive gospel, drink-drenched disaster merged with the blues, Robert Johnson was the doomed Picasso incorporating a hedonistic, soulful cry of the human condition with consummate technique and a poet's sense of the language. When Son House and Willie Brown laughed at the young Johnson's ambition to be a traveling bluesman, the undeterred and fully determined young artist headed out to the crossroads, to the intersection of highways 49 and 61, heading west and north out of the Delta. There, like Daniel Webster before him, he supposedly sold his soul to the devil for the ability to play and sing the blues like no other man. Several of his songs would reflect the mythic deal: "Hellhounds On My Trail," "Crossroads Blues," "Me and the Devil Blues," "Stones in My Passway," and "If I Had Possession Over Judgment Day" all contain lyrics that describe a man haunted by his decisions and powerless to change them, doomed and strangely defiant. Thousands of artists would record versions of the twenty-nine songs he composed during his short career.

Contrary to most surviving accounts, Johnson did receive a measure of acclaim during his lifetime, but he was a feverish traveler, always ready to move to another place. For most of his later years, he would hole up in Helena, Arkansas, when not roaming about up and down the Mississippi River playing in levee camps, for road gangs, on courthouse steps busking, or in the juke joints dotted about the Delta countryside. Most of the great bluesmen from the era made their way through Helena. Sonny Boy Williamson, Willie Brown, Robert Nighthawk, Elmore James, "Honey Boy" Edwards, Howlin' Wolf, "Hacksaw" Harvey,

Johnny Shiner, and Memphis Slim were among the countless itinerants who flopped down and jammed in West Helena's many hot spots and nightclubs.

It was in one of these little joints called Three Forks just south of Arkansas in Greenwood, Mississippi, where Johnson last played and met his demise. He was known to love the ladies, and being fond of whiskey, he was easily poisoned by someone, perhaps the owner of the Three Forks, whose woman had been spending a little too much carnal time with the bluesman. After a set performed with Sonny Boy Williamson, perhaps the greatest harmonica player of all time, Johnson took ill, could sing no longer, and struggled, dying slowly for the next two weeks before his body gave up on August 16, 1938. One of the century's most mercurial and influential musicians was buried in a wooden coffin furnished by the county, just next to the highway as his song, "Me and the Devil Blues" had predicted. "You may bury my body down by the highway side / So my old evil spirit can catch a Greyhound bus and ride."

Eric Clapton, the Rolling Stones, Led Zeppelin, the Red Hot Chili Peppers, ZZ Top, the Doors, the Grateful Dead, Van Morrison, Megadeth, Tesla, and numerous other rock bands claim Johnson as an influence, and every blues artist that followed him found themselves affected by the long shadow he cast. His lyrics and guitar techniques are utterly original and contain a power that is hard to describe, but has haunted every listener fortunate enough to hear them.

> When the train, it left the station
> With two lights on behind
> Well, the blue light was my blues
> And the red light was my mind. ("Love in Vain")

It has been said that the blues ain't nothing but a good man feeling bad, but the blues feels like an absence, an ache, a place where the well of the spirit is filled with dust, where the imagination has run dry, the life-force squandered. Willie Dixon wrote:

> I'm a thousand generations of poverty and starvation
> I'm the dog of the United Nations
> I am the blues.

Another poet has written, "I can't get no satisfaction," and this is the blues. When Gabriel Garcia Lorca spoke of the gypsy's despair and its *duende*, its black sound, I believe he was talking about a version of the blues. In his book *In Search of Duende*, he writes: "Deep song sings like a nightingale without eyes. It sings blind, for both its words and its ancient tunes are best set in the night, the blue night of our countryside." Ralph Ellison also compared the blues to flamenco, gypsies to slaves: "an outcast though undefeated people who have never lost their awareness of the physical source of man's most spiritual moments." Without blues, there is no jazz. Without blues, there is no rock and roll. When Son House sings about the loss of his woman in "Death Letter," he is quickly assaulted by the deep "walking blues," the recognition of unrecovered love, spiraling past his understanding:

> Seemed like 10,000 people standing
> 'Round the burying ground
> I didn't know I loved her
> 'Til they began to let her down.

House is singing about irretrievable loss, loss that takes with it all the energy we commonly take for granted—that energy, Ellison says, "which mocks the despair stated explicitly in the lyric, and it expresses the great human joke directed against the universe, that joke which is the secret of all folklore and myth: though we be dismembered daily we shall always rise up again."

Langston Hughes knew the hot blue jet of deprivation in the heart of this music, and it informed all his poetry with a brooding sense of solitary loneliness, the singular beauty of corrosive sadness. He was just twenty-four years old when his first book, *The Weary Blues*, was published in 1926. Already self-assured and mature in his poetic philosophy, Hughes used his poems to speak not only for himself, but for the entire black community. *The Weary Blues* is split into seven distinct sections with varying themes. The poems have a strong lyrical framework, and were written to be accompanied by music. This first book's success allowed the young poet to attend Lincoln University, where one of his classmates was Thurgood Marshall, a future Supreme Court justice. Ironically, forty-six years before the famous *Brown vs. Board of Education* case, which in 1954 ushered desegregation into the American educational system, Hughes's dynamic mother argued and won her case against the school board of Topeka, Kansas, for refusing to admit her son to a nearby segregated white school because of the color of his skin. The following passage from Langston Hughes's poem "I, Too, Sing America" speaks to this sense of injustice: "I am the darker brother. / They send me to eat in the kitchen / When company comes." What follows, however, is a victorious response: But I laugh, / And eat well /And grow strong."

Because his father emigrated to Mexico and his mother was often away, the young Hughes was raised in Lawrence, Kansas, by his grandmother, Mary Langston, whose first husband had died at Harper's Ferry fighting under John Brown and whose second (Hughes's grandfather) had also been a fierce abolitionist. These adult figures engendered in the boy a keen sense of social justice. As a poet he was also influenced by Paul Laurence Dunbar, Carl Sandburg, and Walt Whitman, and recognized their poignant descriptions of men at work, and of the speech patterns and colloquial expressions of common folk. In this spirit, Hughes invented a character named Simple, a black laborer, and in his name and dialect composed a weekly column for the *New York Post*. What Hughes said of the blues is often true of his own work, that "the mood of the blues is almost always despondency, but when they are sung people laugh." He published more than three dozen books during his life, starting out with poetry and then expanding into novels, short stories, and plays. Many of his plays incorporated musical elements and song, such as the musical *Simple Heavenly*, and his three gospel plays, *Black Nativity*, *Tambourines to Glory*, and *The Prodigal Son*. Hughes authored music guides, including *Famous Negro Music Makers*, and the children's title, *The First Book of Jazz*. He also wrote liner notes for albums by Harry Belafonte and Nina Simone, who recorded a version of his poem, "Backlash Blues."

"What is poetry?" Hughes was asked near his death. He answered, "It is the human soul entire, squeezed like a lemon or a lime, drop by drop, into atomic words." He wanted no definition of the poet that divorced his art from the immediacy of life. "A poet is a human being," he declared. "Each human being must live within his time, with and for his people, and within the boundaries of his country." In 1958 Hughes crossed into the jazz world by reading his work at the landmark Village Vanguard in New York City, accompanied by Charles Mingus and Phineas Newborn. The collaboration eventually resulted in an album, *The Weary Blues*, which united Hughes's voice and words with the music of Leonard Feather and Mingus. The second half of the recording is amazing, with Mingus and his band laying down an organic funky groove that Hughes's mellifluous voice glides upon like a kite or parasail riding behind a moving boat, tipping precisely atop the feathery tide of wind and water.

> And far into the night he crooned that tune.
> The stars went out and so did the moon.
> The singer stopped playing and went to bed
> While the Weary Blues echoed through his head.
> He slept like a rock or a man that's dead. (from "The Weary Blues")

Since the time of Langston Hughes, the blues poem has become a viable form, often in the musical tradition of the blues in which a statement is made in the first line, some slight variation offered in the second line, and a type of alternative, perhaps ironic, declared in the next or third line. Kevin Young (who also has an essay in this collection) is a contemporary poet whose book *Jelly Roll* is a series of bluesy observations and musical effects. He has also edited an anthology collecting many of the poets whose blues-inflected poems he admires. Here is an example of Young's blues impressions, wrested together in a series of haiku-like poems, concurrently comic and tragic, like all true blues:

Locomotive Songs[1]

We were hobos every year.
It was cheap—

Our mother each
Halloween smudged our cheeks

stuffed us in someone
else's clothes—

We hopped houses
like trains

asking for sweets

Much like last night,
empty-armed, at your door

I begged you

———————

Tonight the train horn
sounds like plenty

enough loud
to warm even the autumn—

The night air with a nip
that catches by surprise—

White light, blue
light, fog starting to rise

———————

She has me tied,
a tongue, to the tracks
Her new man's
elaborate moustache

Train comin fast
Can't cry
out to save my life

Drats

———————

I've heard tell
of a town where the train

bound for New Orleans slows
just enough, a turn

that folks place cars
good only for insurance in—

The train cashes them
coming round the bend—too late

to stop, too slow to derail—
That's how I feel

watching you & the station
being pulled away, one hand

hovering the emergency brake
the other

out to wave.

Young's place in the pantheon of contemporary blues poets lies in his ability to synthesize, to capture the black vernacular, or a mood of it, and then stretch the possibilities to achieve a certain surface tension that allows the emotional shudder of the poem to emerge. This comes from a keen sense of listening, of understanding the histories embedded in the repeated oral traditions. His use of the word "Drats," for instance, seems out of place until you see the context. It is a word that Charlie Brown, the maudlin little hero of the Peanuts comic strip, might use, not a hobo bluesman. Young is no hobo bluesman either; he only dressed as one for Halloween as a kid, but the word (drats) he has chosen here is a little anchor in the poem to the present dimension, and a nice completion rhyme to the word "fast" that occurs two lines before. Young's lament is heartfelt, whatever his economic hardship. It is impossible to be wise and in love at the same time. And from the first unrequited love to the last one, deepened by experience, those repercussions can make anyone, regardless of gender or race, a card-carrying member of Bluesville.

Another contemporary poet whose tone is derived from the blues, but capable of almost operatic formulations, is Yusef Komunyakaa. Born in 1947 in Bogalusa, Louisiana, he was raised during the beginning of the Civil Rights movement. He served in the United States Army from 1969 to 1970 as a correspondent and managing editor of the *Southern Cross* during the Vietnam War, seeing action on the front line, where he earned a Bronze Star. Komunyakaa's originality is concentrated on his unerring ability to tackle moral dilemmas in poem after poem. The preoccupation with injustice is one of the blues' most dear characteristics. That and its rhythm.

> Woman, I got the blues.
> Our shadows on floral wallpaper
> struggle with cold-blooded mythologies.
> But there's a stillness in us
> like the tip of a magenta mountain,

writes Komunyakaa in "Woman, I Got the Blues." He concludes the poem by ripening a perfect metaphor for sexual release/relief. "Your breath's a dewy flower stalk / leaning into sweaty air." His poems are loaded with musical imagery: hymns sung in fields, and wounded lovers struggling for redemption. And yet, he manages a copious space for silence and Zen-like contemplation. In "Rhythm Method" he writes about discerning the rhythm of his imagination, or internal body clock, from the variety of sounds in the natural world: "We know the whole weight / depends on small silences / we fit ourselves into," and then later this culmination:

> If you can see blues
> in the ocean, light & dark,
> can feel worms ease through
> a subterranean path
> beneath each footstep,
> Baby, you got rhythm.

Any reasonable study of blues history will surmise that there is satisfaction in action whenever the soul's ailment is called out. The blues are also late-night, feel-good, gutbucket, groove-root music, where sorrow is cancelled out by a deeper yearning for Truth and a general tribally shared recognition of the human condition. Both Young and Komunyakaa define this dichotomy in different ways. Young has said: "You see, I listen to the blues to feel better, not worse—it transforms us as listeners, takes our troubles away not by pretending they don't exist (like much other early pop music) but by naming them. *Good morning blues, how do you do?*" It was this shake rag hip tremble and sanctified gospel shouting that made a young Elvis Presley's pelvis recognize the rhythm of his future. "The blues are the three L's [says B.B. King], and that would be living, loving, and hopefully, laughing—in other words, the regular old E formation on the guitar with the regular three changes. The blues is like a tonic. There's a blues for anything that bothers you." The blues live in both the sacred and the secular worlds. "Blues / don't care how many tribulations / you lay at my feet," writes Komunyakaa. "I'll go with you if you promise / to bring me home to Mercy."

The point where poetry separates itself from the academy, and curls its legs around the blues, is mainly in tenor and amplitude of language. Someone once said of Wordsworth that he used plain words instead of the right ones. And it can be argued that modesty of speech should be the aim of any sentences yearning to communicate, but poetry's effectiveness lies in the honesty of speech hard-won, with magnetic verb play, with discoveries, associations, or imagery that until a moment before the mind would not have connected. Marina Tsvetaeva writes: "the condition of creation is a condition of being overcome by a spell. Until you begin, it is a state of being obsessed; until you finish, a state of being possessed. Something, someone lodges in you . . . that which through you wants to be." (Feiler 6)

Rhythm is what lodges in a poet, for language and rhythm cannot be separated, just as the same word in voodoo means drum and dance simultaneously. Poetry is the language of hidden things in commerce with one another, and it cleans the dust of the everyday from our spirit. All great art must resonate; and poems live in the air, shimmering rhythmically from the body of the poet to be assimilated into the reader. Thus a poem is a living organism, filled with moving parts, and to build them "you have to let the devil use your head for a drum," says Komunyakaa.

When composing the following poem, I wanted to emphasize the universality of the blues, the dislocation from identity, or place, the inability to stay connected to any one thing for too long. We are beings in constant flow, which also means we are being constantly transmogrified, energy in transition, and these momentary islands of exile and torment seem like bedrocks in the blues tradition. In the ninth of Rilke's *Duino Elegies*, he instructs us not to tell the gods about glory, or even the reflected glories of their presence, but to talk about the creatures and faces we know, the heroic accumulation of things and days.

The Blues

Last night I dreamed of my wife,
two years gone, the traces of feeling
in men, like marble in meat,
the hypnotic interiors that highlight
the soul's confusion, like a moth trapped
in a glass or under a hat on the floor.
Nothing rises, not History which requires two,
or marriage with its schizophrenic feeling,
half longing, half belonging, like living
in a homeland constantly occupied by
a different neighboring country.

                                   Her curls
wind-whipped in a field, the old comfort
of our lust rolling through the weeds
in a Welsh meadow of bluebells, and the
cratered places where our bodies had been,
the weight of absence, or the inertia of images,
the half-traced alcove of a piazza's blueprint,
the eclipse of the moon, the plaster casts
of bodies faced with death, contorted together
in Pompeii beneath an age of ash, a single
feather on a beam of wind from atop Chichen
Itxa fastened alone on a journey to the Mexican
jungle.

    I can feel my eye breaking on the coastal
plain, a piece of shoestring tied to a wire,
the silent mouth screaming in an o-ring of
pleasure or fear, all the questions, curdled milk
streaming from a cracked carton into the waves.
I have wondered, if by these details one could
inhabit or comprehend another, by what method
do we understand the spires of an incomplete
building stabbing out at Time whose face
is hidden?

    Camped on a cliff, can we become
complete as one gull battles a crater of saltwater
with its crushed wing, while the flowers ferment

under concrete pressure, and the smell of a muse
that cannot be viewed, flays with a strange violence
in my brain? The fossils rise, their pearly skulls
drained of local color. There is no coupling
of natures, no merger of worlds.
                                    The dead name us,
taking the first fork they find and bending it to suit
their own peculiar path. Ever speak of this and their
voices run wild. Just ask anybody, wandering
half-lit by the moon on a country road at night,
where the shadows announce themselves and
disappear, their presence overblown in a land
scape of broken ruses, and the ending is the blues.

In James Cameron's juggernaut *Avatar*, the natives of the planet Pandora, the Na'vi, have braids of hair the length of their spine, with root-like fibers on the end, that are able to connect, or be roped into the nervous system of the animals on the planet, especially the trees, which store the sacred souls and voices of all life forms that have previously existed there. There is an attempt in this poem to reattach the speaker to the past, which is impossible, of course. No man stands in the same river twice, but we make our peace when we recognize the common bond of that yearning. The blues is the closest music ever comes to imitating the human voice in all its complexity and tone, which is why the blues is the Rosetta Stone for the genres that have followed it, or blended into it, to form the con-silience of all popular music to follow, folk, gospel, jazz, or rock. "If I can sing it, then I know it's a song," says Bob Dylan. "If I can't, then I call it a poem."

When a woman in a certain African tribe knows she is pregnant, she goes out into the wilderness with a few friends and together they pray and meditate until they hear (or together compose) the song of the child. They recognize that every soul has its own vibration that expresses its unique flavor and purpose. When the women have completed the song, they sing it aloud over and over, then they return to the tribe and teach it to everyone else. When the child is born, the community gathers and chants the child's song. When the child passes through the initiation to adulthood, the people again come together and sing. At the time of marriage, the couple's individual songs are sung together. Finally, when the soul is about to pass from this world, the family and friends gather at the person's bed, just as they did at their birth, and they sing the person over the other side, to the next life. The only other time the tribe sings a person's song, during his or her life, is if the person commits a crime or some other aberrant social action. Then the individual is called to the center of the village and the people of the community form a circle around the offending person. The tribe sings their song to them, recognizing that the correction for antisocial behavior is not punishment; it is love and remembrance of joy, the recovery of identity. "The poet must be continually watching the moods of his mind," said Thoreau, "as the astronomer watches the aspects of the heavens." Thoreau realized that expression is the act of the whole man and that the body "must conspire with the mind." In this combination, the voice of the poet becomes whole. He can sing for himself, of himself, to the tribe, and for the tribe, clarifying the values that have become obscured. Music becomes the common currency that gives those values worth. Music, like poetry, cannot be faked. It is authentic or it is ignored. Music is thus a moral law, whose great heart springs open like a net, unrolling from its loom. Whatever is not stone, is light, *and aware*, the blues upright, walking like a man.

Note

1. "It Don't Mean a Thing" © 2010 by Kevin Young. "Locomotive Songs" reprinted from *Jelly Roll: A Blues* published by Alfred A. Knopf. © 2003 by Kevin Young. Both reprinted by permission of the author. All rights reserved.

Works Cited

Cox, Ida. "Fogyism." Music and lyrics by Jesse Crump. Paramount, 1928.

Dixon, Willie, and Don Snowden. *I Am the Blues: The Willie Dixon Story*. New York: Da Capo, 1989.

Dixon, Willie. "I Am the Blues." *I Am the Blues*. Columbia, 1970.

Dylan, Bob. *Chronicles, Volume 1*. New York: Simon & Schuster, 2005.

———. *The Essential Interviews*. Ed. Jonathan Cott. New York: Wenner Books, 2006.

———. *Writings and Drawings*. New York: Borzoi Books, 1981.

Ellison, Ralph. "Flamenco [review]." *Saturday Review* 11, December 1954.

Emerson, Ralph Waldo. *Essays, First and Second Series*. Gloucestershire, UK: Dodo Press, 2007.

Feiler, Lily. *Marina Tsvetaeva: The Double Beat of Heaven and Hell*. Durham, NC: Duke University Press, 1994. 6.

Ferris, William. *Give My Poor Heart Ease: Voices of The Mississippi Blues*. Chapel Hill, NC: University of North Carolina Press, 2009. 202.

Flynn, Keith. *The Golden Ratio*. Oak Ridge, TN: Iris, 2007.

———. *The Rhythm Method, Razzmatazz and Memory: How to Make Your Poetry Swing*. Cincinnati: Writer's Digest, 2007.

Gordon, Robert. *Can't Be Satisfied: The Life and Times of Muddy Waters*. New York: Little, Brown, 2002.

Hoffman, Mark, and James Segrest. *Moanin' at Midnight: The Life and Times of Howlin' Wolf*. New York: Pantheon, 2004.

House, Son. "Death Letter." *Death Letter*. Paramount, 1930.

Hughes, Langston. "I, Too, Sing America." *Selected Poems of Langston Hughes*. London: Vintage Classics, 1990. 275.

———. *The Collected Works of Langston Hughes: Essays on Art, Race, Politics and World Affairs*. Ed. Christopher C. De Santis. Columbia: University of Missouri Press, 2002. 74.

———. *The Collected Works of Langston Hughes: The Poems: 1921–1940*. Ed. Arnold Rampersad. Columbia: University of Missouri Press, 2001. 408.

———. "The Weary Blues." *Selected Poems of Langston Hughes*. London: Vintage Classics, 1990. 33–34.

Hugo, Richard. "Writing Off the Subject." *The Triggering Town: Lectures and Essays on Poetry and Writing*. New York: W. W. Norton, 1992. 5.

Johnson, Robert. "Love In Vain." *King of the Delta Blues Singers, Vol. 2*. Rec. 1937. Columbia, 1970.

———. "Me and the Devil Blues." *King of the Delta Blues Singers*. Rec. 1938. Columbia, 1961.

Jones, LeRoi. *Blues People*. New York: William Morrow, 1963.

Kaufman, Bob. *The Ancient Rain*. New York: New Directions, 1981.

Komunyakaa, Yusef. "Blue Light Lounge Sutra for the Performance Poets at Harold Park Hotel." *Pleasure Dome: New and Collected Poems*. Middletown, CT: Wesleyan University Press, 2001. 252–53.

———. "No-Good Blues." *Pleasure Dome*. 427–30.

———. "Rhythm Method." *Pleasure Dome*. 420–21.

———. "Woman, I Got the Blues." *Pleasure Dome*. 113–14.

Lorca, Federico García. *In Search of Duende*. 2nd ed. Ed. Christopher Mauer. New York: New Directions, 2010.

Massa, Ann. *Vachel Lindsay: Fieldworker for the American Dream*. Bloomington: Indiana University Press, 1970.

Matthews, William. *The Poetry Blues: Essays and Interviews*. Ed. Sebastian Matthews and Stanley Plumly. Ann Arbor: University of Michigan Press, 2004.

McKinney, B. B., ed. *The Broadman Hymnal*. Nashville, TN: Broadman, 1940.

Rainey, Ma. "Black Dust Blues." Music by Ma Rainey, lyrics by Selma Davis. Paramount, 1928.

Rilke, Rainer Maria. *Duino Elegies and the Sonnets to Orpheus*. Trans. Stephen Mitchell. New York: Vintage, 2009.

Rolling Stones. "(I Can't Get No) Satisfaction." Music and lyrics by Mick Jagger and Keith Richards. *Out of Our Heads*. London, 1965.

Shelton, Robert. *No Direction Home: The Life and Music of Bob Dylan*. New York: Beech Tree, 1986.

Wallace, Sippie. "Don't Advertise Your Man." *Sings the Blues*. Storyville, 1966.

Young, Kevin. *Jelly Roll: A Blues*. New York: Alfred A. Knopf, 2005.

COUNTRY MUSIC LYRICS: IS THERE POETRY IN THOSE TWANGY RHYMES?

JILL JONES

Songs, deservedly or not, often receive the label "lowbrow" and poetry receives the more glittery label "highbrow." Country music might be considered the lowbrow of the lowbrow. This article by British literature scholar Jill Jones seeks out the common ground between poetry and country lyrics by focusing on rhetorical tropes and schemes that both poets and country music lyricists frequently utilize. As Jones explains in this essay, "You can't have your Kate and Edith, too," is far more than a funny country line but part of a shared literary and oral history.

"Highbrow" and "lowbrow" are terms literary critics and social scientists have been using since the phrenology movement of the nineteenth century. For decades sociologists have used country music as a register of the lowbrow taste associated with the lower socioeconomic class in American society. Their studies in the 1990s put classical music on the top of the scale and country music at the bottom.[1] Most often country music was associated with rural, unsophisticated, less well-educated audiences, mainly from the South or Midwest. But in the last couple of decades, a gigantic industry has evolved that has brought country music to a larger audience, not necessarily rural or unsophisticated or poorly educated. Country has incorporated elements of folk, blues, bluegrass, rock, and rap that have enabled it to appeal to a broader audience, an audience that has become international in scope. The glitzy, sophisticated "red carpet" awards shows, the technologically sophisticated videos, and performers with movie star status, all reflect a new age of country music. Fans speak with their purchases of CDs, iTunes selections, and concert tickets; the thousands who show up for concerts in Houston, Atlanta, or Los Angeles, paying hundreds of dollars for tickets, represent a wide fan base of people who are not on the lowest rung of the socioeconomic ladder. A lucrative $1,009,143,800.00 industry in 2008[2] has blossomed with such crossover stars as Garth Brooks, Carrie Underwood, and Taylor Swift. According to a Pew Research study of America's musical tastes, 27 percent often listen to country and another 34 percent sometimes do, for a total of 61 percent of listeners.[3] Anyone who wants to understand the American experience or the American psyche could well look to country music for insights. The lyrics of these popular songs reflect the values, interests, and dreams of a large segment of the population.

Certain universal features of country music lyrics may well explain its popularity. Since the beginnings of human history, stories told through song have played a key role in most cultures. American country music fulfills the same function as a conveyor of cultural values and as an inspiration to its listeners. It does this while providing a continuum with traditional forms of poetry. Some may think of writing poetry as a highbrow activity and writing country music lyrics as a lowbrow activity, but actually the poet and the country music lyricist have much in common.

The word "lyric" means something a bit different to the two. To the songwriter, lyrics are the words that are set to music. Historically, to a poet a lyric is any poem about an individual's feelings. One major difference is that while poetry often has a specified rhythm (e.g., iambic pentameter or trochaic trimeter), it generally is not meant to have musical accompaniment. Of course, exceptions exist. A popular example is W. B. Yeats's poem "The Lake Isle of Innisfree." Chorale groups sing it on university campuses, soloists like Bill Douglas have written an arrangement for it, and even the popular group the Cranberries has recorded it. Such interrelationships between poems and musical scores simply reinforce the point of their interconnectedness. Many people are comfortable with musical lyrics, and by looking at the lyrics to a song like "Strawberry Wine" while listening to the heavy rhythm of the guitar in Deana Carter's version, the metrics of poetry can be elucidated. Playing the music along with reading the lyrics can make the rhythmic element more obvious.

Country song lyrics lean heavily on music for effect and, thus, lose a major part of that effect when read apart from the music. But, that is as true of Shakespeare's "Hey nonny nonnies" in his songs as of John Michael Montgomery's "Sold" with the staccato auctioneering rhythms missing. Also, the repetition and choruses do not hold up well on the written page. The interconnectedness of the music and the lyrics has to be conceded, but still, there are similarities in the words of lyrics and words of poems. Song lyrics are more similar to traditionally structured poetry than to more modern forms; there is little kinship with modern poets' taste for free verse and their disdain for rhyme. With the beat of the musical score and a preference for sound devices such as rhymes, consonance, and assonance, country lyrics hark back to conventions of Renaissance or Vic-

torian poetry. One example of a country song that uses extensive rhyme or assonance is Toby Keith's "I Wanna Talk About Me" (italics throughout this article
are added for emphasis):

> We talk about your *work*, how your boss is a *jerk*.
> We talk about your *church* and your head when it *hurts*...
> We talk about your *friends* and the places that you've *been*.

Admittedly, the rap influence is strong here; Keith borrows the rapper's sing-
song rhythms, cataloging of details, and emphasis on rhyme. Rhyme occurs not
only as end rhyme, but as internal rhyme, in a manner reminiscent of the Old
English caesura tradition with repetition of sounds in midline. These rhyming
lyrics are part of a long tradition and provide a link with those hundreds of years
prior to the rise of modernist values that disparage rhyme.

Another trait these song lyrics share with good lyric poems is attention to
the particular. Poems voice the emotion of one man or one woman and often detail particular places and events. Examples from some well-known poets include
William Stafford, who in "Traveling Through the Dark" tells of hitting a deer on
a dark drive home. Robert Frost talks about "stopping by woods on a snowy evening." Wendell Berry says, "Once there was a man who filmed his vacation. / He
went flying down the river in his boat / with his video camera to his eye." Emily
Dickinson asserts, "I heard a fly buzz, when I died."[4] In many good poems, readers find themselves in a very particular place at one very particular time. Such
is also true of country music lyrics. They maintain the narrative element, just
as many excellent poems do, with most of the songs telling stories of particular
experiences in particular locales. Songs deal with the universal human emotions
of love, fear, jealousy, and joy, but they deal with specific experiences. In "What
Was I Thinkin'," Dierks Bentley talks about Becky, whose father may have done
"a little time in the slammer." In "Where Have You Been?" Kathy Mattea sings,
"Claire had all but given up / When she and Edwin fell in love." Collin Raye in
"Love, Me" tells us, "I read a note my Grandma wrote back in 1923. / Grandpa
kept it in his coat, and he showed it once to me." Song after song deals with
specific people with their personal stories. Of course, the ballads of Kenny Rogers, like "The Gambler," and "Coward of the County," continue a long tradition of
story-telling ballads.

In country music, a taste for the particular is obvious in the clear preference
for lists or catalogs of items. The list of what she talks about in Toby Keith's "I
Wanna Talk About Me," above, is an example, as is the list of all the different
people in his "I Love This Bar": winners, losers, chain smokers, boozers, yuppies,
bikers, thirsty hitchhikers, cowboys, truckers, broken-hearted fools and suckers,
hustlers, fighters, early birds and all-nighters, and veterans, among others. This

technique is not unlike the epic catalogs found in the classic works of Homer or Virgil or Milton. From Walt Whitman's *Song of Myself* to Ginsberg's *Howl*, American poets have delighted in enumerating people, jobs, events, activities. Critic Paul Fussell points out Theodore Roethke's use of listing in "Elegy for Jane" and asserts that "enumeration is the essential method of countless other modern free-verse poems" (79).[5] It proves to be an essential method for country music lyricists as well. In "That's What I Love About Sunday," Craig Morgan enumerates what goes on in church and then all Sunday afternoon, concluding with this particular image:

> Cat nappin' on the porch swing,
> You curled up next to me,
> The smell of jasmine wakes us up.

He then catalogs their activities: a "walk down a dirt road," going fishing, carving their names in a tree, and stealing a kiss at sundown. Mark Wills in "Nineteen Something" reminisces in one verse about the 1970s with *Star Wars*, Pac-Man, Stretch Armstrong, Roger Staubach and baseball cards, Evil Knievel, and the death of Elvis and in another verse about the 1980s with microwaves, Rubik's Cubes, Daisy Duke, skating rinks, black Trans-Ams, big hair, and parachute pants, among other things. Josh Thompson tells about how his nine-to-five job "puts beer on the table" and provides him with what he needs:

> It puts the gas in my truck, butter on my biscuit,
> Couple bucks when I'm itching for a scratch-off ticket.
> That poker makes me broker every Saturday night.

The job enables him to pay his water and light bills and have a fun Friday night with his friends. He concludes that "working hard all week puts beer on the table."

Admittedly, certain conventions set country music apart from lyrics of other musical genres. Certain subjects are conventional: relationships, love of the country life, patriotism, and drinking at honky tonks. Writers also must follow certain expectations about language—colloquial diction, dialectal forms, nonstandard grammar, clichés, and simple vocabulary. Those who think of country music as lowbrow are very conscious of the colloquial language and non-standard grammatical forms. For example, Brooks & Dunn sing about the chances of falling in love and conclude:

> Me and you girl we just walked up on it.
> Feels good, don't it.

There are three non-standard grammatical forms there: "Me and you," "don't it," and the "we" after "Me and you girl." These three constructions are common to country lyrics, as are "ain't," sometimes in a double negative like "ain't got no," and "them" instead of "those," as in "she looks good in them boots." Some of the fans of country music would speak that way but some would not. The truth is that if lyricists chose to use highly formal, standard forms, they would be violating expectations for the genre. The genre requires a particular type of "voice"; the subjects of some particular songs require the singer to sound uneducated. This is not so different from conventions followed by such poets as Robert Burns, D. H. Lawrence, Paul Dunbar, Rudyard Kipling, or Wendell Berry, who in their poetry capture the voices of working people who do not speak standard English. Most know Burns's "The best laid schemes o' mice an' men / Gang aft a-gley."[6] His "Tam o'Shanter" begins:

When chapman billies* leave the street,	*pedlar fellows
And drouthy* neebors neebors meet,	*thirsty
As market days are wearing late,	
An' folk begin to tak the gate;*	*road
While we sit bousing at the nappy,*	*strong ale
An' getting fou* and unco* happy	*drunk, very
We think na on the lang Scots miles,	
The mosses, waters, slaps,* and stiles,	*gaps (in walls)
That lie between us and our hame,	
Where sits our sulky sullen dame,	
Gathering her brows like gathering storm,	
Nursing her wrath to keep it warm.[7]	

That unhappy, angry wife waiting at home for her drunken husband is a subject familiar to country music fans. D. H. Lawrence, who grew up in the coal-mining district of northern England, begins "A Collier's Wife," one of his many dialect poems, with these lines:

Somebody's knockin' at th' door
Mother, come down an' see!
—I's think it's nobbut a beggar;
Say I'm busy.

It's not a beggar, mother; hark
How 'ard 'e knocks!
—Eh, tha'rt a mard-arsed kid,
'Ell gie thee socks[8]

When looking at written lyrics of country songs, as in these dialectal poems, the apostrophe to indicate contractions, particularly indicating that it is "knock-in'" and not "knocking," is standard fare. Classical ballads in non-standard English, important in the history of the development of country music, are often printed as poems in anthologies and school textbooks with the dialects recorded graphically ("Barbara Allen" or "Twa Corbies," for example). A requirement of the country music form is, thus, some non-standard forms. "You and I have just walked up on it. Feels good, doesn't it?" simply would not be an appropriate replacement for "Me and you girl we just walked up on it. / Feels good, don't it?" nor would "If I Were a Teddy Bear" for "If I Was a Teddy Bear" or "Jolene and I" for "Me and Jolene."

Of course, some country music songs do use standard English and do not adopt this colloquial, lowbrow voice. Take Garth Brooks's "The River," for example. He begins:

> You know a dream is like a river, ever changing as it flows.
> And a dreamer's just a vessel that must follow where it goes.

He maintains standard English and develops the extended comparison of life as a river:

> Like a bird upon the wind, these waters are my sky.
> I'll never reach my destination if I never try,
> So I will sail my vessel 'til the river runs dry.

Lee Ann Womack's "I Hope You Dance" is another example of the lyricist using standard English. The songwriter chooses, based on the type of song, whether to adopt the dialect form or more standard usage.

Another notable practice of country lyricists that some highbrow listeners disdain is the use of clichés. These lyricists love clichés. In one short stanza of "Till My Dyin' Day," Brooks and Dunn manage to work in three:

> I'm gonna walk on the road less traveled
> Yeah, sit tall in the saddle
> Know when I pick my battles

Country music lyrics abound with such phrases as "a row to hoe," "ain't worth a dime," "like a moth to a flame," "through thick and thin," "tied around her little finger," "a month of Sundays," "the sky's the limit," "right on the money," "short end of the stick," and "till my dyin' day." While these expressions would seem to be metaphors which add no originality or special touch to the lyrics, country music lyricists prefer to give the expected phrase and sometimes delight in word play that creates striking effects with the clichés, as in Garth Brooks's "Friends in Low Places" or Josh Thompson's "Working hard all week to put beer on the table."

Some of the clichés turn into puns which used to be held in higher esteem than they are now. Elizabethan poets, including William Shakespeare, Philip Sidney, and Ben Jonson, delighted in punning and distinguished three kinds: antanaclasis, paronomasia, and syllepsis. Country music lyricists heavily use all three, whereas contemporary literary poets occasionally use antanaclasis and syllepsis. Tim McGraw sings, "There's bars on the corners and bars on the heart," a clear example of antanaclasis, repetition of a word in two different senses. Toby Keith says, "I'm not as good as I *once* was, but I'm as good *once* as I ever was," and, "a high *maintenance* woman don't want no *maintenance* man." Kenny Chesney sings of going into a bar and asking for "the good stuff." The bartender asserts he won't find it in there, playing on a double meaning of "good stuff." To the bartender, the "good stuff" is holding his new baby, remembering a gift of pearls he gave his wife when their son married, wearing a "Grandpa" T-shirt, and holding his wife's hand when she died. He asserts: "Yeah, Man, that's *the good stuff.*"

Paranomasia is a pun using words alike in sound but different in meaning; examples would be "Overnight Male" and the humorous line, "You can't have your Kate and Edith, too." Probably the most common type of pun is syllepsis, where a word is understood differently in relation to two or more other words that it modifies or governs. When we first hear George Strait say, "She let herself go," we think she is broken-hearted over losing her lover and has neglected herself, but the song goes on to show that she "let herself go" in a different sense. She let herself go on her first blind date and let herself buy a brand new car and drive to the beach he had always thought was too far. She "Let herself go on a singles cruise, / To Vegas once, then to Honolulu. / Let herself go to New York City." Michael Peterson sings, "She's not too good to be true," and turns the phrase to say, "She's just too good to be true to you." George Strait misses his lady in "A roundabout way [. . .] 'round about the time that midnight rolls around." When Randy Travis uses the transition phrase "on the other hand," he gives it a twist to say:

> But on the other hand, there's a golden band
> To remind me of someone who would not understand.
> On one hand I could stay and be your loving man
> But the reason I must go is on the other hand.

The line between puns and creative ambiguity, a highly valued aspect in modern poetry, is often a precarious one.

Puns are only one rhetorical scheme used effectively by country music lyricists. Poets have manipulated the language for special effects since the first scops entertained an Old English audience. The sonneteers of Queen Elizabeth's court in the sixteenth century practiced the courtly skill of writing lyric poetry, including hundreds of sonnets in sequences like Sidney's *Astrophil and Stella* or Spenser's *Amoretti* or Shakespeare's collection of 154 sonnets. Back then schoolboys learned over 200 tropes and schemes in their study of Latin poetry and prose, practiced the patterns, and left a legacy for poets of the future. Today's students still learn simile, metaphor, parallelism, oxymoron, onomatopoeia, and alliteration, maybe metonymy and synecdoche. In short, there are patterns of language we expect in lyric poetry. These patterns are easily recognizable in country music lyrics as well. Similes and metaphors abound. Jimmy Buffett in "It's Five O'Clock Somewhere" asserts, "the work day passes like molasses." Garth Brooks asserts, "Lord, I need that little woman / Like the crops need the rain." Randy Travis says his love is "honest as a robin on a springtime windowsill." Brooks and Dunn sing,

> Like a fool playin' with fire . . .
> Like a slave to blind desire
> Oh, I keep hangin' on.

Their "My Baby's Everything I Love" has simile built on simile. Within five lines are four similes: "like a honky tonk," "like a neon light," "like a punch in a barroom fight," "like a smooth shot of whiskey." They go on to enumerate: "My baby's like a Coupe Deville . . . like a trip to town . . . like a country song . . . like a jukebox rocking," with details about each comparison. They conclude, "I'm after her like a hound on a rabbit / She's got it all and I got to have it."

Lonestar likes metaphors. In "I'm Already There" they sing:

> I'm the sunshine in your hair
> I'm the shadow on the ground
> I'm the whisper in the wind

And conclude:

> I'm the beat in your heart
> I'm the moonlight shining down.

The most striking metaphors go throughout a song, creating what a poet would call a conceit. In Garth Brooks's "The Dance" the comparison of life with her to a dance is clear throughout: "Yes, my life, it's better left to chance. / I could have missed the pain, / but I'd have had to miss the dance." In his "Two of a Kind, Workin' on a Full House," the playing card image pervades:

> Yea, she my *lady luck;*
> Hey, I'm her *wild card man.*
> Together we're buildin' up a real *hot hand.*

A classic number is George Jones's "The Race Is On," where he uses imagery from the horse track to describe his broken love affair:

> Well, the race is on and here comes pride up the backstretch.
> Heartaches are going to the inside.
> My tears are holding back tryin' not to fall.

Almost every line in the song has a racetrack image. He continues:

> My heart's out of the running, true love scratched for another's sake,
> The race is on and it looks like heartache and the winner loses all.

Brooks and Dunn use Christian imagery to talk about a secular love situation in "Brand New Man":

> I saw the light
> I've been baptized

He has been baptized by "the fire" in her touch and "the flame" in her eyes and asserts:

> I'm born to love again,
> I'm a brand new man.

Josh Turner piles on the fire images when talking about his love in "Firecracker," particularly in the chorus. He compares her to dynamite:

> When I light the fuse I gotta get back quick.
> You gotta be careful with a dynamite stick.

Then he compares her to particular kinds of fireworks:

> And she packs a punch like a Roman candle.
> She's a pack of black cats in a red paper wrapper.

An effective use of synecdoche (using a part of something to represent the whole) can be found in Dierks Bentley's assertion, "I was thinkin' 'bout a *little white tank top,* / Sittin' right there in the middle by me," in "What Was I

Thinkin'?" That "little white tank top" was not literally what he was thinking about; it represents a more complicated whole.

On the sentence level, country music lyricists habitually use some rather sophisticated rhetorical schemes. A favorite is alliteration, the repetition of initial or medial sounds in two or more adjacent words. Jo Dee Messina piles on the "l" alliteration in "Lesson in Leavin'," a remake of Dottie West's '80s hit, when she sings, "It's like you to love 'em and leave 'em / Just like you loved me and left me. / It's like you to do that sort of thing." Garth Brooks talks about the "mud and the muck" in "The Rodeo," and Tim McGraw describes "Where the Green Grass Grows." Another favorite rhetorical scheme is anaphora, the repetition of the same word or group of words at the beginning of successive clauses. Shania Twain tells her lover:

> Don't be stupid. You know I love ya.
> Don't be ridiculous. You know I need ya.
> Don't be absurd. You know I want ya.

Tim McGraw's "I wents" and repeated "I's" are another excellent example:

> I went skydiving
> I went Rocky Mountain climbing
> I went 2.7 seconds on a bull named Fu Man Chu

He shifts to "And I" in the next two lines:

> And I loved deeper and I spoke sweeter
> And I gave forgiveness I'd been denying.

Another example is the chorus of Alan Jackson's "Who's Cheatin' Who?" a remake of the 1980 #1 hit by Charly McClain:

> Who's cheatin' who, who's being true,
> Who don't even care anymore?
> Who's doin' right to someone tonight

A particularly poetic Alan Jackson song is "If Love Was a River." He begins each stanza with a different supposition: "If love was" a river, a mountain, a firefly, a party, or a fast train, what would she do? In the poetic "The Firefly's Song" he talks about "a young man's voice / a young man's heart and a young man's choice."

Sometimes the anaphora is combined with other schemes such as epistrophe, which is the repetition of the same word or group of words at the ends of successive clauses. A popular variation is to compose various stanzas that logically end with the same phrases. Examples are Tim McGraw's "Don't Take the Girl" and "My Next Thirty Years," George Strait's "The Best Day," and Brooks and Dunn's "Red Dirt Road." The trick is to compose the lyrics so that the last line can be used in each stanza. Edmund Spenser perfected this technique in his poem to his bride celebrating their wedding in 1594, "Epithalamion." He has each stanza of his narrative poem flow into the same final line: "That all the woods may answer, and your echo ring."⁹ In "Don't Take the Girl" Tim McGraw uses the same technique and relates three separate events: his dad taking him fishing when he was eight years old, a jump to ten years later when he is dating the girl he didnot want to go fishing with earlier and is mugged outside the movie theatre, and then five years later when her life is threatened in childbirth. Each time he pleads, "please don't take the girl." The five stanzas of his "My Next Thirty Years" all end with "in my next thirty years." In George Strait's "The Best Day" the refrain, "This is the best day of my life," comes after stanzas about the young boy, again, going fishing with his dad, then the fifteen- year-old son getting an old Corvette as his first car, and finally, the son getting married. Brooks and Dunn have each stanza of "That Red Dirt Road" end in "that red dirt road." Diamond Rio in "Unbelievable" use epistrophe on the word level by exaggerating the repetition of ending syllables for a dramatic effect. They repeat the *–able* ending thirty-four times, using eleven different words, and the *–ent* ending eight times, using four different words:

> She's so *kissable, huggable, loveable, unbelievable*;
> She ain't *typical*; she ain't *predictable*; she's *available*; It's a *miracle* . . .
> [She's] so *kissable, huggable, loveable, unbelievable*.

They repeat the *–able* chorus five more times.

Three other classical rhetorical schemes used often by country music lyricists are polyptoton, antithesis, and antimetabole. Polyptoton often accompanies alliteration because it designates the repetition of the words from the same root close together. Some titles provide good examples, for example "One of Those *Nights Tonight*" by Lorrie Morgan, and "*Lonely* Won't Leave Me *Alone*," by Trace Adkins. Antithesis is the juxtaposition of opposites, a popular device, as this list of examples demonstrates:

> "A little *less talk* and a little *more action*" (Toby Keith)
> "*Live* like you were *dying*" (Tim McGraw)
> "*Beautiful Mess*" (Diamond Rio)
> "I wish I didn't know *now*, what I didn't know *then*" (Toby Keith)
> "Much too *young* to be this damn *old*" (Garth Brooks)
> "I got the *jeep*, she got the *palace*" (Mark Chesnutt)

"Wanna go *left* where the world goes *right*" (Lorrie Morgan)

"*Man*, I feel like a *woman*" (Shania Twain)

"Gimme just *one more last* chance" (Vince Gill)

"I'm *old* enough to know better, but I'm still too *young* to care" (Wade Hayes)

"Spirit of a *boy*, wisdom of a *man*" (Randy Travis)

The emotional power of putting opposites together in a striking way probably accounts for the appeal of antithesis. Antimetabole appeals because it is such an attention-getter. It involves the repetition of words in successive clauses that are in reverse order, an xyyx pattern:

"I treat that *bad woman good*. / Lord, I need a *good woman bad*" (Josh Turner)

"You can take the *girl* out of *the honky tonk* / but you can't take *the honky tonk* out of the *girl*" (Brooks & Dunn)

"I'd be *doing* what I *love* and *loving* what I *do*" (Clay Walker)

"She's *done* what she *should* / *Should* she *do* what she dares?" (Reba McEntire)

"I'm *drinking* because I'm *alone*, and I'm *alone* because I'm *drinking*" (Tim McGraw)

"I've been *fooled* by a *feeling*, now I'm *feeling* like a *fool*" (Barbara Mandrell)

This device makes a good memorable "hook" for a song, but it can create a groaner like "I'd rather have a *bottle in front of me* than a *frontal lobotomy*" (Randy Hanzlick).

Country music songwriters deserve credit for their inventiveness and facility with the language. The lyrics use the same rhetorical devices as some of the greatest poets of the English language. Actually, there exist in many country songs complex rhetorical devices and sophisticated linguistic acrobatics. The characters created in the songs attract fans, and these characters have to be taken seriously. As Pam Tillis sings about her lover in "Maybe It Was Memphis":

Read about you in a Faulkner novel;

Met you once in a Williams play;

Heard about you in a country love song.

The same characters that people highbrow literature populate country music lyrics, and country music lyricists use the same poetic devices as literary poets.

Notes

1. See:

Peterson, Richard A., and Roger M. Kern. "Changing Highbrow Taste: From Snob to Omnivore." *American Sociological Review* 61. Oct. 1996. 900–907.

Bryson, Bethany. "What about the Univores? Musical Dislikes and Group-Based Identity Construction among Americans with Low Levels of Education." *Poetics* 25. 1997. 141–56.

Zill, N., and J. Robinson. "Name That Tune." *American Demographics*. Aug. 1994. 22–27.

Malone, Bill C. "Don't' Get above Your Raisin': Country Music and the Southern Working Class." Chicago: University of Illinois Press, 2005.

2. "2008 Consumer Profile." Recording Industry Association of America. 10 Feb. 2010. www.riaa.com.

3. Taylor, Paul, and Richard Morin. "Forty Years after Woodstock, A Gentler Generation Gap." Pew Social and Demographic Trends. 12 Aug. 2009. www.pewsocialtrends.org.

4. These poems can all be found in *The Seagull Reader: Poems*. 2nd ed. Ed. Joseph Kelly. New York: W. W. Norton, 2009.

5. Fussell, Paul. *Poetic Meter & Poetic Form*. Rev. ed. New York: McGraw-Hill, 1979.

6. Burns, Robert. "To A Mouse, On Turning Up in Her Nest with the Plough, November 1785." *The Wadsworth Anthology of Poetry*. Ed. Jay Parini. Stamford, CT: Wadsworth, 2005. 1345–47.

7. Burns, Robert. "Tam O'Shanter." *The Norton Anthology of English Literature*, Vol. 2. 8th ed. Ed. Stephen Greenblatt, et al. New York: W. W. Norton, 2006. 139.

8. Lawrence, D. H. "A Collier's Wife." *The Selected Poems of D. H. Lawrence*. Ed. Keith Sagar. London: Penguin, 1989. 35–36.

9. Spenser, Edmund. "Epithalamion." *Amoretti and Epithalamion*. Whitefish, MT: Kessinger, 2004.

Works Cited

Adkins, Trace. "Lonely Won't Leave Me Alone." *Big Time*. Written by Jody Alan Sweet and Mary Danna. Capitol, 1998.

Bentley, Dierks. "What Was I Thinkin'?" *Dierks Bentley*. Written by Deric Ruttan, Brett Beavers, and Dierks Bentley. Capitol Nashville, 2003.

Brooks and Dunn. "Believer." *Red Dirt Road*. Written by Ronnie Dunn and Craig Wiseman. Arista Nashville, 2003.

———. "Brand New Man." *Brand New Man*. Written by Kix Brooks, Ronnie Dunn, and Don Cook. Arista, 1991.

———. "Feels Good, Don't It." *Red Dirt Road*. Written by Kix Brooks, Ronnie Dunn, and Mark Wright. Arista Nashville, 2003.

———. "My Baby's Everything I Love." *Red Dirt Road*. Written by Kix Brooks, Ronnie Dunn, and Craig Wiseman. Arista Nashville, 2003.

———. "Red Dirt Road." *Red Dirt Road*. Written by Kix Brooks and Ronnie Dunn. Arista Nashville, 2003.

———. "Till My Dyin' Day." *Red Dirt Road*. Written by Kix Brooks and Paul Nelson. Arista Nashville, 2003.

———. "You Can't Take the Honky Tonk Out of the Girl." *Red Dirt Road*. Written by Bob DiPiero and Bart Allmand. Arista Nashville, 2003.

Brooks, Garth. "The Dance." *Garth Brooks*. Written by Tony Arata. Capitol Nashville, 1990.

———. "Friends in Low Places." *No Fences*. Written by DeWayne Blackwell, Earl Bud Lee, and Garth Brooks. Capitol, 1990.

———. "Much Too Young (To Feel This Damn Old)." *Garth Brooks*. Written by Randy Taylor and Garth Brooks. Capitol, 1989.

———. "The River." *Ropin' the Wind*. Written by Victoria Shaw and Garth Brooks. Liberty, 1992.

———. "Rodeo." *Ropin' the Wind*. Written by Lary Bastian. Liberty, 1992.

———. "Two of a Kind, Workin' on a Full House." *No Fences*. Written by Dennis Robbins, Bobby Boyd, and Warren Dale Haynes. Capitol, 1990.

Buffett, Jimmy, and Alan Jackson. "It's Five O'Clock Somewhere." *It's Five O'Clock Somewhere (Single)*. Written by Jim "Moose" Brown and Don Rollins. Arista Nashville, 2003.

Chesney, Kenny. "The Good Stuff." *No Shoes, No Shirt, No Problems*. Written by Craig Wiseman and Jim Collins. BNA, 2002.

Chestnutt, Mark. "Goin' Through the Big D." *What a Way to Live*. Written by Mark Wright, Ronnie Rogers, and John Wright. Decca, 1994.

Diamond Rio. "Beautiful Mess." *Completely*. Written by Shane Minor, Clay Mills, and Sonny LeMaire. Arista Nashville, 2002.

———. "Unbelievable." *Unbelievable*. Written by Al Anderson and Jeffrey Steele. Arista Nashville, 1998.

Gill, Vince. "One More Last Chance." *I Still Believe in You*. Written by Vince Gill and Gary Nicholson. MCA Nashville, 1992.

Hanzlick, Randy. "I'd Rather Have a Bottle in Front of Me than a Frontal Lobotomy."

Hayes, Wayne. "Old Enough to Know Better." *Old Enough to Know Better*. Written by Wade Hayes and Chick Rains. Columbia Nashville, 1995.

Jackson, Alan. "The Firefly's Song." *Like Red on a Rose*. Written by R. L. Castleman. Arista Nashville, 2006.

———. "If Love Was a River." *What I Do*. Written by Adam Wright and Shannon Wright. Arista Nashville, 2004.

———. "Who's Cheatin' Who?" *Everything I Love*. Written by Jerry Hayes. Arista Nashville, 1997.

Jones, George. "The Race Is On." *The Race Is On*. Written by George Jones and Don Rollins. United Artists, 1964.

Keith, Toby. "As Good as I Once Was." *Honkytonk University*. Written by Toby Keith and Scotty Emerick. DreamWorks, 2005.

———. "High Maintenance Woman." *Big Dog Daddy*. Written by Toby Keith, Danny Simpson, and Tim Wilson. Show Dog Nashville, 2007.

———. "I Love This Bar." *Shock'n Y'all*. Written by Toby Keith and Scotty Emerick. DreamWorks, 2003.

———. "I Wanna Talk About Me." *Pull My Chain*. Written by Bobby Braddock. DreamWorks, 2001.

———. "A Little Less Talk and a Lot More Action." *Toby Keith*. Polygram/Mercury, 1993.

———. "Wish I Didn't Know Now." *Toby Keith*. Written by Toby Keith. PolyGram/Mercury, 1994.

Lonestar. "I'm Already There." *I'm Already There*. Written by Gary Baker, Frank J. Myers, and Richie McDonald. BNA, 2001.

Mandrell, Barbara. "Fooled by a Feeling." *Just for the Record*. MCA Nashville, 1979.

Mattea, Kathy. "Where Have You Been?" *Willow in the Wind*. Written by Jon Vezner and Don Henry. Mercury Records, 1989.

McEntire, Reba. "Is There Life Out There?" *For My Broken Heart*. Written by Susan Longacre and Rick Giles. MCA Nashville, 1991.

McGraw, Tim. "Don't Take the Girl." *Not a Moment Too Soon*. Written by Craig Martin and Larry W. Johnson. Curb, 1994.

———. "Live Like You Were Dying." *Live Like You Were Dying*. Written by Tim Nichols and Craig Wiseman. Curb, 2004.

———. "Where the Green Grass Grows." *Everywhere*. Written by Jess Leary and Craige Wiseman. Curb, 1997.

———. "My Next Thirty Years." *A Place in the Sun*. Written by Phil Vassar. Curb, 1999.

Messina, Jo Dee. "Lesson in Leavin'." *I'm Alright*. Written by Randy Goodrum and Brent Maher. Curb, 1998.

Montgomery, John Michael. "Sold (The Grundy County Auction Incident)." *John Michael Montgomery*. Written by Richard Fagan and Robb Royer. Atlantic, 1995.

Morgan, Craig. "That's What I Love About Sunday." *My Kind of Livin'*. Written by Adam Dorsey and Mark Narmore. Broken Bow, 2005.

Morgan, Lorrie. "One of Those Nights Tonight." *Shakin' Things Up*. Written by Susan Longacre and Rick Giles. BNA, 1997.

Peterson, Michael. "Too Good to Be True." *Michael Peterson*. Written by Michael Peterson and Gene Pistilli. Reprise, 1997.

Raye, Collin. "Love, Me." *All I Can Be*. Written by Skip Ewing and Max T. Barnes. Epic, 1991.

Rogers, Kenny. "Coward of the County." *Kenny*. Written by Roger Bowling and Billy Ed Wheeler. United Artists Group, 1979.

———. "The Gambler." *The Gambler*. Written by Don Schlitz. United Artists Group, 1978.

Statler Brothers. "You Can't Have Your Kate and Edith, Too." *Big Country Hits*. Columbia, 1967.

Strait, George. "The Best Day." *Latest Greatest Straitest Hits*. Written by Dean Dillon and Carson Chamberlain. MCA Nashville, 2000.

———. "Overnight Male." *Pure Country*. Written by Richard Fagan, Kim Williams, and Ron Harbin. MCA, 1992.

———. "Roundabout Way." *Latest Greatest Straitest Hits*. Written by Steve Dean and Wil Nance. MCA Nashville, 2000.

———. "She Let Herself Go." *Somewhere Down in Texas*. Written by Dean Dillon and Kerry Kurt Phillips. MCA Nashville, 2005.

Thompson, Josh. "Beer on the Table." *Way Out Here*. Written by Ken Johnson, Josh Thompson, and Andi Zack. Columbia Nashville, 2010.

Tillis, Pam. "Maybe It Was Memphis." *Put Yourself in My Place*. Written by Michael Anderson. Arista Nashville, 1991.

Travis, Randy. "Deeper Than the Holler." *Old 8x10*. Written by Paul Overstreet and Don Schlitz. Warner Bros., 1988.

———. "On the Other Hand." *Storms of Life*. Written by Paul Overstreet and Don Schlitz. Warner Bros., 1986.

———. "Spirit of a Boy, Wisdom of a Man." *You and You Alone*. Written by Trey Bruce and Glen Burtnik. DreamWorks, 1998.

Turner, Josh. "Firecracker." *Everything Is Fine*. Written by Shawn Camp, Pat McLaughlin, and Josh Turner. MCA Nashville, 2007.

Twain, Shania. "Don't Be Stupid (You Know I Love You)." *Come on Over*. Written by Robert John "Mutt" Lange, and Shania Twain. Mercury Nashville, 1997.

———. "Man, I Feel Like a Woman." *Come on Over*. Written by Robert John "Mutt" Lange and Shania Twain. Mercury Nashville, 1997.

Walker, Clay. "If I Could Make a Living." *If I Could Make a Living*. Written by Alan Jackson, Keith Stegall, and Roger Murrah. Giant, 1994.

Wills, Mark. "19 Somethin'." *Greatest Hits*. Written by David Lee and Chris DuBois. Mercury Nashville, 2002.

Womack, Lee Ann. "I Hope You Dance." *I Hope You Dance*. Written by Mark D. Sanders and Tia Sillers. MCA Nashville, 2000.

SIMILARITIES AND DIFFERENCES BETWEEN SONG LYRICS AND POETRY

PAT PATTISON

*Are songwriters our great American poets, as some fans and music crit-
ics have proposed? If the genres are distinct, what criterion distinguishes
each? This essay explores the complex question of how contemporary poetry is similar to and different from contemporary song lyrics in form,
content, and purpose. Pat Pattison, who holds an M.A. in literary criticism, has published numerous books on lyric writing, and is a songwriting professor at Berklee College of Music, offers his perspective on this
complex topic.*

Since the invention of the printing press, poetry, once spoken and performed, has been delivered mainly to the eye. Lyrics are delivered mainly to the ear. Many consequences follow from this simple fact.

One simple consequence is that the poet can depend on the reader being able to stop and go back, even to look up words while reading the poem. A
lyricist can't.

Since readers can pause and continue reading at their own pace, the poet can
use quite complex language: less familiar words, ambiguity, multiple meanings,
intricate metaphor. The density of poetic language is a poet's way of "harmoniz-
ing" ideas. Like putting chords under your words, it adds a new level of emotion.
Poetry eats the whole animal and says the most it can with the least amount of
words. Phrasing, form, and poetic meter add to this "musical" underpinning. A
good example of this is "After Long Silence" by William Butler Yeats:

> Speech after long silence; it is right,
> All other lovers being estranged or dead,
> Unfriendly lamplight hid under its shade,
> The curtains drawn upon unfriendly night,

> That we descant and yet again descant
> Upon the supreme theme of Art and Song:
> Bodily decrepitude is wisdom; young
> We loved each other and were ignorant.[1]

This poem has lots of nifty words. Just look at "descant." Why not say "talk about?" There are several definitions in the dictionary that provide depth and color to the idea "talk about." Etymologically, *descant* means a voice (cantus) above or removed from others. It also means a lengthy discourse on a subject; or a counterpoint melody sung or played above the theme. One dictionary defined it as: "To discuss at length; To sing or play a descant."

"That we descant and yet again descant": These multiple meanings give texture to the idea, creating tone and depth, just as chords and melody would in a song. The language resonates on several levels, creating something akin to harmonic overtones.

The rhyme scheme adds another undertone. There are two "In Memoriam" stanzas, rhyming abba cddc, using consonance rhyme for the inner lines, dead/shade, song/young. The "In Memoriam" stanza is taken from Alfred Tennyson's poem of the same name, a eulogy. The form is a fitting choice for this descant on ageing. The way this rhyme scheme moves creates a feeling of longing all by itself (motion creates emotion), and adds that emotion to the rest of the poem.

The language of a lyric can be simpler and more straightforward. There'll be plenty of extra color given by the notes that join the words, their relationships to other notes, and the rhythm they embody. If you think of melodies as nouns, then chords—the textures that color them—are the adjectives. Rhythm is the verb. It activates the melody and harmony—it supplies the action. So the words themselves get a lot of help, as in the following example, "My Girl" by Smokey Robinson:

> I got sunshine on a cloudy day
> When it's cold outside, I've got the month of May
> I guess you'd say, "What could make me feel this way?"

You can't help yourself. You hear the whole thing in your head. It all happens at once: not only the instruments and melody, but an expressive human voice.

There's a lot going on, and it's one time through. In most cases, there is no stopping, no looking. No checking the dictionary. Even if we could, we usually wouldn't want to stop ourselves. The pleasure is in the continuous movement forward.

So, the more complicated a lyric's language, the more it limits its audience to those who understand complicated language easily. Not a majority. Take a look, for example, at the Genesis album, *Selling England by the Pound*. It's rife with allusions and quotes from Eliot's *The Waste Land*. Steely Dan's song "Home at Last" is an oblique retelling of the story of Odysseus and the Sirens. The lyrics beg for explication—if you're interested enough to explicate—limiting the audience to those who care. Many people simply move on, not having been allowed entry on the first listen. For those who stay awhile, it may be for other reasons. If the guitarist or the singer is good, perhaps oblique lyrics will be ignored or put on the back burner while the singer wails and the guitarist flashes lick after lick.

It's a matter of choice: how deep do you want the lyrics to go? Most often, it's a trade-off: if the lyric is dense, the music is simple, and conversely. Songwriter "poets" like Bob Dylan and Leonard Cohen generally use pretty straightforward melody and harmony. Usually, something's gotta give: if everything is dense, nothing much is clear and there's limited communication—or at least, communication to a narrower audience.

Of course, the matter of density also affects poets. From pop poets like Rod McKuen to the density of T. S. Eliot or Ezra Pound, choice of language limits and determines audience. Between poets and lyricists is more a difference of degree than kind. Some lyrics may use more complicated language than some poems. Some poems may use simpler language than some lyrics. But still, poems must stand on their own ground. Lyrics have extra modifiers to color their words.

Another distinction between songs and poems is that since the end of a line in poetry is a visual cue, a poet can end a line, yet let the grammatical meaning continue on to the next line, creating tension, but not confusion. An example of this is from "Birches" by Robert Frost:

> You may see their trunks arching in the woods
> Years afterwards, trailing their leaves on the ground
> Like girls on hands and knees that throw their hair
> Before them over their heads to dry in the sun.

The tension between line three's ending and the idea continuing into the next line feels like the girls are actually tossing their hair.

In a song, the end of the lyric line usually has a sonic cue—the end of a melodic phrase. Because the song is aimed at the ear, if a lyricist tries to carry a thought into the next melodic phrase, it usually creates confusion, since there is a disconnect between the melodic roadmap and grammatical structure. I've arranged these lines from "Eddie My Love" by Aaron Collins to match the musical phrasing:

> Eddie please write [pause]
> me one line
> Tell me your love is still only mine

Or take a look at this example from "I Still Believe" by Doug Johnson, again arranged according to the melodic phrases:

> Sometimes it's easy and sometimes it's not
> Sometimes I can't think of one thing we've got [pause]
> In common to keep us from falling apart

The result is almost comical. The melodic phrases give the ear its roadmap. The lyric phrases lose their way.

Because we can see lines on a page, poetry is able to counterpoint line against phrase. Because we only hear songs, the marriage of musical phrase with lyric phrase is essential.

With the recent movement toward performance poetry in spoken word and slams, poetry is once again being directed to the ear rather than the eye, where the grammatical phrase, once again, rules the roost. Like prose, it is grammatically driven, and where the natural phrase ends, it ends. When you don't see lines, counterpointing line against phrase is no longer a compositional option, and we are dealing with a poetry of phrases.

The fundamental unit of composition for prose is the grammatical phrase, building into sentences, paragraphs, sections etc. In slams and spoken word, the phrases build a flow, and are often done with rhythm and syncopation, utilizing the opportunities that a performance by a human voice can give: tone of voice, stopping and starting, extending syllables, modulating pitches—in short, many of the things that the music of the song provides the lyric. Both are ear-directed.

In contrast, poetry uses two fundamental units of composition: the grammatical phrase (tied to meaning) and the line (independent of meaning). It is made for the eye as well as the ear. It is a poetry of both lines and phrases.

These two fundamental units of composition for a poem—the grammatical phrase and the line—are both dependent on the page; a few consequences occur simply because a song lyric is often solely a sonic event. Because a song lyric is directed to the ear, rhyme is important since it provides a roadmap for the ear by showing relationships between lines, creating forward motion, creating either stability or instability in sections, and telling the ear where sections end.

Though rhyme is common in poetry, it is less important, since the reader can see where a line or a section ends. Even when poems rhyme, the rhymes don't necessarily announce a phrase's end or a section's end, as in Percy Bysshe Shelley's "Ode to the West Wind":

> O wild West Wind, thou breath of Autumn's being,
> Thou, from whose unseen presence the leaves dead
> Are driven, like ghosts from an enchanter fleeing,

Yellow, and black, and pale, and hectic red,
Pestilence-stricken multitudes: O thou,
Who chariotest to their dark wintry bed

The winged seeds, where they lie cold and low,
Each like a corpse within its grave, until
Thine azure sister of the Spring shall blow

Her clarion o'er the dreaming earth, and fill
(Driving sweet buds like flocks to feed in air)
With living hues and odours plain and hill:

Wild spirit, which art moving everywhere;
Destroyer and preserver; hear, oh, hear!

Clearly, the compositional strategies of the poet differ dramatically from the lyricist's. The vast majority of poems, whether fixed form, blank verse, or free verse, are linear journeys, moving from idea to idea, line to line, until the end. Except in rare cases, such as the rondel, poetry's compositional strategy does not use repetition of content. Older ballade poetry sometimes uses repetition, but note that it was performed, and directed to the ear rather than the eye.

Lyrics depend heavily on repeated content, usually refrains or choruses. The development of the lyric's ideas must take account of the repeated sections, and in the ideal case, transform or deepen the meaning of that same content each time we hear it. Watch the phrase "What'll I do" from Irving Berlin's song gain weight in each section because of the focus each section provides. First, the thought of distance from you; second, the danger you might be finding someone new; and finally, the heartbreaking news that our love is over:

What'll I do
When you are far away
And I am blue,
What'll I do?
What'll I do
When I am wond'ring who
Is kissing you,
What'll I do?
What'll I do
With just a photograph
To tell my troubles to,
When I'm alone
With only dreams of you

That won't come true,
What'll I do?[2]

Another practical concern that is often overlooked is the fact that a lyricist has extremely limited space to work with. Normal commercial songs, lasting from 2½ to 3½ minutes, limit space dramatically. A commercial song can't be too long nor too short. Not counting the repeated choruses or refrains, the average commercial song contains twelve to twenty lines. There are, of course, some exceptions, but not many: "McArthur Park" (Jimmy Webb), "Vincent" (Don McLean), "Scenes from an Italian Restaurant" (Billy Joel), "Paradise by Dashboard Light" (Jim Steinman). Few long songs have commercial radio success; they take up too much time that could be spent making revenue by playing commercials. This space limitation no doubt affects, to some degree, choice of topic. Of course, that's equally true for fixed poetic forms: sonnet, terza rima, haiku, etc. But for the most part, the poem can be as long or short as it needs to be.

Lyrics are far more dependent on regular rhythm than poems, since a lyric's rhythm is joined to musical rhythm. A regular lyric rhythm prepares the words to snuggle into the alternating strong/weak/strong/weak patterns of 4/4 time. Or the strong/weak/weak pattern of all the triple times, 3/4, 6/8, and 12/8. Because it can extend a syllable's length or syncopate its regular lyric rhythm, music can transform what would be mind-numbingly regular, if spoken, into an interesting journey.

Great poetry contains its own theme and variation, setting a rhythm and syncopating against it. Look at the first two lines of John Keats's "Ode On a Grecian Urn":

Thou still unravished bride of quietness　　- / - / - / - / - -
Thou foster child of silence and slow time　- / - / - / - - / /

The first four feet of line one are strictly iambic (- /, or weak-strong). The last foot is pyrrhic (- -, or weak-weak), creating a diminuendo that supports "quietness." The first three feet of line two are strictly iambic. The fourth foot is pyrrhic, supporting "silence," while the final spondee (/ /, or strong-strong) slows the line down, reinforcing the slowness of time. Neat.

And look at the rhythmic strategy of "After Long Silence" by William Butler Yeats: rhythm is again at work creating additional texture and making its own commentary. The poem is written on an iambic pentameter pulse, using substitutions expressively. In the first three lines, the rhythm seems to be shaking itself awake—clearing its throat after long silence: "Spéech áfter lóng sílence; it is right." This nine-syllable line has a defective first foot, missing the unstressed syllable of the iamb, followed by a trochee (/ -, or strong-weak), a spondee, and a pyrrhic before the final iamb. None of it moves forward. It creaks from age and disuse. None of the feet feel like substitutions, since a pulse has yet to be established:

> Áll óther lóvers béing estránged or deád.

After an opening spondee, the rhythm begins to move iambically, though "being" threatens to feel like two syllables, disturbing the iambic motion:

> Unfriéndly lámplight híd únder its sháde.

The iambic pattern has been established by the time we reach "under," a marvelous trochaic substitution that creates the feeling of being hidden beneath the shade. It interrupts the iambic motion at a particularly sensitive position—the fourth foot. It's hard to hear the last foot as an iamb, so the pattern is broken and must be re-established by the next line.

> The cúrtains dráwn upon unfriéndly night.

"Upon" is probably best scanned as a pyrrhic substitution. This is close, but we have yet to feel a perfectly iambic line. And so now we are prepared to arrive at the rhythmic tour de force of the poem:

> That wé descánt and yét agáin descánt.

This rhythmic release into the smooth iambic actually feels like we can't stop ourselves from talking. The rhythm itself, from the first line to this line, would have had the same effect without using words at all, just tapping it with a stick on a table. We would feel the fifth line release and push smoothly forward. The rhythm carries its own message. It assists the words.

Yeats meant to do all this. It is part of being a poet—to understand how to use the whole of language—its sounds, its rhythms, its stacked meanings. It's not simply a matter of jotting your feelings and insights down in chopped up sentences. Poetry is com-position, from "posito/positare—to place or arrange; to position" and "com"—a prefix meaning "together, in relation to." Art is composed—it places things together for a reason—it creates, in Aristotle's words, a "unity." Everything working together.

Because a poem stands on its own ground, making its own rhythm and music, setting great poetry to music is about as futile and pointless as writing a lyric to a Beethoven piano concerto.

The literary critic and philosopher of art Suzanne K. Langer nicely overstated the point when she said, "There are no happy marriages in art—only successful rape." That is to say, when combining works of art, say music and poetry, one or the other must always be in a position of servitude. Consider setting: "Thou foster child of silence and slow time" (scanned- / - / - / - - / /) to music. The line's rhythm makes its own "music." It makes a statement with the pyrrhic substitution in the fourth foot, creating a diminuendo that creates "silence," while the spondee in the fifth foot slows down, supporting the idea "slow time" nicely.

Music has two choices here: to create a different rhythm of its own, and therefore ruin the rhythmic statement of the line (rape), or bow to the line's rhythm and orchestrate it. Note that in orchestration, the music is in service of something else. It does not create something musically independent. Something else is driving the bus. Of course, setting light verse to music is easier to accomplish, since it thrives on regular rhythms, rhymes, common meter, or matched tetrameter couplets—qualities typical of lyrics. But we're generally not talking about great poetry.

This is not to say that you shouldn't try to orchestrate a poem. But to actually try to create a beautiful stand-on-its-own melody and harmony and stay precisely true to the music of the poem itself is a task. Musical motion makes its own demands, often tempting the composer to step away from the poem's music in favor of his own composition—to create a Piece. The raft of unfortunate settings of Frost poems should be enough to warn off any would-be composer. There's a reason they fail so universally, and it's not that the composers are bad composers. Their music is, by itself, rather lovely and creative. But alas—while the music is out on the town having a real good time, it mostly leaves the poem disheveled and wandering along the nighttime roadside, hoping to hitch a ride home.

When talking about the differences between songs and poems, one has to consider history. And 1066 was a pretty big year for poetry. The Norman (French) invasion of England (Celtic) produced a collision, not only of cultures, but of languages. To that point, poetry in England was accentual—that is, drawn from a Germanic base featuring a wide dynamic range between stressed and unstressed syllables—so much so, that stressed syllables were all that mattered in their poems. Celtic poetry usually consisted of lines of three or four strong stresses usually accompanied by caesura at the half-line. Unstressed syllables weren't counted at all. Some of this strategy is preserved in nursery rhymes:

Hickory Dickory Dock	(three stresses)
The mouse ran up the clock	(three stresses)
The clock struck one, the mouse fell down	(four stresses)
Hickory Dickory Dock.	(three stresses)

Across the Channel, William the Conqueror was mobilizing his army to invade England. He spoke French. But French is not an inflected language, meaning, among many things, that one hears little difference between stressed and unstressed syllables. Thus Norman, or French poetry, was a syllabic poetry, counting syllables. The usual line of French poetry consisted of twelve syllables, often called a hexameter line.

As these two languages inevitably blended, the result was modern English. Poetry beginning with Chaucer began to merge French and English poetic devices resulting in accentual-syllabic verse which counts both the number of syllables and the number of stressed syllables. William the Conqueror had no idea that he was creating the language of Shakespeare and Yeats, but he was.

Because English doesn't use the end of a sentence or thought for grammatical purposes (as does Latin or Spanish), English is restricted to position; adjectives and nouns don't identify their alliance via the way they end, so they must be physically adjacent. Typically, English sentences are ordered—they start with the subject—the noun or noun phrase. Nouns are identified as nouns by using an unstressed article, *the, a, an,* a grammatical function. So, the typical English sentence starts unstressed, and moves to the stressed noun, creating instant iambic motion from weak to strong. Thus, English is iambic.

Poetry uses the dynamic contrast between syllables to create rhythms, to set a "groove." Most poetry in any language, in its creation of lines, strives to create the longest line possible—a line that feels like one thing—that does not feel like it breaks, or subdivides into smaller units. If you think of strong syllables as having weight, the strong syllables in Germanic poetry are quite heavy, only allowing three or four of them to sit on the branch before it breaks, making us feel like another line has appeared. The medial caesura in Germanic poetry attests to the density of the stressed syllables; they need to catch their breath in the middle of the branch.

French poetry's stressed syllables, its meaning functions, are much lighter (they don't weigh as much in this "branch" metaphor), and you can line twelve of them on the branch (six units of two) without some of them falling off into the next line. In English poetry, which is less inflected than German and more so than French, the branch can hold five feet (five iambs) without breaking—without subdividing into smaller units as we can see with these lines by Frost:

> When Í see bírches bénd to léft and ríght
> Acróss the línes of stráighter dárker trées

Whereas with seven stresses in a line:

> When I see birches stánd alóne and bend to left and right
> Across the lines of óak and élm and straighter darker trees

the branches get too heavy, and break into:

> When I see birches stand alone
> and bend to left and right
> Across the lines of oak and elm
> and straighter darker trees

Even hexameter lines (six feet) tend to subdivide from:

> When I see birches stand and bend to left and right
> Across the lines of elm and straighter darker trees

into:

> When I see birches stand
> and bend to left and right
> Across the lines of elm
> and straighter darker trees

So, the longest non-subdividing line in English poetry is the pentameter line—a line of five feet. And the basic rhythmic figure of English is the iamb, moving from weak to strong. Thus, the staple line of the majority of poetry written in English is iambic pentameter, such as we see here:

> When I see birches bend to left and right
> Across the lines of straighter darker trees

Because of Western music's love affair with two-, four-, and eight-bar phrases, the standard lines of lyric are usually tetrameter (four strong stresses) and trimeter (three strong stresses). The typical song lyric is built either on common meter ("Mary Had a Little Lamb") such as Bob Dylan's "Tangled Up in Blue":

> Shé was wórkin' in a tópless pláce   (four stresses)
> And Í stopped ín for a béer,   (three stresses)
> I júst kept lóokin' at the síde of her fáce   (four stresses)
> In the spótlíght so cléar.   (three stresses)

or on matched tetrameter couplets ("Eenie Meenie Miney Mo") such as these lines from Sting's "Stolen Car":

Láte at níght in súmmer héat.	(four stresses)
Expénsive cár, émpty stréet	(four stresses)
There's a wíre in my jácket. Thís is my tráde	(four stresses)

The only lyric form consistently employing five-stress lines is blues:

My báby léft me, I'm só alóne and blúe	(five stresses)
Yes, báby léft me, I'm só alóne and blúe	(five stresses)
I cry all níght, I dón't know whát to dó	(five stresses)

For the lyric's line lengths, musical considerations drive the bus. The two-bar building block of Western music creates the format for the lyric: since two bars of 4/4 time contain a total of four stressed positions, the lyric relies on a heavy diet of four-stress and three-stress lines, adjusting to the confines of the two-bar phrase. The five-stress lines of blues live in four-bar phrases.

There are other differences between song lyrics and poetry, but this ought to suffice to put the stink on the often-heard claim, "Her lyrics are pure poetry." No, they aren't. Those making this claim are probably responding to lyrics written in fresh, interesting language; language using provocative images and startling metaphor; lyrics containing some remarkable insight into the human condition. That is, they are responding to what is being said—to meaning, certainly something that great poetry and great lyrics share in common.

Robert Frost defines poetry as "that which is lost in translation," meaning images and metaphor can generally be translated accurately. The specific rhythm of a poem can't be translated accurately, nor can its specific arrangement of sound and rhyme, or the counterpointing of line and phrase. And these are the elements that give poetry its depth—its identity as a complete use of the language. These elements create the music that underlies great poetry. These are the elements that lyrics don't contain by themselves; they depend on melody, harmony, and the rhythm of music to create it for them.

A great poem, like a great symphony, stands its own ground. It contains everything it needs.

So does a great song. But a great lyric, by itself, doesn't. A lyric is made to be married. As in an earlier age, there is a division of labor: one partner learns to cook, sew, and raise the children. The other plows, hunts, and builds shelter. Together, the team survives quite nicely. Apart, they usually create defective poetry and muzak.

Poetry is made for the eye. Lyrics are made for the ear.

Notes

1. Reprinted with the permission of Scribner, a Division of Simon & Schuster, Inc., from *Collected Poems* by William Butler Yeats. Copyright © 1933 by The Macmillan Company, renewed 1961 by Bertha Georgie Yeats. All rights reserved.

2. "What I'll Do?" by Irving Berlin. © Copyright 1924 by Irving Berlin. © Copyright Renewed International Copyright Secured. All Rights Reserved. Reprinted by Permission.

Works Cited

Dylan, Bob. "Tangled Up in Blue." Music and lyrics by Bob Dylan. *Blood on the Tracks*. Columbia, 1975.

Frost, Robert. "Birches." Ed. Lathem, Edward Connery, and Lawrance Thompson. *Robert Frost Poetry and Prose*. Holt, Rhinehart and Winston. New York. 1972. 54–56.

Greenwood, Lee. "I Still Believe." Music and lyrics by Doug Johnson. *God Bless the USA*. UMG, 1994.

Keats, John. "Ode on a Grecian Urn." Ed. Matlak, Richard, and Anne Mellor. *British Literature 1780–1832*. Heinle, 2006. 1297–98.

Shelley, Percy Bysshe. "Ode to the West Wind." Ed. Matlak, Richard, and Anne Mellor. *British Literature 1780–1832*. Heinle, 2006. 1101–02.

Sting. "Stolen Car." Music and lyrics by Carl Terrell Mitchell and Gordon Matthew Sumner. *Sacred Love*. A&M, 2003.

The Teen Queens. "Eddie My Love." Music and lyrics by Aaron Collins, Maxwell Davis, and Sam Ling. *Eddie My Love*. RPM, 1956.

The Temptations. "My Girl." Music and lyrics by William "Smokey" Robinson and Donald A. White. *The Temptations Sing Smokey*. Motown, 1964.

Whiteman, Paul. "What'll I Do?" Music and lyrics by Irving Berlin. 1924.

Yeats, William Butler. "After Long Silence." *The Collected Poems of W. B. Yeats*. New York: Simon & Schuster, 1996. 265.

WORDS AND MUSIC: THREE STORIES

WYN COOPER

"In January 1993 Bill Bottrell and Kevin Gilbert, Sheryl Crow's producer and keyboard player, took a break from recording her first CD, Tuesday Night Music Club, *for want of better lyrics to a tune they already had in mind. They went around the corner to Cliff's Books in Pasadena, where they found a used copy of [*The Country of Here Below, *Wyn Cooper's first book]. They liked the poems, thought they fit the raw feelings they were after in her songs, and bought the book. They took it back to Sheryl, and asked her to sing 'Fun' to the music." The song became her multi-platinum, Grammy-winning song "All I Wanna Do." In this essay, Cooper talks about how that one song altered his writing and his life, and discusses in detail two of his many writing projects that merge poetry with music. As both a poet and a songwriter, Cooper is uniquely situated to offer his insights into what each genre may learn from the other.*

Some people don't know what to think when you tell them your two biggest influences are Lightnin Hopkins and Robert Frost.
—Townes Van Zandt

When I was a college sophomore in the late 1970s, I took poetry workshops from a noted narrative poet. The first week of class, he gave us a handout of poems and song lyrics, without identifying the authors. Not whole poems or entire lyrics, just snippets. We were asked to differentiate the poems from the lyrics. Not all song lyrics rhyme, and some of the poems he gave us did, so it wasn't as easy as it might sound. It was his way of showing us that poetry is superior to song lyrics, and we would have long discussions about the differences. They were enthusiastic discussions, because there was always someone—sometimes me—arguing that the Leonard Cohen fragment was better than the Dickey or the Snyder.

Looking back now, something strikes me as strange that didn't then: unlike many poets of his generation, my teacher was and is a narrative poet whose poems tell stories, just as many song lyrics do. I don't think he was opposed to the storytelling qualities of the lyrics he selected; it was more that he thought poetry is superior to song lyrics, and was perhaps worried his students would start basing their work on Dylan, Cohen, Joni Mitchell, and other songwriters. He wanted to draw a line in the sand, but in a certain way he was on the side of the line he didn't think too highly of, whether he knew it or not. For the record, he was a great teacher, if a bit old-school.

Much of the power of poetry, which began as song, is found in its sounds, whether hard or soft, vowel or consonant, whisper or wail. Listening to poetry requires concentration, as there's no music to listen to along with it. Whereas when I hear a song for the first time (and many times after that), I don't pay attention to the words. It's the music that moves me, makes me care or not care, and after that I can listen to the words. Listen to them consciously, that is. The words come through the mist of the music, so to speak, and our unconscious minds hear them whether we're trying or not. The words may be perfect as poetry, but if the music isn't compelling I turn it off.

Poetry began as something that went with music, words that were read to the accompaniment of the lyre (those Greeks!), thus the word *lyric*. Only very gradually, and only in some cultures such as ours, did a divide grow between the two. My former teacher's insistence on the difference between poetry and lyrics isn't so much a prejudice of his as a quirk of the cultural/historical moment, not a Truth but a chance meeting of place and time. To many people, the idea that poetry could exist without music is unfathomable. The printing press helped take music away from poetry, and recording technology helped bring it back.

In 1984, while in graduate school at the University of Utah, I wrote a poem which I called "Fun." I sent it to many magazines for publication, with no luck. When I gave readings, I always read the poem, because I believed in it. I put it in my first book of poems, *The Country of Here Below*, published in an edition of 500 copies in 1987. From that time on, I never saw it in a bookstore anywhere. But in January 1993 Bill Bottrell and Kevin Gilbert, Sheryl Crow's producer and keyboard player, took a break from recording her first CD, *Tuesday Night Music Club*, for want of better lyrics to a tune they already had in mind. They went around the corner to Cliff's Books in Pasadena, where they found a used copy of my book. They liked the poems, thought they fit the raw feelings they were after in her songs, and bought the book. They took it back to Sheryl, and asked her to sing "Fun" to the music.

I wasn't there, but I'm told that it worked. They needed the song to take place somewhere, so they set it in Los Angeles, on Santa Monica Boulevard, by adding a chorus that repeats words from the first line of the poem. They took some of my words out as well, including "the genetic engineering lab," and you can hear why: it's hard to sing that phrase. Out of the original thirty-six-line poem, thirty lines are used, and four are replaced by the chorus. Here is the poem:

Fun

"All I want is to have a little fun
Before I die," says the man next to me
Out of nowhere, apropos of nothing. He says
His name's William but I'm sure he's Bill
Or Billy, Mac or Buddy; he's plain ugly to me,
And I wonder if he's ever had fun in his life.

We are drinking beer at noon on Tuesday,
In a bar that faces a giant car wash.
The good people of the world are washing their cars
On their lunch hours, hosing and scrubbing
As best they can in skirts and suits.
They drive their shiny Datsuns and Buicks
Back to the phone company, the record store,
The genetic engineering lab, but not a single one
Appears to be having fun like Billy and me.

I like a good beer buzz early in the day,
And Billy likes to peel the labels
From his bottles of Bud and shred them on the bar.
Then he lights every match in an oversized pack,
Letting each one burn down to his thick fingers
Before blowing and cursing them out.

A happy couple enters the bar, dangerously close
To one another, like this is a motel,
But they clean up their act when we give them
A Look. One quick beer and they're out,
Down the road and in the next state
For all I care, smiling like idiots.
We cover sports and politics and once,
When Billy burns his thumb and lets out a yelp,
The bartender looks up from his want-ads.

Otherwise the bar is ours, and the day and the night
And the car wash too, the matches and the Buds
And the clean and dirty cars, the sun and the moon
And every motel on this highway. It's ours, you hear?
And we've got plans, so relax and let us in—
All we want is to have a little fun.

People have approached me over the years to tell me that when they heard "All I Wanna Do" on the radio, they knew it must be based on a poem, that there was just too much going on for it to be a traditional song lyric. I love these people and have had conversations with them about other song lyrics, whether based on poems or written as lyrics. There's never a consensus about which might be better, but to know that people still discuss such things is quaint, and lovely. I lean toward the opinion that if a lyric has to have music to make it art, it's not poetry. And it may not be poetry to begin with, as it wasn't intended to be treated as anything other than a lyric. Admittedly, "Fun" was written as a poem, not a song lyric. On the other hand, the lyrics I've written were certainly not meant to be considered poetry. They were written with music in mind.

I like the fact that Sheryl and her producer and the boys in the band were willing to take a chance on a poem—musicians generally aren't used to doing such things. Most of the money in music is in songwriting, so this was a song that, as co-writers, they knew they would make less on, should it prove to be a hit. In the long run, it worked out pretty well for everyone, with over nine million CDs sold, an unknown number of downloads, two Grammys, and radio airplay to this day. I am the first to admit that I may well be the luckiest poet in America, at least in terms of the number of people who have heard the words of my poem sung all over the world. And I had the rare treat of pulling up next to a car at a stoplight, while listening to the song on the radio, and was able to witness the woman in the car beside me not only also listening to it, but singing it at the top of her lungs.

With every success story, however, there's a downside. To this day, seventeen years since the song came out, when I meet someone and they ask (because they're American) what I do, I say that I'm a poet. "How do you make a living, though?" they ask, to which I reply that I'm also a songwriter. "Any songs I might have heard?" they ask. And when I say "All I Wanna Do," they almost invariably say, "Oh, you're *that* guy." Which means that they read the *People* magazine piece, or the *New York Times Sunday Magazine* piece, or heard the *All Things Considered* story on NPR, or saw me on television. And then, whatever their literary or other intelligence might be, they ask what Sheryl Crow is like. They rarely ask about my other poems.

Here's a bigger downside: one night years ago my late friend Bill Ripley, hoping to keep the party going, said to me, "All I want is to have a little fun before I die." I remembered the line, and used it to begin my poem "Fun" the next day. When my book came out, he didn't seem to care about the poem, but when it became a hit song, he tried to sue me for a very large amount of money. You can't copyright something you say, but he and his lawyers were undeterred. I had just quit my teaching job at Marlboro College, eager to write for other musicians, and suddenly my royalties were frozen for a year. I had no income and had to hire several lawyers to defend myself. I "won," so to speak, but Bill and I never spoke again.

David Broza is an Israeli pop star with an international following who grew up in Spain and Israel, and lived just outside New York for much of the 1990s. Most of his songs, whether in Hebrew, Spanish, or English, are based on poems. When I met him in the mid-nineties he told me that when he moved here he tried to make sense of America by reading its poets. What an idea! This led him to set their poems to music: Walt Whitman, Anne Sexton, Theodore Roethke, Elizabeth Bishop, Alberto Rios, Liam Rector, Matthew Graham, and, eventually, me. David told me that in Israel about half the songs on the radio are based on poems by Israeli poets. Which made me wonder what the songs on our radio stations might sound like if half of them were based on poems.

When David and I sat down under a tree on a summer day in Vermont, he had his guitar and I had my first book of poems. He asked me to read some poems aloud, and he strummed a little, here and there. But when I read "Opal, Wyoming," he grabbed the book from my hands, read it himself, and started to play. He asked me to help him add one line to each stanza to make it fit his music, and by listening to the music, my job was made easier. In less than an hour the song was done. It has appeared on two of his CDs as "A Night in Wyoming," and was turned into "Night in Masada" for the concert at Masada, Israel, that was then turned into a PBS special called "David Broza at Masada: The Sunrise Concert." So a poem that I wrote in Virginia about a town in Wyoming that was turned into a song in Vermont became a song that takes place in Israel. Here is the poem:

Opal, Wyoming

If you never left this place
you might believe the world
was dust and wind and sky,
the days so hard that no one
save your mother doesn't drink.

A jukebox floats in smoke
in the Red River Bar
when you drive the nine miles
to get Pabst on tap,
and your eyes turn red.

At home your wife frowns,
thinking you're drunk, so you
stand on a chair on one foot
and juggle three apples
until she leaves the kitchen.

It's late when you check
on the horses and hogs
and tell them to sleep,
so late the cool air
comes down from Montana

and you button your shirt,
standing in the red dirt
beside the barn watching
the parade of stars,
watching the world.

Many musicians have set poems to music, too many to list here. One of my favorites is Van Morrison's version of William Mathieu's musical setting of W. B. Yeats's "Crazy Jane on God." Mathieu and Morrison are mostly true to the poem, except for a few added words, two stanzas inverted, one stanza used twice, and the last line of each stanza repeated twice, which echoes the chorus feel of that repeating line. This sounds like a lot of changes, but the song still sounds like the poem. It's a bluesy version, using more repetition than the poem contains, and I think poets can learn something from using that kind of repetition. As my friend Mike Fleming pointed out to me, repetition in music illuminates a possible rationale for distinguishing poetry from lyrics: music provides a context of patterning that gives the repetition of words a different meaning and a different value than if the music were absent.

But what if half the songs on the radio, or on CDs, or available for download, started out as poems? Which of course begs the question, what if the poems they use are terrible poems? What kind of message does that send? Are we back to the line in the sand drawn by my teacher? No, we're not. A bad poem is no better than a bad lyric. At least in the ear, and mind, of the listener.

I went to graduate school at Hollins College with the novelist Madison Smartt Bell thirty years ago, and we've been friends ever since. In 1997 he sent me a rough draft of a novel called *Anything Goes*, which was published by Pantheon in 2002—his eleventh novel at that time. Normally a very private person who doesn't talk much if at all about current projects, he sent me this version and asked me to read it, then write a song lyric from the point of view of one of the characters. The novel concerns the bass player in a blues-rock band, so it made sense. Nonetheless, I was honored. I wrote the lyric, sent it to Madison in Baltimore, and a week later got a cassette in the mail. He had set it to music and sung it while playing guitar. I wrote another one. He set it to music. Before we knew it we were in the studio, making a demo, while I still wrote my poems and he continued revising his novel.

Madison said he had always liked my poem "On Eight Mile," which appeared in my second book, *The Way Back*. It's based on my friendship with my cousin Roby Warren, who once owned a strip bar called The Silent Woman on Eight Mile Road in Detroit, not far from where I was raised. When Madison set it to music for the demo, we both knew it was one of our best. Here's the poem:

On Eight Mile

She appears as if at the edge
of a screen, her brown hair black
in this light, her legs moving the way

she wants you to want them to move.
It's hard to see the woman you loved
dance naked in a room full of men

and come up to your table after
and ask for a light, and the light
in her eyes is still the same,

only her job has changed. So she changes
into clothes and we cross the street
to a quiet place where we can talk,

and the talk turns to me, to what
I do that makes me think I'm better
than her. I'm not and I know it,

but she won't be convinced. Nothing
I can say will sway her the way
she sways on stage. And nothing
can make me look away.

Madison dropped three words and added one, mostly sang it as it was, and it worked. On the demo, he added a guitar solo at the end that to my mind mimics a stripper taking off her clothes, intricate and fast and almost confusing, loud but also satisfying as it crescendos. We hired singers to sing the songs on the demo, thinking we would try to get others to cover the songs, but in two instances we couldn't find singers who could sing in the right key, so Madison sang them. When we got a record deal from Gaff Music, the only caveat was that we had to use the singer on this song and the other song that Madison sang on. Scott Beal, who ran Gaff Music, didn't know it was Madison singing those songs.

Madison said he'd see if the singer was available. It turns out he was. The guitar on the final version matches Madison's invention.

That CD, our first, is called *Forty Words for Fear*. We had the astounding luck to have it produced by Don Dixon, who had co-produced, with Mitch Easter (who became our engineer), most of the first two REM albums. Prior to the recording session, I mailed Don some poems that were new at that time, postcard poems, and he told us before we even began recording that our second CD should be based on these poems. It's not too much to say that he had us figured out before he even met us, and more important, he had seen to the heart of what we were trying to do. Sure enough, our second CD, *Postcards Out of the Blue*, is based on poems from my third book, *Postcards from the Interior*. In both cases, Don insisted that I read poems which were then set to music, not as songs but as spoken-word pieces that are mixed with other sounds that approximate what's going on in the poems, including the use of short wave radio and salt and pepper shakers. Two such poems are on each CD, and the rest of the songs are just that, songs, sung by Madison. Some are based on my poems, and others are based on lyrics I wrote specifically for each project. Madison would sometimes e-mail me a title, or a line, or some kind of idea for a song, which made my job that much easier. Following an assignment, for me, is much more pleasant than staring at a blank page in a notebook, or a blank computer screen, or whatever writers are staring at these days.

One roadblock Madison and I occasionally run into while collaborating is that I send him poems I think might make good songs, and he points out that they're lyric poems that don't tell a story. I often then write a song lyric that does tell a story, because it would be too strange to write a narrative poem after going so long without doing so. I'm perfectly aware of the artificial distinction I'm making. I guess what that teacher said so long ago has stuck, like it or not. When I write poems, I read them aloud over and over to make sure the sound is right; when I write lyrics, I sing them aloud repeatedly, not just to see if they *can* be sung, but to see how certain words and phrases sound in a singing voice. Singers obviously *sing* as they write; poets are less likely, in my experience, to be as preoccupied with sound as I am. Maybe I'm in the right business after all.

Much of the popular opinion regarding the difference between poems and song lyrics comes from expectation: higher for poetry, lower for lyrics. The poetry snob in me wants to say that poetry is the higher art, and, as I said at the beginning of this essay, poems have to stand on their own, both on the page for silent reading, and in the air as sound. Good ones have the music in their lines to sustain a reader's attention; bad ones don't. Lyrics have the added dimension of the music they're set to, and shouldn't be compared to poems on the page alone. Music makes lyrics easier to remember, to the point that many of us know hundreds if not thousands of songs by heart, but can recite far fewer poems. Songs have shaped our collective consciousness far more than poetry has, for better or worse. This may not be true for all poets, but it's true for the wider community we all belong to, poets or not.

Works Cited

Bell, Madison Smartt. *Anything Goes.* New York: Pantheon, 2002.

Bell & Cooper. *Postcards Out of the Blue.* Dogjaw, 2008.

Bell, Madison Smartt, and Wyn Cooper. *Forty Words for Fear.* Gaff, 2003.

Broza, David. "A Night in Wyoming." *Painted Postcard.* Music by David Broza, lyrics by Wyn Cooper. Rounder, 2002.

Cooper, Wyn. "Fun." *The Country of Here Below.* Boise: Ahsahta, 1987.

———. "On Eight Mile." *The Way Back.* Buffalo: White Pine, 2000.

———. "Opal, Wyoming." *The Country of Here Below.* Boise: Ahsahta, 1987.

———. *Postcards from the Interior.* Rochester, NY: BOA Editions, 2005.

Crow, Sheryl. "All I Wanna Do." *Tuesday Night Music Club.* Written by David Baerwald, Bill Bottrell, Wyn Cooper, Sheryl Crow, and Kevin Gilbert. A&M, 1993.

David Broza at Masada: The Sunrise Concert. The Angel Group/WTTWN, 2007.

Morrison, Van. "Crazy Jane on God." *A Sense of Wonder.* Lyrics by W. B. Yeats, music by William Mathieu, arranged by Van Morrison. Recorded 1983. Mercury, 1985.

Part Two

ANALYSIS OF TWENTIETH-CENTURY SONGWRITERS

THE TRIUMPH OF ICARUS:
SAM COOKE AND THE CREATIVE SPIRIT

PETER GURALNICK

Sam Cooke's enormous crossover success started in 1957 with "You Send Me," his own composition and his first pop single. The song beat out Elvis Presley for the Number One position on the pop charts and led, Guralnick explains, "to an outpouring of criticism from the church" and an exodus of prominent gospel singers following in Cooke's wake. Along with Ray Charles, Sam Cooke created a template for the gospel-based R&B that came to be called "soul music." In this essay, Guralnick takes a close look at Sam Cooke's careful compositional approach and pinpoints just what it was that gave his songs (from new gospel standards like "Jesus Be a Fence Around Me" to "A Change Is Gonna Come") their unique place in American vernacular culture.

Write about what you know, write about what you've experienced, write about what you observe. Write about natural things. You've got to get back to what you knew when you were a little kid.
—Sam Cooke to aspiring young songwriter Don Covay, ca. 1962

The secret is really observation. If you observe what's going on and try to figure out how people are thinking and determine the times of your day, I think you can always write something that people will understand.
—Sam Cooke to TV host Dick Clark, April 4, 1964

Sam Cooke was a singer's singer ("Sam was the one and only," said Ray Charles. "*Nobody* sounded like him—I mean, nobody even came close").[1] He was the preeminent gospel singer of his day ("Sam brought sex into the church," said Bobby Womack). His enormous crossover success with "You Send Me," his first pop single under his own name, led to an outpouring of criticism and an army of quartet singers who followed in his wake, creating in the process a template for what came to be called "soul music."

Sam Cooke wrote his own songs, owned his own publishing company, and built his own record label, on which he recorded a wide range of singers, both gospel and r&b, who for the most part interpreted Sam Cooke compositions in a rougher, more exhortatory style than he was accustomed to employ on his own pop hits. His ambitions at the end of his life (he was killed at thirty-three, in what his friend and business partner, J. W. Alexander, would always describe as "a senseless waste") realistically encompassed Las Vegas, a movie career, and turning his record company, SAR, into the kind of full-service pop label that Berry Gordy's Motown would soon become. He was, it was perfectly evident, charismatic in a way that affected everyone with whom he came in contact: friend, fan, family member, or business colleague.

He was complex and contradictory, and, more than anyone I have ever written about, I feel certain that if he were alive today, at age eighty, he would still be making his mark, whether in the field of politics, business, or the arts. But at the heart of his achievement, one can be equally certain, would lie the creative impulse, the need to express himself in a way that gave free rein to the same imaginative vision that fueled his songs. In the end what seems to me most remarkable about Sam Cooke, the man whom legendary Atlantic Records executive Jerry Wexler called "the best singer who ever lived, no contest," was his *inner* voice, the drive to find a form to reify the thunderclap of revelation that animates the creative imagination in every field.

Sam Cooke was constantly writing. At first he wrote down his song ideas on napkins and scraps of paper—he dashed them off in restaurants, backstage, in hotel rooms, in the car on the way to a gig. Later, he formalized the process in a series of spiral notebooks that he filled with his sketches as well as his lyrics. His imagination was kindled not just by his experience but by his reading, first by the Bible stories he recast in his gospel songs, then by the books that captivated him from childhood on—everything from Mark Twain's *Huckleberry Finn*, one of his favorites as a kid, to Tolstoy's *War and Peace*. This was not just an idle pursuit. He was introduced to the formal study of black history by John Hope Franklin's *From Slavery to Freedom*, and he was inspired by James Baldwin's social commentary. At the urging of his friend, the DJ Magnificent Montague, he read poetry by Countee Cullen, Paul Laurence Dunbar, and James Weldon Johnson and even set some of the poems from Dunbar's 1895 collection, *Majors and Minors*, extemporaneously to music (his own "Laughin' and Clownin'" can be seen in many ways as a restatement of Dunbar's most famous poem, "We Wear the Mask"). On his own he read books like William Shirer's 1200-page *The Rise and Fall of the Third Reich*, Aristotle's *Poetics*, and Winston's Churchill's history of World War II.

"You couldn't get him out of his books," his protégé, Bobby Womack, just nineteen when he first started touring with Sam, recalled. "We'd go to a motel, and [his brother] Charles and them would be wanting to get chicks, and they'd be saying, 'We have to get all these goddamn books for Sam.' When he wasn't chasing, he was reading. And the more history he read, the more [he would talk about it.] 'Do you know about this? Do you know about that?' He said, 'Bobby, if you read—the way you write now, you writing songs you ain't even lived. You ain't even *been* with a woman, so how you gonna write about a woman?' I said, 'I know people that have, and I see what they go through.' But he said, 'Bobby, if you read, your vocabulary, the way you view things in a song—it'll be like an abstract painting, every time you look back you'll see something you didn't see before.'

"He'd say, 'You have to be universal. You have to be all the way around. You just work every day at your craft.' It wasn't like he was trying to sell nothing, he was out having a good time. He kept saying, 'Bobby, a star, that's the one you can touch.' He would just sit up and listen to people, listen to people talk. He said, 'That's where you get your hooks.' He said, 'It's easy to write the truth, it's hard to tell a story. You've only got three minutes. You gotta hit 'em, it's gotta be strong, and you've got to stick to the script. It's got to be about feeling, but if you're telling a story, you've got to make a believer out of the person that's listening.'"

Sam developed his storytelling skills at an early age. With the Highway QCs, the teenaged gospel quartet he joined at sixteen, he showed that ability by establishing a clear narrative line for familiar Bible tales, a skill he developed even further after he was recruited at nineteen to sing lead for the Soul Stirrers, the most celebrated gospel quartet of the era. The Reverend Goldie Thompson promoted every spiritual program in the St. Petersburg and Tampa area, and his daughter, Ann, just five at the time, met Sam in 1951, shortly after his Soul Stirrers debut. Both on and offstage she remembers him as different from any of the other singers. When he read to her from the Bible, "he would just go through it like a story. Everything to him was a story. I don't know if he was just able to read it that fast and develop it, but he kept you in total suspense—he was just that way." Clarence Fountain of the Five Blind Boys of Alabama, who frequently traveled with the Soul Stirrers in those days, recalled how Sam would read to the Blind Boys and bring the story dramatically to life. "He could just stop and read you a book. He'd ride with us all the time, and he'd read us westerns and things of that nature, and he could almost put you there, right back in the same time when the book was wrote and how things were going on—he had a good eye for reading."

Because of his facility at rearranging well-known verses and his own highly distinctive vocal approach, he was credited with authorship of a number of traditional songs in his early years with the Soul Stirrers, but it was not until he first started thinking about crossing over to popular music, in 1955, that he actually began writing songs in earnest. The *idea* of crossing over presented itself to him in exactly the same manner that it did to everyone else in the music business at that time: it was prompted by the unprecedented success of Ray Charles's "I Got a Woman."

There had been great "inspirational" hits leading up to the Ray Charles number, certainly—Faye Adams's "Shake a Hand" and the Orioles' "Crying in the Chapel," both #1 r&b smashes in 1953, as was Roy Hamilton's even more successful "You'll Never Walk Alone" the following year. These songs provided a kind of faith-based hope, they mimicked the musical language, and much of the tradition, of gospel music. But they were *not* gospel songs, and in fact there had never been a widely embraced r&b hit that merely attached secular lyrics to a well-known gospel track.

That was precisely what Ray Charles did in November 1954, and he was denounced for it by preachers from coast to coast who declared the singer to be an apostate and the record an unutterable abomination. "He's crying sanctified. He's mixing the blues with the spirituals," said bluesman Big Bill Broonzy indignantly. "He should be singing in a church!" And yet, almost irrespective of commercial impact, the power of the music turned out to be a force that could neither be denied nor turned around. Harmonica player Little Walter was working on a Willie Dixon–authored blues called "My Babe." In the immediate wake of Ray Charles's breakthrough, Dixon set his lyrics to the melody of "This Train," a spiritual popularized by Sister Rosetta Tharpe, and the record climbed to #1 on the r&b charts. Record company owners and gospel singers alike simply could not ignore the explosive potential of the new "crossover" market. "Try to write words in the blues field to songs in the Gospel field that have been hits in the past," Specialty Records owner Art Rupe wrote to one of his lesser-known spiritual artists, even as he remained determined to keep the Soul Stirrers strictly in the spiritual camp. Little Richard was the direct result of Rupe's search for his own secular star with the crossover sound. Little Richard, he noted appreciatively, was "all fervor, embellish[ing]every song with little grace notes and exclamations in the style of gospel singing."

Sam felt the pressure from all sides. Little Richard's producer, Specialty A&R director Bumps Blackwell, in open defiance of Rupe's dictum, seized every opportunity to urge Sam to leave the Soul Stirrers and sing pop—and to take Bumps with him as his manager and musical guide. Newark deejay Bill Cook, who had guided his own protégé, Roy Hamilton, to a career in which he enjoyed almost as much popularity with whites as with blacks with a big-voiced, gospel-based style, saw in Sam the potential to equal if not exceed Hamilton—so long as he engaged the East Coast–based Cook as his manager. Meanwhile, Sam was getting much the same advice from his friend, mentor, and fellow gospel singer J.W. Alexander, second tenor and manager of the Pilgrim Travelers, the Soul Stirrers' closest rivals. J.W., who had begun *his* singing career in the 1930s with a barbershop quartet, played Negro League baseball, and worked as an extra in Hollywood films before joining the Travelers, had first met Sam not long after he joined the Highway QCs. "He was warm and friendly," J.W. said of the fresh-faced seventeen-year-old. "Even as a kid he had something special. I thought to myself: *This guy's a jewel.*" To Alexander, Sam had the potential to surpass Sonny Til, the handsome lead singer for the Orioles, because he could appeal not just to black teenaged girls but to whites. J.W. saw Sam's future more as a matter of destiny than of choice. The way the women screamed for Sam in the churches, there was no way they would not scream even louder if he was singing about love. "I didn't see how he could miss."

Most of all, though, Sam felt the weight of his own expectations. He and his seven brothers and sisters had been taught from early childhood never to accept limitations, whether from within or without ("If you're going to shine shoes," the Reverend Charles Cook told his children, "be the best shoeshine boy out there. Whatever you strive to be, be the best at it"). Sam more than any of the others took his father's lesson to heart. "Anytime you can make a step higher, you go higher," his father told him. And that was what he intended to do. He was determined to do better, financially, materially, artistically—and he was certainly not going to set a ceiling on the scope, or the nature, of that success. From the very beginning he had believed he could reach everyone with his music, irrespective of age, color, or social class, and with the rapid growth of gospel in the late 1940s and early 1950s, he had seen no reason to doubt that he could do so within his chosen field. Now, with the astonishing ascendancy of this new hybrid music, and the almost instant decline in gospel bookings and sales that it created ("We could see how it was affecting us," said Pilgrim Travelers baritone singer Jesse Whitaker. "We could *see* it"), he found himself faced with a new creative challenge, but not one from which he was about to shrink.

It was around this time that Sam and J.W. Alexander got ukeleles, with which they would accompany themselves on the road, mostly just fooling around with pop standards. "Then Sam began to write, and I got a book in New York on 'How to Write a Hit Song and Sell It'—I forget who wrote the doggone thing. But I just told Sam to make it simple, to where little children could hum it. Housewives or truckdrivers or what have you. You write that kind of melody, and lots of people will remember it. And make it danceable, that's really the key." Sam absorbed all of the book's lessons—song structure, the function of verse and chorus, how to construct a bridge— and by the time that guitarist Leroy Crume joined the Soul Stirrers in the spring of 1956, he was using the songs he had started to write, love songs for the most part predicated on a string of metaphorical truisms ("A fish was made to swim in the ocean / A boat was made to sail on the sea / But as sure as there are stars above / You were made for me"), as a kind of social introduction. "We'd have a roomful of people sometimes," Crume said (Sam later dubbed him Crumé—after the manner in which, he said, the French would pronounce the name). "He'd get on my guitar and I'd sing back-up, and we'd sing all those songs to the ladies, try them out and see if they were acceptable. And for the most part they were!"

At first his idea appears to have been not to record these songs himself but, through Bill Cook, now functioning as unofficial manager for a career that had yet to be decided upon, to submit them to either Roy Hamilton or another r&b act, the Platters, with whom the Newark deejay had considerable influence. The Platters' huge mainstream success (in 1955 and 1956 alone they had two #1 pop and r&b hits) was in fact just one more manifestation of the new mixed market that was beginning to open up not just for Ray Charles and Roy Hamilton but for Chuck Berry, Little Richard, and Elvis Presley as well. Bumps Blackwell argued that Sam could achieve the same kind of popularity as Morton Downey, the Irish tenor from the thirties known as "the man with the choirboy's voice." Bill Cook undoubtedly had a somewhat different perspective, and in the end it is hard to say just how much Cook actually exerted himself to get Sam's songs to either Roy Hamilton or the Platters. His intent, clearly, was to get Sam himself into the studio, and in August 1956 he succeeded. The Soul Stirrers were in New York to play an all-star gospel revue at the Apollo, and, unbeknownst to the other members of the group, Sam slipped quietly into the Nola Studio on Broadway to record half a dozen of his own compositions under Cook's supervision.

Then, in December 1956, Specialty owner Art Rupe finally gave in to the urgings of both Cook and Bumps Blackwell and sent Sam to New Orleans to record his first official pop session with Bumps producing in the same studio where he had cut all but one of Little Richard's hits to date. Sam revisited the songs he had demoed in New York, but the principal focus of the session was "Lovable," a note-for-note translation of the Soul Stirrers' recent gospel hit, "Wonderful." "Lovable" offered the same kind of verbal substitutions that Ray Charles and Little Walter had employed ("God is so wonderful" became "My girl is so lovable"), and when the single was released in early 1957 under the name of "Dale" Cook (Sam had not yet added the "e" to his last name), the ruse fooled absolutely no one. It was a measure, though, of how conflicted Sam continued to be not so much about the musical course on which he was embarking as its assurance of success, and it caused J.W. Alexander to urge him to stop worrying about the consequences of failure and take the plunge once and for all. "You can't stick your head in the sand like an ostrich," said J.W. "You can't be Dale Cook. You got to be Sam Cook as you are."

"Lovable" was not in any case a very good representation of Sam Cook as he was. As can be gleaned from the lyrics, it was more like a facsimile than the real thing, representing Sam at his best neither as singer nor as songwriter. Several of the "little love songs" he had already written were in fact far more indicative of his pop potential, and a new number he came up with that spring brought together all of the elements he had learned from the songwriting instruction book to create the kind of direct emotional connection that J.W. was always talking about.

"You Send Me" consisted of little more than a single four-line verse, three of whose lines were the title phrase or the variant "You thrill me," along with a bridge right out of "How to Write a Hit Song and Sell It." The verse was repeated six times, and the bridge was strictly rudimentary, but the charm with which Sam put it across, along with the emotional release and impeccably timed delivery of the climactic fourth line, "Honest, you do," created a sense of drama that "Lovable" never approaches. It was, as J.W. suggested, "simple to where little children could hum it," the kind of melody that in J.W.'s formulation the world would long remember, and, when it was released on the Keen label in the fall of 1957, the record sold almost two million copies, catapulting Sam not just into the front ranks but, in a virtually unprecedented achievement for a debut release on a debut label, to the top of the charts and the top of the pop world.

Sam's course at this point was clear, but if anyone had wanted to hazard a guess as to the scope of his songwriting ambitions, they would have been better served taking a look at the gospel songs he had been writing with increasing frequency and fervor over the last two years. These gospel numbers were the first evidence not just of the facility but of the growing complexity of his work. "Touch the Hem Of His Garment" is perhaps the best example of the former quality, emerging from a February 1956 Soul Stirrers session for which Sam had failed to create enough material in advance. On the way to the session Stirrers manager S.R. Crain complained to Sam that without a strong original composition they would be selling their audience short. According to Bumps Blackwell, who was riding to the studio with the group, Sam scarcely blinked. "He just said, 'Hand me the Bible,' and they handed Sam [a] Bible, and he was thumbing through it, skipping and skimming through it, and he said, 'I got one. Here it is right here,'" and he put the song together on the spot. "The guitar started playing these two little chords, and Sam started singing, quoting right from the Scripture, where Jesus was coming into the marketplace and he met the woman at the well." The song was one of Sam's most eloquent Bible tales, and as much as anything, it made a believer of Bumps, an auto-didact and religious skeptic who had been "looking down my nose at [gospel singers as] untrained, undisciplined people. An ability like this turned me completely around." It also provided him with a striking new view of the future.

Sam in his own way had seen the future all along. "Touch the Hem of His Garment" may have indicated the ease of his writing, but an earlier number is an even clearer demonstration of its breadth. "Nearer to Thee" turns on much the same device as Irving Berlin's "Always," where the key word or phrase—in this case the spiritual song title, "Nearer My God to Thee"—changes meaning, and achieves greater emotional impact, with each fresh use. Sam continued to develop the song after the group first cut a studio version in February 1955, until, by the time that Bumps and Art Rupe recorded the Soul Stirrers in a live gospel program in Los Angeles that summer, it had taken on almost epic proportions. As with so many of Sam's later pop hits, the song begins with an everyday scene.

"The minister was preaching," Sam sings, "and the crowd was standing near . . .":

> The congregation was singing a tune
> In a voice that was so loud and clear
> You know, the crowd that stood all around him
> They were crying, I could plainly see
> For the song that they sang
> Was so touching
> They were singing "Nearer My God to Thee."

From there Sam travels in a series of verses from comfortable homiletics to increasingly passionate personal testimony until, at the end, he paints a picture of his mother at once so deeply felt and so broadly identifiable that the entire auditorium erupts in a transport of shared emotion.

"I remember when I was a little boy," Sam sings:

> Mother used to steal off, steal off all alone
> I used to wonder
> What my mother was doing (help me, Lord)
> I crept out one morning, I found Mother with folded arms
> And Mother had her eyes open,
> She was looking up toward the sky
> And I, I saw the tears
> As they fell down [from] my mother's eyes
> But I could still hear the song
> Mother was singing,
> "Nearer My —", "Nearer My God to Thee."

The extent to which Sam is able to engage the audience—and it is a very *considerable* extent—should be seen, ultimately, as the result not so much of a performance trick or a tease but, much like his minister father, as a fully developed exploration of his text. For Sam this consisted of making vivid by every means at his disposal the profound meaning of words and music. "Song," Sam declares tellingly in the fourth verse of "Nearer to Thee," "is the only thing that will console me, Lord / When I know that trouble's about to come," and indeed one senses by the very reworking of his material the hold that song has on him, the degree to which, like any great poet or songwriter, he is reaching for something beyond meaning while at the same time seeking to elevate inspiration through the conscious application of craft. It is the same dedication that Sam would bring to all of his best pop songs, from "Wonderful World" to "A Change Is Gonna Come," each of which takes off from a common expression, each of which achieves a kind of unassuming lucidity while simultaneously suggesting a depth of field that encourages open-ended interpretation.

Sam wrote or cowrote nearly every one of his familiar hits. "You Send Me," "Chain Gang," "Cupid," "Only Sixteen," "Having a Party," "Bring It On Home to Me" all bear his unmistakable stamp, both as singer and writer. Every one offers a kind of instant accessibility due not just to the charm of Sam's singing style but to their simplicity of structure and direct conversational approach. What makes them so enduring, though, are not the surface qualities but the emotion and artful arrangement that lie underneath, the subtlety of a subtext that suggests whole other dimensions and planes of meaning.

To Sam it was hardly worth singing a song unless you gave yourself to it wholeheartedly and without reservation. But, just as important, you had to present it in a manner that mirrored some universally recognizable human experience. Even in his most lighthearted novelty numbers, throwaway songs like "Everybody Loves to Cha Cha Cha," "Another Saturday Night," and "Twistin' the Night Away," he conceived of himself as a kind of reporter, building the story line around a scene he had observed either directly or indirectly (convicts he had seen on a chain gang in the Carolinas; high society twisting at New York's Peppermint Lounge in a televised report on the latest dance craze) but for which in every instance he created an imagined framework. He was not wedded to the literal picture in the least (in "Chain Gang," for example, he focused as much initially on the prisoners' "women at home / in their silken gowns" as on the chain gang itself) but instead created a world peopled with invented characters and propelled by a plot that helped bring the subject to life. "Another Saturday Night" transformed the real-life comic contretemps in which Sam and J.W. Alexander found themselves when they were told they could not have female company in their London hotel suite. In real life, of course, they simply switched hotels, but almost before they did, Sam had turned the experience into a song. Not a song in which a sophisticated entertainer is thwarted by the management of an exclusive Mayfair hotel but, rather, one in which a decidedly unsophisticated working-class narrator faces one romantic embarrassment after another, with the basic thrust of the story articulated in the chorus.

> It's another Saturday night and I ain't got nobody
> I got some money 'cause I just got paid
> How I wish I had someone to talk to
> I'm in an awful way.

Two of Sam's best-known songs, "Wonderful World" and "Rome Wasn't Built in a Day," were written from finished compositions by other writers who in each instance enthusiastically embraced the transformation that Sam's seemingly minor adjustments made to their song. In the case of "Wonderful World," as transcendent as any of Sam's romantic classics (this is the one that memorably starts out, "Don't know much about history / Don't know much biology / Don't know much about a science book / Don't know much about the French I took"), Lou Adler and Herb Alpert had given up on their own effort, dismissing it as hopelessly inconsequential, out-of-date, and trite. Sam kept returning to it, though, said Adler, as if he sensed something in it that its authors did not. "He kept asking us, 'What about that song?' And then he'd start on it again. His idea—since [in the original version] it was all about reading and books and what you *didn't* have to do in order to [find love]—was to take it more towards school. That's how it evolved." And in the end the simple elements coalesced in such a way as to form a whole much greater (and far more memorable) than the sum of its parts. What Sam did, as Lou saw it, was to create a conversation with the listener. "It was light, it wasn't, 'Listen to this song.' Sam always told me, 'You got to be *talking* to somebody.' Even if the lyric was heavy, his approach to it wasn't that intense."

Herb Alpert, unlike Lou a trained musician, was amazed at what Sam could get out of a lyric. If you looked at the words on paper, Alpert said, if you simply followed the chord structure, the song might seem corny, "but he had a way of phrasing, a way of presenting his feelings that was uniquely his. I mean, he was talking right *to* you, he wasn't trying to flower things up with words that didn't connect."

He also had his own way of presenting the song, his own philosophy when it came to producing a session. "He told me something once," said Herb, "that's riveted to me like a permanent memory. He said, 'People are just listening to a cold piece of wax, and it either makes it or it don't.' When I asked him what he meant, he said, 'You know, you listen to it, you close your eyes—if you like it, great. If you don't, nobody cares if you're black or white, what kind of echo chamber you're using. If it touches you, that's the measure.'"

He took his lesson from no less unlikely a source than Louis Armstrong ("Don't listen to the voice, listen to the phrasing," he told a disbelieving Bobby Womack) and built his songs entirely around Armstrong's conversational style. "You just talk the story," he told Bobby. "That's how you get people to come to you—because it's not like a song, it's like two people rapping, only with a melody attached. But then when you come to the hook ('That's the sound of the men working on the chain gang'), then you're free, everybody's gonna sing that part, you want to get *everybody* to sing along."

That is just what Sam did. You can hear the invitation in almost every song he wrote. "Having a Party," for example, became a kind of anthem in live performance, bringing everyone on the show, from Solomon Burke to Dionne Warwick, out on stage to sing with Sam while the audience joined in. What saves it from becoming just another exercise in self-indulgent nostalgia, though, is the quality of sadness at its core. Its enduring appeal, like the magic of so much seemingly transparent art, lies in its carefully disguised underpinnings, the mournful counterpoint of cellos and violas that Sam built into the arrangement, the sixth chord that he will so often fall back on, hinting at the sonority of a minor key without ever explicitly embracing it. It's even in the words, which, however explicitly celebratory they may be, call up times that the singer strongly suggests may never come again. "So please, Mister DJ," Sam croons almost wistfully, "Keep those records playing / 'Cause I'm having such a good time / Dancing with my baby."

You listen to a song like "Nothing Can Change This Love," with its lushly orchestrated arrangement and finely calibrated evocation of apple pie, cake, and ice cream (pretty much literally), and you feel as if you are in for the most clichéd version of romantic love. But then, as the song unfolds, you catch the tart undertone, you realize that what you are hearing is not the embrace but the *denial* of illusion, set forth in a tone of deeply ambiguous regret. It is similar to the way one gets swept up in the emotion of Sam's best-known song, "A Change Is Gonna Come," written as a kind of summary of the Afro-American experience in the twentieth century and embraced almost instantly by the civil rights movement. As you listen, you cannot help but wonder what it is that has allowed this song, written about a specific time and a specific place, to live on in a manner that permits it to offer hope in the midst of hopelessness to every age. If you listen to it carefully, you will hear the doubt that it expresses ("It's been too hard living / But I'm afraid to die / I don't know what's up there / Beyond the sky"), the deepseated skepticism from which it stems ("I go to my brother / And I say, 'Brother, help me please' / But he winds up knocking me / Back down on my knees")—and yet it has stood for over forty years as a source of solace, resurrected most recently in the wake of Katrina to confirm that a change is gonna, a change almost *has* to come.

There is an inspirational quality to it, certainly, but the question naturally arises: are people misunderstanding the song, or, more likely, are all of us simply—*humanly*—inclined to put art to our own ends? Well, that is certainly undeniable, but at the same time the richness of the song, its very ambiguity, are attributable to the same qualities (clarity of tone, directness of story line, straightforwardness of language) that Sam brings to all of his writing, an openendedness that ensures that meaning is never altogether embedded in text. The fact that he can so often wrest profundity from the commonplace stems from his ability to put his finger on the pulse not just of his audience's but of his own often inaccessible feelings. Sam Cooke's music, like so much great art, represents the achievement of what appears to be effortless spontaneity, but only by dint of great effort. A song like "That's Where It's At," yet another of Sam's strangely elegiac celebrations, required a full thirty-eight takes to find its oddly off-kilter voice, the sense that what you have just encountered is little more than a natural marriage of fluidity and surprise. It is what Sun Records founder Sam Phillips liked to call perfect imperfection, the fortuitous combination of inspiration and circumstance that might in many ways be seen as the hard-won epiphany of art.

Sam Cooke was no more in control of his muse than any other creative artist; he merely attempted to be in control of the way he presented it. He told his friends and family that he was afraid of "A Change Is Gonna Come," as much as anything because he could not place its source. "The song just came to me," he told Bobby Womack. "I never scuffled with the words or anything. It was like it was somebody else's song." He shied away from it, too, he confessed, because of his concern that it might alienate some of his audience. He was afraid of it—but he could not deny it. Just as his father had taught him to reject all social and racial ceilings, he was no more inclined to accept limitations of aspiration that, in pursuit of commercial success, he might place on himself. Like all true artists, he was prepared to follow his inner voice, and like all true artists his work continues to live on in ways that are neither measurable, predictable, nor even in conformity with the intentions of their author.

My biography of Sam is called *Dream Boogie: The Triumph of Sam Cooke*. The "Dream Boogie" part is easy enough. It derives from the Langston Hughes poem which points to the inextricable link between the cultural and the political ("Good morning, daddy! / Ain't you heard / The boogie-woogie rumble of a dream deferred?"). But why the subtitle, people sometimes ask, particularly given the "senseless waste" of his death? Under the circumstances, wouldn't "tragedy" be better suited?

Well, I don't know—I guess I just don't see death as a scorecard. I had originally thought of subtitling the book "The *Education* of Sam Cooke," because of Sam's deeply analytic cast of mind, his remarkable ability to soak up anything and everything that was put in front of him and then move on. But it was Anne Sexton's poem, "To a Friend Whose Work Has Come to Triumph," that summed up my sense of Sam best, that summed up my belief that in the end it is aspiration as much as achievement that matters, it is the restless spirit of exploration that is the truest measure of creativity. Sexton's poem is, of course, about the myth of Icarus, whose father, Daedalus, fashioned wings of feathers and wax so that he and his son could escape from imprisonment in the Labyrinth, an impenetrable maze on the island of Crete. Glorying in the freedom of flight, Icarus disobeyed his father's instructions, flew too close to the sun and, when its heat melted the wax of his wings, fell into the sea and drowned.

> Consider Icarus, pasting those sticky wings on,
> testing that strange little tug at his shoulder blade,
> and think of that first flawless moment over the lawn
> of the labyrinth. Think of the difference it made!

There below are the trees, as awkward as camels;
and here are the shocked starlings pumping past
and think of innocent Icarus who is doing quite well.
Larger than a sail, over the fog and the blast
of the plushy ocean, he goes. Admire his wings!
Feel the fire at his neck and see how casually
he glances up and is caught, wondrously tunneling
into that hot eye. Who cares that he fell back to the sea?
See him acclaiming the sun and come plunging down
while his sensible daddy goes straight into town.

That to me is Sam: the casualness, the grace, the fall—but, above all, the triumph of simply daring to be one of those "wild men," in Dylan Thomas's vivid evocation, "who caught and sang the sun in flight." That is what Sam did, that is what art seeks to do, to soar higher, to stop the sun in its tracks, to invoke freedom—for us all.

Note

1. All quotes are from interviews by the author, except for the Big Bill Broonzy quote which is from Don Gold's "Big Bill Broonzy: A Man and the Blues," published in *Down Beat*, February 6, 1958; the Art Rupe quote; and the excerpt from the Ann Sexton poem "To a Friend Whose Work Has Come to Triumph." Also, thank you to ABKCO Music, Inc. for permission to quote Sam Cooke's lyrics from "Nearer to Thee" and "You Were Made for Me" both written by Sam Cooke and published by ABKCO Music, Inc.

THE JOE BLOW VERSION

DAVID KIRBY

David Kirby visits Macon, Georgia, to research his book on Little Richard and finds himself thinking about the different versions of Otis Redding's song "I've Got Dreams to Remember." As he describes in his essay, "There's a much more tortured version of 'Dreams' on the Stax Profiles CD that Steve Cropper compiled and that's called simply Otis Redding." *As Kirby explores the different versions of the song, taking the reader along with him to Macon landmarks such as Nu-Way Weiners, Macon City Auditorium, and Hummingbird Soundstage and Tap Room, Kirby confronts the idea of variability itself—and how that might be the norm when discussing poetry and songs.*

'm having a beer, or more than one, with Newt Collier in the Hummingbird Soundstage and Tap Room on Cherry Street in Macon when a big man comes in. A really big man, as a matter of fact, maybe six feet six, 280 pounds. Newt, whose first gig was with the Pinetoppers, which was Otis Redding's original backing band, says, "That's what Otis looked like when he walked into a room." This makes sense, because, when his father contracted TB, Otis dropped out of high school and took up well-digging, which, in the day, probably involved a lot more picks and shovels than power tools.

Newt used to play trombone for Sam and Dave, and he tells me they had a gimmick called "getting the Holy Spirit," which means they'd be working up a sweat and "rocking back and forth the way church people do" when suddenly Dave would fall out and the roadies would rush over to revive him. And just when it looks as though the show will have to be called off and everybody given their money back, Dave leaps to his feet and rushes back to his mike—*I'm a soul man, bah-bah-bah-bah-bah-bah-bah-bah-bah!*

Newt says Otis told manager Phil Walden he *never* wanted to be on the bill with Sam and Dave again, because Otis couldn't dance, and he couldn't stand it when Sam and Dave would "pull out that goddamned Holy Spirit gimmick every goddamned show!"

Even though it was a good gimmick, getting the Holy Spirit was a gimmick nonetheless, and after a while, gimmicks become tiresome. Otis was only twenty-six when he died, but already critics were getting on him for that gotta-gotta-gotta gimmick he used more and more frequently in every show.

I'm in Macon to research my book on Little Richard and especially "Tutti Frutti," the song that, as Keith Richard says, turned the world from one color to many. Earlier that day, I'd had lunch at the Market City Café with Karla Redding-Andrews, who was only four years old when her father died. She had a salad, I had the meatloaf sandwich, and then we decided to split a serving of the Market City's deservedly famous banana pudding, which comes in a cinnamon-dusted pastry shell.

It is, hands down, the best dessert in the world. I've been back to the Market City Café many times, and I always get the banana pudding. Now banana pudding is one of those things that turns folks prideful, and every time I tell somebody in Macon that I know where to find the world's best banana pudding, it's a little like claiming that the baby you just saw is more beautiful than all the other babies in town. "I'll put my banana pudding up against theirs any time," they'll say, or "No, baby, you got to try my mama's before you can say you had real banana pudding."

But no matter how good it is, when you're splitting a banana pudding with Karla Redding-Andrews, you've got to be a better man than I am not to salt your creamy dessert with your own tears, because Karla's the spitting image of her dad. So I'm okay as long as I'm asking her what makes a song a standard as opposed to a piece of pop fluff that's here today and gone tomorrow ("I don't mean to be rude," Karla says, "but do you think that, in ten years, anybody is going to be singing a song by _____," and here she says the name of a popular R&B artist whom I'd better not identify, either for fear that I'll want to write about him one day and he'll snub me or, worse, beat my ass). But if I let myself think "I'm having lunch with Otis Redding's daughter!" I hear "Security" and "Mr. Pitiful" and "Dock of the Bay" and begin to tear up.

But I hang in there, and after I finish my lunch with Karla, who likes the banana pudding so much that she gets a to-go order for Zelma, her mother, I hit the streets, looking for places to go and people to talk to. When I realize that I kept my camera in my pocket the whole time we were eating banana pudding and forgot to get a picture, I track Karla down at the Macon City Auditorium where she's meeting Zelma to plan the tribute concert they're having to commemorate the fortieth anniversary of Otis's death. There I meet Zelma and get pictures of Karla and Zelma, Karla and me, Zelma and me, and Karla and Zelma and me.

Otis was only twenty-six years old when his plane went down, and Zelma was barely out of her girlhood. At the funeral, she broke down as Joe Simon sang

"Jesus Keep Me Near the Cross," and there are people in Macon today who still recall with horror her screams.

Sometimes interviewers want to know what dead people I'd like to have dinner with, but my answer to that is nobody. I mean, I wouldn't mind following Dante around and seeing who he talks to and where he shops and what his writing schedule is, but can you imagine trying to have a conversation with Dante? Yeah, he wrote the greatest poem ever, but his worldview would be totally different from mine, plus his temper was supposed to have been terrible.

Shakespeare wouldn't say anything, probably; he'd be storing up bits for his next play. Whitman would probably talk your head off, and then you'd be bored and not like his work as much as you used to. No, I don't want to have dinner with anybody.

But if I could time-travel, I'd like to go to Jamaica in 1967 and be sitting at a table and drinking a Red Stripe in the after-hours club where Bob Marley is playing, and Otis Redding, who is touring the island, comes in "like a god," according to eyewitness accounts, and Bob Marley looks up and begins to sing "These Arms of Mine."

Wow. I wouldn't be myself. I'd be Troilus or Tristan or Lancelot, crying my eyes out for Cressida or Isolde or Guinevere. She'd be on the battlements of a castle in Troy or Wales or England, all beautiful and sad-eyed, and I'd be clanking up a storm as I drop my lance and brush back my visor and pound the table with my mailed fist while all the rastas look at me and say, "I and I a-go cool out wit' a spliff, mon!" "But if you would let these arms, if you would let these arms of mine, oh, if you would just let them hold you, oh, how grateful I would be."

Back in the Hummingbird, Newt is telling me Otis's secret. "He's a torch singer," Newt says. "Everybody puts him in with Little Richard and James Brown, but that's rhythm 'n' blues and funk." I agree vaguely, not knowing what a torch singer is, exactly, but when I get back to my hotel, I look it up on Wikipedia, which defines "torch song" as "a sentimental love song, typically one in which the singer laments an unrequited or lost love, where one party is either oblivious to the existence of the other, or where one party has moved on." (The phrase comes from "'to carry a torch for someone', or to keep aflame the light of an unrequited love.") Of the sixty-six notable torch singers listed in the Wikipedia article, only one, Frank Sinatra, is a man.

Add Otis Redding to the list. Wait, I just did—I logged into Wikipedia and entered Otis's name between those of Ma Rainey and Della Reese.

And of all his songs, none is torchier than "I've Got Dreams to Remember," or at least one version of that hymn to heartbreak is.

Back at the Hummingbird, Big Man is sitting at the bar looking sad, and when a man that size is sad, he's *really* sad, so sad that you have to work hard at not being sad yourself. Big Man's throwing them back like nobody's business, like he's cruising to get a DWI for not having enough blood in his alcohol stream. If he keeps up at this pace, Big Man's going to be toxic. If rattlesnakes bite Big Man, they'll die.

And I wonder if he isn't thinking about a girl, which is when I think of "I've Got Dreams to Remember," which is Otis's saddest song. And that's saying a lot, because he had a lot of them—even his happy songs are sad—though the saddest of them all is "I've Got Dreams to Remember," the standard version of which tells of a man who sees his baby in another man's arms, and the woman says that other man was just a friend, and the singer says, yeah, but I saw you kiss him again and again and again, and every time he says "again," it's like a door slamming on your hand, a pipe coming down on your head, a nail going into your heart again and again and again. You can find that one on *The Very Best of Otis Redding*, which is the CD most people are likely to have; it's also the only version you'll hear on oldies stations.

But there's a much more tortured version of "Dreams" on the Stax Profiles CD that Steve Cropper compiled and that's called simply *Otis Redding*. Cropper played guitar on and helped produce all of Otis's studio sessions at Stax between 1962 and the singer's death in 1967, and in his liner notes, Cropper says that "Otis had the gift of getting musicians to play things they normally wouldn't play." On this song, the singer gets something out of himself that appears nowhere else in his music, something so painful that it seems to come from the underworld, a razor-wire tentacle to draw you down into the fire as you claw at the ground and grab at the roots of the trees and try to hang on to the last happiness you'll ever know.

You'll have to hear it to experience it. Here, though, suffice it to say that, in this version of "I've Got Dreams to Remember," the singer says he dreamed they were walking down the street together, him and his girl, and Joe Blow comes up and grabs her, and she just turns and walks away with him.

And you think, Joe Blow? Not Sam Cooke or Elvis or Muhammad Ali, but Joe Blow, i.e., anybody, any mullygrubbing, chicken-and-biscuit eating dipstick, only now he's got your baby and you're, like, dead, I mean, you can see what's going on around you and hear people talking and laughing and having fun, only you're not having any of it, and you feel the way Muslims feel when they undergo the "torments of the grave," which is when you die and are grilled by the angels Munkar and Nakir, and if you give the right answers, a window to paradise opens and you go back to sleep and wait to travel to the wonderful place you've just had a glimpse of, whereas if you answer wrong, demons are unleashed on your front and back, the grave closes in, and your ribs break. Where's my baby? Where are my friends? Fuck! Lemme out of here!

What do dreams mean, if anything? In his *The Interpretation of Dreams*, Freud says every dream is a wish fulfillment, which is not especially comforting if you've just dreamed that you hacked your mother to death with a butcher knife (unless, of course, that's something you're dying to do). Freud being Freud, he'd say the problem there is not examining the dream fully, looking at its every feature, even the minor ones—in fact, especially the minor ones.

The classic example in *Interpretation* of a dream that is morbid on the surface but nonetheless expresses a healthy wish is the one in which a troubled young woman comes to see Freud because she has a recurrent dream in which she is at the funeral of a nephew she loves. Does this mean she wants the little boy to die? By going over the dream with his patient repeatedly and getting her to describe the funeral in detail, Freud finally elicits her memory of a shadowy figure, a young professor she has a crush on and whom she saw once at another funeral, this one also of a child.

That's the wish, then: not for the boy to die, but for the dreamer to be near the man she loves, yet in a situation that calls for the utmost decorum, that is, one where there is absolutely no chance of her betraying her feelings.

Freud was to change his mind about the nature of dreams in *Beyond the Pleasure Principle*. After treating shell-shocked World War I veterans who repeatedly dreamed of their woundings, he conjectured that not all dreams were wish fulfillments.

Most recently, it's been suggested that the main function of dreaming is merely physiological in nature rather than psychological. In a November 9, 2009, article in the *New York Times*, Benedict Carey writes that, according to Harvard sleep researcher J. Allan Hobson, the dreaming brain is simply "warming its circuits, anticipating the sights and sounds and emotions of waking."

Yet Freud's wish fulfillment idea remains the most satisfying way to think about our dreams, *even if it's wrong*. Why? Because it compels us to do the two things that the distressed young woman did, which was, first, to look at all the evidence (including the adorable professor), not just the dominant bits (the dead nephew), and, second, to interpret. We look at poems that way, and a dream is an unedited poem of sorts, which is why, though Freud may be dead to cognitive behavior therapists, he will always be important to readers of poetry.

So what is the singer in the Joe Blow version of "I've Got Dreams to Remember" saying? One of Freud's central tenets is that we have mixed emotions even about those we love, a revolutionary idea in his lifetime. For millennia before Freud, civilization had been in denial, even though Sophocles and Shakespeare told us otherwise; now we take it for granted that, simultaneously, we can feel desire and repulsion and a dozen other urges.

So maybe the singer's trying to get the girl to rush to him, to say there is no Joe Blow, to declare her love. Or maybe he's trying to drive her off! Maybe he doesn't love her anymore, and maybe he's not ready to admit that, and this is the worse of two thoughts for many of us; sometimes it's easier for us to have our hearts broken than to break another's.

Or maybe the singer is just having a good time feeling bad. Sometimes you want to induce what Keats calls a "waking dream," and that can mean an intense dream rather than a pleasant one.

After an evening of watching Big Man try to drown his miseries and, perhaps in half-conscious empathy, ordering at least one drink to every two of his, the next morning I am on my way to Nu-Way Weiners on Cotton Avenue for their hang-over cure, even though they don't call it that. I'm talking about the Scrambled Dog Platter, an open-faced hot dog smothered in chili and—and I suggest you not laugh at this, reader, because by doing so you would be exhibiting a churlish disregard for one of the great dishes in the roadside diner repertory—oyster crackers, crunchy hexagons that contrast nicely with the rich stew of beans and bread and meat.

On my way to the Nu-Way, whom do I run into on the sidewalk but Zelma, who is coming out of the Nu-Way and heading to the Macon City Auditorium again with two chili dogs, one for Karla and one for herself. We chat for a minute, and then I wash my Scrambled Dog Platter down with a pot of black coffee and head over to the Georgia Music Hall of Fame to talk with then-curator Joseph Johnson.

When I tell him about my obsession with this one song, Joseph shows me a piece of paper with the chorus of "I've Got Dreams to Remember" in pencil in Zelma's schoolgirl hand. Again, I tear up. Zelma was in her early twenties and close still to the blush of first love when she wrote these words. Otis was away on tour, and according to an e-mail from Jared Wright, current curator of the GMHF, Zelma meant to say she "had all her memories of Otis to keep her company while he was gone."

So you're thinking how handsome your sweetheart is, how much you love him, how you'll part one day, sure, but that won't be for years. And then you find out it's one year, the plane falling out of the Wisconsin night, trumpeter Ben Cauley alone surviving by unbuckling himself and grabbing the seat cushion that keeps him afloat and listening to the others as they thrash and scream in the icy water. When I even think about those lyrics in Zelma's handwriting, I suffer the tortures inflicted on the unworthy dead by the angels Munkar and Nakir.

When you're fighting against death, though, sometimes that's when you feel the most alive.

Jared Wright continues the story of the song's composition in his e-mail:

> When Otis returned from the road, she gave those handwritten lyrics to him, saying that she had written out an idea for a song. Otis took the paper and later added

the verses, which significantly changed the meaning of the song. [. . .] The hand-
written copy that you're thinking of is the one she gave to Otis which contained
the eventual 'dreams to remember' hook plus some other lines that were left out of
the version that was recorded.

So there are at least three versions of "I've Got Dreams to Remember": the
canonical one on *The Very Best of Otis Redding* that everyone knows; the virtually
private "Dreams" on the *Otis Redding* album; and the original manuscript that
contained the song's most important words as well as the ones Otis ignored during his rewrite but without which there would be no song at all. (Credit is given
to both Otis and Zelma on both albums, as "Redding/Redding" on the first and
"O. Redding–Z. Redding" on the second.)

And we can only speculate about the lost versions that were sung in live performance but never recorded; I have a feeling that the Joe Blow Version is a variant on one of these. After all, in shows, so many songs become anthems, liable
to change at any moment and seemingly without end. Cosimo Matassa, who
produced the "Tutti Frutti" that changed music forever, told me that song would
go on for twenty minutes or more, "and if you walked into the club wearing a
blue suit, you'd be in the song! 'See the man with the blue suit on,' etc."

Some of the songs that get under our skin the most aren't written so much
as assembled. In *The Old, Weird America*, cultural historian Greil Marcus writes
that so many songs are made out of "verbal fragments that had no direct or logical relationship to each other, but were drawn from a floating pool of thousands
of disconnected verses, couplets, one-liners" and eventually achieved "a kind of
critical mass."

Ted Anthony's *Chasing the Rising Sun: The Journey of an American Song* is the
story of one such song and one that does its best to crack the listener's ribs as
least as much as "Dreams" does. Anthony writes of what he calls the "floating
lyric," that is, one that occurs originally in one song but then migrates to another where it might be more appropriate. The result is what he calls "handmade
music" on one page and "mongrel music" on another. The latter isn't a negative description, as Anthony uses it; our mix of "heritages and experiences and
outlooks and travails makes us stronger and healthier," he writes, "both in our
culture and in the music. [. . .] We come from what we believe is a single world,
but it is so many, all existing at once."

The worlds that flow into the single matrix that is "The House of the Rising
Sun" include, for starters, New Orleans, the forbidden city, the home of Mardi
Gras, the festival of masks. There's the house itself, most likely not a mere bor-
dello but an all-purpose sin palace, a temple of gambling and drink and dope and
the pleasures of the flesh. There's family: the mother who sews for a living, the
father who is never there, the brother (or sister, depending on the version) who

must be protected from the life of "sheer misery" from which the singer can't escape.

Like "I've Got Dreams to Remember," "House" exists in different versions, and in some, "The House of the Rising Sun" seems like a prison. But the real jail here is the one the singer has built for himself. The verse that haunts the most is one that occurs late in the song, the one that says:

> One foot is on the platform
> and the other one on the train.
> I'm going back to New Orleans
> to wear that ball and chain.

These lines shake with horror. The singer has escaped—he's not even in New Orleans anymore—yet he can't stay away. He knows he should stay in Cleveland or Detroit or wherever he is; he's got enough scratch for a train ticket, so he can just keep moving, if he wants to, can join the tide of drifters and grifters and lowlifes that ebb and flow along the rail lines, in and out of cities great and small, just in reach of a handout or a day of backbreaking labor, just out of sight of the law.

Instead, the singer's already got one foot on the step of that train car. He's going back to New Orleans, to the thing that will kill him, yet the thing he can't resist, just as the singer in "I've Got Dreams to Remember" knows he can't stay away from the woman who will destroy him. In both cases, it's like being offered the Hope Diamond: It's going to take your life, but you can't say no.

Most of us will never face such a dilemma. Yet each of us is to some degree a slave to the poison in our own veins, to the darkness that we fear and despise and that makes us human.

When I write my colleague Anne Coldiron, a textual scholar, about my interest in the instability of the lyrics to "I've Got Dreams to Remember," she says this: "Your Otis example stands in a venerable line. Some of us more recent textual scholars say that variability *is* the norm, and that the older ways of handling texts, ways of attempting to stabilize, to create and/or to declare 'definitive' editions, to establish copy text (a loaded term in this field), and so on, are not just out of date but do not reflect the truth of things."

Coldiron describes the canon making that shaped the literature curriculum for decades and that broke only under the call for new texts that began in the sixties and continues today: "The nineteenth century in particular was an age of canon founding," she writes, "and thus of efforts to establish copy text, fix authorship, lay out national literary histories, and set up curriculum."

Of course, canon making extends well beyond the confines of the university English department, just as it goes back much farther in time. The Bible that is the basis for every form of Christianity was assembled in the fourth century by a papal synod that included the books we have today and excluded others, notably the Gnostic books.

And Shakespeare's plays exist in different versions, notably in the case of *King Lear*. Apparently some versions include lines by someone other than the bard of Stratford. Shakespearean scholar Christie Carson writes in "The Quarto of *King Lear*": "Over time the text of *King Lear* has changed drastically owing to the work of editors and theatre artists. From the outset *King Lear* existed in two very different versions, the Quarto of 1608 and the Folio of 1623. While there are many hypotheses about the origins of the Quarto editions all that is certain is that they appeared in Shakespeare's lifetime—but the playwright seems not to have been involved in their creation. [. . .] Some would argue that the differences between the Quarto and the Folio reflect changes made to the play as it was performed in Shakespeare's theatre—changes in which the playwright may or may not have had a hand."

Today textual scholars work less to create literary canons and more to show how variants not only exist but challenge, enrich, and, as I say of the Joe Blow version of "I've Got Dreams to Remember," exceed the accomplishments of the better-known variant. W. H. Auden notoriously revised his poems, and his literary executor, Edward Mendelson, writes this in his introduction to the *Selected Poems*: "By revising his poems, Auden opened his workshop to the public, and the spectacle proved unsettling, especially when his revisions, unlike Yeats's, moved against the current of literary fashion. In the essays he wrote in the later part of his career, Auden increasingly called attention to the technical aspects of poetry, the details of metrical and stanzaic construction—much as Brecht had brought his stagehands into the full view of the audience. The goal in each case was to remove the mystery that surrounds works of art, to explode the myth of poetic inspiration, and to deny any special privileges to poetry in the realm of language or to artists in the realm of ethics."

So, too, does a musical "textual scholar" like the Steve Cropper who preserved the Joe Blow version of "I've Got Dreams to Remember" remove the mystery and, in so doing, heighten the pleasure. In Cropper's version of Otis's song, the first sound you hear is a producer saying "Three, four" and Otis starting to sing and then saying "Al, don't say four, because then I'm on you" as the producer counts "One, two, three," and the song starts over.

So you songwriters and poets, keep revising—keep changing up your pitches. And you Steve Croppers, Anne Coldirons, Edward Mendelsons, and Christie Carsons, keep doing what I have done here, which is to argue for one version over another, sure, but, mainly, show all the versions in their variety.

For what works in art is that which startles and surprises, and what doesn't work is the rote, the familiar—the tired "gimmick," as Newt Collier calls a hack piece of showbiz trickeration. In *Gravity and Grace*, Simone Weil writes of the "monotony of evil: never anything new [. . .]. That is hell itself."

We should ask of art no less than we ask of life, which, as they say, is full of surprises. When I run into Zelma Redding outside of Nu-Way Weiners, we chat awhile, and I wish her luck with the tribute concert, and I start to walk away, and then I turn and say, "Oh! Zelma! Wasn't that banana pudding good?"

And Zelma says, "What banana pudding?"

Works Cited

Note: I have identified sources by other authors in the text. While most of what I contribute to the discussion is new, I have pillaged past writings of mine. These include my book *Little Richard: The Birth of Rock 'n' Roll*, as well as three poems about my Macon experiences: "Big Man's Got the Blues," "These Arms of Mine," and "What Zelma Found Out at the Nu-Way." In addition, some material appeared earlier in two newspaper pieces by me, an article about Macon (in the *Washington Post*) and a review of the Ted Anthony book (the *Christian Science Monitor*).

Anthony, Ted. *Chasing the Rising Sun: The Journey of an American Song*. New York: Simon and Schuster, 2007. 4.

Carey, Benedict. *New York Times* 9 November 2009.

Carson, Christie. "The Quarto of *King Lear*—representing the early stage history of the play?" *Treasures in Full: Shakespeare in Quarto*. British Library website, 2 February 2010. www.bl.uk/treasures/shakespeare/lear.html.

Coldiron, Anne. "The Unstable Lyric." E-mail to the author, 23 February 2010.

Collier, Newt. Personal interview, August 6, 2007.

Cropper, Steve. "Liner notes." *Stax Profiles*. Stax, 2006.

Crosby, Fanny. "Jesus, Keep Me Near the Cross." Music by William Doane. Before 1869.

Freud, Sigmund. *Beyond the Pleasure Principle*. New York: Barnes and Noble, 2006.

Freud, Sigmund. *The Interpretation of Dreams: The Complete and Definitive Text*. Trans. James Strachey. New York: Basic, 2010.

"The House of the Rising Sun." Traditional folk song.

Johnson, Joseph. Personal interview.

Keats, John. "Ode to a Nightingale." *The Complete Poems of John Keats*. New York: Modern Library, 1994.

Little Richard. "Tutti Frutti." *Here's Little Richard*. Specialty, 1956.

Marcus, Greil. *The Old, Weird America: The World of Bob Dylan's Basement Tapes*. New York: Picador, 2001. 116.

Matassa, Cosimo. Personal interview.

Mendelson, Edward. "Introduction." *Selected Poems*. By W. H. Auden. New York: Vintage, 2007. xxvii.

Redding, Otis. "(Sittin' On) The Dock of the Bay." *The Dock of the Bay*. Volt/Atco, 1968.

———. "I've Got Dreams to Remember." *Stax Profiles*. Written by Otis Redding, Zelma Redding, and Joe Rock. Stax, 2006.

———. "I've Got Dreams to Remember." *The Very Best of Otis Redding, Vol. 1*. Written by Otis Redding, Zelma Redding, and Joe Rock. Rhino, 1992.

———. "Mr. Pitiful." *The Great Otis Redding Sings Soul Ballads*. Written by Steve Cropper and Otis Redding. Volt/Atco, 1965.

———. "Security." *Otis! The Definitive Otis Redding*. Rhino, 1993.

———. "These Arms of Mine." Volt Records, 1962.

Redding-Andrews, Karla. Personal interview, August 5, 2007.

Redding, Zelma. Personal interview, August 5, 2007.

Sam & Dave. "Soul Man." *Soul Man*. Music and lyrics by Isaac Hayes and David Porter. Atlantic, 1967.

"Torch song." *Wikipedia*. en.wikipedia.org/wiki/Torch_song.

Weil, Simone. *Gravity and Grace*. Trans. Emma Craufurd. London: Routledge, 1988. 62.

Wright, Jared. "Looking for Otis." Email to the author, February 1, 2010.

A NOBEL FOR DYLAN?

GORDON BALL

This article argues for Bob Dylan's nomination for the Nobel Prize in Literature. Traditional criteria for the award include outstanding idealism and work that benefits mankind, criteria that are easily met in Dylan's case, given his activism in early 1960s civil rights, antiwar compositions, and beyond. Yet questions have been raised concerning Dylan's eligibility for such an award. Can a literary prize go to a writer of song? Past Nobels in Literature display a breadth that admits such a lineage, and the connections between music and poetry have been noted by Laureates Rabindranath Tagore and W. B. Yeats. The Literature Prize has gone to historians and philosophers as well. From whatever standpoint Dylan's work is viewed, this article argues that it deserves consideration for literature's highest prize.

For decades I have admired the work of Bob Dylan, whom I saw at Newport 1965; my memoir *'66 Frames* relates first contact with his music, and he has a small cameo in my chronicle of years on a farm with Allen Ginsberg and others.

In August 1996 I first wrote the Nobel Committee, nominating Dylan for its literature prize. The idea to do so originated not with me but with two Dylan aficionados in Norway, journalist Reidar Indrebø and attorney Gunnar Lunde, who had recently written Ginsberg about a Nobel for Dylan. Ginsberg's office then asked if I would write a nominating letter. (Nominators must be professors of literature or linguistics, past Laureates, presidents of national writers' groups, or members of the Swedish Academy or similar groups.) Over the next few months several other professors, including Stephen Scobie, Daniel Karlin, and Betsy Bowden, endorsed Dylan for the Nobel.

Examining Prize criteria, I learned that Alfred Nobel's 1895 will specified that in literature the work must be "'the most outstanding . . . of an idealistic tendency'"; and that "'during the preceding year'" the honorée must "'have conferred the greatest benefit on mankind'" (Frenz, Introduction vii). As Horst

Frenz reports in *Nobel Lectures: Literature*, the second stipulation was interpreted by Nobel Foundation statutes "to mean that awards should be made 'for the most recent achievements in the field of culture' and that older works should be considered only in cases where their importance 'has not become apparent until recently'" (Introduction vii).

However, a review of awards and their presentation statements since 1901 suggests considerable latitude in terms of recent achievement and revised appreciation of earlier work. While some Nobel presentations focus more on an author's latest creation (or, as with Faulkner, on a new view of his entire oeuvre), others seem to take in a whole career. In the case of Icelandic novelist Halldor Laxness (1955), the most recent work cited was published nine years earlier. T. S. Eliot was over a quarter century removed from *The Waste Land* when he received his Nobel recognition.

Though a recent statement from the Swedish Academy emphasizes literary and artistic values (Allén and Espmark 47), in the earliest years Nobel's "idealistic tendency" was taken to mean that it was "not primarily a literary prize" but also one recognizing elevating views of humanity (Espmark 10). However, the senses of "idealistic tendency" have varied greatly over time, and have even included "uncompromising integrity in the description of the human predicament" (Allén and Espmark 47).

Few would challenge Bob Dylan's "uncompromising integrity" in depicting the "human predicament." Yet many may ask whether the Nobel Committee should break with perceived tradition for a writer and performer of song. Is Dylan's work truly of sufficient literary quality to join that of time-honored masters of the pen? Can an icon of popular culture, a "song and dance man," stand shoulder-to-shoulder with literary giants? Bobby Zimmerman alongside Jean-Paul Sartre, Albert Camus, and Gunter Grass?

In 1900 Nobel statutes defined "'literature'" as "'not only belles-lettres, but also other writings which, by virtue of their form and style, possess literary value'" (Espmark 4). In fact, music and poetry have been historically linked, and Dylan's work has helped renew that vital connection. The art of poetry is thousands of years old; it began in performance and has survived in good part on oral strengths, less through the rather recent convenience of moveable type. In our era Bob Dylan has helped return poetry to its primordial transmission by human breath; he has revived traditions of bard, minstrel, troubadour.

This vital connection between music and poetry had been weakened, at least in the United States, from the 1930s into the 1960s by New Critical emphasis on poem as written text to be explicated, de-emphasizing orality. In revitalizing this relationship it is as if Dylan had heeded Ezra Pound's observation that ". . . both in Greece and in Provence the poetry attained its highest rhythmic and metrical brilliance at times when the arts of verse and music were most closely knit together, when each thing done by the poet had some definite musical urge or necessity bound up within it" ("The Tradition" 91). And Pound referred to poetry and music as "twin arts" (91). Greek lyric poetry is said to have been sung and accompanied; indeed, even the figure of Homer singing with harp or lyre (as some conceive) may not be as distant from the blue-eyed son prophesying with his guitar as the millennia between them suggest. For Pound, so important was the musical aspect of verse that he proposed: "For practical contact with all past poetry that was actually *sung* in its own day I suggest that . . . universities combine in employing a couple of singers who understand the meanings of words. . . . A half-dozen hours spent in listening to the lyrics actually performed would give the student more knowledge . . . than a year's work in philology" ("How to Read" 39).

Needless to say, I do not mean to suggest that the Greek "singer of tales" and "the vagabond who's rapping at your door" share an interchangeable identity. Homer was an epic poet; Dylan can be seen as a lyrical one. The music we might associate with the entity or consciousness called Homer may have been more elemental: perhaps he intoned, rather than sang; translator Robert Fitzgerald claims not to know the precise relationship between voice and verse and instrument (489). In the view of some scholars, including Robert Fagles and Bernard Knox, Homer "may have known a rudimentary form of writing" (Fagles ix), though Knox allows that Homer "probably did sing in performance" (7). In any case, the link between poetry and music is historic. As W. B. Stanford tells us, "In Greek and Roman education music and poetry were kept together in the discipline called <u>mousiké</u>" (27). He also asserts that "Poetry's earliest name in Greek . . . primarily meant 'song'; and the poet was called a singer . . . long before he was called a maker. . . ." (27). Whether Dylan is first poet or musician is open for debate, as it has been, evidently, in Dylan's mind. Christopher Ricks (11–12) has demonstrated this with Dylan's own words. If we select some of Dylan's comments on the issue and place them in chronological order, we can see his own varying views of the subject over time:

> "The words are just as important as the music. There would be no music without the words." (1965)
> "It's the music that the words are sung to that's important." (1968)
> "It ain't the melodies that're important man, it's the words." (1971)
> "I consider myself a poet first and a musician second." (1978)

My point, then, is rather modest: poetry and music share time-honored ground, are often bound closely together, and Dylan's great gifts may be appreciated within such a performative lineage.

Moreover, some Nobel awards have demonstrated that media overlap and merge, yet deserve this highest recognition. The Prize has gone to nine dramatists, whose work depends on performance by others skilled in a mixed media range of arts and crafts: lighting, acting, set design, music, dance. Even the literature prize to Sir Winston Churchill—one of two historians to win it—was awarded in part for his "'brilliant oratory'" (Frenz, *Nobel Lectures* 487).

In 1997 the Nobel went to Dario Fo. Some observations by Burton Feldman in *The Nobel Prize: A History of Genius, Controversy, and Prestige* may apply: ". . . many consider [Fo] not a dramatist but a writer of scripts for his own performances. He is a vivid and popular actor of farce and satire. . . . In each performance he improvises at will, so that his scripts are never quite available in permanent form, but remain prompt-books. He is the first postmodern 'playwright'—or performance artist—in the Nobel list" (87).

Idealism and benefiting humanity often, of course, move hand in hand, and Dylan's idealistic, activist songs have helped change our world. His 1963 Tom Paine Award (an earlier recipient, Bertrand Russell, was one of three philosophers—not counting Sartre—to win the Nobel in Literature) came after "Blowin' in the Wind," "Oxford Town," and other works, as well as his going south for voter registration ("In the days when you could get shot for it," said Mississippi novelist Barry Hannah [283]). An attitude in his 1965 "It's Alright, Ma (I'm Only Bleeding)"—"even the President of the United States / sometimes must have / to stand naked" (*Lyrics* 157)—may have helped revise our view of presidential authority, encouraging inquiry into what became Watergate.

For a generation raised in conformity, Dylan validated imagination and independence of thought; his work was central to the creativity of the 1960s in the U.S., and has affected others elsewhere. Asked if growing up in West Germany he had an "American dream," German Foreign Minister Joschka Fischer replied "'Not an American dream, but my very own dream of freedom. That was for me the music of Bob Dylan'" (qtd. in Noack 33).

Nor has Dylan's idealism been wholly confined to one period, as later songs have shown: the sentimental fatherly idealism of "Forever Young"; the extraordinary songs of religious idealism such as "Every Grain of Sand"; the expression of an aesthetic ideal—against a torched historical landscape—in the brilliant but fated blues singer Blind Willie McTell, who would recognize that "power and greed and corruptible seed / Seem to be all that there is" (*Lyrics* 478); the search for a classical character trait, "Dignity." And if I may offer a personal example: here at VMI, trudging along in uniform past fortress-like barracks, returning salutes from cadets, I have of a sudden heard a haunting, familiar voice from far away and behind the wall, calling for a new world of human possibility.

To return to the relationship of poetry and music, and Dylan's literary value: Rabindranath Tagore, Nobel winner in 1913, set many of his own poems to music. Yeats, quoting a Bengali speaker as he introduced Tagore's *Gitanjali*, reported, "'He is as great in music as in poetry, and his songs are sung from the west of India into Burmah wherever Bengali is spoken'" (viii). And the 1923 award to

Yeats himself noted that in his verse "There is a greater element of song than is usual in modern English poetry" (Hallstrom 196).

If there is, thus, recognition of this linkage of poetry and music in the case of past Nobel winners, we might ask whether Dylan's works—on the page—can rest companionably with enshrined works of literature. The answer is decidedly positive. Dylan's ability to evoke an entire milieu with a few swift words is reminiscent of Chekhov. The opening of "Just Like a Woman" with its suggestion of a whole social scene ("Nobody feels any pain / Tonight as I stand inside the rain" [*Lyrics* 202]) brings to my mind that of "Lady with a Dog": "A new person, it was said, had appeared on the esplanade . . ." (412). Dylan's view of life as a journey, as well as his assuming the role of prophet or *voyant*, recalls visionary Arthur Rimbaud. And his prophecy has been borne out time and again. Consider a line from "A Hard Rain's A-Gonna Fall" in terms of recent conditions here: "I saw guns and sharp swords in the hands of young children" (*Lyrics* 59). And across our planet: "Where the pellets of poison are flooding their waters" (*Lyrics* 60).

Dylan's eclecticism and inventiveness can be compared to Yeats. That is, in Yeats Celtic and English coalesce; in Dylan linguistic and musical idioms of ancient folk music and contemporary rock and roll become as one. In Bob Dylan, Scots balladeers meet Little Richard. That his imagery resists numerous attempts at schematization by hosts of scholars ("'People *dissect* my songs like rabbits,'" he once remarked [qtd. in Brown]), testifies to its power as poetry.

In examining the human condition Dylan can be as grim and unappealing as William Faulkner; indeed, much of his work ("Visions of Johanna," "Most of the Time") shows "the human heart in conflict with itself" that Faulkner, receiving his Nobel, required for "good writing" (Faulkner 444). Surely his experimentalism and variety are as rich as Faulkner's: love songs of bittersweet poignancy ("Most of the Time") and shocking realism ("Ballad in Plain D"); stark indictments of human nature ("I Dreamed I Saw St. Augustine"); adaptations of earlier songs, including "A Hard Rain's A-Gonna Fall," that inspired revision of "Lord Randall." There are works that seem foremost aesthetic, or about the power of art, such as "Mr. Tambourine Man"; there are songs of wisdom ("My Back Pages") and, as we have noted, from the beginning, songs of social protest, songs of prophecy.

One of Bob Dylan's recent releases, so to speak, is *Chronicles*, the first in a planned three-volume series of personal recollections—and finalist for the 2005 National Book Critics Prize in Biography and Memoir and winner of the 2005 Quill Book Award in biography/memoir. I know a little about memoirs; I have read a few, and have published two. And so I was intrigued to learn of Dylan's, eager to examine it with certain basic questions in mind. Will I find the obfuscation that colored certain earlier autobiographical depictions of his life, especially in interviews? Will someone who not merely seems to value but cherish privacy reveal *anything* of significance? He has invited familiarity in "You may call me Bobby, you may call me Zimmy" (*Lyrics* 402)—but in song, where we recognize the principle of persona. In memoir, we may like to think, we can get closer to truth.

Overall, I find the value of *Chronicles* extraordinary, though, true to form, Dylan denies being "the conscience of a generation" (115). Here are accounts from the whirlwind's center: the unknown nineteen-year-old from the provinces driven by a sense of destiny into the heart of New York's folk music scene; the star in his late twenties, hostage to fame, shocked when asked by Robbie Robertson, "'Where do you think you're gonna take . . . the whole music scene?" (117).

Those early days are vividly recalled in *Chronicles*: his reading Thucydides's *Athenian General*, "which would give you chills" (36); Mike Seeger, "the supreme archetype" folk musician who "could push a stake through Dracula's black heart" (169); how "the bells went off'" when first he read Rimbaud's formulation of the unstable nature of the self—"*Je est un autre*" (288).

Along with his oratory, the 1953 Nobel award cited Churchill for his "mastery of historical and biographical description" (Frenz, *Nobel Lectures* 487); perhaps Dylan's three volumes, when completed, will constitute a lasting and complex personal, historically central, and cultural record that only this individual could offer. As the Nobel presentation to Churchill claimed, "There is something special about history written by a man who has himself helped to make it" (Siwertz 490).

Having sketched some of the idealism and benefits to humanity in the works of Mr. Dylan; having considered them within the context of poetry; having brought his lyrics shoulder-to-shoulder with literary masters and examined his most recent publication in light of an earlier Prize; we might note one other concern associated with the awarding of a Nobel: that the work so honored meet the test of experience or examination of experts (Nobel Foundation). Dylan, of course, has satisfied both criteria.

As for the former, it is apparent today that Dylan's work has not merely survived the course of forty-five years, but—as Faulkner in Stockholm 1950 predicted of mankind (qtd. in Frenz, *Nobel lectures* 445)—it has prevailed. Just a few of the countless indications: the 1996 adaptation of "Knockin' on Heaven's Door" by a Scottish anti-gun campaign; Dylan's performance for the Pope and 300,000 others in 1997, with John Paul quoting from a Dylan song already then a quarter century old; Dylan's appearance on a major American news magazine interview program in 2004, with interviewer Ed Bradley insisting, despite his guest's disclaimer, that in the minds of many he's been gifted with special insight on the level of a prophet (Dylan, "Interview"). Indeed, one can see that Yeats's prediction about the future of verses of Tagore ("travelers will hum them on the highway and men rowing upon rivers. Lovers . . . murmuring them" [xv]) has been realized many times over by Dylan.

As for meeting the examination of the experts: various academic textbooks, including the Norton *Introduction to Literature* (2005) and the *Portable Beat Reader* (1992), have reproduced his lyrics. The enlarged edition of the *Princeton Encyclopedia of Poetry and Poetics* included an entry on the "Rock Lyric," where specific songs by Dylan are given as examples of the incorporation of "elements of modern poetry": "Alienation as objectified in a dissociated modern sensibility . . . Dylan's 'Desolation Row' (which refers specifically to Pound and Eliot) . . . Surrealism—used . . . to render a sense of social chaos (Dylan's 'Memphis Blues Again') . . . Highly complex wordplay and intricate themes: Dylan's 'Subterranean Homesick Blues.'"

Forty-six years ago, critic Ralph Gleason declared Dylan "the first American poet to touch everyone, to hit all walks of life in this great sprawling society" (28). More recently, Danny Goldberg's *Dispatches from the Culture Wars* concluded with a warning to the American Left that demonstrates the timelessness of a Dylan theme: "Bob Dylan's message of four decades ago still works: 'You better start swimming or you'll sink like a stone, for the times they are a changin'" (312).

Poet Andrei Codrescu once exclaimed, "'Dylan? He's the best living American poet there is, man!'" (qtd. in Spitzer). In 1996, poet and Distinguished Professor Allen Ginsberg told me his works were "prolific and memorable, and memorableness is a mark of great poetry." Proposing him for the Literature prize, Ginsberg wrote: "Bob Dylan is a major American Bard & minstrel of XX Century, whose words have influenced many generations throughout the world. He deserves a Nobel Prize in recognition of his mighty & universal poetic powers."

Returning from India in 1963, Ginsberg heard "A Hard Rain" and wept: "The torch," he said, "had been passed to another generation" (*No Direction Home*). In 1971 he wrote: "For Dylan's genius, one of his greatest works is 'September on Jessore Road.'" And Ginsberg—who had begun composing music himself after the Chicago convention 1968—dedicated his 1975 volume of lyrics, *First Blues: Rags, Ballads & Harmonium Songs*, to "Minstrel Guruji [little guru] Bob Dylan." Every third line of Dylan's, he once told me, is one of genius.

The 2000 Polar Music Prize, presented in Stockholm by the King of Sweden, cited Dylan's "musical and poetic brilliance" (Stig Anderson). Mr. Andrew Motion, British Poet Laureate, has noted "'the concentration and surprise of his lyrics . . . the dramatic sympathy between the words and the music. . . .'" (qtd. in Kelley 7).

Equally important—and a more direct sign of how Dylan has enriched our collective experience—are the many phrases from his lyrics that have become part of our everyday lexicon: "the times they are a-changin'"; "I was so much older then / I'm younger than that now"; "Nobody feels any pain." According to Professor Daniel Karlin, Dylan "'has given more memorable phrases to our language than any comparable figure since Kipling'" (qtd. in Indrebø). Most recently, editor David Lehman, explaining the presence of the lyrics to "Desolation Row" in his *Oxford Book of American Poetry*, wrote that, unlike with "Some Enchanted Evening" and other standards, "the lyrics have an existence apart from the music" (xix).

The American poet Michael McClure has written, "Bob Dylan is a poet; whether he has cherubs in his hair and fairy wings, or feet of clay, he is a poet" (33). "Dylan," he explains, "has slipped into people's dream baskets. He has been incorporated into their myths and fantasies" (34).

Many are the writers who have titled their works with phrases from Dylan, or made dedications to him. For novelist Barry Hannah, author of *Yonder Stands Your Orphan*, Dylan is "a master of spiritual geography" (283); fiction writer Joyce Carol Oates has dedicated her most frequently reproduced short story, "Where Are You Going, Where Have You Been?" to him; activist publisher Raymond Mungo titled his personal history of the 1960s Liberation News Service *Famous Long Ago* (1970).

Recent years have witnessed a surge of new books on Dylan's work, including a new edition of Michael Gray's remarkable exploration, *Song and Dance Man III: The Art of Bob Dylan* (2000), and Christopher Ricks's provocative study, *Dylan's Visions of Sin* (2003). Though Professor Ricks and I have debated the issue of whether Dylan should be accorded the Nobel, his volume offers, among other things, one of the most extended expositions of Dylan's poetic gifts I've seen. Years ago he reflected (qtd. in Brown): "Dylan is an artist of a kind we have very few of now. He is like Shakespeare or Dickens—great writers who communicated across class. He has a Shakespearean size and ambition in the themes he explores and what he achieves. I don't think there's a British or American poet today more sensitive and imaginative about how he uses language than Dylan is." And Ricks's summing-up is among the best: "'If the question is does anybody use words better than he does, then the answer in my opinion is no'" (qtd. in Glaister).

At this point I would like to introduce two further considerations. Late in 1996, after our Nobel letters were in, Ginsberg remarked, "I don't think Dylan particularly cares about it." So, I would like to offer a little perspective here: Dylan does not have to win the Nobel. He has won so many accolades and awards, will one more really matter? If he were to win, of course that would occasion joy and celebration for many—possibly even Dylan would be pleased. But with or without a Nobel, his work remains triumphant.

William S. Burroughs once said that the habit of denial, the refusal to acknowledge anything other than an official version of reality, was so strongly ingrained in America several decades ago that if an elephant had mounted the dais at Roosevelt's inauguration, and made deposits before walking off, it would not have been reported.

In *Chronicles* Bob Dylan tells us that:

Things were pretty sleepy on the Americana music scene in the late '50s and early
'60s. Popular radio was at a sort of standstill and filled with empty pleasantries. . . .
What I was playing at the time were hard-lipped folk songs with fire and brimstone
servings, and you didn't need to take polls to know that they didn't match up with
anything on the radio, didn't lend themselves to commercialism. (5–6)

The songs that affected the young Dylan recently arrived in the Village, as he
puts it, "could make you question what you'd always accepted, could litter the
landscape with broken hearts, had power of spirit" (14). "Folk songs," he recalls,
"were the way I explored the universe . . ." (18). He further stipulates:

Songs about debauched bootleggers, mothers that drowned their own children,
Cadillacs that got only five miles to the gallon, floods, union hall fires, darkness
and cadavers at the bottom of rivers weren't for radiophiles. There was nothing
easygoing about the folk songs I sang. They weren't friendly or ripe with mellow-
ness. They didn't come gently to the shore. . . . They were my preceptor and guide
into some altered consciousness of reality. (34)

Dylan was, first in the folk songs he chose, soon and for decades thereafter
in songs he composed, singing of "real" things, regardless of "official" or commercial reality. As William Carlos Williams once said of Allen Ginsberg, "'He
had something to say'" (qtd. in Breslin 30). That has been one of Dylan's great
strengths—telling us what we may not want to know or acknowledge; defying
the protocol of accepted discourse, whether within the folk song community of
the 1960s, or among legions of followers who think they have, as Eliot's Prufrock
worried, gotten him "formulated, sprawling on a pin" (57), "pinned and wrig-
gling on the wall" (58). He has surprised us, he has moved us, he has altered the
way we think, feel, speak, and imagine. He has, as the saying goes, moved moun-
tains: helped change the course of history in the United States. He is not merely
a decorative versifier, but a singer of great substance reviving and re-creating
some of our most time-honored poetic traditions as he gives us melody matched
by matter: he has inspired, enriched, and disquieted us.

To close with some personal perspectives: broadly, literature is aesthetically
charged language, and poetry depends on oral performance. Of course there are
exceptions and complications and matters of degree, but that is how I see poetry's vital core. Though I do not deny the considerable effect that Ginsberg's *Howl*
has (fortunately) had on the page alone, what is there may only approximate
what is in the air, in the poet's—the singer's—voice. America's Beat Generation was born overnight, so to speak, at a poetry reading at the center of which
was Ginsberg's first public rendering of *Howl*. According to Jack Kerouac's *The*

Dharma Bums, it was "wailed" by the poet, "drunk with arms outspread" and "everybody . . . yelling 'Go! Go! Go!' (like a jam session)" (14). A decade later, *Howl* did not come alive for me till I heard Ginsberg declaim it.

Poetry and music have shared common ground, from Greeks to Pound to Ginsberg; categorize Dylan's work as you will, its literary qualities are exceptional; its artful idealism has contributed to major social change, altering and enriching the lives of millions culturally, politically, and aesthetically; the voices acclaiming it are many and distinguished. The Nobel Prize for Literature, which in over a century of being awarded has covered a territory broad and diverse, is a deserved form of recognition for such extraordinary accomplishment.

Works Cited

Allén, Sture, and Kjell Espmark. *The Nobel Prize in Literature: An Introduction.* Stockholm: Swedish Academy, 2001.

Booth, Alison, J. Paul Hunter, and Kelly J. Mays, eds. *The Norton Introduction to Literature.* 9th ed. New York: Norton, 2005.

Breslin, James E. B. "The Presence of Williams in Contemporary Poetry." In *Something to Say: William Carlos Williams on Younger Poets.* Ed. Breslin. New York: New Directions, 1985. 5–37.

Brown, Mick. "Messiah of the twentieth century? It ain't me babe." *Sunday Correspondent.* 4 Feb. 1990: 20.

Chekhov, Anton. *The Portable Chekhov.* Ed. by Avrahm Yarmolinsky. New York: Viking, 1968.

Dylan, Bob. *Chronicles: Volume One.* New York: Simon & Schuster, 2004.

———. "Interview with Ed Bradley." *Sixty Minutes.* WBRA, Roanoke, VA. 5 Dec. 2004.

———. *Lyrics 1962–2001.* New York: Simon & Schuster, 2004.

Eliot, T. S. "The Love Song of J. Alfred Prufrock." *The Waste Land and Other Poems.* New York: Harvest/Harcourt, 1962. 3–9.

Espmark, Kjell. *The Nobel Prize in Literature: A Study of the Criteria behind the Choices.* Boston: G.K. Hall, 1991.

Fagles, Robert. "Translator's Preface." *The Iliad.* By Homer. New York: Penguin, 1990. ix–xiv.

Faulkner, William. "Acceptance." Frenz 444–45.

Feldman, Burton. *The Nobel Prize: A History of Genius, Controversy, and Prestige.* New York: Arcade, 2000.

Fitzgerald, Robert. "Postscript." *The Odyssey.* Trans. Fitzgerald. New York: Doubleday, 1963. 465–507.

Frenz, Horst, ed. *Nobel Lectures: Including Presentation Speeches and Laureates' Biographies: Literature 1901–1967.* Amsterdam: Elsevier, 1969.

Frenz, Horst. "Introduction." Frenz VII–IX.

Ginsberg, Allen. *First Blues: Rags, Ballads, & Harmonium Songs, 1971–1974.* New York: Full Court, 1975.

———. Letter to the Nobel Committee of the Swedish Academy. 20 Nov. 1996. Unpublished personal communication.

Glaister, Dan. "It's Alright, Ma, I've Just Been Nominated for the Nobel Prize for Literature." *The Guardian* [London]. 28 Sept. 1996: 1.

Gleason, Ralph J. "The Children's Crusade." *Ramparts*. Mar. 1966: 27–34.

Goldberg, Danny. *Dispatches from the Culture Wars: How the Left Lost Teen Spirit*. New York: Akashic, 2003.

Gray, Michael. *Song & Dance Man III: The Art of Bob Dylan*. New York: Continuum, 2003.

Hallstrom, Per. "Presentation." *Frenz* 194–98.

Hannah, Barry. "Constant Time for Bob Dylan." *Studio A: The Bob Dylan Reader*. Ed. Benjamin Hedin. New York: Norton, 2004. 280–84.

Indrebø, Reidar. "Press Release #2." Rev. May 24, 2002. 4 Jan. 2010. www.expectingrain.com/dok/art/nobel/nobelpress2.html.

Kelley, Tina. "Keats with a Guitar: The Times Sure Are A-Changin'." *New York Times* 9 Jan. 2000, sec. 4: 7.

Kerouac, Jack. *The Dharma Bums*. New York: Penguin, 1976.

Knox, Bernard. Introduction. *The Iliad*. By Homer. Trans. Robert Fagles. New York: Penguin, 1990. 3–64.

Lehman, David, ed. Introduction. *The Oxford Book of American Poetry*. Oxford: Oxford UP, 2006. vii–xxi.

McClure, Michael. "The Poet's Poet." *Rolling Stone* 14 Mar. 1974: 33–34.

Mungo, Ray. *Famous Long Ago: My Life and Hard Times with Liberation News Service*. Boston: Beacon Press, 1970.

Noack, Hans-Joachim, and Gabor Steingart. "Ein unheimliches Gefühl." *Der Spiegel* 18 May 2002: 32–35. Translated by Patricia Hardin.

Nobel Foundation. "Statutes of the Nobel Foundation." 2006. 12 Dec. 2006. nobelprize.org/nobel-foundation/statutes.html.

No Direction Home. Dir. Martin Scorsese. DVD. Paramount, 2005.

Pound, Ezra. *Literary Essays of Ezra Pound*. Ed. T. S. Eliot. New York: New Directions, 1954.

——— "How to Read." *Pound* 15–40.

———. "The Tradition." *Pound* 91–93.

Ricks, Christopher. *Dylan's Visions of Sin*. New York: HarperCollins, 2003.

"Rock Lyric." *Princeton Encyclopedia of Poetry and Poetics*. Enlarged ed. 1974.

Siwertz, S. "Presentation." *Frenz* 488–92.

Spitzer, Mark. "Bob Dylan's *Tarantula*: An Arctic Reserve of Untapped Glimmerance Dismissed in a Ratland of Clichés." 21 Feb. 2003. *Jack Magazine* 2.3. 4 Jan. 2010. www.jackmagazine.com/issue7/essaysmsptizer.html.

Stanford, W. B. *The Sound of Greek: Studies in the Greek Theory and Practice of Euphony*. Berkeley: U of California P, 1967.

Stig Anderson Music Award Foundation. "Polar Music Prize." 2000. 6 Jan. 2010. www.polarmusicprize.com/newSite/2000.shtml.

Yeats, William Butler. Introduction. *Gitanjali (Song Offerings)*. By Rabindranath Tagore. New York: Macmillan, 1916. vii–xxii.

LYRIC IMPRESSION, MUSCLE MEMORY, EMILY, AND THE JACK OF HEARTS

CLAUDIA EMERSON

This essay by Pulitzer Prize–winning poet Claudia Emerson analyzes Bob Dylan's "Lily, Rosemary, and the Jack of Hearts." As Emerson explains, "Some of the ongoing discussions and debates about whether or not this or that song is also a poem, or this or that songwriter is also a poet intrigue and vex me in equal parts because I haven't felt the attraction to debating the borders of genre. It seems that there have been and will always be places where a certain song will share characteristics with a poem. Dylan's songs will continue to be examined for their 'poetry'—and for whatever makes people talk about the particular multifaceted lens that is poetry, I am ever grateful. Part of Dylan's impact for me lies in the ways he can situate his songs at the point where song forever departed from poetry and in so doing, keep alive the vestigial imprint of older poetic traditions."

Some years after I began teaching and writing with great intensity, I volunteered for the further immersion of being a literacy tutor in Pittsylvania County, Virginia—a large rural county in Southside with an unusually high rate of illiteracy. I was assigned to work with Cecil, a man in his mid-fifties who worked in a local lumber mill. Cecil's goal was to be able to read the stock-car results in the paper. He had never learned the alphabet. So we began.

After the first session, he asked the most basic and, for me, profound question. We'd been talking about recognizing and memorizing the letters, and, following my instruction manual, I dutifully taught him that we have two kinds or categories of letters, consonants and vowels. So, Cecil looked up and asked what the difference was. Difference? What's the difference between vowels and consonants? I don't think I'd ever thought about it, not as an adult anyway, and if I had thought about it as a child, I was, as most children are, just learning what I was told. AEIOU, right, sometimes Y.

But after a few minutes, it came to me that *a* difference at least is that you need your teeth, tongue, and lips to "sound" consonants, and you don't need them for vowels. Cecil was satisfied with that, and we returned to the lesson.

Later, on the drive home, however, the obvious came to me with stark rawness: letters are symbols for sound we make with our physical bodies. We evolved and agreed to order these sounds in an extremely sophisticated way, and that's what writing is, an agreed-upon ordering of these symbols for sound.

My adult reaction to the obvious brought me back to Dickinson's famous "The brain is wider than the sky" poem with added excitement about the word choice of brain—not *mind*, but *brain*, the physical place of the mind and the place with real, tangible heft in the physical reality of the world. I also thought again about Dickinson's famous quote: "If I read a book [and] it makes my whole body so cold no fire ever can warm me I know that is poetry. If I feel physically as if the top of my head were taken off, I know that is poetry."

Dickinson's poem and her reaction to poetry became all the more amazing—and relevant—because her response to poetry is not intellectual, not of the pure mind but physical, of the brain as it is indivisible from the body.

We all know that poetry is not one thing; the spectrum from lyric to narrative in the category of "poem" is vast and encompasses much; so, too, the spectrum of formal to freer verse. The same goes for song, for music itself. So some of the ongoing discussions and debates about whether or not this or that song is also a poem, or this or that songwriter is also a poet intrigue and vex me in equal parts because I haven't felt the attraction to debating the borders of genre, or, more important, to making some definitive decision about the topic. My thinking about the separation of poetry from music—and from song, regardless of various similarities—was and continues to be greatly influenced by H. T. Kirby-Smith, my former teacher at the University of North Carolina at Greensboro. He introduces his brilliant book *The Celestial Twins: Poetry and Music through the Ages* (University of Massachusetts Press 1999) in part by suggesting that while we should consider poetry's "indebtedness to music," we must also recognize its decisive "separation from it" (2).

After all, there will be, regardless of genre or artistic medium, places of intersection, genre blurring; there have been and will continue be places where a certain song will share characteristics with a poem, where a long poem will share much with a short story, where a poem could be and will be "set"—after its conception as poem—to music. And I hope there will continue to be obviously distinct genres that make the shifting interstices so compelling.

Songs are, for the most part, obviously different from a great number of poems because songs are blatantly physical, meant to be heard—nodded and danced to, learned, reinterpreted through performance, etc. They are meant to be remembered—memorized—for their words and musical progressions, their rhythms and chords, all integral parts of the song's meaning. I have never really thought that the genre of song is made of words and music; the two, whatever the order of their genesis are ultimately fused—one creation.

The "music" of the poem is far more subtle, the measures inherent in English's (as well as other languages') accentual syllabic system. Unlike the songwriter, the more formal poet will create according to a prescribed measure, but will, for the most part, pray you will not think to tap your foot to it and instead will feel most accomplished when you don't even notice the measure at first. Despite the fixed forms that require repetition (villanelle, sestina, etc.), poems often work best to the contemporary ear when they don't repeat as blatant part of their construction, but succeed as something more linguistically understated.

Edgar Allan Poe in his famous "The Poetic Principle" writes about the concept of a poem's impression, insisting a long poem cannot make a lyric impression, that, in fact, "'a long poem' is simply a flat contradiction in terms"—while also warning that a poem can be too short and unrealized, failing to make "a profound or enduring . . . effect."

Despite my realization all those years ago that letters are symbols for sound, I had to remind myself too that for a long time the symbols of text were not common or shared; for centuries, many more people like Cecil were illiterate and the production of shared texts rare. What creates impression in older, oral poetic works, then, crafted to be heard, would logically share more with the elements of song that create impression, or make any work memorable.

Many of us credit Bob Dylan for the multi-faceted importance of his art, for its political, social, spiritual, and musical relevance, for its groundbreaking innovation as well as for its many allusions to musicians and poets who came before him. It's no wonder then that many of us continue to be drawn to the study of this body of work in our desire for greater understanding of it. Another essay in this collection, Gordon Ball's "A Nobel for Dylan," for one example, discusses how Dylan's work should be considered for a Nobel in literature even though that prize is primarily reserved for novels and poetry.

Dylan is a songwriter often tagged as a poet, and the words to some of his songs have often been anthologized as poems, though he didn't create them that way or release them into the world as poems. Again, whatever argument people want to make about it they are certainly free to do, but I don't see why I would want—besides for the sake of studying a part of a whole—to separate out the text from its music and insist that it belongs in one category over another.

Still, as an admirer of Dylan's longer songs, I have noticed that in many of them (some more and some less narrative), he employs ordering principles that are less traditionally song-like and instead hearken back to quite ancient oral-formulaic traditions that work to create the "impression" Poe is looking for—lyric constructions that accomplish a narrative impression, or an emotional one—without relying much on chorus or even musical progression and repetition to make the song memorable.

The measure in some of Dylan's longer songs, such as "Masters of War," "A Hard Rain's A-Gonna Fall," "Desolation Row," "Visions of Johanna," "Tangled Up in Blue," and "Lily, Rosemary, and the Jack of Hearts," to name a few, connotes the Anglo-Saxon, with a recurring pattern of alliteration, consonance, or assonance woven within the lines in addition to the expected end-rhyme we look for in songs; and while not employed with the deliberate regularity of the accentual meter in *Beowulf*, the pattern is regular and discernible enough to effect Poe's desired impression, and make the song memorable despite its lack of the typical strategies of most songs—the mnemonic elements that, regardless of subcategories (country, soul, pop, etc.), many songs share: rhyme, refrain, chorus, bridge, a "hook" repeated often—all working with the connotations of key and rhythm, minor keys more somber, the polka rhythm festive, etc. Such Dylan songs are not merely long, they are word-rich, so that without the patterning of sound, the brain would have too little to hold on to for the song to be memorable past its melody or a phrase here and there.

Again, thinking back to that long-ago lesson with Cecil, I realize that memorability is not only an act of the intellect, but also of muscle memory, the brain finding pleasing the repeating movements of the fingers on the keys or strings, or the tongue on the back of the teeth or the roof of the mouth.

For one example "Lily, Rosemary, and the Jack of Hearts" (1975) is long (8:50) and narrative, a puzzler, a mystery. There are a lot of players and much action. While the verses are made up of tightly rhyming couplets, the song employs no refrain or any chorus except variations on the "Jack of Hearts" that closes each verse and rhymes only itself. The melody, while compelling, creates part of the song's impression by way of simplicity—its measures falling within a limited range, the urgent tempo imparting part of the song's driving suspense. But more important to this song's memorability is the distinct patterning of sound within the lines. Look at the first two lines of the fifth verse:

> Rosemary combed her hair and took a carriage into town,
> She slipped in through the side door lookin' like a queen without a crown.

The repeating hard "c" of "combed" in the first line sounds in the back of the line in "carriage" which also rhymes internally with "hair," followed by "took" pairing with "town." In the second line, "slipped" resonates with "side" as "queen" does with "crown."

> She fluttered her false eyelashes and whispered in his ear,
> "Sorry, darlin', that I'm late," but he didn't seem to hear.

Continuing in a similar fashion, "fluttered" echoes "false" which anticipates "lashes," and the first syllable of "whispered" can be heard gently to rhyme with "his"—while in the next line, "darlin'" waits for the balancing "didn't."

While there are many places throughout the song where we can find patterned alliteration and assonance, there are also more subtle instances of patterned consonance. The first two lines of the seventh verse offer an example:

> Lily was a princess, she was fair-skinned and precious as a child,
> She did whatever she had to do, she had that certain flash every time she smiled.

Notice that "princess" quite obviously looks for "precious," but the "s" and "sh" also resound in "skinned" and "precious." Similarly, in addition to the patterning of initial consonants in the second line of this verse, the first "she" after the caesura finds itself in the final letters of "flash."

Of course, any skilled poet or songwriter will use patterned sound inside the lines to pull the ear away from strong end-stops or too many exact rhymes, most preferring a joining of sound akin to a dovetail or mortise and tenon effect over the driven nail of too-obvious end rhyme. But in this case, the technique is so audible throughout, I am persuaded it is a key part of the song's mnemonic strategy, and not simple variation.

In addition to the patterning of sound that connotes the ancestral accentual measure, Dylan employs the mid-line caesura also characteristic of the older verse. Whether or not he places his repeating sounds neatly on either side of it, Dylan regularly crafts a caesura, "cutting" or pausing the line with a comma or coordinating conjunction. The ninth verse opens with two good examples, the first line seesawing on "and" and the second on its middle comma:

> Rosemary started drinkin' hard and seein' her reflection in the knife,
> She was tired of the attention, tired of playin' the role of Big Jim's wife.

Surely those compelled to argue that Dylan is a poet, or more poet than songwriter, mean to compliment, assigning the designation as an artistic elevation from songwriter (with or without apologies to the songwriters whom I do not consider lesser in their otherness). And of course, it's always writing that will withstand close study that attracts the attentions of such readers.

And yet, I am most impressed in the end that those with little background in the study of poetry have also been drawn again and again into linguistically complex songs to be influenced, inspired, entertained, and delighted with the songs despite perhaps not recognizing the underlying poetic strategies, even as they most certainly understand them. We don't have to know how an engine works to understand driving a car with great skill and confidence—and joy.

Dylan's songs will continue to be examined for their "poetry"—and for whatever makes people talk about the particular multifaceted lens that is poetry, I am ever grateful. Part of Dylan's impact for me lies in the ways he can situate his songs at the point where song forever departs from poetry and in so doing, keep alive the vestigial imprint of older poetic traditions.

Cecil learned to read. When he and I stopped working together, he could comprehend at the third-grade level, and enjoyed reading about the stock car race he had often watched on television just the day before. But the happiest I ever saw him was the day he arrived to tell me that after all the years he had driven the road from Pelham, North Carolina, where he had lived his entire life, to his job in Chatham, Virginia, he had been able to read the sign that said *Pelham*. He had been able to sound it out. The ability to read what he already knew changed nothing in one sense, every muscle in his body having learned the way, and yet, in a most vital sense, that place was made new to him in another understanding of it: the syllable from the sound.

Works Cited

Dickinson, Emily. "The brain is wider than the sky." *The Poems of Emily Dickinson*. Ed. R. W. Franklin. Cambridge, MA: Belknap Press of Harvard University Press, 1999. 598.

Kirby-Smith. *The Celestial Twins: Poetry and Music through the Ages*. Amherst: University of Massachusetts Press, 1999.

Dylan, Bob. "Desolation Row." *Highway 61 Revisited*. Columbia, 1965.

———. "A Hard Rain's A-Gonna Fall." *The Freewheelin' Bob Dylan*. Columbia, 1963.

———. "Lily, Rosemary and the Jack of Hearts." *Blood on the Tracks*. Columbia, 1975.

———. "Masters of War." *The Freewheelin' Bob Dylan*. Columbia, 1963.

———. "Visions of Johanna." *Blonde on Blonde*. Columbia, 1966.

———. "Tangled Up in Blue." *Blood on the Tracks*. Columbia, 1975.

Poe, Edgar Allan. *The Poetic Principle*. Fitchburg, MA: Quill Pen Press, 2008.

DON KHAN AND TRUCK-DRIVING WIVES: DYLAN'S FLUCTUATING LYRICS

BEN YAGODA

In live performance (often captured on recording), Bob Dylan has almost obsessively offered new versions of his lyrics. Some critics have suggested that he does this because he's forgotten the old ones; others maintain that Dylan knows very much what he is doing, and that the alteration is part of his project as an artist. In this essay, Yagoda will consider both interpretations and address the larger issue of an artist who continuously and methodically changes his creations.

They're songs. They're not written in stone. They're on plastic.

—Bob Dylan, 1991 interview

I was at Madison Square Garden in 1974 to see Bob Dylan in his first concert tour in five years. With the opening notes of the opening song, "Most Likely You'll Go Your Way (And I'll Go Mine)," it was clear (to quote another Dylan song) that "revolution was in the air." This was most definitely not the "Most Likely" familiar from the album *Blonde on Blonde*, on which it had originally appeared. Dylan and his accompanists, The Band, changed the tempo, the arrangement, even the melody. On the record, singing the opening lines— "You say you love me / And you're thinkin' of me, / But you know you could be wrong"—Dylan's voice descends to the tonic on that last word, "wrong." But at the Garden, backed by Robbie Robertson's urgent lead guitar, it ascended in a defiant lion's roar: "WROOOONNNGGGG!" It was a thrilling moment, as you can hear in the crowd reaction on the album recording the tour, *Before the Flood*.

A template was set. I have seen Dylan at least a dozen times since then, most frequently in the last decade or so, as he proceeds on his "Never-Ending Tour," and each performance of each song is reimagined, sometimes to within an inch of its life. But even the out-there versions are welcomed by me and most other Dylan fans, as a reminder that he is not presenting and will never present the moribund just-like-a-record renditions of so many other performers and bands. It is performance as creative act.

With that in mind, it stands to reason that Dylan should have sometimes changed his lyrics in performance; what's surprising, actually, is that he has not changed them more often. I would put forth two explanations. First, in many if not most of its forms, music is conducive to improvisation and variation, both planned and extemporaneous. The blues, jazz, and rock traditions are in some ways based on the idea of performers continually reimagining a given harmonic structure. That's not the case with rhymed lyrics—or at least it wasn't the case till rap and hip-hop came along, and, despite his early talking blues and the declamatory and still startling "Subterranean Homesick Blues," Bob Dylan is no rapper. Second, interviews Dylan has given over the years make it clear that he values his lyrics more than his melodies and harmonies. (I don't agree with him, but that's not important for this discussion.) He frequently says that he only knows four chords, that he borrowed this or that tune from an old English folk song. As a Romantic-surrealist-confessional-troubadour-Beat hybrid, Dylan writes lyrics that have an extemporaneous, stream-of-consciousness feel, but, paradoxically, he talks about them with a palpable pride and, sometimes, awe. Clearly, he would let the precise words slip away only after solemn deliberation.

So the fact that he has in fact sometimes done so deserves attention; it's not a whimsical fancy. As he commented of one such alteration in a 1985 interview, "I didn't change it 'cause I was singing it one night and thought, 'Oh, I'm bored with the old words.' The old ones were never quite filled in."

Dylan's lyric changes can be divided into a small number of categories. The first consists of times when he forgot or botched the words. Again, this is rarer than you might think, but it has happened, most frequently early on in his career, when he was often allegedly under the influence of ingested substances. One example is his "Like a Rolling Stone" at the Isle of Wight in 1969 (available on YouTube), where he appears to have only a minimal familiarity with his most famous song; in the first verse, instead of "You used to laugh about," he sings what sounds like "You and you feel so proud."[1]

The second category comprises one-off variations for specific occasions or moments. In performances in 1974–75, as the Vietnam War seemingly refused to end, he changed the second verse of "Knockin' on Heaven's Door." "Mama, put my guns in the ground. / I can't shoot them anymore" became "Mama, wipe the blood from my face, / I'm sick and tired of the war." (In subsequent performances, he has kept the arresting blood imagery but presented varying second lines to the couplet, including, "I can't see through it anymore.")

Dylan presented probably his most bizarre variation in a 1986 tribute to Martin Luther King Jr., while performing "I Shall Be Released." The song would have worked perfectly in its original form, with its dreamlike imagery and message of faith in the face of darkness and pain: "Any day now, any day now, / I shall be released." For some reason, Dylan chose to insert into the chorus the line "I don't need no doctor or no priest" (King having been both, loosely speaking). And in what could only be taken as a tasteless reference to King's extramarital affairs, he sang, "He [J. Edgar Hoover?] will find you where you're stayin', / Even in the arms of somebody else's wife." More tastelessly still, Dylan concluded the verse with the advice, "You're laughin' now, you should be prayin', / To be in the midnight hour of your life."

Deserving of a category of its own is "You Ain't Goin' Nowhere," a delightful (seemingly) nonsense ditty, with an airy tune that has launched a thousand jams. It exists in two distinct versions. Dylan wrote the song for the "Basement Tapes" he recorded in 1967 with The Band, but that wasn't released until 1975. Meanwhile, Roger McGuinn of The Byrds heard that version of the song and included it on the group's highly influential 1968 album, *Sweetheart of the Rodeo*.

The plot thickened in 1971, when Dylan recorded a folky take on the song with the veteran Woodstock picker Happy Traum on guitar. It turned out so well that it was included on that year's album *Bob Dylan's Greatest Hits Vol. II*. (Never mind that Dylan had never before even released the song, much less had a hit with it.) By virtue of being on such a big-selling compilation, that version is the one many Dylan fans (including me) associate with the tune. The chorus ("Whoo-ee, ride me high / Tomorrow's the day / My bride's gonna come . . .") is the same but the verses are totally reworked, with a marked improvement in the first one. The vague and telegraphic "Clouds so swift, rain won't lift, / Gate won't close, railings froze" becomes a marvelously specific dreamscape that name-checks the Byrds' frontman:

> Clouds so swift and rain fallin' in
> Gonna see a movie called Gunga Din
> Pack up your money, pull up your tent, McGuinn

Later, Dylan changes the puzzling and somewhat flat "Genghis Khan, he could not keep / All his kings supplied with sleep" to "Genghis Khan and his brother Don / Couldn't keep on keepin' on," thus importing into the song one of the most resonant phrases in the history of popular music. "Keep On Keepin' On" was a song recorded by Woody Herman and the Thundering Herd in 1955, presumably heard by young Bob Zimmerman back in Hibbing, Minnesota. The soul singer O. C. Smith recorded his own song by that name in 1969, and Curtis Mayfield one with more formal diction, "Keep on Keeping On," in 1971. All told, the web site allmusic.com lists 183 tracks with one of the two titles. Dylan fans do not need to be told that he used the phrase in 1974: "And when finally the bottom fell out, I became withdrawn. / The only thing I knew how to do was to keep on keepin' on . . ."[2]

Those lines are from "Tangled Up in Blue," the lead-off song on the album *Blood on the Tracks*. I am not alone in considering that disk, along with *Blonde on Blonde* (1966), the best in his distinguished career; "Tangled Up in Blue," meanwhile, perennially vies with "Like a Rolling Stone" in arguments about Dylan's greatest song. It's interesting, therefore, that "Tangled" and two other memorable songs from "Blood on the Tracks"—"Idiot Wind" and "Simple Twist of Fate"—should be the ones whose lyrics Dylan has most vigorously reinvented.

Each song on *Blood on the Tracks* is a different take on the same scenario: basically, boy gets girl, boy loses girl, that's it. Part of the brilliance of the album is how very different—emotionally, philosophically, and musically—the songs are from each other. Hitherto known for the bilious kiss-off ("Positively Fourth Street," "It Ain't Me, Babe," and so many more), Dylan here invokes what seems suspiciously like emotional maturity, acknowledging (as he sings in one song) "yer gonna have to leave me now, I know," but refusing to point fingers or cast blame.

Well, except for on "Idiot Wind," the one hate song on the disk—and what a big bowl of hate it offers up. Dylan has traveled quite a distance from the like-titled "Blowin' in the Wind"; now, instead of banning weapons, he would clearly like to shoot them. "You're an idiot, babe, / It's a wonder that you still know how to breathe," he spits out. What saves the song is the way it expands its contempt, from an individual to the singer himself and then to humanity itself.

Complicating any discussion of *Blood on the Tracks* is the well-known fact that after recording the album (in New York, in the fall of 1974), Dylan re-recorded the three songs mentioned, plus two others, in Minnesota in December, and included these later cuts on the album. For "Idiot Wind," the two versions of the lyrics are substantially different in detail (if not in theme). In New York, he sang:

> I threw the I-Ching yesterday, it said there might be some thunder at the well.
> Peace and quiet's been avoiding me for so long it seems like living hell.

In Minneapolis that became:

> I ran into the fortune-teller, who said beware of lightning that might strike.
> I haven't known peace and quiet for so long I can't remember what it's like.

Near the end, this couplet:

> I been double-crossed too much, at times I think I've almost lost my mind
> Lady-killers load ice on me behind my back, while imitators steal me blind

turned into:

I been double-crossed now for the very last time and now I'm finally free,
I kissed goodbye the howling beast on the borderline which separated you from me.

So which versions of lyrics are the "original" ones? In concert, Dylan favored the bloodier-on-the tracks New York version until the late 80s. In a 1991 interview he said, "Yeah, you know, obviously, if you've heard both versions you realize, of course, that there could be a myriad of verses for the thing. It doesn't stop. It wouldn't stop. Where do you end? You could still be writing it, really. It's something that could be a work continually in progress."

One hundred eighty degrees different is "Simple Twist of Fate," which he introduced in the 1979 performance captured on the *At Budokan* album with the words: "Here's a simple love story, happened to me." Maybe not so simple, but certainly the song has the feel of a lovely and rueful short story. (In his book *Chronicles, Part I*, Dylan intimates that the entire album was an attempt to reimagine Chekhov's short fiction). Or maybe it's more like an impressionistic film: light bursts through a "beat-up shade," while somewhere a far-off saxophone plays; the lonely protagonist "walks along with a parrot that talks, / Hunts her down by the waterfront docks."[3]

As chronicled by Eyolf Østrem on dylanchords.info, Dylan almost continuously changed the lyrics of the song from the release of the album through the late 1980s. He sang a substantially new version on the Rolling Thunder Revue tour of 1975. The talking parrot is gone, alas; now, the forlorn lover "hunts for her through the city blocks." The "cheap hotel" of the original becomes "a river front hotel," sometimes altered to the Rio Grande Hotel, or the St. Claire Hotel. Dylan's 1984 European tour, Ostrem reports, saw the most dramatic changes. Now the hotel has a desk clerk dressed in white: "With a face as black as night, / He said: 'Check-out time's at eight.'" Dylan's performance in Barcelona on June 28 of that year included the white-clad clerk, as well as a new version of almost every line in the song. Some contain arresting images ("He woke up and it sure was dim / He could feel her eyes looking at him"), but the message and the mood of the song are always the same. The constant changes, one imagines, are directed at his listeners who know or feel they know the song by heart; he wants to trouble their familiarity. Or maybe in part he wants to tell himself that the "simple love story" isn't over yet.

Of the three songs, "Tangled Up in Blue"—midway between the other two in mood and tempo—is the most protean. It's a winding, picaresque cross-country and time-traveling tale, Dylan's version of *On the Road*. For a while the lyrics took as many detours and excursions as the characters. One interesting variation concerns the protagonist: in the Minneapolis (album) version, this character is "I" in the opening—"Early one morning the sun was shining, / I was laying in bed"—and remains so throughout, but in the (earlier) New York version and subsequent live performances, he alternates between the first person and the third. The effect is to call identity into question—always a key theme in Dylan's music and his life.

Throughout the 1970s, Dylan fiddled with the details in the song. In the album version "I" drifts down to New Orleans and works on a fishing boat "right outside Delacroix." In the New York version, it's L.A. where "he" tries his luck: "Working for a while on an airplane plant, / Loading cargo onto a truck." On a live version he sang on tour in 1978, he goes to New Orleans, where's he's "lucky not to be destroyed. / Almost died of the bulldog clap / Two miles outside of Delacroix." Later in the song, "the people we used to know" keep changing jobs. On the album, "some are mathematicians, some are carpenters' wives." In New York: "some are doctors' wives." On the Rolling Thunder Revue in 1975: "some are truck-drivers' wives." And on his 1978 tour: "Some are bricklayers, some are bankrobbers, / Some are burglars and some are truck-drivers' wives."

On that same tour, he made some intriguing changes in the middle section, where the main character encounters "you" working in a bar and renews their acquaintance. The "topless place" of album is now "the Flamingo Hotel" and the woman has a new line of dialogue: "You know it ain't no accident that you came." In both 1974 versions, the woman shows the narrator a book of poems "written by an Italian poet from the thirteenth century." In 1978—the time of Dylan's well-publicized exploration of Christianity—she opens up a Bible and starts quoting from Chapter 17 of the book of Jeremiah. From night to night, Dylan specified different verses, but he always mentioned verse 33, which, in that chapter of Jeremiah, does not happen to exist.

Six years later, he completely recast the song, with major changes to every verse. In this version (captured on the 1984 disk *Real Live*) there is a flurry of new details: she's married to a man "four times her age"; "he nearly drowned in Delacroix"; she's working at "the Blinding Light"; there's no poetry book or Bible. This "Tangled" also shifts slightly from the picaresque to the confessional. Though Dylan has consistently disputed this interpretation, *Blood on the Tracks* has always been taken to be about, or at least inspired by, the fissures and tensions in his marriage; at the time of its creation, he was separated from his wife, Sara Lowndes, and they would divorce in 1977. In its original version, "Tangled Up in Blue" takes a long and complicated relationship and shoots it through the prism of a prodigious fancy. On *Real Live* the song is more intimate, almost confessional, and at times feels like the transcript of a therapy session. On the couple's first separation, in the first verse: "She said, 'I wish I could tell you all the things that I never learned how to say." Later, the singer admits he "had one too many lovers."

The final verse is less hopeful than ever. Before, the singer vowed, "I'm going back again, / I've got to get to her somehow"; no more. The mathematicians and truck drivers' wives, who always seemed like colorful extras in a Frank Capra movie, have vanished as well. Now, when Dylan scans the population, he finds, "Some are ministers of illusion, / Some are masters of the trade, / All under strong delusion . . ." He ends the song with another pronoun switcheroo. The original version concluded, "We always did feel the same, / We just saw it from a different point of view. / Tangled up in blue." The sense is of a rueful acknowledgment of separateness, even for two people who on some level will always be connected. Now, he sings: "We always did love the very same one. / We just saw her from a different point of view." Does "we" refer to two separate men? Is this some kind of ménage? Or is Dylan referring to his own inevitable and sad state of shifting identity? The latter interpretation seems more likely to me, but everything is too tangled up in blue for us to ever know for certain.

In a 1985 interview, Dylan said he wrote this version of the song in a hotel room in Amsterdam. "When I sang it the next night, I knew it was right." That same year, in the liner notes to his *Biograph* collection, Dylan called this "Tangled" the "finished" work: "It's more like it should have been. I was never real happy with it. I guess I was just trying to make it like a painting where you can see the different parts but then you also see the whole of it."

But that's not the end of the story. Dylan had a revelation in 1987 while touring in Switzerland with the Grateful Dead: in an interview, he described an intensive feeling that "I have to go out and sing these songs, they mean something to others, The Dead play them better than me." Shortly thereafter, Dylan assembled a stellar band, and hit the road for an ongoing regimen of some 100 concerts a year: his "Never-Ending Tour." And from that point on, even in "Simple Twist of Fate," "Idiot Wind," and "Tangled Up in Blue," he has jettisoned all the lyrical variations and gone back to the original album versions of his songs. One senses that he has traveled far enough from the moment of their creation—in years and emotion—that they have become artifacts. The issues he was working out have been resolved or set aside or forgotten. His music is still plastic, but at this late date the words have indeed been set in stone.

Notes

1. My quotation from Dylan lyrics in this essay comes from three sources: the official lyrics at www.bobdylan.com, performances as captured on YouTube videos, and Eyolf Østrem's transcriptions on his indispensable website, dylanchords.info.

2. Yet another rendition of "You Ain't Goin' Nowhere," captured on the *Basement Tapes* album, shows the difference between inspired nonsense and just plain nonsense. Dylan is clearly singing whatever comes into his mind—he starts out, "Now look here dear Sue, you best feed the cat / The cat needs feedin', you're the one to do it" and things go downhill from there.

3. A parrot that talks plays a key role in Chekhov's story "The Shooting Party."

THOUGHTS ON "ME AND BOBBY MCGEE" AND THE ORAL AND LITERARY TRADITIONS

DAVID DANIEL

Kris Kristofferson began writing songs while pursuing his Masters in English Literature as a Rhodes Scholar at Merton College, Oxford. More than any other popular songwriter of his time, Kristofferson's crafted songs exhibit this pedigree and provide an ideal opportunity to examine the relation between traditional poetry and popular song of the rock and roll era. In this essay, David Daniel analyzes "Me and Bobby McGee" because it is an example of the traditional ballad form; because it has been covered by dozens of recording artists, whose versions are various enough to compare them; and perhaps most importantly because the song, more akin to great poetry in this regard, is remarkably compressed in its storytelling, and its compression creates precisely the sort of mystery and richness that is at the heart of all literary tragedy.

The story is well-known. Between gigs flying a helicopter in the Gulf of Mexico for an oil company, Rhodes Scholar–turned-struggling-songwriter/pilot Kris Kristofferson gets a call from Fred Foster, his boss at Combine Music, who tells him to write a song called "Me and Bobby McKee." "And here's the hook," he said: "Bobby McKee is a she." Bristling a little at being told what to do—and at what seemed like a horrible idea to him—Kristofferson hid from Foster and did nothing about it for months. But the idea stuck. Kristofferson was on the verge—or just over the verge—of losing everything. He'd lost his marriage and family, was buried in child support and grief, had failed as a songwriter, and was about to be fired from the pilot job for not letting twenty-four hours pass "between bottle and throttle." Somewhere in the middle of that, he'd seen Fellini's *La Strada*—a road movie, after all—at the end of which Anthony Quinn's character gains his freedom but loses what he

193

too-late discovers he cherishes most and ends up alone, howling at the stars. It made an impression.

Then one night driving to the airport on his way home in heavy rain, the windshield wipers began slapping time. Bobby McKee (the real name of song-writing great Boudleaux Bryant's secretary) became Bobby McGee; and the free-dom Kristofferson sensed and even enjoyed while, as he puts it, "I nearly trashed my act," became "just another word for nothing left to lose." By the time he made it back to Nashville that night, the song—one of the greatest road songs of all time—was finished and soon became a hit for Roger Miller; then, in a consider-ably different, gender-re-bent form—the most famous of over three hundred re-corded versions since—it became a number one hit for Kristofferson's girlfriend, Janis Joplin, who recorded it a few days before her death.

We often think of the oral tradition as a sort of old-fashioned memory device, which is fair enough, but it's also, and maybe more importantly, a creative force as it culls and recombines, forgets or misremembers. And in an important sense, at least within cultural boundaries, it—or the force that drives it—acts as the great communal artist, a sort of artist-God, that speaks for all of us whether we know it or not—and often more deeply than we care to recognize. This is what is often called the art of the people: the myths, fairy tales, bibles, folk songs, etc. The converse, in a sense, is also true: The individual artist, whether or not he or she knows it, is driven by the same force and sorts through the debris of life, including the art around him or her, and shapes it into something he/she thinks is his/hers. Just as we remember only a handful of significant memories from the millions of events that make a childhood, forgetting all the rest in order to construct a coherent self that's relevant as we live our lives in the present, so too does the oral tradition create a coherent cultural identity by forgetting all that is not essential to it at the time. In a sense, the measure of a song or poem—or a life—may be taken by how richly it participates in and expands that tradition, consciously or not.

There's something in the origin of "Me and Bobby McGee" that sounds like a fast-forwarded version of the oral tradition as it works to create and refine: a title slightly misremembered, tangled with a traveling circus story from a for-eign film that itself echoes King Lear's horrendous and foolish loss; a desperate personal situation, a car, a little rain, an order from a boss—all leading to a kind of mash-up, but one that sits comfortably in a traditional form as old as song itself. And who knows if Kristofferson's version of this creation story, the one I'm retelling, one he told thirty years or more after the fact, is the real story at all—or if I'm getting it and giving it straight right now. It can be hard to tell a recollection from a re-creation. A bunch of accidents, our writing and yakking, that somehow finds a form to hold it and pass it along, at least if it's any good.

"Me and Bobby McGee" has long reminded me of "Barbara Allen," that as-tonishing folk song/poetry anthology standard that stretches back for half a millennium at least. In it, Sweet William (or one of his many aliases depending on the version) loses the love of his life, Barbara Allen, because, it seems, he made a drunken public toast to women in general without, well, including his Barbara—a mistake, it turns out; he dies of the loss, of a broken heart, of Barbara's cold rejection of him and his pleas, before she, overwhelmed by grief or guilt perhaps, dies immediately after. In one of the most enduring images in all art, at the end of the song, the two are finally brought together as a rose and briar grow into a lovers knot above the local chapel. Dave Marsh's illuminating essay "Barbara Allen"[1] (required reading!) tells us that the song, in its hundreds of variations shaped over so many centuries, so many places, never loses its rose and briar—or the deep, essential, painful mystery at the heart of that image. In love and life, we'll simply never understand the force that shapes our lives, that heaps on tragedy as a consequence of the most trivial, well-meant, momentarily prideful—*whatever*—decisions we make.

Is "Barbara Allen" an origin story of how the rose got its thorns? Yes, and of how the rose became such a potent symbol of love, if we dare look deeply enough, or even just glimpse: beautiful, sensuous, sweet (like William), short-lived, fragile, terrifying to reach for, painful, sexy, bloody, and usually stinking by the end. In any case, as it was passed down in oral or written form, what is essential to "Barbara Allen" stuck. The rest could be stripped away or modified to keep the song relevant, to keep it alive so the next generation could keep it alive and so on. Nothing too tricky in this, of course, or particularly insightful, but it bears mentioning that when a poem or story or song stays with us, it does so because it speaks to us, so songs and poems that have lasted can be seen not as relics but as a repositories of all the things we, as a culture, simply couldn't live without but that, in a way, we can't accept directly. It has to come wrapped in a song, a poem, an image.

The words "Rhodes" and "Scholar" appear in virtually every reference to Kristofferson over the last forty years, including this one, and that's not just to show that he's a smart guy; instead, it comes up because it's such shocking news: Oxford and songwriter rarely go together, much rarer still a Nashville songwriter writing for country artists. Country songwriters and artists are, we suppose, un-schooled, unsophisticated children of the soil, more likely associated with NAS-CAR and deer rifles than with punting on the Thames; these are people for whom the simple sentimentality of country music comes as naturally and inevitably as bass boats to a lake behind a TVA dam. (That "naturally" is a joke—because whatever "natural" means, it doesn't easily accept "bass boat" or "TVA dam.") In other words, it's a class issue, which, more than any other single factor besides the passage of vast amounts of time, determines what can exist as either a poem or a song. The bass boat–riding equivalent of a thousand years ago wrote or sang most of what we call the poetry from his or her time. Kristofferson, because of his fancy pedigree, confuses and confounds. He's a freak—smart and properly educated, but able to communicate brilliantly with everyone; hence people label him (along with a handful of other songwriters), if somewhat bashfully, "poet" as if it were an honorific, as if it were an Oxford tie to wear.

But other than the obvious difference of lyrics being set to music that's integral to its meaning and poetry being set only to the music integral to its language and therefore its meaning, the important and unacknowledged practical difference between poetry and lyric is that lyrics remain deeply tied to the oral tradition. They can and will gleefully be altered by anyone with a guitar or a voice who wants to make them relevant and/or make a buck—copyright be damned. We own them together—they are ours, for better or worse. Phil Ochs's estate has, for example, recently given permission for his classic protest songs to be updated and made relevant to the specifics of the now—a process that, pre-twentieth century, would have occurred naturally in the oral tradition. Poetry, on the other hand, remains almost completely static and is bound to die but for those elements that participate in the tradition that lives within them. No one, so far as I know, has contacted Mr. Eliot's estate.

Just as hundreds of years of (granted, lunatic) scholars have resisted the idea that Shakespeare the actor and businessman could possibly have written the plays associated with his name, so too the intellectual culture generally—that is, not just the loonies—cannot accept the notion that the unschooled can create something as grand as poetry, something untouchable. But the question of whether or not lyrics are poetry is beside the point, since "poetry" at this point is about as meaningful as "natural." The question is really whether or not they deserve to be studied seriously (a given with poetry, in thought if not action); that is, whether they hold something essential to what it means to be human, and the answer to that is a heavily reverbed "yes." Because songs like these, once as much a part of our consciousness as fairy tales, tend to flow over us now like water as our posture toward them has become more passive and our choices so overwhelmingly large. And the process of culling and altering them through the oral tradition has, for the most part, been eliminated by the massive digital archives we carry in our pockets or on our desks—nothing need ever be deleted. But that, of course, is the real job of education, to cull, to present what is essential.

So what is essential in "Me and Bobby McGee"? First, it's the clock that got it going in the first place: the windshield wipers, as unpromising as they sound on a page of prose. Before I knew Kristofferson had said so, I believed they were the song's heart—as no doubt most people do—and the likely start of the lyric itself, the shaping force of all the disparate elements the song contains. Shakespeare's "When I do count the clock that tells the time" no doubt had a related beginning—he notices the clock of the sun going down, the clock of a day, the clock of the seasons, all of which lead him to a meditation on mortality and the desire to escape it somehow—that time by having children. He does this a number of times in the sonnets, of course, generally taking his cue from an image in nature, from things more traditionally poetic. That these clocks are all around us goes without saying; we just tend to ignore them, generally without disastrous result. But Kristofferson, driving along in the quintessential twentieth-century American symbol of freedom and individuality on the great symbolic American highway that promises to lead you wherever the hell you want to go, cannot escape that ticking and the fundamental lesson it teaches about all such concepts: freedom, love, hope, progress, whatever. As the chorus tells us: "Freedom's just another word for nothing left to lose: / Nothing left is all she left for me. / Feeling good was easy, Lord, when Bobby sang the blues."

The first verse sets the physical scene, where the music of its language—with its B's and D's sounding loud, with its S's snaking through and cinching the whole thing together—is brilliant and alive, echoing the excesses of Hopkins in the third line, and again more gently with each of the first three lines starting with a heavily accented repetition of B, F, B, & D sounds, respectively. The first three lines of that verse are: "Busted flat in Baton Rouge, heading for the trains / Feeling nearly faded as my jeans. / Bobby thumbed a diesel down, just before it rained." Astonishing, really, how precisely such souped-up language sets such a rich scene without calling attention to its complex artistry—and how much we discover.

With the second verse the tone is set—a blues feel, and we learn (as is so often the case with the great ones) that this is a song about songs, particularly the blues. He's blowing sad tunes on the Aeolian harp of the masses (but it's *our* breath, our *pneuma*—not the wind—blown through reeds screwed between wood and tin) and she's singing the blues: *all* of the blues. "I took my harpoon out of my dirty, red bandanna, / And was blowing sad while Bobby sang the blues." We're the driver and the listener to both those blues and this song, the one who's carrying them along.

The third and fourth verses, after the chorus, are considerably looser, more abstract, and are therefore more expendable, and this is where Joplin, predictably, made her most significant changes, and where, no doubt, despite our iPods, the future will too. If these verses are less inspired—and I think they are—it's likely because the certainty of the external world—its cars and highways, its trains, its promises—have themselves slipped away into abstraction, no longer providing the pleasure or protection they once did. But the one line that will, that must persist, like the rose and briar in "Barbara Allen," is uttered like a prayer: "Somewhere near Salinas, Lord, I let her slip away." Just as Anthony Quinn's Zampano left Gelsomina sleeping on a roadside bench in *La Strada* (literally, *The Road*); just as Lear, sleeping through his life, let Cordelia slip away, only to wake up, finally alive, howling at her death, so does our hero in "Bobby McGee" lose Bobby. There's no lesson here, no moral. Just love—rose and briar.

If you love her, set her free—wait, is that right? More like: If you set her free, you will really love her—just too late. Ask Barbara Allen who's free. Or Linda Loman, who, after Willy's suicide, is "free and clear . . . we're free." Or Oedipus, who is free at last of everything. Even poor Satan in *Paradise Lost*. One thing, at least, is true and positive: They are all free of any illusion that they'll ever know anything with certainty, which is known generally as wisdom, or at least as literary wisdom. Great art in any form doesn't answer questions; it enacts them, and the related fact that what we think we know tends to mock and ruin us. Did poor William deserve his fate? Or Oedipus? Any of these? No, of course not. It just doesn't add up. "Deserve" is a word that belongs to us, that comforts us, but it's unknown to the dark god that rules our lives and our lasting art. King Lear, holding the dead daughter Cordelia in his arms, might just have well had cried, "Somewhere near the castle, Lord, I let her slip away," instead of "Thou'll come no more / Never, never, never, never, never."[2] That is just before he trades all his tomorrows for one single yesterday, as he leans to hear her (imagined?) whisper, then joins her in death, in full understanding at last—joining too Barbara Allen and Sweet William, the briar and the rose, the rose and the briar, and all the rest.

Kristofferson—Rhodes Scholar—ran away from academic life, from his conservative family, from everything he was bred to be, just as so many others were running away during that war, during the sixties, disillusioned maybe, a little too smart maybe, a little too drunk for sure. While I don't think he—or Shakespeare or Barbara Allen's anonymous author or most any other significant artist or we as a culture—chose a path, really, he did end up on one, as accidental and inevitable as life itself, a highway littered with the trash of life, with the jewels of it, leading, as they all do, to the same rich, indelible place.

Notes

1. Marsh, Dave. "Barbara Allen." *The Rose & the Briar: Death, Love and Liberty in the American Ballad.* Ed. Sean Wilentz and Greil Marcus. New York: W. W. Norton, 2005. 7–18.

2. Shakespeare, William. *King Lear.* Ed. Barbara A. Mowatt and Paul Werstine. New York: Simon & Schuster, 2004.

THE SOUP THAT COULD CHANGE THE WORLD

BETH ANN FENNELLY

Poet Beth Ann Fennelly discusses folk-alt/country singer Caroline Her-
ring's album Golden Apples. *One song in particular catches her atten-*
tion, "The Dozens," which is dedicated to author and political activist
Larry Levine. As Fennelly writes in her piece, "When I hear 'The Dozens,'
I remember that girl and her gumption. Like The Clash's 'I Fought the
Law,' like Public Enemy's 'Fight the Power,' like Bob Marley's 'Get Up,
Stand Up,' Herring's 'The Dozens' is a fight song, but it's also a song about
youth she couldn't have written when she was young." This essay artfully
weaves the personal with the analytical as Fennelly reflects on her own
life and poetry in regards to those selves who we once were.

aroline Herring earned her MA in Southern Studies at Ole Miss, where I
teach. She graduated before I got here but I've been listening to her new
album lately, so I asked one of my colleagues what she'd been like as a
student. "Memorable," he answered, and described how, on the first day
of class, he had the students go around in a circle and say why they were
interested in Southern Studies. Herring replied, "I'm looking for honest Chris-
tians." Apparently, she found some: Her thesis was on the 1920s' Association of
Southern Women for the Prevention of Lynching. All of which would make me
guess her music is a touch too earnest for my taste, but it's not.

A Southern woman herself, Herring moved to Austin to earn a Ph.D. in American Studies, but while playing weekly gigs at a happy hour found herself a following, then a record label, and after being named Best New Artist in Austin left
her studies for full-time music. Since then she's put out several albums, most
recently Signature Sounds' *Golden Apples of the Sun.* If you recognize the title as
from Yeats's poem "Song of the Wandering Aengus," you're the right kind of listener for these story-songs that make references, at times, to Dante, Pablo Neruda, Wendell Berry, and the Gulf Coast artist Walter Anderson. Lest you fear the

album is too black-beret highbrow, too "do-you-know-the-secret-handshake," however, Herring also covers not only the traditional blues "See See Rider" but also the Cyndi Lauper hit "True Colors," which is revealed to have a surprising depth in Herring's clear, pure vocals.

Golden Apples is the album of a woman who has come into her powers as a singer-songwriter, claiming as her stomping ground the territory where folk meets alt-country. There's a Chinese expression that says, "He who reads one hundred poets sounds like one hundred poets. He who reads a thousand poets sounds like himself." Caroline Herring has read her thousand poets—one discerns the great J trio of Joan Baez, Judy Collins, and Joni Mitchell—but she sounds like herself. Which is a pretty good thing to sound like, I'd say: Her voice is both intimate and resonant. Her producer, David Goodrich, wisely decided to leave the arrangements uncluttered, and the stripped-down approach does justice to Herring's emotional range.

The album's fifth song, "The Dozens," is dedicated to an author with less name recognition that Yeats or Neruda. Larry Levine published his *Black Culture and Black Consciousness* in 1977, which Herring read and admired; she tracked him down in Washington, D.C., and the two became friends. Spare, unadorned—composed of just her vocals and two guitars, Herring's and Goodrich's—the song recalls Levine's efforts at community building to fight segregation. In his book, Levine describes a game of words called "the dozens" which consists of trading insults. (To "a white girl from a segregated town"—Herring is from Canton, Mississippi—it made sense to think of the rounds of "your Mama" putdowns like a dance she could recognize, in this case, "a veiled quadrille round.") A player "wins" the dozens by staying cool, by not getting mad or violent, so the game becomes a strategy for toughening up, steeling oneself against larger injustices.

In "The Dozens," Herring remembers driving to Memphis to hear Levine speak, traveling with fellow activists in "a Ford station wagon / So full of us it was dragging." A powerful public speaker, Levine emboldens the group to create social change, and they depart later having "made our plans / To hoist the flag and rule the world." The speaker's relationship continues with Levine and his wife—"meals with you and Cornelia / were my most precious memories." But the song takes an elegiac tone when the speaker recalls her last visit to Levine. She finds him "with a shock of white hair," and reflecting sadly on his son's illness as well as his friend who was killed by a garbage truck—"They threw him down / Then they picked him up." This time, when Herring's chorus begs Levine, "Let's play the dozens," we sense a different urgency; after years of receiving inspiration from him, she wishes to return the favor, to imbue him with the fighting spirit. That she can't—his death is implied—is what gives the song its emotional power, its poignant nostalgia. Her voice softens and takes a step back from the chord-throbbing guitar as she sings, toward the end, "I would vote for you for president / But you're floating with the butterflies."

Herring is missing not only Levine, but the person she was when she knew him. And we listen to the song to recall the selves we miss, for that is one reason we turn to music: to become the person we become when we hear it. Baudelaire wrote, "A poet must be a professor of the five senses," and I think he meant that artists must be attuned to the ways in which sensory experiences can be powerful time machines. For Proust, the taste of madelines dipped in tea brought him back to his childhood. I can return to my eighth-grade spring through the smell of Love's Baby Soft perfume or Bonne Bell 7-Up flavored chapstick. Such time travel is automatic, site-specific. It's a bigger accomplishment when the item that transports us wasn't there in our youths, but feels like it was. For while I never heard Herring's music when I was in college, that's where I return when I hear "The Dozens." Who was I then? Oh, reader, you wouldn't recognize that girl. Listening to the song, I see her now, a freshman at Notre Dame, which might not sound like a bastion of progressive activism but consider where she was a few months before: at an all-girl, private, Catholic boarding school, complete with plaid kilt and knee socks (dear reader, it's been twenty years and she still can't wear plaid). Suddenly she's part of conversations more serious than which lipstick to wear. There are all-night talks in the cinderblock dorm hallways on philosophy and politics. She discovers feminism and this opens the door to considering race and class and all the things she's been taught not to talk about at the dinner table. She is enthralled. She thinks in a few years she'll persuade the Catholic Church to accept women priests; that apartheid is about to be eradicated, and with it all vestiges of racism; that the Cold War and the threat of nuclear arms are moving into past tense. She carries her mail up to her dorm room and sinks onto her bed beneath its outsized black and white poster of Paul Simonon of The Clash about to smash his bass onstage, and she studies the cover of *Time* magazine. The Berlin wall has fallen. No: not fallen; has been *dismantled*, and when she looks at the photo of the dismantlers with their blue-jeaned legs dangling from atop the graffitied concrete, she recognizes them for who they are: her people. People her age are tearing down walls. Watch out; she will be one of them.

Several years ago I tried to write a poem that dealt, in part, with my certainty then that a well-meaning protest could change Catholicism:

> At Notre Dame, our fight song ended,
> "While her loyal sons are marching onward to victory,"
> and I was one of those who yelled, "and daughters"—
> so likewise I decided
> to stop picturing God as a white-haired old white man
> stop singing *Him* in hymns
> picture instead a genderless breeze who valued
> women and animals and gays and birth control and masturbation,
>
> I didn't know then that the threads I pulled
> ten years later would still be unraveling—

The poem goes on to deal with this confusing unraveling in which I exchanged righteousness for a tentative, at times painful, fumbling towards clarity. The double perspective of the then/now self is what fuels the poem's anxieties.

We feel nostalgia for those younger selves at their fighting weights, maybe because nostalgia has a kind of condescension to it—isn't it cute to have been so spunky, so full of gumption—that helps mask the true pain we feel at the compromising of our moral fervor. It's the fact that time has passed that allows me to write about who I was then, to see her as a different person from whom I am now. Similarly, "The Dozens" is underscored with a tension created by juxtaposing the events of the song and Herring's recalling of them. Hearing the song a second time, the listener better understands the pathos of the opening lyrics, which begin, after all, "I had a few more questions / I never knew to ask." Clearly, the speaker fully knows those questions now, though it's too late to ask them, so she doesn't.

Like The Clash's "I Fought the Law," like Public Enemy's "Fight the Power," like Bob Marley's "Get Up, Stand Up," Herring's "The Dozens" is a fight song, but it's also a song about youth she couldn't have written when she was young. It's not so much that the fight has gone out of her as that the fight has changed, become a touch world weary, and she misses the purity of the early days when villains were so easy to spot they didn't need to wear black Stetsons. "Let's eat some democratic soup," she asks Levine, needing a dose of his inspiration and a sign that she "won't bottom out in seconds flat." Unlike revenge, such soup is a meal best served hot, and she gazes across the years and through the steam at the girl she was—inviting us, too, to gaze back at the dreamers we'd been—and she lifts her spoon. She'll spend the rest of her life trying to recreate how good that first bite tasted.

Works Cited

The Clash. "I Fought the Law." *The Cost of Living*. Lyrics and music by Sonny Curtis. CBS, 1979.

Herring, Caroline. "The Dozens." *Golden Apples of the Sun*. Signature Sounds, 2009.

———. *Golden Apples of the Sun*. Signature Sounds, 2009.

Lauper, Cyndi. "True Colors." *True Colors*. Music and lyrics by Billy Steinberg and Tom Kelly. Epic, 1986.

Levine, Lawrence W. *Black Culture and Black Consciousness: Afro-American Folk Thought from Slavery to Freedom*. Oxford: Oxford University Press, 1977.

Public Enemy. "Fight the Power." *Do the Right Thing* (original soundtrack album). Music and lyrics by Chuck D, Eric "Vietnam" Sadler, Hank Shocklee, and Keith Shocklee. Tamla Records, 1989.

The Wailers. "Get Up, Stand Up." *Burnin'*. Music and lyrics by Bob Marley and Peter Tosh. Tuff Gong/Island Records, 1973.

Yeats, William Butler. "Song of the Wandering Aengus."

LAUGHING IN TUNE: R.E.M. AND THE POST-CONFESSIONAL LYRIC

JEFFREY ROESSNER

While Michael Stipe's lyrics have always received something of a mixed response, everyone agrees that his lyrics are difficult to understand in part because of Stipe's own muddled enunciation and the way the vocals are mixed. In this essay, Jeffrey Roessner embraces this sense of lyrical obfuscation and considers it for what it is. Instead of dismissing the lyrics as nonsense, teasing out underlying meanings, or forgiving Stipe for his lyrical indulgence, Roessner investigates the assumption that lyrics should provide literal meanings. In this essay, Roessner suggests an alternative view that places "R.E.M.'s lyrics in the context of contemporary verse, particularly Language poetry. As in experimental work by poets such as Charles Bernstein and Bruce Andrews, Stipe develops an anti-confessional poetics by rejecting the singer's position as the confessional 'I' in the songs, abjuring a representational style, and ultimately inviting listeners to co-create rather than simply receive meaning from the lyrics."

n the early 1980s, R.E.M. arrived as the antithesis of almost every trend in corporate rock music. In the era of ubiquitous hit albums such as Prince's *1999*, Bruce Springsteen's *Born in the U.S.A.*, and Duran Duran's *Rio*, top-forty rock was hyper-produced, strident, and awash in synthesizers; in marked contrast, R.E.M.'s style was murky, understated, and laden with chiming guitars. Rock was big city, multinational, stadium-sized; R.E.M. was local, quirky, Southern, and the band represented a burgeoning underground scene created and sustained by college radio. Significantly, mainstream rock also continued to trade on the clichés of confessional lyrics, in which authenticity was granted by the singer's personal expression of deep emotion, almost always related from a first-person point of view. Here again, R.E.M. forged an original approach. On their early records, particularly their first album, *Murmur*, the band promoted a radically different poetics for popular music, one that formed a more oblique and compelling connection to their fans.

Although R.E.M.'s intimate relation to the audience was crucial to their early success, the responses to singer Michael Stipe's lyrics for R.E.M. were mixed from the beginning. Beyond near universal agreement that the words are difficult to decipher—due both to Stipe's strangled enunciation and to the low volume of the vocals in the mix—fans and critics alike have tended to have one of two reactions. Either they dismiss the lyrics as nonsense more interesting for their sonic qualities than for meaning, or they strike a note of indulgence as they forgive Stipe's eccentric verbal incoherence (Greer 58; Sullivan 52–53). In both cases, however, the responses suggest a deep attachment to literal, referential meaning—as though songs ought to deliver a clear message, and when they don't, the choice is to either ignore them or make excuses. Here I want to suggest an alternative view that places R.E.M.'s lyrics in the context of contemporary poetry, particularly Language poetry. As in experimental verse by poets such as Charles Bernstein and Bruce Andrews, Stipe forges an anti-confessional poetics by rejecting the singer's position as the confessional "I" in the songs, abjuring a representational style, and in so doing, ultimately inviting listeners to co-create rather than simply receive meaning from the songs.

From the beginning, R.E.M. evoked a mysterious aura, and crafted a romanticized image of both the band and the music. The kudzu sprawling across the cover of *Murmur* announces the arrival of eccentric Southern poets of place. As for the album title itself, it connotes a heart murmur and the exposure of closely guarded inner secrets, all of them delivered in an indistinct whisper. The suggestion is that you'll have to listen closely to make out the intimate confessions here. Ultimately, the mystique is solidified in the very appearance of Michael Stipe, whose flowing locks suggest nothing less than a reincarnation of late-sixties Roger Daltry. As the singer and de facto frontman, Stipe anchors the band's appeal, and his sand-and-gravel voice, with its deep resonance and pleading highs, draws listeners inexorably into the emotional vortex.

As a reaction against rock clichés, R.E.M.'s enigmatic woolliness solidified the band's early appeal. But it has also led many critics to dismiss the cryptic lyrics as irrelevant nonsense, "stitched together primarily out of regard for their assonance and consonance" (Greer 48). Still others contort the lyrics in an attempt to wrangle literal sense out of the songs, and generally still end up dismissing them as impenetrable. In describing "Radio Free Europe," for example, Johnny Black writes, "The lyric that appeared on the final single included such unforgettably mysterious lines as, 'Raving station, beside yourself / Keep me out of country in the word / Deal the porch is leading us absurd,' but how closely they resemble what [Stipe] sang while composing is anybody's guess, as is precisely how they related to the concept of the song" (49).

Such critical confusion and often utter derision is somewhat perplexing, given that the band has repeatedly spelled out exactly the intention behind its approach to lyrics. Peter Buck explains,

> Michael and I used to say how much we hated most rock'n'roll lyrics. . . . We had this idea that what we'd do is take clichés, sayings, lines from old blues songs, phrases you hear all the time, and skew them and twist them and meld them together so that you'd be getting these things that have always been evocative, but that were skewed just enough to throw you off and make you think in a different way. (Black 34)

Far from being an assemblage of random nonsense, the band's poetics arose out of a considered rejection of the lyric tradition and a fascination with the materiality of language. Stipe removes phrases from the context that gave them meaning and puts them together in unconventional ways. In so doing, he calls attention to an important element of his approach. The language itself generates meaning beyond his conscious control, and the emphasis lands firmly on the listener's response; As Buck insists, this approach makes "you think in a different way"—hardly the aim of most lyrics produced by a rock and roll band.

In fact, such experiments with language represent a serious assault on the typically confessional voice of much recent poetry and song lyrics. As David Yezzi argues, the confessional approach depends upon the revelation of deeply personal truth: In such work, "The 'I' of the poem is meant as a direct representation of the flesh-and-blood poet. Through its enumeration of sins, the confessional poem emerges as a tragic self-portrait." In larger historical terms, Yezzi rightly identifies conflation of the poet and the speaker of the poem as a reaction against modernist impersonality. Since the 1950s and the work of Robert Lowell, Sylvia Plath, and Anne Sexton, the confessional approach has remained a dominant thread in verse, apparent not only in autobiographical soul-bearing poetry, but also in the invective-laced goading of performance poetry. And of course, the honest expression of personal truth underpins many song lyrics, whose impact often hinges on the singer's emotionally charged delivery of them.

In this context, it's clear that Stipe's approach from the start was radically anti-confessional. As Marcus Gray notes, Stipe "had no great interest in using the songs as soapboxes or confessionals, and . . . he even took to comparing such baring of the soul to the physically violent act of evisceration. 'I'm not about to split myself open, to gut myself on stage and spill myself all over people'" (Gray 61). The quest for impersonality reflects a desire for self-protection, obviously, but also a renunciation of literalism. Not wanting to mount a soapbox, Stipe resists ingrained habits of reading and listening, and actively thwarts those who so desperately want concrete sense. Given this approach, it is more helpful to read the lyrics in the context of contemporary poetry than rock and roll.

Stipe's skewed lyrics put him in the company of other poetic radicals, especially Language poets, who sought an alternative to confessionalism. Although the work of Charles Bernstein, Bruce Andrews, Susan Howe, and others is decidedly non-lyrical—that is, much of the work exhibits more affinity to visual art than music, and sometimes resists being read aloud, let alone sung—the movement nonetheless offers a profound challenge to the dominant confessional tradition. The nature of this assault on clichéd conventions is spelled out starkly by Bruce Andrews: Aiming to disrupt writing grounded in "reference, representation, transparency, clarity, description, reproduction, positivism," an alternate poetics would be "those of *subversion*: an anti-systemic detonation of settled relations, an anarchic liberation of energy flows" (16–17). The project to unsettle language and our relation to it would of necessity have profound implications for the speaker's relationship to the words, and that detonation would in turn produce a confused reaction in some listeners. As Charles Bernstein argues, such works may

> discomfort those who want a poetry primarily of personal communication, flowing freely from the inside with the words of a natural rhythm of life, lived daily. . . . An influence of work that appears to be of this (other) type is the sanctification of something that gets to be known as its honesty, its directness, its authenticity, its artlessness, its sincerity, its spontaneity, its personal expressiveness. (Bernstein 94)

Those critical of Stipe's lyrics are absolutely right: He confronts them with language that defies all their interpretive habits. It makes sense that critics—steeped in the lyrical history of the genre—would likely be among the confounded. If we want to read Stipe on his own terms, then, we have to start with a different question: What happens when the lyrics require us to rethink our relationship to language?

On *Murmur*, Stipe takes a major step toward inventing a subversive poetics for rock and roll. Despite his appearance as the romantic poet, he systematically strips the album of personal references. Although the language gains resonance from his impassioned delivery and the slurred texture of his voice, the words themselves remain starkly detached from Stipe himself as the speaker. As J. Niimi notes, "*Murmur* has no *I*": Of the twelve songs on the album, nine contain no first-person singular or "I," and in one other track, "9—9", the "I" only occurs as part of a child's prayer ("Now I lay me down to sleep," etc.) (100). References to "me" or "my" are also rare on most of the tracks. Three songs on the album do seem highly personal: "Catapult," "Perfect Circle," and "Sitting Still." Although these songs are exceptions on the record, critics often seize on them for comment, because they present the most accessible references and, on "Catapult" at least, seemingly clear connection to Stipe's childhood (Gray 65). But even here Stipe does not deliver confessions—and if he did, they are so veiled that any attempt to uncover them remains fruitless. The impersonality of the record under-cuts one common point of identification in song lyrics: we cannot easily connect with the singer's feeling when he himself does not own them (Niimi 111).

In place of the first-person confession, Stipe develops other tactics to draw listeners in. Along with downplaying personal pronouns, he consistently elides the subject in his lyrics, engaging in what J. Niimi calls "subjective ambiguity" (103). One of his most frequent strategies is to employ an understood subject, and open his lines with verbs. For example, "Radio Free Europe" contains the phrase, "Put that put that put that up your wall"; "Laughing" offers "Lock the door, latch the room," "Run the gamut, settled new," and "Find a place fit to laugh"; and "Perfect Circle" includes the unexpected instruction, "Pull your dress on and stay real close." In fact, only two songs on the album don't contain this construction: "Sitting Still" and "Shaking Through." In several, it's the first line: "Pilgrimage" ("Take a turn . . . Take our fortune"), "Moral Kiosk" ("Scratch the scandals in the twilight"), "Perfect Circle" ("Put your hair back"). In the case of "Perfect Circle," of course, the lyric can be read as narrative, with the speaker addressing the other main character. But in general, the grammar aims the lines directly at audience members, who are syntactically embedded in the lyric and thus asked to play a role in construing meaning.

Moreover, when Stipe does identify subjects in his lines, he gravitates toward inclusive pronouns about shared experience. References to "we," "our," and "us" abound, occurring almost twice as often as the first-person-singular pronouns on the record. So even in a song reputedly heavily invested in personal experi-ence such as "Catapult," the connection to listeners is made through plural pro-nouns: The song opens with the lines, "Ooooooh, we were little boys / Ooooooh, we were little girls." Stipe immediately blurs the gender of the speaker and opts to universalize childhood experience rather than tie it to his specific memory. He further invites listeners in with the pervasive childhood plea disguised as a question, "Did we miss anything?"—again, not asking us to share his memory, but to recall our own. The repeated question prepares the launch into the chorus and the chant, "catapult," which deftly captures the propulsive energy of being young.

This invitation for listeners to participate in the construction of meaning be-comes, in fact, the key element of Stipe's early poetics, and ties the work firmly to the project of Language poetry. Not only does he rarely take subjective control of the lyrics, but he actively undermines his authorial control over the words themselves. J. Niimi describes this as the "tension in hearing a song sung and not really knowing whose song it is—the singer's, the subject's, yours?" (110). Investing in such ambiguity, R.E.M. made the conscious decision not to offer a lyric sheet with the early albums. And in one interview, drummer Bill Berry claims, "Sometimes people will send Michael what they think the lyrics are in the hopes that he'll tell them what they are. . . . Sometimes Michael will change the lyrics to what people thought they were" (Walters 78). Stipe has also been known to alter the lyrics to suit the particular occasion of their performance. Fan and friend Keith Altomare notes, "If you would be at more than one show, it would be different words. He might know the phone book in the town they were in or he would throw in whatever he was reading. He liked my name and he would scream it during the bridge [of 'Catapult']" (Sullivan 56). The indeterminate language sutures the lyrics to a context, and undermines the notion that any particular song has a definitive version or universal, stable meaning. For Altomare, the fungible nature of the words doesn't erode their significance, but rather heightens the relationship to the audience: "It really showed they were conscious of their people and their fans" (56).

Given the uncertain and protean language, listeners don't simply receive but actually confer meaning on the lyrics, and nowhere is this more apparent than through the fan culture of the internet, which has produced multiple versions (and hence multiple readings) of the songs. Part of a refrain in "Radio Free Europe," for example, is frequently rendered, "Raving Station beside yourself." Other versions offer language seemingly dictated by the title: "Radio station beside yourself." The chorus of "Sitting Still" has also been variously heard as:

> Up to par and Katie bars the kitchen signs but not me in
> Setting trap for love making a waste of time, sitting still.

Or alternatively as:

> Up to par, and Katie buys a kitchen-size, but not me in
> Sit and try for the big key, a waste o' time, sitting still.

Listeners insert or omit punctuation, shift words, and modify the rhymes at will. Which versions are "correct"? Except for the rare instance in which Stipe has confirmed a lyric, there is no easy answer to that question. For some, such a stance confirms the pointlessness of the lyrics; for others, it stokes an obsessive quest to locate a definitive version. Both approaches share an unshakeable, rigid belief in the stability of meaning and the coherence of the speaking subject who delivers it—precisely the lyrical conventions that Stipe challenges. If we have no definitive version of a lyric, then seeking one becomes an irritable grasping after fact that neither illuminates the "meaning" nor helps clarify what Stipe is up to here.

Aside from ambiguous words and shifting lyrics, Stipe more radically opens the field of language as he deconstructs the very syntax of his lines. As Bill Berry notes, "He leaves out essential parts of speech. . . . People try to guess the next word before he says it. Then when it's not there, they completely lose it" (Fricke 50). Such elisions can be fairly simple, as in these lines from "Pilgrimage": "Rest

assured this will not last, / Take a turn for the worst"; if we insert the understood subject and verb ("it will") between them, the lines make complete sense,
and hardly baffle even the casual listener. In many instances, though, grammar
is strained much further, beyond the point of breaking. The very first words on
Murmur appear in "Radio Free Europe": "Beside yourself if radio's gonna stay."
We could attempt to parse this by reading it as an inversion and supplying missing words: "If radio's going to stay, then it's going to stay beside you." But when
we do this, we are immediately aware that we are *adding*, not finding, meaning.
Language here is not a transparent medium through which Stipe expresses his
meaning; rather, language itself becomes generative, producing meanings that
are beyond Stipe's control. Other songs even more defiantly resist our attempts
to master them. "Sitting Still" opens with "This name I got we all were green /
See could stop stop it will red." Faced with such resistance, some listeners "completely lose it," as Berry notes. At the very least, we must accept that the songs
do not honor our casual assumptions about the invisible structure of language.
Exposing the seams of language, Stipe disrupts our utilitarian control of it—we
exist as part of the field of meaning that language creates.

One other favorite tactic of Language poets also emerges as part of the disintegration of literal meaning here: parataxis. Not only do listeners confront
missing parts of speech and contorted syntax, but the individual lines are often
jarringly disconnected from those around them. To be sure, the melody, vocal
delivery, and rhymes often confer a sense of unity on the lines, tautly weaving
them together outside a referential frame. But it's often distinct lines that catch
our attention, and resist integration into the "sense" of the lyric as a whole (Niimi 106). In "Laughing," for example, Stipe sings, "Know them more, emotion
bound / Martyred, misconstrued / Lighted in a room, lanky room." In "Moral
Kiosk," we hear, perhaps, "She was laughing like a Horae / Put that knee in dour
landslide / Take this step to dash a roving eye." The center of locution remains
obscure, the speaker and the spoken to both unmoored. These constructions
produce a collage-like effect: Lines arise in your mind after listening to the album, but it's often difficult to identify their part in specific songs.

In the context of such linguistic experiments, the line "Laughing in tune" provides a central metaphor for the album. Laughter signifies beyond literal meaning, and any attempt to explain why something is funny kills the joke. Approach-
ing Stipe's lyrics with this metaphor in mind may help us understand why so
many who try to *explain* the lyrics fail: Any perceptive reading would have to be
tentative, open, flexible, generative. Unfortunately, most attempts at exegesis
read like high school English papers, with the authors hoping once and for all to
expose the real meaning behind a song. The otherwise highly perceptive Marcus
Gray, for example, claims that "the opening line of 'Time After Time,' 'Ask the
girl of the hour / By the water tower's watch' is Stipe-speak for, 'ask the girl what
time it is by the water tower clock'" (67). Such a reading deflates and devalues the

lines—the "girl of the hour" certainly suggests a more fraught character than someone who simply tells you the time. Literalism produces reductive readings that take us further from rather than closer to the compelling sounds that hook our ears, destabilize our being in language, and render us less able but more compelled to speak for ourselves.

By 1985 much had begun to change for R.E.M. Leaving behind the retro aesthetic of original producers Mitch Easter and Don Dixon and Reflection Studio in North Carolina, they flew to London to record their third album, *Fables of the Reconstruction*, with producer Joe Boyd. This shift in scenery brought new songs, of course, but also new production values and a new direction for Stipe as singer and lyricist. You can sense the palpable relief in Johnny Black's assessment of this period in the band's history. After attempting to wrestle sense from the lyrics of the first two albums, Black claims that—although the "precise meaning" of the songs remains elusive—the album is a "remarkable development, especially for Stipe": He "seems to be spinning little stories, fashioning oblique cameos, about people he had met.... These are all songs about people" (107). At long last, then, the turn toward referential meaning and clarity in vocal style: Listeners can identify what these songs are "about" from Stipe's point of view. To be sure, *Fables* is a remarkable achievement for the band. And on it as well as subsequent releases, Stipe largely continues to eschew a confessional stance, often through the use of impersonal narrative ("Wendell Gee") or all-consuming irony ("The One I Love"). But *Fables* reflects a notable shift away from the compelling, experimental Language poetics of the first albums that so actively engaged listeners and launched the band's career.

Works Cited

Andrews, Bruce. "Writing Social Work & Political Practice." *The L=A=N=G=U=A=G=E Book*. Ed. Bruce Andrews and Charles Bernstein. Carbondale and Edwardsville: Southern Illinois UP, 1984. 133–36.

Bernstein, Charles. "Stray Straws and Straw Men." *The L=A=N-G=U=A-G=E Book*. Ed. Bruce Andrews and Charles Bernstein. Carbondale and Edwardsville: Southern Illinois Press, 1984. 94–99.

Black, Johnny. *Reveal: The Story of R.E.M.* San Francisco: Backbeat, 2004.

Buckley, David. *R.E.M. Fiction: An Alternative Biography*. London: Virgin, 2002.

Fricke, David. "R.E.M." *Rolling Stone* 460 (7 Nov. 1985): 49–50.

Gray, Marcus. *An R.E.M. Companion: It Crawled from the South*. New York: Da Capo, 1992.

Greer, Jim. *R.E.M.: Behind the Mask*. Boston: Little, Brown, 1992.

Niimi, J. *Murmur*. New York: Continuum, 2010.

Platt, John, Ed. *The R.E.M. Companion*. New York: Schirmer, 1998.

Sullivan, Denise. *R.E.M.: Talk About the Passion*. Lancaster, PA: Underwood-Miller, 1994.

Walters, Berry. "Visions of Glory" *Spin* 2.7 (Oct. 1986): 52+.

Yezzi, David. "Confessional Poetry and the Artifice of Honesty." *New Criterion* 16.10 (1998). *Academic Search Complete*. Online. EBSCO. 23 Apr. 2010.

SWEETNESS FOLLOWS: MICHAEL STIPE, JOHN KEATS, AND THE CONSOLATIONS OF TIME

ERIC REIMER

Michael Stipe's attention to the musicality of language was undermined, especially early in his career, by what many perceived to be willful obscurantism; with 1992's Automatic for the People, *however, Stipe realized a consistently stunning balance between semantic content and auditory richness. In this sense, the album's songs can nearly be described as Keatsian. Indeed, the album's concluding song, "Find the River," one of the band's most serenely beautiful tracks, recalls the last of Keats's great odes, "To Autumn," and in so doing begins to measure the greatness of Stipe as a poetic songwriter. In addition to revealing the emotional amplitude of the song and drawing out the intricacies of Stipe's nuanced poetics, the comparison helps listeners understand two speakers—and two writers—seeking grace from the painful confrontation with time and transience.*

Even after three decades of writing and performing for R.E.M., Michael Stipe's status as one of rock's most accomplished and poetic lyricists remains obscured for some by the perception of an opaque composing style governed by free association, playful but frivolous word salads, and semantic enigmas. This reputation was largely forged through his work on the band's very first album—1983's *Murmur*—but has been reinforced by any number of individual songs since that time and, at least very early in his career, was further accentuated by his famously indistinct vocal delivery. All of this heightened the effect produced by the appearance of the full lyrics to one track—"World Leader Pretend"—on 1988's *Green*, the first time the band had made any lyrics available in an album's packaging.[1] Ironically, Stipe's own humility, good humor, and self-deprecating sensibility relative to his writing have also perhaps helped to deny him some of the acclaim he deserves as a lyricist; he'll both readily admit to songs that make little sense even to him and quickly privilege the emotional experience and interpretation of the listener over any authorial intent and pride of craft.[2]

By the time 1991's *Out of Time* arrived, however, Stipe had moved determinedly toward a more direct and personal voice in his lyrics.[3] Then, in 1992, *Automatic for the People* subsequently introduced some of the most consistently affecting and emotionally accessible lyrics of his entire career, and this in addition to his usual attention to auditory richness, internal complexity, and the felicities of language. Always reluctant to think of his work as poetry, Stipe would undoubtedly be amused to hear the cycle of songs on *Automatic* described as Keatsian. With the thematic emphases on youth, aging, memory, and a mutable world, with the ongoing search for aesthetic epiphany, and, ultimately, with the grace and acquiescence emerging from the painful confrontations with time and transience, these songs match up in intriguing ways with the great ode cycle of Keats. Moreover, Stipe, like Keats, reveals a sophisticated ability to match form to manifest content, to write lyrics full of sensuous immediacy and "emotion worked through on the level of sound" (Stewart 135), to manage the resources of rhythm and the musicality of language, and to use the lyric "I" to alternate "between the specular and the acoustic, sense and sound, cognition and sensation" (Blasing 85). In each case, these writers, through both their intellects and their ears, honor the poet Christian Wiman's belief that poetry should reflect "some density of experience, some sense that a whole life is being brought to bear both on and in language" (135). At twenty-three and thirty-two, respectively, when much of the writing occurred for these two sequences, Keats and Stipe seem nearly too young to be inhabiting perspectives that so insightfully calculate one's losses, even as they, less surprisingly, articulate their yearnings.

The echoes of a Keatsian aesthetic and awareness are perhaps nowhere more evident than in "Find the River," the concluding song on *Automatic for the People* and one of the band's most serenely beautiful. Although it seems audacious to seek commensurability between a poem often cited as one of the greatest in the English language and a melancholy pop song, "Find the River" recalls the last of Keats's odes, "To Autumn," and, in so doing, begins to measure the greatness of Michael Stipe as a poetic songwriter. Like "To Autumn" and so many Romantic lyrics, generally, "Find the River" seems to be underwritten by an alienated if not tragic vision, motivating a writer who has apparently been "profoundly touched by the spirit of transience" (Macksey 855) to seek understanding and solace as a temporal being. The path to this understanding requires the intellect, for sure, but is also governed by a musical coherence that gestures beyond semantic clarity; in a lyric that transcends its textuality, logical reasoning combines with the sonority of the language and the musical elements of the song to offer the experience of "a hearing just beautifully ahead of knowing" (Plumly, *Posthumous* 344).

In the end, "Find the River," like the Keats ode before it, finds comfort and grace in a universalizing and musical lyric voice; its combinatory meaning allows us, as the best poetry always does, "not only to bear the tally and toll of our transience, but to perceive . . . a path through the grief of that insult to joy" (Hirshfield 35). The song—through both its words and its music—manages paradoxically to suggest both finality and time's continuance. When we listen to its words, carried by the beguilingly sweet musical accompaniment, we're always conscious that it will end, as it must, after the allotted time; still, the reflections its mysteries and poetic indeterminacies invite, by "replacing chronology with epiphany" (Baker 239) and by making us desire repeat experiences, displace and extend the actual time of the engagement. Jane Hirshfield could be assessing "Find the River" as surely as "To Autumn" when she notes that "good poems provide an informing so simultaneously necessary and elusive that they are never, it seems, taken in fully, can never be fully used up" (28).

M. H. Abrams, describing "the greater Romantic lyric," recognizes a formula common to many Romantic poems. Conducted by "a determinate speaker in a particularized, and usually a localized, outdoor setting" (527), and one who is often in the presence of a silent auditor, these poems feature a meditative engagement with both the landscape and the speaker's situatedness in time. In almost every case, the poems reveal speakers and poets whose confrontation with time begins with an almost desperate desire to recover a sense of lost wholeness. Thus, in Wordsworth's "Tintern Abbey," the speaker uses the word "again" four times in the opening fourteen lines, as if willing himself back into the ecstatic experience he enjoyed on the banks of the river Wye five years ago; in Keats's "Ode to a Nightingale," the speaker tries a variety of measures—wine, poetry, and even a flirtation with death—to prevent the fading of the bird's "plaintive anthem" (l. 75). Often, and certainly in these poems, sound and hearing figure prominently in the speakers' conflicts—in part because, as John Minahan observes, "to hear is to perceive duration" (115), and to perceive duration is to be reminded of the present's painful tendency to become the past. The greater lyric typically proceeds with the speaker's strenuous efforts to absorb loss and restore hope, to find what Wordsworth's speaker refers to as the "abundant recompense" necessary to transcend the "still, sad music of humanity" ("Tintern Abbey," ll. 88, 91). As the speaker finally resolves the sense of lacerating loss, usually through the healing tendencies of Nature and the assuagements of the poetic mind, the greater lyric often "rounds upon itself to end where it began . . . with an altered mood and deepened understanding" (Abrams 528).

Especially because it lacks an identifiable speaker who self-consciously meditates on a natural setting, Keats's "To Autumn" does not obviously conform to the contours of Abrams's greater Romantic lyric. Experienced as the final ode in a sequence of six that complexly reveal "sets of mutual relations" (Vendler, *The Odes* 4), however, we nevertheless sense the presence of an intimate, observing voice that is no less preoccupied with the problems attendant to a painful temporal awareness. Across its three stanzas, the poem moves literally from sunrise to sunset and figuratively from birth to death, thus allowing that observing consciousness to consider his own place in the passage of time. Keats formalizes this awareness in many of the poem's individual details, perhaps most memorably with the "sticky feel" (Minahan 181) and the rapt attention to the "last oozings" (l. 22) of the cider-press, which suggest an attempt to defy time's insistence on succession and its guarantee of betrayal. Whereas hearing initiates the sense of conflict in the aforementioned greater lyrics—"again I hear / these waters, rolling from their mountain springs / with a soft inland murmur" ("Tintern Abbey," ll. 2–4)—it seems to resolve that conflict in the final stanza of Keats's final ode. Here the richly ambivalent music of Nature—the choir of gnats, the bleating of lambs, the singing of hedge crickets, the whistling of redbreasts, the twittering of swallows—manages to help the implied human observer understand, as W. Jackson Bate explains, that "the present has meaning only in terms of what is past and what is to come" (47–48).

Much as the serenity and peaceful acceptance eventually achieved in "To Autumn" are made more meaningful by the speaker's apparent ability to resolve the agonizing problems introduced in the preceding odes, the speaker's quest in "Find the River" gathers increased significance from the song's position as the last track of *Automatic for the People*. Appearing after songs focused on the death of parents ("Sweetness Follows"), the quiet desperation of daily life ("Everybody Hurts"), reflections on a full life ("Try Not to Breathe"), nostalgic invocations of youth ("Man on the Moon"), and memories of hallowed summer nights and physical vitality ("Nightswimming"), "Find the River" not only concludes what has been called R.E.M.'s "most mature album" (Gray 129) but implicitly carries the weight of sundry losses. The lyric commences with an older speaker directly addressing a younger auditor who must "go to task in the city / where people drown and people serve" (ll. 3–4).[4] Having posited the enervating aspects of urban life as the immediate threat to wholeness and personal fulfillment, he then urges his possible protégé to find the courage and endurance to earn his "just deserve" (l. 5), even if there are still "light years to go" (l. 6) in his journey. Perhaps having emerged from his own such "service," however, either recently or earlier in his life, the speaker realizes that he himself must depart to pursue a more natural and artistic life; as for himself, he indicates, "my thoughts are flower strewn / ocean storm, bayberry moon. / I have got to leave to find my way" (ll. 7–9).[5] At this point the lyric embarks on a rather traditional quest structure, governed by such familiar components as a river voyage and the search for self-awareness. In its effective simplicity, the lament that "nothing is going my way" (ll. 12, 21) suggests the impediments that will make finding the river difficult; repeated at the end of the second and fourth stanzas, the line both brilliantly deadens the lyric's metrical progression and suggests the speaker's loss of moorings, allowing Stipe to match form to content. The speaker seeks his own courage, then, to "leave the road" in order to find that with which he knows he shares affinities: "A need to leave the water knows" (l. 14). Additionally, both the river and the speaker have a goal: "The ocean is the river's goal" (l. 13), we are told, and although the speaker's is far more uncertain and appropriately undefined, we surmise that it involves a reconciliation with time. If not a kind of spiritual apotheosis, the speaker may at least find, with the river, a sense of twilight vitality that will allow him to "chase the ride" (l. 25) as he reaches the latter stages and days of his life.

Though not a quest poem in the same manner as "Find the River," "To Autumn" nevertheless postulates that "whoever seeks abroad" (l. 13) may encounter and learn from an autumn that refuses to "enact her own dissolution" (Vendler, *The Odes* 251). Beyond any specific journeys into unknown territory, though, these lyrics both remain centrally concerned with and governed by a sense of motion. Before it eventually reaches its state of exhausted but satisfied passivity in the second stanza, Keats's ode is intensely kinetic, accumulating a cluster of active verbs in the opening stanza. Autumn seeks a partner with the "maturing sun,"

> *Conspiring* with him how to *load* and *bless*
>   With fruit the vines that round the thatch-eaves *run*;
> To *bend* with apples the mossed cottage trees,
>   And *fill* all fruit with ripeness to the core;
> To *swell* the gourd, and *plump* the hazel shells
>   With a sweet kernel . . . (ll. 3–8; emphasis added)

The subtler forms of movement in the poem include the diurnal progression of sunrise to sunset across the three stanzas which, in an increasingly metaphorical way, imply the annual cycle of the seasons and, by further extension, the trajectory of the human life—figured through the poem's fruit from generation to maturation, ripeness, and, finally, sweet rottenness. Then—perhaps most brilliantly in terms of Keats's accomplishment, and as Helen Vendler so perceptively recognizes in her reading—the poem conducts a steady sense of movement in space, to which the reader responds in a palpable, bodily way. Concentrated at first near the human dwelling of the thatched cottage, the integrated reader is carried outward to the apple orchards and beehives, then onward to the outlying buildings and harvested fields, then still further, beyond the stubble-plains and on to the river, hilly bourn, hedgerows, and garden-croft at the furthest reaches of the farm. At this point, producing a sensation that feels simultaneously spiritual and physical, the reader's gaze is directed upwards into the expansive skies, "where gathering swallows twitter" (l. 33).[6] We are reminded, perhaps, that the odes, as Stanley Plumly argues, "in their embodiment, want to involve as much of the whole body and brain as possible" ("Between Things" 113).

In part because of its narrative development but perhaps more interestingly because of Stipe's attentive management and alternation of meter, rhythm, and sound qualities, "Find the River" also moves in palpable and complicated ways. Echoing Plumly to some degree, William Matthews describes the effect of a poetics—here realized by Stipe—that allows us to experience words and their music in a physical way: "'Form' is what we call it when it's dormant, when the poem is adoze on the page and no reader comes to wake it. But read it with your eyes, speak it in your silent voice, experience it with your body—the reader, too, has a body of work—and you'll find it mutable, swift, varied in its particulars and yet all of a piece, like music or running water." (39)

"Find the River" is mutable before it is swift. Evenly split between iambic and trochaic meters across its thirty-nine lines—with, five times, the interruption of lines with irregular, "sprung" rhythm—the lyric's metrical alternation produces a sense of defiance, nearly, and especially with the trochaic modulations, a sense of "assertive solemnity" (Steele 72). These trochaic lines seem designed to suggest an expression of the spirit's resolve in the face of challenge: "I have got to find the river" (l. 16) and "Pick up here and chase the ride" (l. 25), for example, both follow iambic lines and thus use the change in meter to accentuate the speaker's determination; they produce the same distinguishing and dramatic effect, we might say, as the admonition in the third stanza of "To Autumn" to "think not of them"—those songs of Spring—for "thou hast thy music too" (l. 24). Additionally, with never more than three successive iambic or four successive trochaic lines, Stipe creates, perhaps unwittingly, a kind of countercurrent, a metrical analogue to the undertow that suggests both promise and peril for the speaker late in the poem as his river ride approaches its terminus.

Managing that rhythmic undertow and having overcome the obstructions of the repeated "nothing is going my way" line—which briefly impedes both the speaker's search to find his life's proper channel and, with its successive dactylic feet, the reader's/listener's rhythmic comfort—the lyric, in its final verse of twelve lines, finally achieves an inspired, riverine propulsion. These lines attain a solidly regular metrical alternation, with six iambic and six trochaic lines; more than that, though, their semantic details, lush sonority, and rhyme linkages, especially, create a galvanizing effect across the metrical pattern and reveal a verse constructed with the kind of meticulous poetic care rarely seen in pop or rock lyrics.[7] The assonantal end rhymes are more irregularly patterned than elsewhere in the lyric, but by consolidating them into essentially three cascading clusters—governed by the long "o," long "a," and long "i" sounds—Stipe produces a sense of insistent, headlong movement.

The accumulating momentum of the final verse is augmented by the strategic blending of end rhymes and internal rhymes, most notably with "rose of hay" (l. 33), which picks up multiple payoffs in two directions (i.e., *rose* answers *throw* and *indigo*, while *hay* answers *way*, and then, three lines later, *rose of hay* is answered by *naïveté*), as well as with the *ginger/indigo* and *lemon/stem* pairings that communicate within and across lines:[8]

> There is nothing left to throw
> of ginger, lemon, indigo,
> coriander stem and rose of hay. (ll. 31–33)

Stipe also uses consonance and assonance to rich effect in this coda; the former includes a heavy incidence of "r" and "n" sounds (e.g., the connections between *ginger*, *indigo*, and *coriander* are striking in the above lines) while the latter features long "o" and long "e" sounds (*weary/naïveté*, et al.). Effectively introduced in the opening lines of the verse—"The river to the ocean goes, / a fortune for the undertow" (ll. 28–29)—the long "o" sound, especially, is subsequently woven by rhyming and assonance in complicated ways across such words as *going*, *throw*, *indigo*, *rose*, *overrides*, and *poet*. Despite the preponderance of end-stopped lines in the verse, these kinships create the impression of enjambed fluidity as the lyric, river, and speaker all move irrepressibly towards their final end-stops.

Although he has perhaps found his proper place "chasing the ride" and has been figuratively integrated, the speaker, just four lines before the end, himself seems urgently caught up in the coda's velocity, forced to the almost desperately distilled delivery of the puzzling "river poet search naïveté" (l. 36). If only because they provide something of a tonal and thematic précis of the overall lyric, though, it may little matter that we struggle to attach "naïveté" (i.e., is the poet naïve? Is the poet's search naïve? Is the poet searching for childlike renewal? Is Stipe purely privileging the sound and the expectations of rhyme?). The word sequence fittingly and pleasingly consolidates and recapitulates many of the assonantal and consonantal sound features of the entire verse, and thus again affirms Stipe as a writer who not only writes with an attentive and musical ear, but who uses sound in significant ways to enhance meaning. As Robert von Hallberg argues, "when words cohere musically they allude to significance beyond paraphrase" (143)—or, as Simon Frith similarly observes of powerful pop songs, they "celebrate not the articulate but the inarticulate" (35). Stipe's ear for "the cooperative capacity of words" (Steele 4) and his uniquely realized "taxonomy of poetic surprise" (Hirshfield 29) time and again, but especially in a song like "Find the River," conspire "to make plain talk dance . . . to make ordinary language intense and vital" (Frith 378), and to leave his readers and listeners willing to accept intuited meanings and lingering mysteries. Indeed, then, at the cusp of the lyric's and the journey's apparent conclusion, we are especially satisfied to intuit that "river poet search naïveté" captures the almost manic sense of a speaker and writer desperate to make meaning but lacking the time to do much more than conjoin four suggestive words. We're reminded, perhaps, of Keats's own rendering of the desperate fear of finality in a poem like "Ode to a Nightingale," when the speaker is left "forlorn" by the vanishing of the last note and the reality of the fled music.

Vendler observes that "the constitutive trope of the ode 'To Autumn' is enumeration, the trope of plenitude" (*The Odes* 266) and, indeed, the poem is "o'er-brimm'd" (l. 11) with a catalog of fruits, nuts, flowers, grains, and animals. This abundance appears formally, as well, in the dense textures of Keats's poetic line, in the subtleties of sound and rhythm, and, as H. T. Kirby-Smith adds, "in a wealth of vocalic resonances, echoes, and reflections" (225) that finally turn the poem over to the music of autumn in the final stanza.⁹ When Keats, in an 1820 letter to James Rice, and in the grips of illness, observes "how astonishingly does the chance of leaving the world impress a sense of its natural beauties on us" (Grant 419), his reverence and equanimity help us understand "Find the River" as surely as his own "To Autumn." Stipe, too, loads his poetic line with carefully considered sound elements, and creates a speaker whose cornucopia of spices and scents—referencing, as he does, bergamot, vetiver, ginger, lemon, indigo, coriander stem, rose of hay—articulates his own pursuit of sensuous abundance and the sense of the sublime in the ordinary.

What neither writer or speaker possesses in abundance, though, is time, and thus each lyric proceeds with the painful awareness that what now is "loaded," "swelled," and "o'er-brimm'd" must finally fall, turn to "last oozings," or reach the ocean. Amidst all the temporal and spatial movement, the poetics of each lyric also ironically strive to produce stoppages and stasis, seeking to arrest the flow of time with challenging syntax, rhythmic variation, and metaphor. In "To Autumn," one thinks not only of the stickiness of those "last oozings," but also the unceasing sibilance of the first stanza, which both slow down the reader and trick the bees into thinking "warm days will never cease" (l. 10). John Minahan also usefully points out the signifying power of the "half-reap'd furrow" (l. 16) which, "like the poem at large, like time itself," constitutes an image that "moves forward toward full reaping and circles back toward not-yet-reaped" (181). The exquisitely paradoxical blending of life's stages (e.g., "full-grown lambs" [l. 30]) and the blending of life and death (e.g., "barred clouds bloom the soft-dying day" [l. 25]), culminating with the mysteriously evocative and uncertainly comforting connotations of the gathering swallows, collect time in such a way that "every moment is part of every other moment" (Minahan 183); what passes may yet return, we infer the human observer to realize.

Stipe, of course, manages the progression of time most obviously with his masterful rhythmic variations and metrical anomalies. In addition, the obliqueness of some of his phrasings (e.g., "bergamot and vetiver / run through my head and fall away" [ll. 17–18]), the tactical breaks with syntactic convention (e.g., "river poet search naïveté"), and the Hopkins-like coined phrases (e.g., "bayberry moon" [l. 8]) all serve to slow down the reader's experience of time, and thus work brilliantly *with* the thematic content of "Find the River" even as they work *against* those rhythmic elements that sweep one along in its current. As a lyric, then, "Find the River" stops, rearranges, and even at one level transcends the problems of time in the way that poems can; as a musical composition and auditory experience, however, the song accedes to a sense of linear inevitability, proceeding from the soft opening strums of the acoustic guitar to its preordained conclusion after three minutes and fifty-two seconds. Because music happens to us in "real time," argues Matthews, "to change the time of a piece of music is to alter, as it were, its cellular makeup, and for the worse" (38); to violate the flow seems to do a kind of violence to it. Although it's repeatable and we can find the river over and over again, we always necessarily swim in different waters—it is always, at some level, an experience of one-timeness. While its meditative content and formal qualities do, as we've seen, extend the reader in time, the semantic coda of "Find the River" does not exhibit the expressive qualities of what Barbara Smith calls "weak closure" (250): the last line, in which the speaker, seemingly again addressing the young auditor, promises that "all of this is coming your way" (l. 39), feels so declarative, so wise, and so full of final significance as to secure strong closure.[10]

If, though, we consider, as we should, the musical elements that surround and complement Stipe's words, then, when the rushing stateliness of the final verse seems at last to capitulate to the unforgiving linear nature of time, we realize Stipe receives help from his bandmates.[11] We're delivered definitively and emotionally to that final end-stop, but yet the song, in its very last moments and just after Stipe's voice has exited, yields to the soft repetitive strums of the acoustic guitar, which fade gently as if loath to leave, and as if the notes—and we the listeners—are being stretched like gossamer in an unending present: like "permanence wrung out of wane," as Rilke writes in his poem "Gong." We think, perhaps, of Plumly's assessment of Keats, that "at his best, in the odes, time is not only suspended but extended to an edge, to where the running-over almost spills" (*Posthumous* 344). This is poetry's "timeless, time-bound business," writes Linda Gregerson, "to trace both portal and mortality, to write against death, yes, but also into it" (263).

Just as Keats's poem provides that exhilarating spatial sensation of veering upwards into the expanse of sky, "Find the River" widens out to the ocean and the horizon as the river dramatically approaches the estuary. In each case, we ultimately experience a poetic work "whose visionary size transcends its local space" (Plumly, *Posthumous* 172). Richard Macksey proposes that the resolution and acceptance that infuse the last of the great odes puts Keats at the threshold of a new poetics. By "achieving the serene tone of a new music," writes Macksey, "Keats succeeded in creating a poem that marks the crossing from the poetry and poetics of Romanticism" (855, 883). Something similar might be said of the Michael Stipe of 1992 who, with his work on *Automatic for the People* and especially on a song like "Find the River," reached a new level of poetic presence.

Moved by his sophisticated balancing of words as sense and words as sound, we emerge from "Find the River" and its musical packaging realizing that it seems to "mean" something even apart from its semantic content. Trying to describe it is like trying to narrate an emotion, and may leave us agreeing with the proposal that "the poem must resist the intelligence / almost successfully" (Stevens ll. 1–2).

We can infer that "Find the River" represents a "crossing" for Stipe and R.E.M. as well. The song stands near the point at which Stipe shed some of his previous inhibitions to become a more personal, introspective, and spiritually insightful lyricist; marshaled in the service of more focused subject matter, his earlier dispensation for inveterate musicality as a writer would now begin increasingly investing the ordinary with a defamiliarizing "affective force and kinetic grace" (Middleton 229). Although Stipe is typically reluctant to discuss individual lyrics in detail, we also learn something about the song's significance (and meaning) based on its role in a galvanizing emotional moment for R.E.M., at a time when the band still had unresolved feelings regarding the sudden departure of drummer Bill Berry. When, at a 1999 concert in Atlanta's Chastain Park Amphitheater, Stipe dedicated "Find the River" to Berry, whose 1995 brain aneurysm precipitated his decision to leave the band, the drummer subsequently came on stage to embrace his three former bandmates. As reported by Johnny Black, bassist Mike Mills deemed the moment "his most magical musical memory" of his two decades in the band (247). One imagines the lyrical power of "Find the River"—a song R.E.M. has rarely played in live shows—and the melancholy simplicity of the concertina-like keyboard refrain being especially poignant and consoling that evening.

As convinced as Keats was in his last year that he'd leave little of value behind in his poetic work, no one any longer, of course, needs to argue for his legacy or for that of his odes. Using "To Autumn" as an ongoing reference point in a discussion of Stipe's "Find the River" in no way implies an equivalency of stature or accomplishment—the latter will never, after all, appear in a single poetry anthology. All the same, "To Autumn" uniquely helps to reveal the thematic and emotional amplitude of "Find the River," as well as to draw out the intricacies of Stipe's nuanced poetics. Considered together, however improbably, we value these two lyrics because they convince us that the imaginative can be situated "in a harmonious relation to the natural" (Vendler, *Music* 126) and in so doing they provide recompense and instructions for our experience of time. By being so resolutely embedded in the fleeting, both "To Autumn" and "Find the River" teach us how to assimilate the implications of the reaped furrow and the river's arrival at the ocean, and thus to extend ourselves temporally—with grace and with the expectation that sweetness will follow. We are, in turn, perhaps newly appreciative of the "stubble-plain," accepting of the power of the undertow, and welcoming of the expanse (and possibly the void) of the boundless sky and sea.

With sense that "seems to be brought along by chimes of sound" (Hallberg 164), these two lyrics allow us to reach beyond the linguistic, to sense "a cohesion and ongoingness to which we adhere even when we cannot know its ground" (Stewart 331). And if and when there is, indeed, "nothing left to throw," and no more songs of Spring in the sonorous air, these lyrics tell us we can make peace with the accompanying doubts and uncertainties, trusting that *our* figurative last line will be some manner of enjambment and not an end-stop.

Notes

1. At the time, critics would jokingly refer to *Murmur* as *Mumble*. When the record company IRS asked R.E.M. to include a lyric sheet with their debut album, Stipe presented, in a single continuous paragraph, a collage of his favorite phrases from the various songs. IRS subsequently decided not to pursue a lyric sheet. See Gray 101–2 and 106.

2. As Marcus Gray relates, Stipe said of his early lyrics, especially, that they are "a blank chalkboard for people to pick up and scribble over. They can make up any meaning they want to" (116).

3. In 1990, Stipe decided he "would use the first person singular instead of the first person plural. . . . Everything was sounding anthemic, because we were saying 'we' all the time instead of 'I' or 'me' or 'you.' With [*Out of Time*] I wanted to move toward more of a personal politic" (Black 175).

4. For simplicity of reference, and as a kind of terminological halfway point between "lyric poem" and "rock lyric," I will use the term "lyric" to refer to both "To Autumn" and "Find the River." Although some will only hesitantly use "lyric poem" to describe "To Autumn," noting the complete disappearance of the speaking "I" into the poem, others, like Helen Vendler, argue that we nevertheless "read it as a lyric and introspective poem" (*The Odes* 277).

5. Having invoked Abrams's "greater Romantic lyric," we might remember the peril posed by the city in such poems as Wordsworth's "Tintern Abbey" and Coleridge's "Frost at Midnight."

6. For her discussion of the "several great organizing motions" at work in "To Autumn," including the spatial motion, see Vendler's *The Odes of John Keats*, 244–45.

7. Gray is one of the few writers and critics to engage in a sustained discussion and appreciation of Michael Stipe's body of lyrics. See his chapter "Rivers of Suggestion: Approaches to Lyric Writing," 106–40, in *It Crawled From the South: An R.E.M. Companion*.

8. Asked about the meaning of "rose of hay," Stipe replied, "I made it up because I needed, and could not find, something that rhymed with 'way' and 'naïveté.'" See "Ask Michael Stipe #2." *Pop Songs* 07–08. 13 Sept 2008. 20 Mar 2010. popsongs.wordpress.com/2008/09/13/ask-michael-stipe-2/.

9. We remember that the ode has an implicit relationship to music, having its origins in Greek as a choral song. Interestingly, the backing harmonies of Mike Mills and Bill Berry lend a choral sensibility—and an optimistic one at that—to "Find the River," especially in its concluding verse.

10. Smith's book may still be the definitive scholarly treatment of our readerly expectations and gratifications relative to closure and anti-closure in poetry.

11. "Find the River" has a peculiar compositional history in that, as Gray relates, the entire back-

ing track was provided by bassist Mike Mills, "recorded with Bill on drums and Mike on just about everything else" (255); guitarist Peter Buck doesn't even play on the recorded version.

Works Cited

Abrams, M. H. "Structure and Style in the Greater Romantic Lyric." *From Sensibility to Romanticism: Essays Presented to Frederick A. Pottle*. Eds. Frederick W. Hilles and Harold Bloom. New York: Oxford University Press, 1965. 527–60.

Baker, David. "To Think of Time." *Radiant Lyre: Essays on Lyric Poetry*. Eds. David Baker and Ann Townsend. St. Paul: Graywolf Press, 2007. 235–46.

Bate, W. Jackson. *Stylistic Development of John Keats*. New York: Humanities, 1946.

Black, Johnny. *Reveal: The Story of R.E.M.* San Francisco: Backbeat, 2004.

Blasing, Mutlu Konuk. *Lyric Poetry: The Pain and the Pleasure of Words*. Princeton: Princeton University Press, 2007.

Frith, Simon. *Sound Effects: Youth, Leisure and the Politics of Rock 'n' Roll*. London: Constable and Robinson, 1981 (rpt. 1983).

Gray, Marcus. *It Crawled From the South: An R.E.M. Companion*. New York: Da Capo, 1997.

Gregerson, Linda. "Mortal Time." *Radiant Lyre: Essays on Lyric Poetry*. Eds. David Baker and Ann Townsend. St. Paul: Graywolf, 2007. 247–63.

Hallberg, Robert V. *Lyric Powers*. Chicago: University of Chicago Press, 2008.

Hirshfield, Jane. "Poetry and the Constellation of Surprise." *Writer's Chronicle* 40:2 (Oct./Nov. 2007): 28–35.

Kirby-Smith, H. T. *The Celestial Twins: Poetry and Music Through the Ages*. Amherst: University of Massachusetts Press, 1999.

Macksey, Richard. "Keats and the Poetics of Extremity." *MLN* 99:4 (Sept. 1984): 845–84.

Matthews, William, and Stanley Plumly, eds. *William Matthews: The Poetry Blues: Essays and Interviews*. Ann Arbor: University of Michigan Press, 2001.

Middleton, Richard. *Studying Popular Music*. Philadelphia: Open University Press, 1990 (rpt. 2002).

Minahan, John. *Word Like a Bell: John Keats, Music and the Romantic Poet*. Kent, OH: Kent State University Press, 1992.

Plumly, Stanley. "Between Things: On the Ode." *Radiant Lyre: Essays on Lyric Poetry*. Eds. David Baker and Ann Townsend. St. Paul: Graywolf, 2007. 113–16.

———. *Posthumous Keats: A Personal Biography*. New York: W.W. Norton, 2008.

R.E.M. "Everybody Hurts." *Automatic for the People*. Warner Bros., 1992.

———. "Find the River." *Automatic for the People*. Warner Bros., 1992.

———. "Man on the Moon." *Automatic for the People*. Warner Bros., 1992.

———. "Nightswimming." *Automatic for the People*. Warner Bros., 1992.

———. *Out of Time*. Warner Bros., 1991.

———. "Sweetness Follows." *Automatic for the People*. Warner Bros., 1992.

———. "Try Not to Breathe." *Automatic for the People*. Warner Bros., 1992.

———. "World Leader Pretend. *Green*. Warner Bros., 1988.

Rilke, Rainer Maria. "Gong." *Poems 1906 to 1926*. Trans. J. B. Leishman. London: Hogarth, 1957.

Scott, Grant F. *Selected Letters of John Keats*. Cambridge: Harvard University Press, 2002.

Smith, Barbara. *Poetic Closure: A Study of How Poems End*. Chicago: University of Chicago Press, 1968.

Steele, Timothy. *All the Fun's in How You Say a Thing: An Explanation of Meter and Versification*. Athens: Ohio University Press, 1999.

Stevens, Wallace. "Man Carrying Thing." *Transport to Summer*. New York: Knopf, 1947. 81–82.

Stewart, Susan. *Poetry and the Fate of the Senses*. Chicago: University of Chicago Press, 2002.

Vendler, Helen. *The Odes of John Keats*. Cambridge, MA: Belknap, 1983.

———. *The Music of What Happens: Poems, Poets, Critics*. Cambridge: Harvard University Press, 1988.

Wiman, Christian. *Ambition and Survival: Becoming a Poet*. Port Townsend, WA: Copper Canyon, 2007.

SWEEPING UP THE JOKERS: LEONARD COHEN'S "THE STRANGER SONG"

BRIAN HOWE

Leonard Cohen, the beloved Canadian musician, won major literary priz-es for his poetry and fiction before issuing a single note of professional music, and never ceased incorporating beloved poems into his songs, even long after he was better known as the singer of "Suzanne" and "Bird on a Wire" than the author of Beautiful Losers *or* The Spice-Box of Earth. *His pungent, artful approach to ancient questions of love and faith was never more focused, more robustly poetic, than on 1967's "The Stranger Song," an early-career* ars poetica *that vividly illustrates how heavily the forms and practices of verse have informed Cohen's songwriting. With its uniquely formal structure and dense, coolly surreal details, it's one of those rare works that holds up as well on the page as in the air—that crucial dividing line between a poem set to music and a song. In this es-say, against the biographical backdrop that is inextricable from the mu-sic, longtime Cohen fan Brian Howe explores some of the structural me-chanics and semantic tics that give "The Stranger Song" its peculiar poetic thrust.*

Many a songwriter has been branded "poetic," but the Canadian Leonard Cohen has a particularly strong claim to poetry. At the Jewish day school Herzliah, he became an acolyte of Irving Lay-ton, to whom Cohen, much later in his life, would dedicate the song "Go No More A-Roving," a setting of a Byron ballad that poignantly capped an itinerant life: "So we'll go no more a-roving / So late into the night." (On the same late-career album, *Dear Heather*, he also set to music a villanelle by Frank Scott.) He plunged headlong into the literary scene at McGill University, where he was president of the debating union and a frequent name in literary journals. He published several well-received volumes of poetry and fiction before gradually becoming a popular folk singer, though even in his pre-recording days he played in a country band called The Buckskin Boys and often supplemented his readings with live, improvised music, in the mold of Allen Ginsberg.

But above all, he emerged as a songwriter with a taste for antiquity that made his music feel pre-modern: like the stuff from which poetry evolved in the first place. His lyrics were mostly narrative, as if reclaiming song's domain of storytelling, not soundbites. The words were laced with modernity—famous blue raincoats and famous hotels—but the pulses animating them were sensual, mythic, often Biblical. Abraham and Andy Warhol cast equally long shadows, as did Joan of Arc and Joni Mitchell. Transubstantiations of flesh and spirit hinged on sex and faith. Drafts of archaic European folk rustled in the finger-picked acoustic strings, as if the music were gusting in from long ago and being revivified by the contemporary. While Bob Dylan made folk music new and loud, Cohen strove to keep it old and quiet. In it he seemed to seek freedom through discipline, as if in the archaic forms escape routes from the conventional could be carefully revealed.

Like many poems, Cohen's songs were intent on the clarification of origins. Never just sin, but original sin; never just love, but original love. His own origins were couched in the stuff of legend. Many wonderful legends that happen to be true are included in *Various Positions*, a 1996 biography by Ira B. Nadel. Nadel reports that one of the first of the Cohens to immigrate to Canada from Lithuania was named "Lazarus," an omen of rebirth that would echo down the line to his great-grandson Leonard, who, Nadel also reports, successfully hypnotized and undressed the family maid as a young man. This second omen predicts the precise nature of the seductive, entrancing magic that Leonard Cohen would weave in song, years later. Both of these claims of Nadel's sound too far-fetched and absurdly symbolic to be anything but true. (In the index of his book, right under "The Stranger Song," we find entries for "suicide, threat of" and "summer camps." This indexical coincidence happens to sum up all of Cohen's music: the idyll and the disaster, holding each other at bay, in precarious suspension.)

Cohen had too much patience to fully embrace beatnik spontaneity, preferring to let the ancient words reveal themselves carefully over time—though he was freer with his music, letting it trace a rough grain against the polished-marble texts. He also had too much passion to ever really settle into bourgeois complacency, and these conflicting affinities for the security of familiar patterns and the allure of unpredictable ones produced "The Stranger Song," an incidental *ars poetica* at the very beginning of his major recording career. (Much, much later, this essential schism in his nature would bear him away to a Zen Buddhist monastery for five years, but we are concerned here with his perspective as a younger man, when motion, not stillness, seemed the key to contentment.) It's right to say *ars poetica*—a personal artistic treatise—because in it, he lays out the whole diagram of the alchemy, which renders poetry back into music, that he continues to refine today, at age seventy-seven. He was in his early thirties when "The Stranger Song" was released, and it provides a vantage from the other end of the tunnel he's peered back through on recent albums like *Dear Heather*. As a beginning, each time you hear it, it feels like the first time.

First you encounter the cover of Cohen's 1967 debut, *Songs of Leonard Cohen*. An impenetrably black border frames a square, sepia portrait, blending the visual aesthetics of twentieth-century vinyl and a nineteenth-century cameo. Already, we know we're in the presence of something old, exhumed into our time. The face peering out has an appropriately doomed and conventional aspect, but the glinting eyes are tinged with sophistication, irony, quietly voracious desire. There is a solid-looking wave of dark hair, a bulb of a nose, and a fine, sad mouth; the intimation of a no-nonsense suit. The cover conveys, in perplexingly equal measure, senses of dusky romance and sullen ordinariness. Unlike many of his peers, Cohen wore his wildness on the inside. If this face appeared at the peephole of your door, you wouldn't be sure whether it meant to sweep you off your feet or sell you a vacuum cleaner.

Then we stand at the gates of the song: its perfectly ambiguous title. Is this a song about a stranger, or is the song itself more strange? And if so, stranger than what? In 1967, Cohen himself was a stranger, having just immigrated to the United States to test his luck in the folk music movement. He came from a distinguished rabbinical line, whose stern incense he never truly shed as he embarked on the usual physical, spiritual, and political unfetterings of sixties New York—art, drugs, protest music, disastrous liaisons. He hung around Warhol's Factory pining hopelessly for Nico, searching for spiritual transcendence against a mythical materialist backdrop. He had affairs and passionate friendships that always seemed foreordained to beautiful ruin, resulting in songs like "Suzanne" and "So Long, Marianne," where grace springs from the essence of women who sheltered him for a time. He's always been a drifter between worlds: sinner and saint, scholar and mystic, trust funded bohemian, singing poet; a traveler through many lands and resident of none.

But the song *is* stranger, too—stranger than the others on the album, certainly. It's startlingly bare, featuring none of producer John Simon's embellishments. (Cohen and Simon sometimes butted heads over the album's arrangement and mixing. Cohen wanted the songs to be spare, while Simon favored the lush stereophonic arrangements of the era. If Simon had had his way, Cohen revealed to *Mojo* in 2001, "Suzanne" would have featured heavy, syncopated piano and drums.) Thank goodness that in the case of "The Stranger Song," Cohen prevailed—because it's so ephemeral and simple, it feels deathless, undated in 2012. The lone guitar part, a hypnotic blur of crepuscular finger-picking, seems to catch Cohen's warm, rich voice between two coursing currents: deep, loping low strings and twinkling, balletic high ones. There's no waiting for a chord progression to resolve—the melody leaps out fully formed, instantly captivating. Like a dream, its rhythm feels strange, intuitive, inexorable.

You can feel the dance of Cohen's hand on the strings, the endless web-weaving quality of the motion, the preparation to incant. If you've ever played any music, you understand the difference in feeling between playing songs with mobile melodies and playing repetitive, rigid structures. In the former case, your mind stays alert, and your hands do this and that, building meaning like they always do. In the latter case, the body becomes a sort of holy machine, fixed and eternal, and the mind goes blank. Time stops. You can feel the stopped passage of time in "The Stranger Song." Or rather, time still flows—flows along the trickling drone of the guitar—but we aren't in it, and neither is Cohen. To call this song "timeless" is more than rhetorical. It begins *in medias res* and fades to black without any proper conclusion. It's like a gate swinging open and closed on an archetypal scene with no beginning or end.

There's also something of the desert or wasteland about this expanse of music, how it shimmers and repeats, imparting a sense of vastness with meager substance. The ear begins to perceive the slightest variation as meaningful, charged with narrative potency, like caught breaths in orated lines. A slip in the arpeggio feels like a whisper of fate, an admission of guilt or glimmer of understanding. Cohen's voice appears like a mirage. On beloved songs like "Bird on the Wire," he let a sort of nasally rowdiness into his singing, but here, he's seductive and subdued, but with a hint of urgency—all velvet and burlap, rough and smooth. The voice has the homely burr of speech, under the fluent notes; the voice of the orating poet. The terse rises and falls in the vocal line are crucial in creating the infinite, down-swirling feel, but the melody mostly seems designed to make you forget it's there, and draw you more fully into the words, so you read it like a poem even as you hear it. Cohen's diction is careful and precise, never letting the melody distort the words past understanding.

"It's true that all the men you knew / were dealers who said they were through / with dealing every time you gave them shelter," Cohen sings at the beginning of the song. It comes out as a single, controlled exhalation, in two roughly iambic lines of eight syllables followed by a prolonged final line that projects precariously into thin air, mirroring the situation of Cohen's foundationless protagonist. (You'll be familiar with the iambic rhythm from Shakespeare's sonnets, where a natural-speech rhythm is formalized along the even short-long pulses of the human heart.) This folding of theme into form is entirely deliberate on Cohen's part, as the uniform guitar part could accommodate lines of any length—it never changes, just respires like the poet's breath behind the words. The jagged but regular cadence of the lines keeps the song feeling appropriately itinerant and mutable. There are many verses and fragmentary refrains, but nothing you'd call a proper chorus. So it just unwinds and unwinds, the repeated lines that close many of the short verses strengthening the sense of poetic formality.

These repetitions make "The Stranger Song" feel less like a folk song and more like a villanelle or a pantoum, two poem forms that function through repeating lines—worrying and circular and indeterminate.

These opening lines establish two characters, the male speaker and the female (we sense) listener, who appear in so many of Cohen's songs, as he works out his love and guilt on the proxies of his own conscience and memory. Yet the ambiguity from the title is held over. "Dealer of what?" does not feel like an insignificant question. In any case the word summons a latent air of danger, mild disrepute, lawless games of chance.

If poetry is an art of strategic omission and unexpected connections, Cohen fulfills both of these obligations from the outset. Instead of simply telling us who this dealer is, he resorts to a different kind of identification. "I know that kind of man," Cohen understates—he is that man. He's always talking to himself on these one-way duets. One of the rare singers immune to disguises, he wears his own face in his songs. We see it alongside Montreal's St. Lawrence River in "Suzanne"; peering into a farm mailbox in Nashville in "Diamonds in the Mine"; inclining toward the music drifting up from Clinton St. in "Famous Blue Raincoat," where he signs off, "sincerely, L. Cohen." "Poetry is just the evidence of life," he once said. "If your life is burning well, poetry is just the ash." But "burning well" didn't necessarily mean happily and easily, as his often-depressive music evinces; It meant burning hard, burning bright.

"I know that kind of man; / it's hard to hold the hand of anyone / who is reaching to the sky just to surrender." So far we still just have hearsay and rumination, yet the plot is already emerging. Something of the old West begins to glint through the invocation of sheltered dealers, of hands reaching to the sky. (Why do we, already, see that sky as raw and huge and grey? I do, at least, though the nature of the sky is never mentioned in the song. I see it as silent, roiling, dwarfing the tiny conversing figures; the clouds sped up and streaming.) The archetypes are beginning to gather like thunderheads, becoming pregnant with implication. We now understand, somehow, that we're talking about a dealer of cards. The whiff of the old West summons the knowledge. Poetry can be an art of chained intuitions; when it works best we always feel one step ahead of the poem in a subliminal way, each line arriving with a surprised "of course!" Cohen confirms our intuition in the next line, "And then sweeping up the jokers that he left behind / you find he didn't leave you very much, not even laughter." The sense of the song expands, now admitting lost laughter, sadness, trickery; the wry tone ("It's true," it began, as if haughtily conceding a point) becomes doleful. The jokers are wild and enigmatic, not funny.

But in fact, Cohen has already tipped his hand. That the wild cards were left behind leaves little doubt as to whether or not they were the ones the dealer was "watching for," the ones "so high and wild / he'll never need to deal another." Now, between the twin poles of shelter and freedom, a dialectic sense enhanced by the intimation of auditor and audience in the lyrics, we feel fully the huge tension that animates the song—the sense that the bohemian, itinerant life isn't an ideal, but a failsafe: that it would be gladly given up if any such thing as a home could be located. Now we feel for our dealer both a sort of revulsion—for we recognize our own capricious longings and infidelities in him—and a profound sympathy, for the same reason. We know already he'll never stop traveling from station to station, leaving only a trail of random cards in his wake. "He was just some Joseph looking for a manger," Cohen repeats twice, in case we missed the implication: of a holy quest, thwarted or perverted; one that plays out eternally in imperfect variations of the ideal.

Having so quickly, cunningly established the song's thematic motion, Cohen now begins to breathe it full of detail, emotion, action, sense. His stranger splits and doubles, seeming always to be coming and going at once. He leans on the windowsill (there is always something rakish about our dealer's body language) and says, "You caused his will / to weaken with your love and warmth and shelter." The love, warmth, and shelter capture our attention, but "weaken" is the key word. For Cohen, contentment was both longed for and feared, an altar for passion that could swiftly turn into a prison. (He never put it better than in "So Long, Marianne": "I'm standing on a ledge / And your fine spider web / Is fastening my ankle to a stone.") And even as he speaks those loaded words—which seem accepting but are actually laying out an exit strategy—he's pulling an old train schedule from his wallet. If the stranger's life is locked into a rhythm of repetitive changes, so is his interlocutor's. Now "another" stranger seems to want her to ignore his dreams; she hates to "watch another tired man / lay down his hand / like he was giving up the holy game of poker." The shelter wants to be filled and the stranger wants to "trade the game he knows for shelter," yet both are shackled to endless boom-and-bust cycles. It's a story about a man and a woman. But it's also about the gap in the self that can never be closed, the divided nature rendered literally.

This archetypal timelessness gives Cohen recourse to clear, simple images that ring out with unaccountable power. What is to my mind one of the finest triplets in English-language songwriting is here: "You've seen that man before / His golden arm dispatching cards / But now it's rusted from the elbow to the finger." The melody line makes each lyric come quick and clean, like a scalpel cut, with meaning flexing over the line breaks: the ominous silhouette of the familiar man, spilling into color and action down the "golden arm dispatching cards"— "dispatching," i.e. "doing away with," a much better choice than "dealing"—and then decaying before our eyes like a time-lapse film. The entire cycle of the song—the stranger appearing mysteriously, burning with fervor, then wearying and moving on—plays out in these three concise lines, like a nested doll.

The ominous lyricism maintains its razor sharpness throughout: as the stranger "talks his dreams to sleep, / you notice there's a highway / that is curling up like smoke above his shoulder." This is just perfect. The mention of dreams and sleep tips us toward a hallucinatory world, which is ratified by the highway "curling like smoke above his shoulder," as if the highway were a part of the stranger, ephemeral and pervasive. (The bracing, mysterious clarity of this line always reminds me of the poet Charles Simic in *The World Doesn't End*). The word "notice" cements the dream-sense with impeccable subtlety, evoking the way that in dreams we suddenly perceive important things that have been in plain view all along. Cohen's meticulous word choices and airtight control over his tone are of poetry, not music.

And as we tip into dream, the song takes a turn, as in a game of cards or at the *volta* of a sonnet. (Charlotte Pence's essay in this collection discusses the *volta* in depth.) Identities begin to loosen and shift. Now, says Cohen, "It's you my love, you who are the stranger." We are fully in the province of metaphor now, the coming and going unfolding in one simultaneous, impossible motion. Even as plans are made to meet "on some endless river," the stranger is gone from the platform, aboard a warm sleeping car. And we leave the song this way: the stranger gliding into the next repetition of the cycle, with the promise to meet again at "the bridge or someplace later" hanging vaguely in the air, twisting the narrative into a Möbius strip. A specific human transaction has been nudged into a general metaphysical one so subtly it's impossible to say when one becomes the other. When I listen to a lot of songs over and over, I'm going back for the melody, or some certain images. But with Cohen, here, it's more about wanting to hear the story one more time; to experience its indelible thrust and to try and come to terms, once again, with some its more penetrating mysteries. "Please understand," Cohen confesses, "I never had a secret chart / to get me to the heart of this / or any other matter." And even as he utters this, he's handing us a scrap of that very chart—partial, almost useless, tantalizingly close to revealing a fundamental secret: "The Stranger Song."

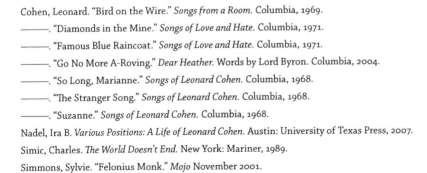

Works Cited

Cohen, Leonard. "Bird on the Wire." *Songs from a Room*. Columbia, 1969.

———. "Diamonds in the Mine." *Songs of Love and Hate*. Columbia, 1971.

———. "Famous Blue Raincoat." *Songs of Love and Hate*. Columbia, 1971.

———. "Go No More A-Roving." *Dear Heather*. Words by Lord Byron. Columbia, 2004.

———. "So Long, Marianne." *Songs of Leonard Cohen*. Columbia, 1968.

———. "The Stranger Song." *Songs of Leonard Cohen*. Columbia, 1968.

———. "Suzanne." *Songs of Leonard Cohen*. Columbia, 1968.

Nadel, Ira B. *Various Positions: A Life of Leonard Cohen*. Austin: University of Texas Press, 2007.

Simic, Charles. *The World Doesn't End*. New York: Mariner, 1989.

Simmons, Sylvie. "Felonius Monk." *Mojo* November 2001.

FACING THE MUSIC: THE POETICS OF BRUCE SPRINGSTEEN

ROBERT P. McPARLAND

Bruce Springsteen's music speaks for people. His work, like a bridge, spans the shores of defiance and despair. The song-poet, emerging from among the people, says things that they want to say. He gives voice to their lives. These lives know family and neighborhood. They know the jobs that they work, the small triumphs, the surprise of love. And they know the darkness out there on the edges, the obstacles, the hurt that enters into the cycle of daily life and how it may overcome them. What does it mean to enter this universe of his songs and what do they say about our lives? How are Bruce Springsteen's songs a form of popular literature? Can we begin to understand them as a form of folk-rock-soul "poetry"? As a way to approach these questions, Robert P. McParland considers three of Springsteen songs: "Born to Run," "The Promised Land," and "The Rising."

The New Jersey Turnpike can feel like a long way—like a long poem. There is more space between the exits than on many other state roads. The landscape seems moonlike in places. Traveling a long road anywhere in the United States, you might want to put on a Springsteen song. Springsteen is good company: His catalog is full of America, rich with poetic life, enduring like the tough sinews of America itself. On the N.J. Turnpike, there is Exit 8 for Freehold and there is Route 33 out to the shore. The terrain of Springsteen's younger days is not exactly Wordsworth's Lake District. Yet, like that poet, he draws upon the voice of the people. Travel north and one sees the blur of the sun, the shadows of the refineries, and the last exit in New Jersey. On I-95 there is the bridge named after George Washington. It's a stretch of America one wouldn't expect a lot of poetry to come from. If a driver misses that last exit, then he or she is at the toll, then onto the bridge, and is plunging into New York

City. As a young man, Bruce Springsteen went by that last exit many times. From New York came a voice and song, flesh and blood and dream that went out across the country, out across the world.

What does it mean to enter this universe of his songs and what do they say about our lives? How are Bruce Springsteen's songs a form of popular literature? Can we begin to understand them as a form of folk-rock-soul "poetry"? Here we will consider three Springsteen songs: "Born to Run," "The Promised Land," and "The Rising." A core of resolve moves through these songs and dozens of others. Springsteen's music speaks for people. His work, like a bridge, spans the shores of defiance and despair. The song-poet, emerging from among the people, says things that they want to say. He gives voice to their lives. These lives know family and neighborhood. They know the jobs that they work, the small triumphs, the surprise of love. And they know the darkness out there on the edges, the obstacles, the hurt that enters into the cycle of daily life and how it may overcome them.

Springsteen tells us stories of our lives. He is a musician who embodies the legacy of rock, soul, and folk, who earns his impact with unmistakable intensity. Bruce Springsteen faces the music—and so do many of his characters, the narrators, whose lives come to us through his songs. He confronts us with the gift of his music. He engages us and calls for life against resistance, summoning up the forces to break through. There is something heroic in that gesture, something tenacious and fundamentally American. The poet's capacity to touch deep sources of emotion is evident in Springsteen's work.

Springsteen's songs are written with music—wedded to music, sometimes dissolving into that music. His songs show many characteristics of poetry or of storytelling. They use poetic devices: figures of speech, metaphor and simile, assonance and consonance, cadence and metrics. But they are songs; we do not call them "poems"—even if they do similar work among us. Visceral, physical, rhythmic, Springsteen songs are rich with themes and they sneak into the heart. They give us voices and imagery, striking stories that ring with truth, helping us to see the world in new ways. The Springsteen song lyric emerges with music, sound and soul and attitude altogether. Always lyrics are born in music. This language begins in sounds; it arises from an emotion, a phrase in the mind, a riff on the piano; guitar chords form its ground. Even if words are written first, music soon follows. A Springsteen song comes to life in music, inseparably, indissolubly linked to performance, open to improvisation. That is to say, Springsteen's lyrics are more than words on a page. They are more like leaves on a tree, taking life in the spring, shot through with life, and then casting out each autumn in an improvisational dance in the wind. Poems and songs are possibilities of emotion and story that are voiced and sung and given life.

Once, music and poetry were connected. Poetry lived in sound, in chant and intonation and rhythm. Springsteen is not far from that at all. Once, poetry was for the ear. With modernity and the printing press, poetry became something for the eye. As poet and pianist John Hollander has put it, there was an "untuning of the sky." People experienced the world differently. That sense of a harmony in all things—a "music of the spheres"—was gone. Poets bring us back. They help us to listen. They get at the roots and remind us to feel. Poems offer vision. They remind us that the world is alive, charged with energy. We don't always have the Telecaster turned up, amps popping, a saxophone splitting the sky. We have something that calls for attention. The poem may speak subtly. Poems are often condensed, compressed language. Words may have multiple meanings. Lines offer suggestions. Images open on ways of seeing.

Springsteen, of course, is a musician. He is not just his words; he is his voice, his guitar, his band. So, what kind of a "poet" is Springsteen? When Allen Ginsberg or Gregory Corso wrote a poem, it was voiced. The Beat poem is something organic. The narrative unfolds as a rhythm, as a voice. Likewise, a Springsteen song is ever alive; it is a performance that is never static. True, it has to be set in a particular recorded form. But its life is more than this. The song happens; it unfolds as a work of imagination. In Springsteen, we are brought past misty beaches and working-class neighborhoods, down long highways, past tongues of fire that leap Inferno-like from New Jersey refineries and the Turnpike's black iron sprawl, across the Meadowlands, into a netherworld: the mythical urban spaces of his first two albums. We travel out to America through the American stories and landscapes of *The River*, *Nebraska*, and *Devils and Dust*. We see images and hear stories of pain and promise. Likewise, when a poet like Robert Pinsky gives voice to humanity in *An Explanation of America* (1979), or in his translation of Dante's *Inferno*, he comes close to song and brings us mythic worlds. Pinsky's translation of Dante is evocative, ever moving forward, like a song. The poet shows a fine ear for tone and his poem reads naturally when read aloud. In this way both Pinsky and Springsteen effectively bring to us what William Carlos Williams called "the American idiom": a variety of forms of American speech.

Poetry is its sounds and its soul. Yet we encounter poetry most often on a page. It is given to us in school settings and we are supposed to "analyze" it. Bring a poem into an educational setting and chances are that we will soon be dissecting it like a frog in biology lab. We start taking it apart, looking at its constituent parts or functions, as one would look at an engine. Yet, just as an engine ignites and becomes energy, so too does a poem. And so does a Springsteen song. To listen to a Springsteen lyric in its musical context—to not just read it "dry" on the page—may remind us that spoken poetry is a living thing. What if we were to speak the poem, to get at the sound and the riddle of it? What if experiencing the poem were more like trying to seize the breeze, to catch a breath, to feel the heartbeat, or seek a meaning? The song or the poem is a process that we enter, allowing it to work on us. Sometimes we work with our heads and sometimes we work with our hearts. When the poem happens for us—even if just a glimmer of light sparks in us—that's a poem.

That's what Springsteen can do: hit us in the gut, open our eyes, light a spark, and we say "Ah-hah! That moves me; it sends a shiver down my spine. That's when I know it is music." Poems can be open, rambling, mystical—like Whitman's "Song of Myself." Or they can be dense, packed, like gems you have to hold to the light at an angle. Figuring them out is more like cutting through the layers of a mid-sixties Dylan song. It's like Walt Whitman says: "The world is written to me and I must get at what the writing means." With an Emily Dickinson poem, for example, one has to stay with it. It's like sitting with a Rubik's cube for an hour. "A poem should not mean but be," wrote the poet Archibald MacLeish. Yet, it's a rare poet who, like the poets of Springsteen's "Jungleland," just stands back and lets it all be. A poem has a life when we bring ourselves to it, when we allow it to "be." Then, maybe it is like suddenly seeing the light on the hill, the glow on the city towers, the gleam on the car you're shining up on your driveway: You suddenly "get it," or it gets you—and that's a poem.

It's those moments that make poetry and song lyrics a means of participation and epiphany. Springsteen is a participatory performer who brings us to such moments. He is ever in dialogue with his audience, often engaging them in strenuous marathons of music. With "Spirit in the Night," he dances into a crowd. With "Tenth Avenue Freeze-Out," he slides to the edge of the stage, as if to touch the audience. This breaks boundaries of performer-audience, across space, geography, class, race, gender, or difference. The song is never only words or notes on a page: It is open to change. Like a match, it is filled with possibility. It just has to strike something.

The song is a happening, a passion, an active rumbling "out on Highway 9." Poems like this go somewhere. They catch the sunlight and stir our senses. So, when you read, first experience the poem. When you listen, first experience Springsteen's song. You may find that music is where words dissolve—into sounds, rhythm, patterns. The lyric hits that point where there are no words— as in "The Rising," all becomes just voices chiming in to the flow together. A song comes alive when it is performed. It is then open to the moment in which it is given voice. That difference, that improvised novelty, is like the breakthrough of a cool rain, or the sudden wash of a warm ray of sun. What is breathtaking is what happens spontaneously. It's that echo across the stage from someone else in the band who suddenly knows—you don't know how—just where all of this is going. The pulse, the rasp, the sigh, the exclamation point: That is music!

The gift of Springsteen is that he knows this in his blood; he so obviously knows it. And he can accomplish it. Like the driver who has crossed the bridge a hundred times, he knows just when and where to turn. He goes past that last exit in New Jersey. He doesn't need a GPS or a map; it is built intuitively into the fiber of his being. That is the poet. He knows in his guts. The technique—he's worked it so many times that it is built in.

In the 1970s Springsteen recognized the darkness on the edge of town. The urge to escape it pulses in songs like "Born to Run." The will to grapple with it lives in songs like "The Promised Land." Music itself is tension and release—and so it is for lives that seek to break out, lives for whom music is a kind of momentary "salvation." This theme of "escape" on *Born to Run* seems modified as we listen to the determination that lives in *Darkness on the Edge of Town*—a hope that cannot be subdued, the promise of an American dream, even if one wonders if and how that dream is possible. To follow Springsteen's journey is to follow the pursuit of that dream.

The first line of "Born to Run" pulses rhythmically, placing that long "i" and "e" of "night" and "we" against the tight, short "e" of "sweat" and the alliterative "streets" with its long "e." The "r's" rumble into "runaway American dream." The lyric is working the "uh" of runaway and "American" and maybe the place is "ugh," or the strain of trying to break out is "ugh." But we are moving like pistons at this point, out to that long "e" vowel of "dream." We are in motion and we have an idea: What is this dream? Can this dream be fulfilled?

The second line springs to life with the "i" of "night" "ride," "suicide" and there is the balance of line lengths and the parallel structure: "by day we"/"at night we." A stark contrast of images all bump into each other. Those "mansions of glory" cast shadows on a world of vehicles going in circles: cars that are as much a death trap as a means of freedom. One can see the teens circling, taking that shore road out to where the big houses keep watch over the ocean. Two lanes can take us anywhere. We are "Born to Run" and dream, libido, blood are fuel. These machines have revved up into life. They are risk, reach, aspiration: "stepping out over the line." The speaker aches for escape from a place that tears at the very fiber of a man or woman: a place they have got to get out of. And they will, with determination, with these engines, with this possibility. But this night is dark; it hangs like a dark cloud, a fog of fumes, and from behind a half-cracked windowpane a radio plays. We're pulling out of here to win. The last lines of "Born to Run" are punctuated—one-two-three: a trinity of punches ("tramps like us"). They are given with affirmation, with a note of destiny.

On record we hear versions of "Born to Run." The single, as Dave Marsh recognizes, is "a pure creation of the studio" (131). Structurally, the song is in AABA form (which is verse, verse, bridge, verse). The ragged, impossible roller-coaster-ride energy of the tempo seems to be the point. The lyrics and music both build toward a critical point of breaking out. In the studio Springsteen and the E Street Band clearly worked toward something like a live sound. They were making a record. This is an art in itself, full of calculations, calibrations, and textures. When we listen, we hear a layering of guitars and the sure rhythm section. The album's songs seem guided by Roy Bittan's piano, or at least centered in the movement of piano chords. The sound is characterized by—indeed deeply marked by—Clarence Clemons's saxophone. Whatever speaks in Springsteen's lyric lives and moves within this setting. The verbal is inseparable from music and performance. "Born to Run" has the layering of a dozen guitar tracks, a fullness of keyboards, the driving rhythm section and signature sax, and touches of bell-like glockenspiel.

The second verse offers a direct address to "Wendy." She could be anyone. Her name is echoed with assonance in the word "let" and "me" balances "be" amid the internal off-rhyme of "in" and "friend." The singer's offer to guard her dreams and visions connects with the sexual "velvet rims" and "engines." There is a request, a plea, the sound of reassurance and dedication, all wrapped up in this line and in this embrace. Engine and flesh are fused in this sharp metaphor into passionate romantic abandonment. That want aspires to know what is wild, to know what is real.

The music itself provides this energy that breaks out from futility. We are brought to that moment with vivid imagery. In the song's bridge, our gaze rises with a picture of the horizon of the amusement park and the vivid image of kids huddled on the misty beach. One sees the distant curve of the park: rides above, beach below, where the kids "huddle." With a declaration, then comes the "everlasting kiss": like a firecracker, an exclamation point! We hear a drum hit, vocal punctuation, and we're off, and an explosive saxophone solo says the rest.

A count of four builds momentum that thrusts us back into the final verse. The highway's jammed with broken heroes. Everybody out on the road has "no place left to hide." The declaration of love is made "with all the madness in my soul." The dream of "someday" flashes again and we arrive at that trinity of punches— "tramps like us"—that brings us back to the title and a conclusion where words dissolve into sound. But "Born to Run" is not just power in a car bound up Route 9 for the Parkway. No, this song is more like John Glenn's rocket. How does it hold together when it takes off and not split apart into pieces?

Poems are like that: little engines. They take our minds somewhere. They beckon for us to open them, to listen to them, to take a ride with them. As in "Thunder Road," a poem pushes the door open "but the ride ain't free." We have to invest ourselves in a poem. We have to give it our time and let it do its work on us. Sometimes the poem is a window, like one cracked open a bit along some street, with music from behind it coming out into the night. Sometimes it sneaks out at you and, sometimes, it's like Emily Dickinson once said: "If it takes the top of my head off, I know it's a poem."

Poetry is a challenge. John Keats's notion of "negative capability" suggests that the artist, the poet, has to learn how to stay with the darkness of uncertainties until the light of an idea appears. Sometimes, so does a reader, or listener. As you read a poem, give the poem time to unfold itself to you. Stay with the poem, with what it may be trying to say. Like the song, if it catches that spark in your mind, it may come alive. You may draw a blank. But maybe an idea will come, and it's a bit like that someone down the street who has opened the window a little and lets the radio play. As Springsteen sings, on "Thunder Road": "Show a little faith. There's magic in the night."

The album *Darkness on the Edge of Town* is connected by constant references to work and the working life. It discloses an America of working men and women who survive with dreams sometimes shadowed by the circumstances of daily reality. The search for America, for integrity, continues: "I want to find out what I got." There is an effort like that of Sisyphus, the character in an ancient myth who rolls a rock up a hill only to have it roll back down again. In Albert Camus's retelling, it is Sisyphus's integrity in this "absurd" situation that counts. He is like the working man, who gets up and goes to work each day, whose monotonous pattern of labor sometimes feels futile. These are the jobs and the people Springsteen writes about: common Americans with uncommon spirits. They are anonymous to the world at large, but loved by their families, connecting with their friends, working alongside their co-workers.

Darkness on the Edge of Town is not only about escape. It is about facing the music, confronting the obstacles. Stark, pounding, propulsive, this album faces life. The lyrics repeatedly anchor in commitment and resolve. "Badlands" begins the album with its insistence on believing in love, hope, and faith in spite of it all. The music of "Adam Raised a Cain" pounds with the spare, solid drive of the music on a night at CBGB in 1976–78: Patti Smith or Television is onstage and a mirror along the right wall catches your reflection as you look at them. The album, as Robert Hilburn once observed, is "moodier" than the previous recording. The wide horizon of *Born to Run* appears to have contracted. Yet the desire to escape, to flee monotony and limitation, is met with the determination to work with what one has and to find a realistic way to break out. Hope endures. Where the screen door once slammed, the narrator now works all day in his daddy's garage and by night chases some mirage. Now he is going to "take charge." As Dave Marsh pointed out in his August 1978 *Rolling Stone* cover article, the "darkness" is not "grim;" it is relentless. The working man endures relentless struggle. The sounds being thrashed out are its complement.

After two pickup drumbeats on the tom-toms and a final roll, "The Promised Land" launches on a harmonica. The song begins with an image of empty vastness and dryness: a poisonous highway twisting into the distance. Paid for his work, after picking up his money, the speaker is wandering out over the county line, "killing time." He has been working all day in a garage and night is that space where he chases a mirage. The verse lands on the assertion that he is going to take charge. The *carpe diem* poet seeks to seize the day, to pull life out of the jaws of death, or, as Springsteen puts it, to "take one moment into my hands." Roy Bittan's piano provides an interlude and Danny Federici's organ playing joins over the top. Gary Tallent does a descending bass run that moves into Springsteen's lyrical guitar lead. This climbs into a saxophone solo, which returns to the hook phrase, with the harmonica. All of this gives us some listening space.

We listen to the phrase from the harmonica: a folk instrument, portable, easily held and carried in the pocket of a traveler. It is like a little orchestra, tuned to a key. In *The Grapes of Wrath*, a story filled with dreams of the Promised Land, John Steinbeck writes of the harmonica, the guitar, and the fiddle (362–63). "The Promised Land" is filled out by the harmonica sounding its central riff. The wind blows from human breath. While the twister would blow away dreams, the human breath asserts, "I believe in . . ." This self-reliance and assertion stands at the center of the song.

Whereas Petrarch wrote in the sonnet form, in two sections of eight and six lines, this modern lyric, in verse-chorus form, comes to us in verse lines of seven and a chorus of five. Like the character in Wystan Auden's poem "The Unknown Citizen," the character in Springsteen's song asserts that he has tried to live justly, dutifully going to work each day. He recognizes that he has struggled and that struggle is vividly described in lines that are as much reality as hyperbole: eyes going blind and blood running cold. The pent-up energy and frustration he feels is set to detonate. In the next verse, a dark cloud is rising and the speaker is heading out into the storm. A "twister" is coming that will "blow away" life. What is a man rooted to, grounded against such forces? A metaphor is at work here. The twister is a symbol. The repetition three times of "blow away," with its parallel structure, is an assertion against what would blow away the promise. One would expect the "twister" to do this blowing away. Yet it is the speaker taking charge against the elements who will "blow away" the resistance to the dreams and those things that break the heart. Guitars are pulled back with Bittan's piano and Tallent's bass over Max Weinberg's drums leading the way. We land on the doubled vocals of the chorus, ending three times on the affirmation of a belief in the Promised Land. The harmonica that closes the song is assertive, jubilant.

Increasingly, after *Darkness on the Edge of Town*, Springsteen's songs open out on a world of uncommon common folks. In the albums after *Darkness on the Edge of Town*, *The River* and *Nebraska*, there is less "flight" and an increasing confrontation with the world. Facing the music—or the world with his music— Springsteen's lyrical world increasingly adopts the voice of characters who live here and who have a variety of stories. The first person narratives tell us these stories, as the landscape broadens. We are in the heartland. *Darkness on the Edge of Town* begins with "Badlands" and "trouble in the heartlands." Dave Marsh, Springsteen's biographer, captures a central theme: "Believe in yourself and the world will work better" (258).

This heartland of America is typified by families like the Joad family of John Steinbeck's *The Grapes of Wrath*. In Steinbeck's novel (1939) and the John Ford film (1940), this Oklahoma family is an exemplar of this striving of hard work, resilience, and conviction in the midst of systems and institutions that are often unresponsive, divorced from the breath and blood of lives. This family soon sees that there are other families who are just like them, who, beset by circumstances, struggle, seek a "promised land," and hold on to their integrity in the teeth of adversity. Springsteen characters, likewise, are extraordinary while ordinary and common. Digging down into folk traditions, on *The Ghost of Tom Joad*, *Nebraska*, and *Devils and Dust*, Springsteen gives us something visceral, sturdy, and enduring about many of these characters. They are at the core and the variety of America and "the American dream" can be explored by listening to these imagined voices. We are drawn to feel for these people, even as some characters fail, or the dream seems to fail.

Springsteen moves across American life through a variety of voices and styles. Songs from *Nebraska*, or *Devils and Dust*, have a dark, storytelling quality. Many move in ballad patterns, rest on guitar chords, and are mixed in a way that draws attention to the vocal and to the story. Built on folk forms, these song patterns reflect those of anonymous ancestors who have sung of their lives from the days of settlement down through Woody Guthrie and Pete Seeger. Springsteen stands in line with this tradition. As much as he is a repository of rock music's legacy, he also grasps the earthy, enduring elements of the people's music, the unique songs, voices, and issues of these lives.

9/11/2001 brought the American people some deeply unsettling issues. Springsteen's song "The Rising" begins by focusing our attention on the spoken-sung voice of a first person narrator. Going through the darkness, he "can't see nothing." From underneath comes a pulse, and then the gated drums' deep, echoing reverb. We are given images: "Mary" in the garden, holding pictures of her children. In the presence of one who offers care, "lay your hands in mine" becomes "your blood mixed with mine": an intimate union of sympathy. You can hear this song move into that large group chorus to the point where words are not necessary and melt into "la-la-la . . ." The song has been interpreted as being voiced by a character that encounters his dying, that thinks of his family, of those he loves. Its title may be interpreted as metaphorical or symbolic of hope, resurrection, or union. Inevitably, that depends upon what the listener, within a community of interpreters, brings to the song.

In Springsteen's repetition of "sky"—of black, of darkness, sorrow, love, tears, mercy—the parallel structure here is Whitman-like. The vocal in the foreground points to "the sky." This is matched by Springsteen's own background vocal, affirming "dream of love" over and over, between the lines. The bank of guitars, mixed back, emerges with overdrive-fuzz, amid overtones, and matches the "la-la" chorus. The song gathers intensity and the drums lead us back into the chorus: voices in unison. This joining in unity seems central to the song: a mixing of blood, breath, and spirit. The song reflects something like the mystic's movement from the darkness of *via negativa* toward illumination and unitive vision, resurrection, and hope. One hears synthesizer chords and a single reverbed guitar chord plays, accenting the end of the phrase. The rest is all mixed back. The voice rests on top of this and leads the chorus. We hear long extended notes of the guitar lead with overdrive and effect on the guitar. We hear the repetition, like a mantra: "Come on up for the rising."

Springsteen songs like this are characterized by their dynamics: shifts in timbre and tempo, pitch, rhythm, and volume. There are peaks and valleys, pacing and inflection. It's like the ocean at Asbury Park that rolls to a crest, crashes, and subsides. The roller coaster at the amusement park hits its peak, accelerates, and, whirling down, makes its turn in a breathless blaze of glory.

The Springsteen lyric often moves toward affirmation. It recognizes the sharp sting of human pain and struggle. For people who move out on highways that get jammed everywhere, pain becomes a universal experience. Hungry hearts have dreams. What is jammed in these lives, trying to break free? Who are these broken heroes? How is this their last chance? Where will this affirmation of passion and life take them? This is the *carpe diem* of the poets—Jonson, Marvell, Herrick. "Someday" is up ahead: that horizon where they can "walk in the sun." But life is now, immediate: so they must seize it. What might it mean to be born to run? One runs *from*—as to escape—but one also runs *toward* something. Hope works against life's resistance. Entropy will not, cannot, subdue the vital spirit.

Works Cited

Auden, W. H. "The Unknown Citizen," *Collected Poems*. New York: Vintage/Random House, 1991.

Camus, Albert. "The Myth of Sisyphus." *The Myth of Sisyphus: And Other Essays*. New York: Vintage, 1991.

Dante. *The Inferno of Dante: Bilingual Edition*. Trans. Robert Pinsky. New York: Farrar, Straus and Giroux, 1996.

Hilburn, Robert. "Some Glory Days Revisited." *Los Angeles Times* (8 November 1998).

Hollander, John. *The Untuning of the Sky: Ideas of Music in English Poetry, 1500–1700*. Princeton: Princeton University Press, 1961.

Kramer, Lawrence. *Music and Poetry: The Nineteenth Century and After*. Berkeley: University of California Press, 1984.

Marsh, Dave. *Bruce Springsteen, Two Hearts*. New York: Routledge, 2004.

———. "Bruce Springsteen Raises Cain." *Rolling Stone* (24 August 1978).

Pinsky, Robert. *An Explanation of America*. Princeton: Princeton University Press, 1979.

Springsteen, Bruce. "Adam Raised a Cain." *Darkness on the Edge of Town*. Columbia, 1978.

———. "Badlands." *Darkness on the Edge of Town*. Columbia, 1978.

———. "Born to Run." *Born to Run*. Columbia, 1975.

———. "Jungleland." *Born to Run*. Columbia, 1975.

———. "The Promised Land." *Darkness on the Edge of Town*. Columbia, 1978.

———. "The Rising." *The Rising*. Columbia, 2002.

———. "Spirit in the Night." *Greetings from Asbury Park, N.J.* Columbia, 1973.

———. "Tenth Avenue Freeze-Out." *Born to Run*. Columbia, 1975.

———. "Thunder Road." *Born to Run*. Columbia, 1975.

Steinbeck, John. *The Grapes of Wrath*. New York: Penguin, 1985.

COMING INTO YOUR TOWN: OKKERVIL RIVER'S "BLACK"

STEPHEN M. DEUSNER

Will Sheff is the singer and chief songwriter for Austin's Okkervil River, who for about ten years now have been making tightly wound, lyrically astute indie rock. A complex and distinctive lyricist, Sheff incorporates literary techniques and dark cynicism into his songs while keeping them straightforward, accessible, and catchy. This essay parses one of his most compelling songs, "Black," which is also one of his most puzzling. It is a story song that constantly undercuts its story. Every detail balances an ambiguity, and what is not disclosed looms larger and larger as the song proceeds. What is the narrator's relationship to Cynda, and what happened when she was abducted? Was it merely a custody battle, or something darker and more damaging? This essay has no interest in reconstructing the events of the story—at least not definitively, as the song's power lies in its unknowability. Instead, Stephen M. Deusner engages closely with Sheff's lyrics and Okkervil River's music to discuss issues of agency, omission, and unreliable narration.

A kidnapped child who grows into a traumatized woman. A devious father who escapes punishment for his crimes. A hysterical, heartsick lover coercing a recovery. These are the strikingly dramatic, yet deceptively mutable elements Will Sheff, singer and songwriter for the Austin, Texas, indie-rock band Okkervil River, uses to create "Black," a harrowing song from the group's 2005 album *Black Sheep Boy*. Even with such clearly drawn characters, a dark mystery remains at the core of the song, as the relationships are all determined by an unspeakable event that happened long ago, a guarded secret known to everyone but the listener—who must lean in closely, pay careful attention, and read between the lyrics to fully comprehend the song and its impact.

It is, in other words, a typical Sheff song. Distinctive among American indie-rock songwriters for his ambitious narrative scope and metaphorical playfulness, he conjures up whole worlds in his compositions, skirting easy readings or concrete meanings. In that regard, "Black" may be his best and trickiest song yet. Its strict plotting suggests a straightforward dramatic monologue set to indie-rock music, not dissimilar to the first-person working-class compositions of Bruce Springsteen or the hood-rat dramas of Okkervil River's peers the Hold Steady, but it also bears the hallmarks of confessional singer-songwriters— namely, intense emotions and romantic subject matter. The song twists, fuses, and inverts these familiar forms in ways that reveal new possibilities in them, calling attention to their limitations while using them to Sheff's narrative advantage.

A former art and music critic, freelance writer, and editor in Austin, Sheff approaches songwriting as a kind of prose poetry, carefully considered and exactingly composed. In the liner notes to each of Okkervil River's albums, the lyrics are printed without line breaks or even paragraph breaks, but as blocks of left-justified copy that appear, when typed out, suspiciously amelodic. At first, they do not resemble songs: writing in complete, grammatically precise sentences, Sheff splits his lines across melodic phrases, interrupting his thoughts and creating a sense of stream-of-conscious extemporaneity. His work is strewn with details, yet his lyrics come across as primarily impressionistic, suggesting rather than showing the whole. Furthermore, his songs change meaning either subtly or significantly depending on the context in which they are heard: "Black" in particular sounds slightly more straightforward on its own, but as one track in a larger album, it magnifies certain of Sheff's themes—rootlessness and restlessness, both emotional and creative—as the characters blend with those in other songs.

Not surprisingly, Okkervil River have been criticized as overly brainy and pretentious in the true sense of the word—i.e., pretending that the form is more than it actually is, that popular music can have self-consciously literary potential—but bolstered by Sheff's performative abandon, his compositions rarely come across as simply clever. Instead, his investment in "Black," as in all of his songs, comprises a form of method acting, an imaginative use of voice and point of view. Given the nature of his songwriting, it's almost imperative that Sheff sing like a madman. He wails, he cries, he screams, he caterwauls, he bellows, he spits, giving emotional weight to his potentially intricate, intelligent lyrics. Sheff's vocal range is limited but he often sings well beyond it anyway, as if trying to express something that is larger than any one voice—least of all his own—could adequately convey. Listening to him sing "Black," it's impossible to determine if he is tearing the song apart with his voice or if the song is all that is holding him together.

No matter how earnestly he inhabits those first-person roles, it's nevertheless dangerous to conflate Sheff with his narrators. In this sense, his songs—especially "Black"—tend toward the rules if not the form of the dramatic monologue in its most literary sense, allowing him to assume personae and absent himself. It is an empathic undertaking, as Sheff has in the past sung from the perspective of a war criminal, a teenage killer, a porn star, or in the case of "Black" a helplessly lovelorn young man. Of course, these narrators possess such skewed, often damaged views of the world that very little they tell us can be taken on faith, and the resulting narrative ambiguity creates songs of unusual melancholic power.

"Black" and *Black Sheep Boy*

To fully comprehend the intricate narrative machinations of "Black," it is imperative to place it in the context of the album on which it originally appeared. At the time of its release in the mid-2000s, *Black Sheep Boy* represented the band's most ambitious musical project and Sheff's most intricate lyrical undertaking to date. He intended it as a loose concept album based on the 1967 song of the same title by Tim Hardin, and *Black Sheep Boy* alludes to the folk singer's biography without being too literal. Born in 1941, Hardin was a fixture on the Greenwich Village folk scene in the very early 1960s, a contemporary of Fred Neil, Karen Dalton, Cass Elliott (later of the Mamas and the Papas), and a very young Robert Zimmerman (later famous as Bob Dylan). Like Neil, Hardin blended folk music with blues and jazz to create a unique sound: earthy and grounded, yet given to fanciful flights of melody. Despite his notoriety and the endorsement of so many of his peers, Hardin had trouble procuring and keeping a record deal, mainly because of his unreliability brought on by heroin use. He released a handful of albums in the late 1960s and early 1970s, including one titled *Suite for Susan Moore and Damion: We Are One, One, All in One*, which was an ode to his wife and son. They left him before it was finished.

Despite his commercial failure as a solo artist, Hardin found more success as a songwriter. Rod Stewart had a minor hit in 1971 with Hardin's "Reason to Believe," although it is more notorious today as the original A-side to the eventual smash "Maggie May." Even more popular was Hardin's "If I Were a Carpenter," which has been covered by artists as diverse as Joan Baez, Johnny Cash, Robert Plant, Bobby Darin, and Leonard Nimoy. Hardin grew to hate the song, and his heroin use increased to the extent that he was barely able to play and sing, let alone record or perform professionally. He struggled throughout the next decade before dying of an overdose in 1980, never achieving success beyond the respect and pity of his fellow artists and the loyalty of a small cadre of fans.

Okkervil River do Hardin the favor of ignoring "If I Were a Carpenter" on *Black Sheep Boy*, instead choosing to cover his "Black Sheep Boy" as the album's overture. After that short, grave opener, Sheff's own songs variously plumb themes of wanderlust and self-negation, following "the family's unowned boy" through a phantasmagorical world of broken homes and busted hearts, of men made animal by desire and tragedy. Yet *Black Sheep Boy* is neither explicitly biographical nor autobiographical. It is not set in the real world that Hardin or Sheff inhabits; in fact, it seems more concerned with the life the former lived in and through his songs. Ultimately, the album inhabits a space where their songs and stories intersect, a harsh landscape marked by departures rather than reunions, by prodigality rather than security.

Released as a promotional mp3 to preview the album—which suggests the band and its label, Jagjaguwar, considered it accessible and representative of the whole—"Black" stands out on *Black Sheep Boy* not only because it echoes the title of Hardin's song, but because it seems to have little to do with the album's implied narrative. It is, ostensibly, a fiction, describing a predicament that bears little obvious connection to Hardin and forgoes much of the language and imagery Sheff uses throughout the rest of the album. There are no horn-headed boys, no hearts made of stone, no haunted radio songs, no metaphors made fantastically manifest. Instead, there are concrete details (dates and names even) and an urgent narratorial voice, which deploys familiar first- and second-person pronouns and speaks from a very singular, very human point of view. Compared to other songs on the album, "Black" sounds strongly rooted in real experience—it is the only one to assign a character a proper name—and yet it proves perhaps most disquietingly ambiguous, evading any attempt at a straightforward interpretation. As Sheff provides concrete details, he withholds crucial information; as he describes the characters' predicament, he muddies their relationships. As he sings "Black," he unwrites it.

Coming into Your Town

"Black" begins incongruously, with a light, bouncy pop-song momentum that grimly contrasts its dark subject matter. The band establishes a buoyant groove in the intro, defined by a streamlined bass line, rapid high-hat clicks, and a spry keyboard theme. These elements coalesce into a forward rush suggestive of travel, into which Sheff's abrupt and slightly breathless narrative intrudes. That first sentence—"I'm coming into your town"—draws together thematic tendrils from the previous songs on *Black Sheep Boy*; in particular, "In a Radio Song," which immediately precedes "Black," ends with a farewell, setting up the introduction to this song and suggesting a picaresque thread running through the album. Immediately the second-person pronoun stands out here, as do the common nouns "town" and "night," the first describing a fixed location where the narrator does not belong and the second implying some impending calamity.

Rather than follow the narrator into town, however, "Black" indulges a flashback, providing strangely specific details: a date, a place, and an action. "April 12th, with nobody else around; you were outside your house (where's your mother?), when he put you in the car, when he took you down the road." This is the root of the song, the wellspring of its angst, and yet, the event remains only obliquely glimpsed, an abduction (perhaps) recounted in worried, cursory language. (It should be noted that the punctuation and absence of line-enders are Sheff's entirely. He includes parenthetical asides, semicolons, and—on "The Latest Toughs," also from *Black Sheep Boy*—blank lines where listeners can add their own lyrics. This essay will reproduce his lyrics exactly as they appear in the liner notes, without corresponding line breaks.)

April 12th may mark a moment when lives were changed irrevocably, but such a specific detail perhaps says less than the pronouns, which Sheff invests with purpose and slippery meaning. "You" has no name or even gender yet, and "he"—especially connected to those two aggressive actions—is full of threatening portent. Sheff will address the former, but leave the latter vague throughout the song. The second-person "you" is a woman or a teenage girl, and she even has a name: Cynda Moore. That abbreviated first name, with its stylish Y, suggests aspiration, vulnerability, and disconnectedness all at once: there is no "I"—a damning first-person substitution that echoes the negation implied by "I can still see where you loved yourself before he tore it all down."

By contrast, "he" remains clouded and creepily vague, shrouded perpetually in the song's many layers of blackness. "Baby daughter on the road," Sheff sings, "you're wrapped up warm in daddy's coat." In these few lines, Sheff intimates conflict and leaves it to the listener to imagine the specifics—a custody battle perhaps, involving an embittered and emboldened father, an unwatchful mother, a traumatized child. Similarly, by writing "daddy's" instead of "Daddy's," Sheff the former editor maintains the song's maddening ambiguity, providing clues and simultaneously rescinding them. Almost out of sympathy for the female character, Sheff never discloses what happened after she was taken: was it simply an abduction, or was it something worse? The irony, whether intended or not, is that by refusing to disclose that information, "Black" only piques the listener's curiosity, leaving those horrors to the imagination and making them central to the song. It's a burden for the audience, especially because Sheff repeatedly exchanges certainty for uncertainty, always insinuating something worse than he is actually describing.

That sensibility actively engages the listener, who becomes an active participant in these harrowing goings-on, an eavesdropper on the narrator's pleadings. As in a dramatic monologue, Sheff trusts—or at least compels—the listener to filter through faulty information to create a more realistic, more complicated situation and in doing so to measure the distance between the world as the narrator perceives it and the world as the listener perceives it. Neither can be finally correct, of course, yet Sheff continually thwarts his listener's perception of that distance by revealing new facets to his characters and their emotional layers. There is no solid ground in "Black," not for the narrator or Cynda, nor for Sheff or the listener.

The Door Is Closed

"Black" is not about Cynda's relationship to the man who is presumably her father; instead, it is primarily about the narrator's relationship to both. His feelings toward the father are obvious: blinding, confounding rage. "And if I could tear his throat, spill his blood between my jaws, and erase his name out for good, don't you know that I would?" His hatred makes him animalistic, echoing the album's central black sheep metaphor. "Or I'd call some black midnight, fuck up his new life where they don't know what he did, tell his brand-new wife and second kid." His threats are hollow; the point of his anger toward the father is the narrator's own impotence. The father looms sinister and grotesque over the song, but the narrator can't "tear his throat." He can neither undo the past nor act as the agent of revenge, which explains the pleading tone of Sheff's lyrics as well as the conditional quality of phrases like "Or I'd call" and "if I could."

The narrator's relationship with Cynda is never quite defined. It's affectionate, albeit perhaps one-sided: depending on her age, the narrator could be a lover or a friend, or perhaps just a one-time hook-up more enamored with her than she with him. Or perhaps, given the meta aspect of the album, the narrator may actually be more like Sheff himself, the artist to her reluctant muse, the pop idol to her fan—two people who know each other only in song. What's clear, however, is that she has closed herself off from him and most likely to others, so "Black" articulates his attempt to move past her formidable defenses; it's futile, perhaps selfish, and certainly more aggressive than seems to be good for either of them. In that sense, he occasionally comes across as adversarial, another domineering male whose attentions, regardless of his intentions, may become harmful and overbearing. Even that ominous first line implies an invasion of privacy and space, yet as he cajoles her to "say his name the way that he said yours," the narrator knows that she is unreachable, that he is "not useful anyhow." Pointedly, Sheff never reveals the father's name, which suggests that Cynda never utters it with the contempt the narrator wants to hear.

What makes "Black" so powerful—what makes it emotionally resonant rather than merely conceptually playful—is how richly these two characters are drawn and how carefully their circumstances are delineated in just 360 words. Sheff offers only fleeting glimpses of Cynda through the narrator's point of view, but even as she remains just out of the songwriter's and his character's comprehension—they are males unable to grasp female angst, although only Sheff is able to imply as much about himself—"Black" suggests that her trauma has made her stronger, albeit stonier. It's unclear whether Cynda is repressing these toxic memories or recovering from them, and her response, as he repeats, is simply that he "'forget it.'" He can't do that, of course. The narrator's reaction is immediate and intense, yet it proves surprisingly complex and changeable, alternating between animal outrage in one verse and tender sympathy in the next. After that rollercoaster, he finally settles on a curious feeling: "Though I know I can't help anyhow, when I watch you I'm proud."

Sheff, however, is sympathetic to his flawed protagonist, neither condoning nor condemning his misguided attempts to comfort Cynda. The narrator's pride is neither selfish nor sinister, but simply pitiful: it's one last desperate means of connection, of inserting himself into her story, by commenting on it and deeming it worthy of a song. In a sense the narrator sees himself as her emotional proxy—aching for her, hating for her, even loving for her—and just as she has come to define herself by her father's actions, the narrator defines himself, in this song at least, by her distance. His only goal is to bridge that rift, but from the very first line it sounds impossible.

In the larger context of the album, "Black" tells a coming-of-age story in which a young man learns how terrible and unfair the world can be and how utterly powerless he is to right such a fundamental wrong. A young woman like Cynda can be permanently scarred, but the perpetrator may never be punished. If the narrator's initial response is anger, by the song's end it has softened into something more complicated, if by no means any less intense. To live in the world is to live with its messiness and its injustices. The narrator ends the last verse with a futile plea: "Let me through that door, baby."

Pop Life

Just as it never settles comfortably into the dramatic monologue form, "Black" plays as an unlikely pop song. Sheff's lyrics are in constant dialogue with other songs, suggesting a mercurial definition of pop (as in popular music, not pop as a specific radio format or genre), yet he does not write in traditional pop forms. "Black," like most of his songs, eschews the commonplace verse-chorus-verse structure for an approach less rigid but no less controlled. Even so, in relating and complicating these central relationships between the three main characters, "Black" takes its shape from that long-running staple of pop music—the romantic triangle. Sheff puts a dark spin on the setup, depicting it not as the woman's choice between two suitors but as the men's exploitation of her. There is something aggressively needy in the narrator's behavior toward Cynda, something selfish in his insistent counsel; it's certainly not as malign as her father's actions, but her only dialogue—"forget it," which she does not state directly but which the narrator quotes—implies that his anger is no comfort but further agitation. Whether the song provides an account of real-world people in a real-world predicament is ultimately beside the point; its considerable impact does not rely on the story being true. But Sheff's persistent undercutting of his own story implies something closer to lived experience than to what the pop-song playbook usually achieves. He bypasses the expected emotions—love, heartache, regret— for something grittier and grislier, for something that bursts the confines of the pop song.

The form pointedly does not match the function: Sheff is placing an especially distressing event within a pop framework, but the fit is neither neat nor natural. In fact, that contrast between the expectations and the "reality" provides a critical commentary on music itself, pointing to the inherent limitations of love songs as vessels for capturing and conveying chaotic human emotions. And yet, fans and songwriters continue to believe in them, to create and consume them, to fashion their own experiences according to the dictates of pop music. Sheff would certainly count himself in that group, yet his dissatisfaction with the form is aggravated rather than ameliorated by the fact that he practices it. As Okkervil River progressed and grew more popular during the 2000s, he engaged with increasing confidence and nuance in the ambitious project of creating a series of sweeping concept albums about the vagaries of the creative and touring life, recounted by someone perpetually coming into towns on dark nights. Capturing the tone and the consequences of devoting oneself to music, "Black" sounds like the origins of the band's future undertakings, the kernel of their later concept albums. Sheff is trying to make pop music mean what it always promises to mean. He's holding it accountable.

The distance between art and life, as irreconcilable as that between the narrator and Cynda, has always been Okkervil River's true subject, inflecting nearly every song before "Black" and since. On *Black Sheep Boy*, this song is only one episode in a larger story, yet it stands out for straining the hardest to remove the pop filter and view the world in all its disarray. In that regard, the album's larger themes of prodigality and wanderlust loosely mirror Okkervil River's very real-world experiences as a touring band. For its creators if not its consumers, pop music is a profession built on travel, playing in a different city and to a different crowd every night and generally giving oneself over to itinerancy. Inspiring countless songs—from Bon Jovi's "Wanted Dead or Alive" to the Ramones' "Touring" to Bob Seger's "Turn the Page"—the business realities of pop music have long supported this historically male pursuit, but lately, especially for a mid-level indie band touring the country in its own van and carrying its own equipment (which was Okkervil River's lot in 2005), that experience has become increasingly formalized through an entrenched system of clubs, promoters, schedules, and venues. What once must have struck eager young artists as a romantic undertaking, an excursion akin to settlers moving westward or Depression-era hobos hopping freights—that old urge to see America—is transforming into a professional obligation, a necessary adjunct to the average career in pop music.

Touring has become a rite of passage especially for indie-rock bands, and yet, pop music remains synonymous with arrested development and stunted growth. Popularly, music allows its practitioners—as well as its listeners, if only vicariously—to remain cocooned in adolescence, to stay forever young. Okkervil River echo this idea in "Black" and elsewhere, albeit with a distinct twist: men, Sheff intimates, aren't made on the road, but by the hard trials of home life. If the coming-of-age concerns lend the song and the album a dynamic thrust while grounding them in a recognizable setting, then the nomadic existence within the music world breeds the strange masculine hysteria that permeates *Black Sheep Boy*. The road represents loneliness, transience, impermanence—and that's not counting equipment malfunctions, unscrupulous club owners, cramped vans, mechanical problems, and other tribulations that arise between playing dingy venues only half-full of half-interested club-goers. If artists must suffer to create, then the price of a song is life and pride.

This kind of road-raw hysteria informs Sheff's wailing performance, but it also infects his lyrics as well. For all the obvious care that has gone into "Black," the song sounds almost spontaneous in its pleading urgency. It's a gut-level response—a feeling before thinking—and it takes a while for the brain to catch up to the heart. Reason enters the song almost undetected, in the form of admissions of powerlessness and pride. And yet, certain events remain unspeakable even in this pop-confessional context, in this case not just the abduction but the subsequent events that Cynda apparently won't reveal. The narrator tries to coerce some sort of disclosure from her, but ultimately he cannot confess to the listener, which only fuels his frustrations as both a lover and a narrator. So, the pop-song format by its very inadequacies and shortcomings can evoke unbearable emotions even if it cannot express it outright. Sheff works with the idea that pop history—all of its formal modes and emotional concerns, going back just a few minutes or several decades—remains ever present, anchored in the present and therefore inescapable, even as it has been so thoroughly absorbed by listeners as to be nebulous, invisible, intangible—an idea reflected in Cynda's dark mystery at the center of "Black." To be a songwriter is to grapple with that overwhelming accumulation of expectations and meanings, to sift through so many expressions of abject pain, and, as Sheff implies, to grow hysterical with frustration.

Works Cited

Bon Jovi. "Wanted Dead or Alive." *Slippery When Wet*. Music and lyrics by Jon Bon Jovi and Richie Sambora. Mercury, 1986.

Hardin, Tim. "If I Were a Carpenter." *Tim Hardin 2*. Music and lyrics by Tim Hardin. Verve Forecast, 1967.

———. *Suite for Susan Moore and Damion: We Are One, One, All in One*. Columbia, 1969.

Okkervil River. "Black." *Black Sheep Boy*. Music and lyrics by Will Sheff. Jagjaguwar, 2005.

———. "Black Sheep Boy." *Black Sheep Boy*. Music and lyrics by Tim Hardin. Jagjaguwar, 2005.

———. "In a Radio Song." *Black Sheep Boy*. Music and lyrics by Will Sheff. Jagjaguwar, 2005.

———. "The Latest Toughs." *Black Sheep Boy*. Music and lyrics by Will Sheff. Jagjaguwar, 2005.

Ramones. "Touring." *Pleasant Dreams (Expanded Edition)*. Sire, 2002.

Seger, Bob. "Turn the Page." *Back in '72*. Reprise, 1973.

Stewart, Rod. "Maggie May" [single]. Music and lyrics by Rod Stewart and Martin Quittenton. Mercury, 1971.

———. "Reason to Believe" [single]. Music and lyrics by Tim Hardin. Mercury, 1971.

STILL HOLDING AT THE SEAMS: MAGNOLIA ELECTRIC CO.'S *JOSEPHINE* AND THE CONTEMPORARY POETIC SEQUENCE

JESSE GRAVES

In recent years, many poetry books and albums seem to belong together less because of any common thematic bond than because of a loose structural coherence, a sense that their individual songs and poems make up a larger poetic sequence. One recent record, Magnolia Electric Co.'s 2009 release Josephine, *stands in particularly close relation to contemporary poetry, both through its reliance on symbols and recurrent imagery, as well as the sense that a definite, though incomplete, narrative holds the album together. This essay explores the use of the poetic sequences in contemporary poetry and albums.*

ontemporary poetry and independent/roots music increasingly resemble twins separated at birth, not exactly identical, but nurtured by the same native sources. Both genres have been set adrift from their traditional methods and outlets of distribution, and both have found greater independence on the web and through new media, but have also found a more diffuse marketplace. Both have small but dedicated followings that cross generational and cultural boundaries, and both exist on the fringes of larger economic entities that more or less neglect their existences. The deepest and most consequential bond, however, exists in the style and subject matter that makes up the work of contemporary poetry and indie music.

For example, listening to the 2007 release *The Stage Names* from the Austin, Texas, band Okkervil River and reading the 2005 poetry collection *The Book of Faces* by Joseph Campana present a strikingly similar set of qualities. In the same way that Okkervil River's album unfolds through a series of cinematic references and situations, beginning with the opening track "Our Life Is Not a Movie, or Maybe," Campana introduces the beguiling actress Audrey Hepburn, in a variety of real and imagined roles, as the muse of his poems. These two works, along with many others in recent years, seem to belong together less because of any common thematic bond than because of a loose structural coherence, a sense that their individual songs and poems make up a larger poetic sequence. One recent record, Magnolia Electric Co.'s 2009 release *Josephine*, stands in particularly close relation to contemporary poetry, both through its reliance on symbols and recurrent imagery, as well as the sense that a definite, though incomplete, narrative holds the album together.

The poetic sequence provides poets with a solution to the question of how to expand on an image or occasion, without acquiescing to the inevitability of narrative resolution in prose fiction, or to the historical and dramatic sweep of the epic. The sequence allows a poet to elaborate on an idea or sensation without necessarily telling a linear story about it. The sequence poem is not a recent development in American poetry. Interestingly, the roots of the genre trace back to the very first distinctly, authoritatively American poetry, Walt Whitman's monumental *Leaves of Grass*. Whitman's poem "Song of Myself" makes a compelling case as a sequence of discreet lyrics, drawn together through the subjective qualities of perspective and sensibility, especially when compared against more traditional long poems such as William Wordsworth's *The Prelude* or John Milton's epic *Paradise Lost*. The contemporary lyric sequence bears at least one thing in common with Whitman's "Song of Myself": The subject matter of the individual poems need not be the same to successfully carry the points of reference and connection through the entire piece.

Magnolia Electric Co. is a touring and recording collective of musicians led by singer and songwriter Jason Molina, begun in 2003 after Molina retired his earlier band name, Songs: Ohia. The band plays a hybrid country/rock style reminiscent of Neil Young and Gram Parsons, solidly based out of the 1960s folk revival sound, a brand of music given a variety of names such as "alt-country" or "Americana." Like another highly literary singer-songwriter, Josh Ritter, Molina attended Oberlin College in Ohio. *Josephine* is the band's fifth album (and the first to pursue a clear sequence of songs), though Molina has released dozens of collaborations, side projects, and single/EP recordings. Not all the songs on *Josephine* are about the speaker's relationship with the character of Josephine, and many songs do not mention her at all. This distinguishes the album from earlier examples of song cycles, or "concept albums," in country and rock and roll music, such as Willie Nelson's classic *Red-Headed Stranger*, which tells the story of a wronged preacher who seeks revenge, and Neil Young's more recent *Greendale*, which documents the lives of a family of characters in a small California town. *Josephine* coheres because the emotional center of the songs revolves around the sense of loss that Josephine represents; even when she is not the direct subject, her absence is felt in the speaker's travels, and the mistakes that he has made in his life seem to lead back to their relationship.

The album's title track (and third song), addressed to Josephine, begins, "I turned your life so upside down / I don't know how you stayed, or why." He continues the verse by saying, "Looking always over my shoulder / Exactly what I was hoping to find was already mine. / Josephine, Josephine." These lines establish both the speaker's mistreatment of his beloved, and also his regret at his behavior. The following lines explain his actions: "But I saw the horizon, and I had to know where it all ends. / I lived so long with the shadows, Lord, I became one of them. / Oh, what a fool I've been, Josephine, Josephine." The lines that shape the emotional center of the whole album come toward the end of the song, and give our best picture of Josephine's isolation, and the speaker's regret: "You lock the door, and put them old records on / I hear you crying along / Oh, what a fool I've been." The song ends with the speaker lamenting at how he tried to hold things together, but finally admitting that he followed the wrong dream, that he chased the horizon instead of showing his love for Josephine. The song doesn't resolve the situation, but simply stakes a claim to be revisited throughout the album, ending with, "O Josephine / You are free / O Josephine." Molina offers personal implications in the lyrics, but they are not quite confessional in the amount of detail revealed, and as in much contemporary poetry, the distinction between the actual and the symbolic remains blurred.

If "Josephine" is the signal track on the album, the establishing shot for the whole sequence, then the song "Hope Dies Last" serves as a crux for all the threads running through the entire collection. The speaker's regret resurfaces when he scans his new landscape, retracing his steps: "I have mapped my falling sky from Harper's Ferry to the Gauley Bridge / Wichita to Omaha, in the imminent bliss / but I made it too hard." The song once again looks to the past—even the album's cover art (designed by Molina) suggests a world long departed, depicting a locket photograph woven into a lace doily of a young woman in nineteenth-century dress. In a lovely unaccompanied duet, Molina sings with a backing vocalist, "I see the arrow climb, climb, climb / I know it finds my heart, every time." The arrow in the heart reappears in the album's closing track, but here re-establishes the pain and loss that drives the speaker's actions: "I make no small plans, my love / and I know hope dies last of all . . . Josephine, Josephine." There is anguish in these lines, but not hopelessness, echoed again in the next song, "The Handing Down," with the lines, "Heart-worn more than most, I guess / But I'm still holding at the seams." Josephine herself is not the only recurring element between songs on the album. Other motifs broaden the canvas, such as the wandering of the speaker, conveyed in "Map of the Falling Sky," and his pervasive loneliness, best seen in "Whip-Poor-Will," with its haunting refrain, "For all you people up in Heaven not too busy ringing the bell, / some of us down here ain't doing very well / some of us with our windows open in the Southern Cross Hotel."

The album closes with "An Arrow in the Gale," another ode both to the speaker's time spent with Josephine and to life on the move. At only one minute, twenty-two seconds, one is tempted to call it a reprise of the earlier song "Josephine," yet the tone in this final track is much lighter, less bound to past mistakes, and more focused on the possibilities of the future. The opening lines are, "Lightning on our tail, we gotta run, run, run / Lightning on our tail, we better go, Jo." Even certain musical phrasings recur throughout the album, when chords and guitar lines repeat, and in the background chant of "Run, run, run" later in the song, behind the lead vocal repeating the name "Josephine," both of which echo the title track and "Hope Dies Last." The final lines of the song present a question: "There's an arrow in the gale / and in the heartbeat / Oh, which one of us is free, Josephine?" The listener is left wondering about how to interpret this track as the album's conclusion: Is it a memory, a reunion, does it suggests a future with Josephine, or is it a look backward toward an intense moment they shared? The song, and the album as a whole, is as inconclusive as any lyric poem, or book of poems-in-sequence, and bears all the compression, imagery, and significant detail that characterizes the best lyric poetry.

There are many examples in contemporary American writing of the poetic sequence, including some of the most celebrated volumes in recent memory. Louise Gluck's Pulitzer Prize–winning collection *The Wild Iris* appeared in 1992, and its inventive use of a speaker in dialogue has made it one of the most discussed poetry books of that decade. Gluck introduces a gardener who engages in parallel discussions with the flowers in her garden, and with the voice of a god, all through a series of songlike lyrics in a sequence of recurring images and conceits. The Pulitzer Prize for Poetry was awarded to volumes that rely heavily on sequence poems in 2006, 2007, and 2010, respectively to Claudia Emerson's *Late Wife*, Natasha Tretheway's *Native Guard*, and Rae Armantrout's *Versed*. Emerson (who writes on Bob Dylan in this essay collection) divides *Late Wife* into three sets of epistolary poems, each examining a different relationship and period of the speaker's life, culminating in a sequence of sonnets to her new husband about living with the death of his first wife. Tretheway also uses three sections for *Native Guard*, through which she intermingles personal trials, including the murder of her mother, with the historical situation of the Louisiana Native Guard, an all-black regiment in the Civil War. Like Emerson, Tretheway displays a mastery of poetic forms, including the sonnet-sequence that makes up the title poem. In *Versed*, Rae Armantrout, once known as a Language poet, employs a far more experimental sense of poetic style, and a more fragmented set of experiences which are held together by an anxiety created by the speaker's illness. As these volumes indicate, the poetic sequence can take many shapes and styles, as well as a variety of subject matter.

Larry Levis's posthumous collections of poems, *Elegy*, has become something of a touchstone for a younger generation of poets, a book that often comes up in conversations with a tone of awe at the accomplishment, as well as a warmth that conveys real affection. More than any of the previously discussed books, *Elegy* folds its connections and linkages through the poems in a way that closely mirrors how the threads of recurrent imagery and thematic continuity are woven throughout *Josephine*. Even repetitions of various versions of elegy, the mode of poetry that mourns or meditates upon the dead, create a sequential effect in the book. For example, the poem "Anastasia and Sandman" by Levis introduces the image of the horse, and the holiness of the horse's natural state of being. The poem opens with a scene:

> The brow of a horse in that moment when
> The horse is drinking water so deeply from a trough
> It seems to inhale the water, is holy.
>
> I refuse to explain.

After this mysterious invocation, and the speaker's refusal to shed any light on what it means, the poem forges the immediate scene—the water in the trough—to its reflection of the infinite, the unknowable:

> When the horse had gone the water in the trough,
> All through the empty summer,
> Went on reflecting clouds & stars. (8)

The poem proceeds through a reverie addressed to "Members of the Committee on the Ineffable" (8), then into a bleak historical vision of Stalin's conquest of Romania, when he confiscated the farmers' horses, leaving them with no means for tending their land. Ultimately the species of the horse outlasts even Stalin's tyranny, and ever-present through the entire sequence is an angel lingering beyond the fields, alighting in a horse's ear; and there is hope, three pages later at the poem's conclusion, that good will prevail:

> I keep going to meetings where no one's there,
> And contributing to the discussion;
> And besides, behind the angel hissing in its mist
> Is a gate that leads only into another field. (8)

Here again the speaker uses indirection and seeming insignificance to guide the speaker into a deeper realization, where in fact the reader is introduced to the main players in the poem's drama, the title characters:

> A horse named Sandman & a horse named Anastasia

> Used to stand at the fence & watch the traffic pass.
> Where there were outdoor concerts once, in summer,
> Under the missing & innumerable stars. (8–9)

Levis establishes the significance of the horse, as well as the mystery of the stars, in "Anastasia & Sandman," and then revisits both symbols throughout *Elegy*. Other details, such as the significance of the year 1967 in the life of the poems' speaker, arise in several poems, but the horses, which appear on the book jacket in a kind of half-erased photographic negative image, are most central in the recurrent sequence. The two particular horses surface again, their relation to the speaker finally revealed, in a long poem from the third and final section of *Elegy*, titled "Elegy with the Sprawl of a Wave Inside It":

> The wooden streets of MacLeod are lost in snow.
>
> I love to say the names, over & over,
> For the luster of their syllables, Vizcaino & Magellan,
> Drake disappearing into mists off the Farallones.

The speaker luxuriates over the language, the sound of names, before introducing the important figure of his grandmother:

> Murrieta, Sontag & Evans, the Skeleton Club,
>
> My grandmother Adah coming home after teaching school in a buggy
> Drawn by the two horses, Anastasia & Sandman,
>
> A small Derringer with a pearl handle in her lap.

All of this prepares us for the poem's actual resolution, which involves the speaker's father, and his unexpected return to his home.

> My father walking halfway over the swaying bridge
> Of the last whaling boat—
>
> Bound for Juneau out of San Francisco Bay &
> Then turning around in the middle, deciding not to. (44)

Anastasia and Sandman also appear in the later poem "Elegy with a Bridle in Its Hand," which presents the speaker's memory of riding the two aged horses when he was a boy. The pervasive, but never openly revealed, significance of the horses in *Elegy* mirrors the elusiveness of the character of Josephine, and the unresolved nature of her relationship with the speaker of Magnolia Electric Co.'s songs about her.

Given the relative predominance of the form, surprisingly little criticism has been written about the lyric sequence. The most wide-ranging study on the subject was published in 1983, *The Modern Poetic Sequence: The Genius of Modern Poetry*, by M. L. Rosenthal and Sally Gall. In the section of their introductory chapter, titled "The 'New' Genre and Organic Form," Rosenthal and Gall consider how the sequence emerges into its own:

> Its presence becomes abundantly obvious, for the modern sequence is the decisive form toward which all developments of modern poetry have tended. It is the genre which best encompasses the shift in sensibility exemplified by starting a long poetic work "I celebrate myself, and sing myself," rather than "Sing, Goddess, the wrath of Achilles." The modern sequence goes many-sidedly into who and where we are *subjectively* [emphasis in original]; it springs from the same pressures on sensibility that have caused our poets' experiments with shorter forms. It, too, is a response to the lyrical possibilities of language opened up by those pressures in times of cultural and psychological crisis, when all past certainties have many times been thrown chaotically into question. More successfully than individual short lyrics, however, it fulfills the need for encompassment of disparate and often powerfully opposed tonalities and energies. (3)

As with other elements of style and structure in poetry, the sequence as mapped out by Rosenthal and Gall has evolved since the period of High Modernist triumph. A reconsideration of how the sequence poem now functions is long overdue. One clear modification over time is that the kind of material that creates a thread of continuity throughout the poem is less overt, the connections are fainter, more subtly construed. The dominant themes in such monolithic poetry as T. S. Eliot's *The Waste Land*, Ezra Pound's *The Cantos*, and William Carlos Williams's *Paterson* announce themselves with a clarity that unifies even disparate parts of the works. These poems are all part of the "American Flowering" of the new genre, which according to Rosenthal and Gall expand upon the promise of Whitman's experiments. In contrast, the unifying elements in Levis's *Elegy*, as well as in Magnolia Electric Co.'s *Josephine*, lie buried in images or correspondences between images. The linking thread that generates coherence in these recent works forms something more like a trail (a "fading trail," to echo an earlier Magnolia Electric Co. album title) than a highway system.

During the week of the album's release, Pitchfork.tv ran a full-length documentary called *Recording Josephine*, in which filmmaker Ben Schreiner observed the band during the recording of the album. Much of the film focuses on in-studio details of how individual songs go through different versions, along with interview segments with the band and their near-legendary producer Steve Albini.

Near the very end of the documentary, however, Schreiner finally asks Jason Molina, the band's singer and songwriter, about the lyrics for the record. Molina is coy, even evasive, about what the songs refer to, and like any true poet seems unwilling to commit the "heresy of paraphrase." Just as he becomes visibly uncomfortable, on the verge of saying something definite, the camera makes an abrupt cut, which signals the end of the film. The band could not have been more forthcoming about the process of recording their instruments, but when it came to discussing lyrics, the secret could not be unveiled. As in a fine sequence of poems, following the thread of images and implications as it winds through *Josephine* gives all the joy, and the satisfaction, of a mystery not quite revealed.

Works Cited

Armantrout, Rae. *Versed*. Middletown, CT: Wesleyan University Press, 2009.

Campana, Joseph. *The Book of Faces*. St. Paul: Graywolf, 2005.

Emerson, Claudia. *Late Wife*. Baton Rouge: Louisiana State University Press, 2005.

Gluck, Louise. *The Wild Iris*. New York: Ecco, 1992.

Levis, Larry. "Anastasia and Sandman." *Elegy*. Pittsburgh: University of Pittsburgh Press, 1997.

———. *Elegy*. Pittsburgh: University of Pittsburgh Press, 1997.

———. "Elegy with a Bridle in Its Hand." *Elegy*. Pittsburgh: University of Pittsburgh Press, 1997.

———. "Elegy with the Sprawl of a Wave Inside It." *Elegy*. Pittsburgh: University of Pittsburgh Press, 1997.

———. "Members of the Committee on the Ineffable." *Elegy*. Pittsburgh: University of Pittsburgh Press, 1997.

Magnolia Electric Co. "An Arrow in the Gale." *Josephine*. Secretly Canadian, 2009.

———. "The Handing Down." *Josephine*. Secretly Canadian, 2009.

———. "Hope Dies Last." *Josephine*. Secretly Canadian, 2009.

———. "Josephine." *Josephine*. Secretly Canadian, 2009.

———. *Josephine*. Secretly Canadian, 2009.

———. "Map of the Falling Sky." *Josephine*. Secretly Canadian, 2009.

———. "Whip-Poor-Will." *Josephine*. Secretly Canadian, 2009.

Nelson, Willie. *Red-Headed Stranger*. Columbia, 1975.

Okkervil River. "Our Life is Not a Movie, Or Maybe." *The Stage Names*. Jagjaguwar, 2007.

———. *The Stage Names*. Jagjaguwar, 2007.

———. *The Stand Ins*. Jagjaguwar, 2008.

Rosenthal, M. L., and Sally Gall. *The Modern Poetic Sequence*. Oxford: Oxford University Press, 1983.

Schreiner, Ben, dir. *Recording Josephine*. Pitchfork.tv. 24 Sept. 2009. pitchfork.com/.

Tretheway, Natasha. *Native Guard*. Boston: Houghton-Mifflin, 2006.

Whitman, Walt. "Song of Myself." *Leaves of Grass*. 1892. New York: Norton, 2002.

Young, Neil. *Greendale*. Warner Bros., 2003.

NOT TO OPPOSE EVIL: JOHNNY CASH'S BAD LUCK WIND

TONY TOST

"The Man in Black" persona of Johnny Cash invites discussion, yet at the same time resists tidy categorization and bends toward the mythic. In this essay Tony Tost explains how ". . . the legendary, the mythic, always exceeds our understanding of it, always operates by its own logic, by truths that do not concede to modern assumptions concerning motivation and causation." Tost discusses the song "Thirteen" written by Glenn Danzig and reflects on how Cash's rendering evokes the complexities involving his own mythology. The result is a song that provides both a sense of a "lonesome fugitive" and of "the lawman on that fugitive's trail."

"There is less trouble in the world," Edward Dahlberg assures us, "when we are reared by streams, animals, trees, as legend says." In "A Boy Named Sue," the Shel Silverstein composition Cash performed for the first time in front of the citizens of San Quentin prison in 1969, the narrator's displeasure is that he has grown up as a kind of comic legend. Because his father deeded him nothing but a woman's name, he has faced a life of mockery and abuse. When Sue discovers his father later in the song and prepares to slay him in revenge, the father pulls a curtain back, revealing the story behind the name: the father knew he wouldn't be there to raise his son, so he named the child Sue to toughen him up in his stead, placing gravel in his gut and grit in his eye. The name came first, and it was up to the son to fulfill it, one way or another. A boy named Sue would have to get tough or die. It's a kind of fable: the boy who was raised not by a father but by a name.

The odd, bawling resonance of "A Boy Named Sue" had to be among the precedents informing "Thirteen," a song about a man born without any name at all. Glenn Danzig wrote the song specifically for Cash's *American Recordings*, and it is a composition that, like "Delia's Gone," "The Man Who Couldn't Cry," and "Sue" itself, toys with the fault line separating tragedy and farce, that broadcasts

261

from the spot where tragedy and farce hold unsteady mirrors to one another. Cash gives the song a hushed urgency, conjuring the feel of uneasy company at a late hour. "Bad luck wind blowing at my back," Cash sings. "I was born to bring trouble to wherever I'm at." The bad luck wind never rises to a gale in Cash's performance, but it never subsides either; it's an undercurrent, teasing but never spilling out. And it sounds like it could be the theme song both for some lonesome fugitive and for the lawman on that fugitive's trail, a sound mapping out the empery of the permanent solitaire, one who discovers his or her own queer means by which to achieve such solitude: an Emily Dickinson or Billy the Kid, a Pat Garrett, Susan Smith, or Howard Hughes. The song's quietness is that of being late and alone with one who is dangerous and close, even if that one is simply one's own self.

On the page, "Thirteen" is a competent genre exercise in lyrical self-pity and generalized menace, nearly a caricature of Cash's persona; it embraces the Man in Black's wanted-man mythology without including either the spiritual ache or the knowing wit that are also in his possession. It is not any scaffolding for the creation of a legendary figure but rather an ornament, a gargoyle to attach to a legend, not to update him but just to reaffirm what Danzig believed that legend contains. "Find me a preacher man, confess him all I've done," Cash sings in an outtake of the song, trying out a Danzig verse he would eventually cut. "You can catch me with the devil, playing twenty-one." But the legendary, the mythic, always exceeds our understanding of it, always operates by its own logic, by truths that do not concede to modern assumptions concerning motivation and causation. Legends are neither born nor made; they are repeated. Danzig was wanting to write down that famous Cashian biblical menace, and there it sat easily in the lyrics, simple and untroubled. But in his unexpectedly restrained, nearly tender embodiment of the song, Cash lifts Danzig's lyrics out from the narrator's own prison house of self-regard and lets the words ride on the bad luck wind that is at that narrator's back, a wind that is not his alone. Cash gets at the fearsome anonymity underlying the song, the kind of anonymity that can be turned into a weapon, as it was for the D.C. sniper and the Green River Killer in their unidentified incarnations, both growing more potent as they seemed more amorphous, more permanently abstract and faceless; for a time, seeming like plain evil itself. "The American intellect is a placeless hunter," Edward Dahlberg wrote. "It is a negative faculty which devours rather than quiets the heart."

The placeless narrator of "Thirteen" moves easily and proves lethal only if perceived. "I pray that you don't look at me," he sings, "I pray I don't look back." He sounds like night itself, quiet and forlorn. It is a sound Cash conjured when he performed "Long Black Veil" as a whispery lullaby for the dispossessed on *At Folsom Prison*. Cash's version of the modern standard, still definitive in its initial recording by Lefty Frizzell, was surprisingly limp and toothless. The quiet, anonymous menace that lets Cash expand "Thirteen" into an anthemic stillness merely dissipated "Long Black Veil," turning it into an eerie ghost story, narrated by everyman and known by everyone. But in Frizzell's voice the song had hit like the possession of a singular life, the tale of an actual, sinful man who elected death rather than dishonor: when he is asked by a judge to provide an alibi for a murder he did not commit, the accused narrator refuses. "I had been in the arms of my best friend's wife," he sings afterward, in death. The alibi would have been more dishonorable than the accused crime. His lover, his best friend's wife, abides by his decision, and watches his hanging without emitting a peep. These two cannot marry but they can make their own vows with eternity: he will agree to the false terms of his death; she will weep forever over his concession. By making these vows, they come to their own kind of honor, slipping away together into a secret only they can know. In place of words of protest, and in place of the dishonorable truth that would have spared the narrator's life, the woman instead selects for herself the costume of legend. She becomes the woman who wanders the hills in a darkened veil, whose steady tears taste by now of the holy.

At Folsom Prison, Cash sang the song as though from the grave, as though a microphone had been set up on the other side of eternity; his voice is burdened, overwrought and over-hushed, and the mood is only broken when Cash gets to the line about being in the arms of his best friend's wife. Just after that line, he stops. Cash has heard one of the prisoners cheering the adulterous line, and he begins to chuckle. "Did I hear somebody applaud?" he laughs. A brilliant moment, it is certainly a more authentic instance of identification between Cash and his audience than Cash's posturing banter between songs on the album. Michael Streissguth notes in his superb book on the making of *At Folsom Prison* that the famous cheers that greeted the "I shot a man in Reno" line on the album's title track were an after-effect: they were spliced onto the recording after the performance was finished. The reaction to "Long Black Veil" was in real time, however, and it speaks to the same sentiment—one that Cash's singing was missing out on, and that needed the prisoner's cheer to be voiced—the simple fact that doing wrong so often feels so right.

Frizzell sang the song not from the grave but as though he was a couple of barstools down from you, maybe a few sheets closer to the wind. It is more startling and complex than Cash's cover because Frizzell sounds so near, so human. "I was not always like this," his version argues. ("It can only be like this," Cash's cover implies.) For Frizzell's narrator, everything changed the moment he chose to accept death as the price for his earlier, adulterous pleasures. He does not renounce the fact that he was in the arms of his best friend's wife; he simply chooses to make things right, a decision that alters his affair with his buddy's wife from being tawdry to being tragic. It is as if, with that choice, he has successfully petitioned the gods for a hearing. His is a song of mythic power, which is not the same as saying it has a spiritual force (the spiritual promises a meaningful escape from the carnal world while the mythic promises a meaningful manner for passing through it; the mythic remains in the world, explaining it). In Frizzell's recording, the narrator sounds like an ordinary man caught up in the currents of fate and myth; the distant cry of a steel guitar hints continually, like a black cloud, that some unwanted rider is making his approach, a bad luck wind at his back. Frizzell's voice quavers when he sings about how the "night winds wail," both ventriloquizing that wail while also lodging a grievance about being caught within it. His aim is not to be the wind but to maintain his humanity inside it, even after death. As the song fades, his voice finally begins its retreat back into eternity. "Nobody knows but me," he repeats.

Cash's misstep on *At Folsom Prison* was his decision to sing "Long Black Veil" as the night and the wind instead of as a man trapped within them. But that same approach salvages his performance of Danzig's "Thirteen," which is a song not about a human being but about evil, and what countenances it comes to bear. Thirteen, born without a name, and born in the soul of misery (whatever exactly that could be), seems to have had no say in the matter: he emerged, pre-destined and marked by fate, sired and raised by some overweening absence. He is what he is. "Sir, I guess there's just a meanness in this world," Charlie Stark-weather likewise concludes at the end of Bruce Springsteen's "Nebraska," in ex-plication of such unvectored violence. Springsteen's narrator chills with his very plainness and modesty; the song passes through pastoral imagery—a young girl twirling a baton in her front yard, a young couple going for a ride in their car—that would not be out of place in a rudimentary American love song. No mask is ripped away from the speaker to reveal the monster lurking underneath; his ac-tions aren't pinned on some past trauma, like the swing that struck John Wayne Gacy in the back of his head when he was eleven, clotting his brain. No such modern diagnostic comforts are offered by Springsteen's speaker; he and his girl killed everything they saw because it was fun to do so. And unlike Cash's killers in songs like "Delia's Gone," "Going to Memphis," and "Sam Hell," Springsteen's narrator maintains a respectful decorum, making him all the more inexplicable. He is all mask.

Like the applauding prisoner interrupting Cash's "Long Black Veil," Spring-steen's Starkweather doesn't pretend there is no sensual charge to sinfulness either. "You make sure," he sings, readying himself for the electric chair, "my pretty baby is sittin' right there on my lap." By rendering his narrator so recog-nizably, unremarkably human, Springsteen makes his evil inextricable from his humanity. Cash and Danzig's Thirteen embodies a different, more ascetic kind of evil; his song is almost an inverse spiritual, refusing as it does the gratifications and torments of the flesh. ("Be primordial or decay," Dahlberg concluded.) How difficult it is to imagine Thirteen driving through a countryside or undressing for pleasure, or even stepping into a grocery store to fondle some avocados and bananas. Given a number instead of a name, this abstemious creature appears destined for a life off the social grid, outside the tethering norms of work and family. But there is also a falseness to his bearing, evident in the bravado line about playing cards with the devil that Cash ultimately cut from the song, but also in the tattoo Thirteen has selected as his brand. The wind at his back may in fact be a harmless summer breeze, but in the theater of his own self it will always be a bad luck wind. It is nearly a child's idea of evil, a face one sees in the lower limbs of the darkening wood or at night in the folds behind an open closet door.

By writing Thirteen as such an otherworldly emanation, Danzig set him outside creation, as some aberration conceived and delivered via inhuman measures. Cash retrieves the song for the human world, however, largely through performance—and just by being Johnny Cash. In his austerity and reserve, Cash pulls Danzig's song inward; it becomes a song sung not to a crowd but to one's own reflection, as a comfort and warning both, a way of voicing one's own worst thoughts about one's own self. Cash sounds like a man who has traveled a long distance in order to say his piece and who in that traveling has winnowed his own expressiveness down to its wounded essence. Instead of proclaiming the song as a boast, Cash gathers it in closer and closer until it becomes nearly ethereal, as though the sensibility giving voice to the words has lifted itself up out of the body of any one man and has exited to become a contagious, injured premonition, ready to assume any physical form. It could be the anthem of anyone's own worst self. The song exists inside the world of *American Recordings* as a mood, a foreboding that hovers behind the other tracks; its bad luck wind will always tug and threaten. Just as the lyrics of "Long Black Veil" revealed the personal traumas hiding behind a mythic figure, Cash's performance hints at the human hurts, vulnerabilities, and solitudes tucked behind even a caricatured figuration of evil.

"The poet's role," wrote Robert Duncan in correspondence with fellow poet Denise Levertov, whom Duncan accused of betraying her art by explicitly protesting the Vietnam War in her work, "is not to oppose evil, but to imagine it." For Duncan, it is "a disease of our generation that we offer symptoms and diagnoses of what we are in the place of imaginations and creations of what we are." This was Cash's challenge: not just to know evil but to know it as it knows itself, a snake sighing back into its skin. In Cash's voice, an epic distance creeps in behind the song's immediately familiar portrait of evil. Thirteen sounds like he has been transformed into some dark angel of history, an elemental instrument by which God—or the gods, or History, or the Cosmos, or whatever name you wish to select—avenges unspoken grievances and wrongs for those who are unable to haunt their tormentors themselves. It is a feel for how the universe sets aside a place for evil, a sense that a Thirteen or a Charles Manson, a Stagger Lee or a Deepwater Horizon is always being brought into the perpetual American historical melodrama in order to be unleashed; these entities never truly understand their historical role but simply operate by the buried codes of the republic itself, revealing and redressing them (see the collected works of Timothy McVeigh).

Their chronic reappearance is always just another round of a familiar story, and we find ourselves accepting not the severity of their vengeance but rather the inevitability of their appearance. We are certain that we have done plenty to deserve such monstrous visitors, and expect more visitations still, though we can never quite recall what it is we have done to invite them.

Works Cited

Edward Dahlberg, *The Sorrows of Priapus* (New York: Harcourt Brace, 1973).

Johnny Cash, "A Boy Named Sue," *Johnny Cash at San Quentin* (Columbia, 1969).

Johnny Cash, "Thirteen," *American Recordings* (American Recordings, 1994).

Johnny Cash, "Thirteen (alternate lyrics)," *Unearthed* (American Recordings, 2003).

Johnny Cash, "Long Black Veil," *Johnny Cash at Folsom Prison* (Columbia, 1968).

Lefty Frizzell, "Long Black Veil," *Life's Like Poetry* (Bear Family, 1992).

Michael Streissguth, *Johnny Cash at Folsom Prison: The Making of a Masterpiece* (Cambridge, MA: Da Capo, 2004).

Bruce Springsteen, "Nebraska," *Nebraska* (Columbia, 1982).

Robert Duncan, *The Letters of Robert Duncan and Denise Levertov*, ed. Robert J. Bertholf and Albert Gelpi (Stanford: Stanford UP, 2004).

GLOSSARY

Note: This glossary is not meant to be exhaustive, but referential to the terms that appear in this collection's essays.

AA Form: Also known as the 8-Bar folk song. The simplest song form that consists of eight measures of 3/4 or 4/4 time. An example is "He's Got the Whole World in His Hands."

AAA Form: Also known as the one-part song. This form consists of several verses, but it does not feature a chorus or a bridge. Instead, the song features a refrain where a line (or often a title) is repeated at each verse's end. An example is "Bridge Over Troubled Water."

AABA Form: Also known as standard form. 32 bars are divided into 8-bar sections: two opening A sections are followed by a B section that contrasts in some way such as with a bridge. The song then reverts back to an A section. An example is "Your Cheating Heart."

AB Form: Also known as Verse-Chorus structure. This song form doubles the 8-bar form. The 8-bar verses tell the story and the 8-bar chorus repeats one lyric such as in "My Darling Clementine."
Please note that all the forms have variants. Other song forms defined in this glossary include 12-Bar Blues (see Bars), Double 16-Bar Form, and Verse/Chorus/Verse Song Structure.

Accent (or **stress**): The vocal emphasis placed on a syllable. In some cases, it is quite clear what the stressed syllable is, but other times it is not. Also, word stress, contrastive stress, and sentence stress all play a role in what is stressed. For example, word stress is what the dictionary will denote as the stressed and unstressed syllables, sentence stress reflects how the stressed syllables may change based on the surrounding words, and contrastive stress is when a word is stressed because it is suddenly key as in someone asking, "Do you want this *in* the microwave or *on* the microwave?" To properly scan a line of poetry, one must consider sentence and contrastive stress over word stress. (Note: some linguists distinguish between "accent" and "stress." Others consider the terms synonymous.) In music, the term refers to any emphasis on a particular note or notes in a sequence, either a sharp increase in volume (dynamic or stress accent), an elongation of the tone (agogic accent), or a modulation of the pitch (pitch or tonic accent).

Accentual verse: Lines that feature a fixed number of stressed beats without patterning the stressed or unstressed beats in specific placements. The most common type of accentual verse is a four-beat line with a caesura in the middle, such as in the Old English poem *Beowulf*, and a few Middle English poems such as William Langland's *Piers Plowman*. Also, three of the four stressed syllables can alliterate (as they do in those two examples), resulting in what is called accentual-alliterative verse. After the Middle Ages, accentual-syllabic verse (poetry with lines that have fixed patterns of stressed and unstressed syllables) eclipsed accentual verse. An argument can be made that some rappers and singers are modern-day practitioners of accentual verse.

Alliteration: The repetition of sounds at the beginning of a word two or more times in a single line, sentence, phrase, or clause.

Assonance: See *slant rhyme*.

Ballad: In both genres, *ballads* used to refer to narratives about an everyman who suffered great tragedy, unrequited love, death, etc. Also, they were often about a community's tragedies, such as a local train crash or local couple's troubled love. In poetry, a ballad is still often reserved for those themes, and the form (also called ballad stanza) is a four-line stanza with the first and third lines being unrhyming iambic tetrameters (four feet) and the second and fourth lines rhyming iambic trimeters (three feet). Ballad meter is similar to common meter which has the same metrical structure but a different rhyme scheme. In common meter, lines one and three also rhyme with each other.

Whereas poets have retained the traditional definition for ballads, songwriters have created new definitions. In pop music, a ballad is a song with sentimental, romantic, or elegiac subject matter, often with narrative elements and almost always played at a slow tempo. In the late twentieth century, *ballad* has come to refer generally to any slow song, such as the rock ballad or power ballad.

Bars (4 bars, 8 bars, etc.): A chord progression pattern determined by the number of measures (or bars) in a verse. For instance, in a 12-bar blues progression (the most dominant type in blues, although 4- and 8-bar patterns are also very common), the chord progression is divided into three segments consisting of four measures each, with a different chord for each segment.

Beat: The basic temporal division of a song, or the stroke of a conductor's hand to denote the beat. In pop music, it can also refer to the rhythmic pattern generated by bass, drums, percussion, or sampler that underlies a song and determines its tempo.

Bridge: A passage of a song or stanza that connects two different, typically more prominent passages. In a verse, the bridge is usually the third line that connects the first two lines to the fourth. In the common verse-chorus-verse song structure, the bridge typically follows the second or third repetition of the chorus and sets up a final recurrence of the most prominent passages.

Caesura: A strong pause midway through a line. This is a feature of accentual verse, but any type of poem, received or open form, or song can employ it.

Chorus: A segment that is repeated throughout a song, usually following a verse or stanza. Originally, a chorus was a performance group at festivals, specifically religious or fertility festivals. The chorus later became an integral part of Greek tragic drama, which the Romans emulated and then Elizabethan dramatists as well.

Common Meter: See *ballad*.

Consonance: The repetition of consonant sounds at the end of a syllable or word such as the "nd" sound in *hand*, *bandage*, and *rind*. See also *slant rhyme*.

Counterpoint: The combination of two melodies or melodic phrases played simultaneously, with each given equal prominence. One element would be considered a counterpoint of the other.

Doggerel: A pejorative term to describe poetry considered poorly constructed and trivial. Features often include monotonous rhythm and rhyme.

Double 16-Bar Form: While all song forms feature variations, this song form has been noted as representing all the variations as many song forms fit the definition in subtle ways. Essentially, this is a long form where the first 16-bars create one section and the second 16-bar section begins like the first, but is then altered midway through.

Dramatic monologue: An outward speech given by one character, often to an implied listener. The writer's personality recedes in this type of approach. Also, in poetry the reader often perceives an incongruity between what the speaker is trying to reveal over what the speaker actually reveals. Some critics refer to this incongruity as "the gap" and others as "dramatic irony." In poetry, dramatic monologues were popular in the Victorian era; currently, songs use dramatic monologues more often than poems do. One example where poetry and songs converge is Richard Buckner's album *The Hill* (2000), which sets to music some of Edgar Lee Masters's dramatic monologues from *Spoon River Anthology* (1915).

End-stopped line: A definite halt that ends a line of poetry. It may be marked with punctuation that dictates a pause such as a period, colon, semi-colon, comma, or no punctuation at all. Either way, the line serves as a complete thought.

Enjambed line: Poetry lines that do not pause at the end, but spill over into the next line. Romantic poets revived the use of enjambment which continues to be a prominent feature of contemporary poetry.

Feminine rhyme: A rhyme composed of two words that are each two or more syllables, such as *curdle* and *hurdle*.

Heroic couplets: A rhyming couplet composed generally in iambic pentameter meter.

Hook: Any part of a song that stands out and grabs the listener's attention, often distinguishing it from other songs within a playlist or sequence. Usually, the term refers to a song's chorus, but it can apply to any element, such as a guitar riff, unusual instrumentation, vocal inflection, programmed beat, or sample.

Iambic: See *meter*.

Iambic pentameter: See *meter*.

Lyric: The Greeks defined *lyric* as words "to be accompanied by the lyre." An *aulos*, which is similar to an oboe, was also used. The term at the time meant to distinguish a type of poetry that was not only accompanied by music, but that also differed from epic, didactic, and dramatic poetry. Contemporary songs still use a definition similar to the Ancient Greek: a word, phrase, or line composed in verse and set to a melody. In contemporary poetry, this term refers to a specific type of poetry—one that is neither narrative nor dramatic. Rather, it is a type of poem that emphasizes emotion over narrative. Also, time in a lyric often becomes suspended as the speaker observes, reflects on, or espouses a feeling, object, or subject.

The lyrical "I": The first-person speaker in a poem who is not the poet, but a persona the poet employs.

Masculine rhyme: A rhyme composed of two monosyllabic words such as *hot* and *pot*.

Measure: A unit of time in a song comprised of an established sequence of beats. Most popular music adheres to a 4-beat measure (often called 4/4 or common time).

Melodic Phrase: A unit of a melody intended to convey a specific musical idea or mood, often defined in parallel with a lyrical line or phrase.

Melody: The arrangements of notes against a rhythm in musical time.

Meter: Originating from *metron*, which in Greek means "measure." In poetry, this term designates a pattern of rhythm—also called organized rhythm. This type of rhythm refers to the stress (or emphasis) placed on each syllable as this is a distinguishing sonic feature of English, as opposed to the length of a syllable in Greek, for example. This feature of stress versus length makes English verse qualitative and Greek verse quantitative. The unit we pay attention to in English is the foot with the most common feet including:

> Iambic: ˘ ´ (unstressed, stressed)
> Trochaic: ´ ˘ (stressed, unstressed)
> Anapestic: ˘ ˘ ´ (unstressed, unstressed, stressed)
> Dactylic: ´ ˘ ˘ (stressed, unstressed, unstressed)
> Spondaic: ´ ´ (stressed, stressed)
> Pyrrhic: ˘ ˘ (unstressed, unstressed)

Notice, except for spondaic and pyrrhic, that one stress is what will determine the foot. Also, the number of feet are designated as the following:

> Trimeter: a line of three feet
> Tetrameter: a line of four feet
> Pentameter: a line of five feet
> Hexameter: a line of six feet

The number of feet and type of meter will often be combined as a descriptor. For example, five feet of iambic meter will be called iambic pentameter.

Off-beat: A note or accent that does not fall directly on the established beat but in between beats.

Off rhyme: See *slant rhyme*.

On-beat: A note or accent that falls directly on the beat.

Persona or **speaker**: The first-person character presented within a poem or song. Readers are to understand that the "I" is not the writer, but a character being presented.

Qualitative verse: See *meter*.

Quantitative verse: See *meter*.

Refrain: A lyrical passage (or melodic passage, in the case of songs) that is repeated at intervals, typically a word or phrase at the end of a line or a line at the end of a verse or stanza.

Rhyme scheme: The system of end-line rhymes within a poetic stanza and song verse, with letters denoting distinct rhyming syllables. For instance, in an ABAA rhyme scheme, the first, third, and fourth lines correspond and the second does not. In ABAB, the first and third lines correspond, and the second and fourth lines comprise a different rhyme.

Rhyme-within-a-line: A line that features a rhyme in the middle and at the end of the line. For example, "picket signs for my wicked rhymes" by Eminem exemplifies this technique with picket/wicked and signs/rhymes. In poetry, this feature is known as internal rhyme.

Slant rhyme: Also called off rhyme, partial rhyme, near rhyme, or pararhyme. This type of rhyme is neither the employment of masculine or feminine rhyme. Some maintain it is, by conventional standards, incomplete. Others maintain it is nuanced and flexible. Some common types of slant rhyme include the following: consonance where the consonants match but the vowels do not, such as *cat* and *cot*; assonance where the vowels match but the consonants do not, such as *mop* and *not*; the use of an unstressed syllable to rhyme, such as *sing* and *running*; apocopated rhyme, where the last syllable of one rhyme is missing, such as *pet* and *netted*; and eye rhyme, such as *plough* and *trough*.

Sprung rhythm: Coined by poet Gerard Manley Hopkins to describe accentual verse, in particular his type of accentual verse. In his Preface to *Poems* (1918), he describes sprung rhythm often in ways that oppose "running rhythm," a term he used to describe standard English meter. For example: "[It] is measured by feet of from one to four syllables, regularly, and for particular effects any number of weak or slack syllables may be used. . . . And hence Sprung Rhythm differs from Running Rhythm in having or being only one nominal rhythm."

Stanza: The structural grouping of lines in poetry—what songs would call the verse.

Syllable: The smallest unit of speech that can be isolated.

Tempo: The speed at which a song or passage is played.

Tetrameter: See *meter*.

Trochaic: See *meter*.

Troubadours: A group of poets who flourished in the south of France between 1100 and 1350. They were often employed by particular courts and commissioned to sing on topics such as courtly love. Most of their lyrics were amorous in nature and are assumed to have been accompanied by music.

Unreliable narrator: Description of a narrator whose credibility is compromised, thus forcing the reader to question the validity, motives, and/or intentions of his/her statements. This type of narrator may be hiding information, concealing negative personal aspects, and/or providing misleading facts. The narrator may also not intend to provide false information, but might do so for reasons such as point of view, trauma, insanity, etc.

Unstressed: Describes the syllable in poetry that does not receive the emphasis.

Verse: The word derives from Latin *vertere* meaning "to turn," and *versus* meaning "a furrow, a turning of the plow"—both of which suggest that the lines turn from one to another. Some people use poetry and verse synonymously, although many debate if that should be the case. In Britain, verse may signify simply a line or a stanza. In music, the term typically applies to a stanza, often with different stanzas containing different lyrics sung over similar or identical musical structures.

Verse/Chorus/Verse Song Structure: Also known as verse/chorus/bridge. This form is an extension of AB Form. Many different patterns may be used with the most common being: Verse-Chorus-Verse-Chorus-Bridge-Chorus. The first verse establishes the song's theme and is followed by the chorus. Then, another verse follows where new details further complicate and expand on the song's theme. Next, a bridge occurs that differs from the verses, lyrically and melodically, and provides a reason for the chorus to repeat. In many ways, the verse/chorus form is similar to the sonnet form in that each verse must provide new information or complication to the song's message similar to how each sonnet stanza will provide new information and/or complication.

ACKNOWLEDGMENTS

Of course, to the contributors of this collection, a thank you is not enough. Without their enthusiasm, talent, and foresight to write on songs in a way that moves the discussions to new areas, this collection simply would not exist. David Daniel, Claudia Emerson, and Keith Flynn saw the possibility of this collection early on, and urged me to pursue it. I am grateful and indebted to their prescience. Jesse Graves and Stephen M. Deusner helped usher in the final project regarding the introduction and glossary respectively, and this collection greatly benefits from their conscientiousness and care. The truth is, however, all of the contributors deserve a special singling out, as each one invested time, energy, and support beyond what duty required, resulting in a collection that is more about collaboration than singular achievements.

I would also like to thank Kathryn Alexander and Tim Jenkins for those first into-the-morning-hours discussions around the kitchen table on songs and their relation to poetry. The time we spent interviewing songwriters and songwriting execs all over Nashville, camera in tow, was foundational research for the development of this collection. Finally, the support from the University of Tennessee, specifically the Hodges Fund, Dr. Allen Dunn, Dr. Amy Elias, Dr. Tom Haddox, Dr. Stan Garner, Dr. Marilyn Kallet, and Dr. Arthur Smith were all instrumental. Writers Marcel Brouwers and Chris Hebert also helped in those final stages when all words began to blur. I would also like to thank my editorial assistant Avery Finch and everyone at University Press of Mississippi, especially Craig Gill. Finally, I would like to thank my family, who not only supported this project, but who did so knowing the result would be less of me. Above all, I would like to thank my best friend and reader—who also happens to be my husband, Adam Prince. I have never known a person to bring such passion and discipline to whatever he does, a combination that I continually find inspiring.

CONTRIBUTORS

Lamar Alexander is U.S. Senator from Tennessee and has been U.S. Education Secretary for President George H. W. Bush, University of Tennessee president, and professor at Harvard's School of Government. He is a classical and country pianist and the author of seven books, including *Six Months Off*, the story of his family's life in Australia after he was governor.

Gordon Ball is a professor of English at Virginia Military Institute and a specialist on the Beat Generation. He is a writer, filmmaker, and photographer who edited several books with Allen Ginsberg and took numerous photographs of the poet. Ball is the author of *'66 Frames: A Memoir*; a volume of prose poems, *Dark Music*; and *East Hill Farm: Seasons with Allen Ginsberg*.

Adam Bradley is an associate professor of English at the University of Colorado, Boulder. He is author of *Book of Rhymes: The Poetics of Hip Hop* (2009) and *Ralph Ellison in Progress: From* Invisible Man *to* Three Days Before the Shooting . . . (2010). He is co-editor of *The Anthology of Rap* (2010) and *Three Days Before the Shooting* . . . (2010), the collected manuscripts of Ralph Ellison's second novel.

David Caplan specializes in twentieth- and twenty-first-century American literature. His scholarly interests include poetics, contemporary poetry, and popular music. He has published *Questions of Possibility: Contemporary Poetry and Poetic Form* (Oxford University Press 2004; paperback 2006) and *Poetic Form: An Introduction* (Longman, 2006), as well as a book of poetry, *In the World He Created According to His Will* (University of Georgia Press/VQR Poetry Series, 2010). He serves as a contributing editor to the *Virginia Quarterly Review* and *Pleiades: A Journal of New Writing*. His current projects include *Rhyme's Challenge* which analyzes rhyme in hip-hop music (under contract to Oxford University Press).

Wyn Cooper has published four books of poems: *The Country of Here Below* (Ahsahta Press, 1987), *The Way Back* (White Pine Press, 2000), *Postcards from the Interior* (BOA Editions, 2005), and *Chaos is the New Calm* (BOA Editions, 2010), as well as a chapbook, *Secret Address*. His poems, stories, essays, and reviews have appeared in *Poetry, Ploughshares, The Southern Review, Crazyhorse, Slate,* and more than seventy-five other magazines. In 1993 "Fun," a poem from his first book, was turned into Sheryl Crow's Grammy-winning song "All I Wanna Do." He has also cowritten songs with David Broza, David Baerwald, and Jody Redhage. In 2003 Gaff Music released *Forty Words for Fear*, a CD of songs based on poems and lyrics by Cooper, set to music and sung by the novelist Madison Smartt Bell. Their second CD, *Postcards Out of the Blue*, was released in 2008 by Dog Jaw Records. Currently, he lives in Vermont and helps run the Brattleboro Literary Festival and serves as a consultant to a think tank founded by the Poetry Foundation.

David Daniel's award-winning book of poems, *Seven-Star Bird*, was published by Graywolf Press. Harold Bloom has called him "an authentic heir to Hart Crane," and poems from his new collection *Ornaments and Other Assorted Love Song* have been published or are forthcoming in the *American Poetry Review*. The longtime poetry editor of *Ploughshares*, Daniel is currently professor of English and director of undergraduate creative writing at Fairleigh Dickinson University, where he also teaches in the low-residency M.F.A. program; a poetry editor for the *Literary Review*; and founder and director of WAMFEST, The Words and Music Festival—a weeklong celebration and examination of the relationship between literature and song.

Stephen M. Deusner, a Tennessee native, is a freelance music journalist based in Chicago. A *Pitchfork* staff writer since 2004, he contributed to the book *The Pitchfork 500: Our Guide to the Best Songs from Punk to the Present*. His writing appears frequently in *Paste*, *Blurt*, the *Memphis Flyer*, the *Village Voice*, and the *Washington Post Express*. He also writes a monthly column for the country music Web site The 9513. His fiction has appeared in *Best of Memphis 2003* and *Southern Voices Volume 5*.

Claudia Emerson received the 2006 Pulitzer Prize for Poetry for her collection *Late Wife*. Professor of English and Arrington Distinguished Chair in Poetry at the University of Mary Washington, she is also Poet Laureate of Virginia. She writes songs and performs with her husband, Kent Ippolito, a musician who plays bluegrass, rock, folk, jazz, blues, and ragtime.

Beth Ann Fennelly is a poet and essayist living in Oxford, Mississippi, and directing the M.F.A. program at the University of Mississippi. She has published three books of poetry: *Open House*, *Tender Hooks*, and *Unmentionables*, as well as *Great with Child*, a book of nonfiction. She has received a National Endowment for the Arts Award, a United States Artist Grant, a Pushcart, and a Fulbright to Brazil.

Keith Flynn (www.keithflynn.net) is the author of five books, including four collections of poetry: *The Talking Drum* (1991), *The Book of Monsters* (1994), *The Lost Sea* (2000), and *The Golden Ratio* (Iris Press, 2007), and a collection of essays, entitled *The Rhythm Method, Razzmatazz and Memory: How to Make Your Poetry Swing* (Writer's Digest Books, 2007). From 1987 to 1998 he was lyricist and lead singer for the nationally acclaimed rock band the Crystal Zoo, which produced three albums: *Swimming Through Lake Eerie* (1992), *Pouch* (1996), and the spoken-word and music compilation *Nervous Splendor* (Animal Records, 2003). He has been awarded the Sandburg Prize for poetry, the ASCAP Emerging Songwriter Prize, the Paumanok Poetry Award, and was twice named the Gilbert-Chappell Distinguished Poet for North Carolina. Flynn is founder and managing editor of the *Asheville Poetry Review*.

Jesse Graves is an Assistant Professor of English at East Tennessee State University, where he teaches creative writing and American literature. He received a Ph.D. in English from the University of Tennessee, and a Master of Fine Arts in Poetry from Cornell University. While at the University of Tennessee, he developed a special topics course called "Writing Roots Music and Culture," which focused on researching the cultural origins and stylistic developments of such folk genres as Appalachian old-time music, bluegrass, and the Delta blues. Graves's first collection of poems, *Tennessee Landscape with Blighted Pine*, will appear in 2011 with Texas Review Press. Essays on the ethics of aesthetic beauty in the prose of James Agee, the natural sublime in the poetry of John Ashbery, and the use of native speech in poetry from Appalachia all appeared in 2010. Jesse recently guest-edited a special issue of the *Southern Quarterly* titled "A Community Across Time: The Poetry and Prose of Robert Morgan."

Peter Guralnick has been called "a national resource" by Nat Hentoff for work that has argued passionately and persuasively for the vitality of this country's intertwined black and white musical traditions. His books include the prize-winning two-volume biography of Elvis Presley, *Last Train to Memphis* and *Careless Love*, which the *New York Times Book Review* declared to be "not simply the finest rock-and-roll biography ever written; it must be ranked among the most ambitious and crucial biographical undertakings yet devoted to a major American figure of the second half of the twentieth century." Other books include an acclaimed trilogy on American roots music, *Sweet Soul Music*, *Lost Highway*, and *Feel Like Going Home*; the biographical inquiry *Searching for Robert Johnson*; and the novel *Nighthawk Blues*. His most recent book, *Dream Boogie: The Triumph of Sam Cooke*, has been hailed as "an epic tale told against a backdrop of brilliant, shimmering music, intense personal melodrama, and vast social changes."

John Paul Hampstead was born in Augusta, Georgia, and grew up in Tennessee. Like his father, he played rugby at the University of Tennessee, where he received a B.A. and M.A. in English literature. He recently began his doctoral work on the Renaissance at the University of Michigan.

Brian Howe is a freelance writer, poet, and multimedia artist living in Durham, N.C. His arts and entertainment journalism appears regularly in *Pitchfork* and other publications, and he is the editor of The Thread, the blog of the Duke Performances series. His poems, sound art, and videos have appeared in many print and online journals, and he has issued three chapbooks of poetry. He makes no bones about the fact that his love for Leonard Cohen's music verges on the immoderate. He blogs at waxwroth.blogspot.com/.

David Kirby has published over thirty books on soul and rock 'n' roll as well as multiple collections of poetry. His work appears regularly in the Pushcart and Best American Poetry series, and readers of the *New York Times* are familiar with his frequent contributions. Kirby has received fellowships from the National Endowment for the Arts and the Guggenheim Foundation. His latest book is *Little Richard: The Birth of Rock 'n' Roll*. And a lot more about David Kirby can be found at www.davidkirby.com.

Jill Jones is Professor of English at Georgia Gwinnett College in Lawrenceville, Georgia, where she teaches British literature, composition, and world literature. Although a fan of country music, her publications generally focus on the British novelist Netta Syrett and other turn-of-the-century literary figures. She has taught English at Southwestern Oklahoma State University, Louisiana Tech University, Louisiana State University at Baton Rouge, and the University of Houston.

Robert P. McParland is the author of *Music and Literary Modernism* (2006) as well as two other books on criticism, *Charles Dickens's American Audience* (2010) and *Writing on Joseph Conrad* (2010). He is Associate Professor of English and chair of the English department at Felician College in New Jersey. His first article on Bruce Springsteen appeared in a high school newspaper, soon after the release of *Born to Run* (1975). His music essays include: "The Geography of Bruce Springsteen: Poetics and American Dreamscapes," *Interdisciplinary Literary Studies*, "A Generation Lost in Space: The Cultural Significance of Don McLean's 'American Pie'"; "Yesterday: Narrative, Memory, and the Beatles"; "The Music That Came After It All," an essay on *Music in the Post-9/11 World*; and "A Sound Education: Teaching with Popular Music Lyrics."

Pat Pattison is a professor at Berklee College of Music where he teaches lyric writing and poetry. Author of *Writing Better Lyrics, The Essential Guide to Lyric Form and Structure*, and *The Essential Guide to Rhyming*, Pattison has also developed three online lyric writing courses for Berklee's online school. Several of his students have won Grammys, including John Mayer and Gillian Welch. Before becoming a songwriting professor, Pattison received an M.A. in literary criticism from Indiana University.

Charlotte Pence recently earned her Ph.D. in English, concentrating in creative writing, from the University of Tennessee. She is a poet who has received a fellowship from the Tennessee Arts Commission, a New Millennium Writing award, and the Discovered Voices 2009 award. Most recently her chapbook, *Branches*, won the Black River Chapbook Competition and is forthcoming from Black Laurence Press. Her work has appeared in *North American Review, Prairie Schooner, Denver Quarterly, Kenyon Review Online, Tar River, Iron Horse*, and many other journals. She is also the author of a textbook written for creative writers teaching composition entitled *The Writer's Path*. Her interest in contemporary poetry, composition, and the influence of having lived in Nashville, country song capital, led her to investigating the blurry line between the genres of song and poetry. While an adjunct at Belmont University in Nashville, she created an English literature course entitled "The Poetics of Country Music."

Eric Reimer is an Assistant Professor of English at the University of Montana, where, in addition to a popular course on literature and music, he teaches courses on contemporary British, Irish, Caribbean, and postcolonial literatures. He is currently working on a series of projects that examine representations of Belfast both before and after the Northern Irish peace process. He has articles forthcoming in the *Journal of Caribbean Literatures* and *Eire-Ireland*.

Jeffrey Roessner serves as dean of the Arts and Humanities at Mercyhurst College in Erie, Pennsylvania, where he teaches classes in contemporary literature and leads workshops in creative writing. In addition to music, his primary research interests include historical fiction and cultural studies, and he has published essays on John Fowles, Angela Carter, and Jeanette Winterson, among others. His essay "'We All Want to Change the World': Postmodern Politics and the Beatles' *White Album*" appears in the collection *Reading the Beatles: Cultural Studies, Literary Criticism, and the Fab Four*. In addition, he has published a book on songwriting, *Creative Guitar: Writing and Playing Rock Songs with Originality*, with Mel Bay.

Tony Tost is the author of *Johnny Cash's American Recordings* (Continuum 2011), a descent into the mythic Americana of Cash's later work. He is also the author of two books of poetry, *Complex Sleep* (Iowa 2007) and *Invisible Bride* (LSU 2004), the latter of which won the Academy of American Poets' Walt Whitman Award for a first book of poetry. He recently completed a dissertation on myth, technology, and modern American poetry at Duke University and currently resides in Seattle with his wife and sons.

Ben Yagoda is a professor of English at the University of Delaware. He is the author of *Memoir: A History*, *About Town: The New Yorker and the World It Made*, *The Sound on the Page: Style and Voice in Writing*, *Will Rogers: A Biography*, and many other books. His writing has been collected in the *Da Capo Best Music Writing 2005* series, and he has contributed to magazines that start with every letter of the alphabet except K, Q, X, and Z.

Kevin Young is the author of seven books of poetry and editor of five others, most recent *Ardency: A Chronicle of the Amistad Rebels*. Past books include *Dear Darkness*, winner of the Southern Independent Bookseller's Award in poetry, and *Jelly Roll: A Blues* (2003), a finalist for the National Book Award and the *Los Angeles Times* Book Prize, and winner of the Paterson Poetry Prize. His anthology *The Art of Losing: Poems of Grief and Healing* appeared in March 2010. This selection is taken from *The Grey Album*, which won the 2010 Graywolf Nonfiction Prize and is forthcoming in 2012. Recently named the United States Artists James Baldwin Fellow, Young is Atticus Haygood Professor of Creative Writing and English and curator of Literary Collections and the Raymond Danowski Poetry Library at Emory University.

INDEX